FIRE FORCE

0

ATSUSHI
OHKUBO

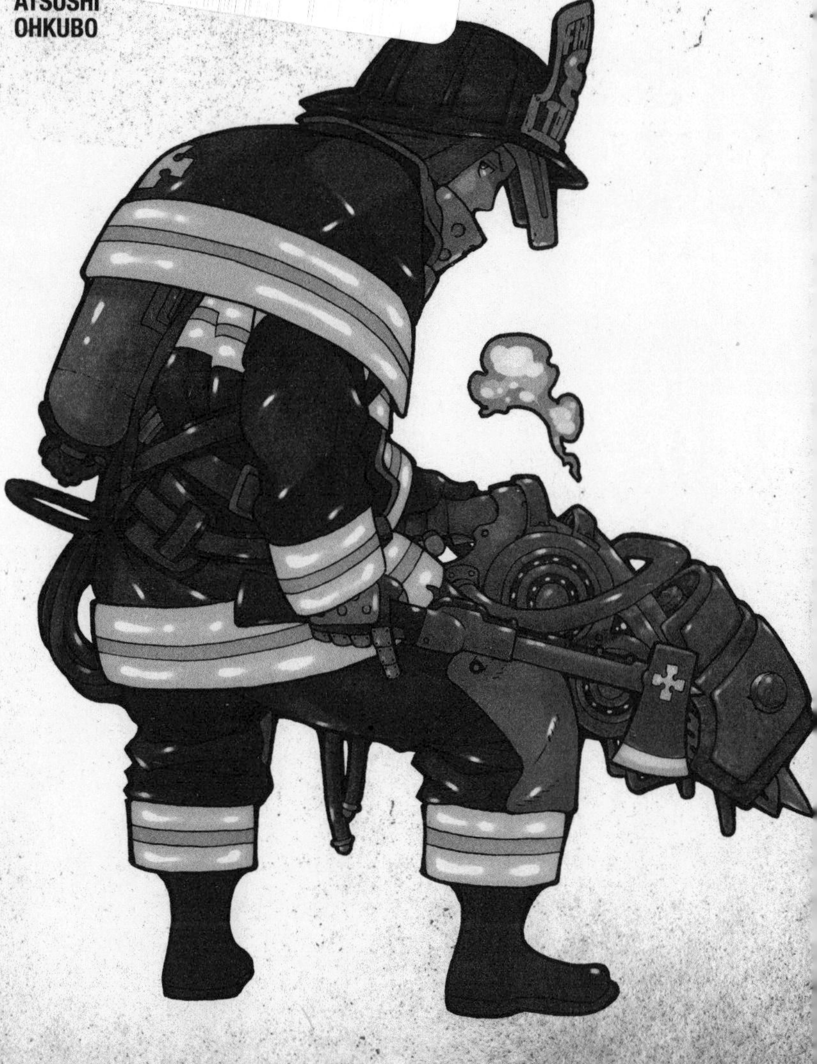

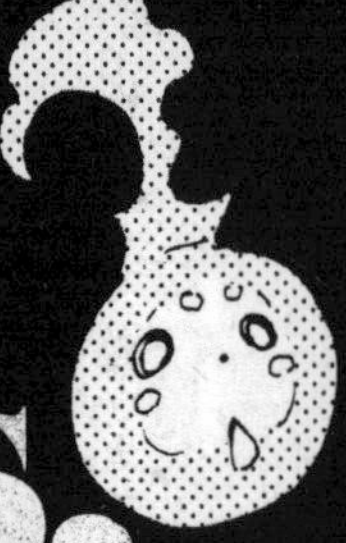

friends, families... planet... nothing.

VOL. 6

ATSUSHI OHKUBO

Before
our
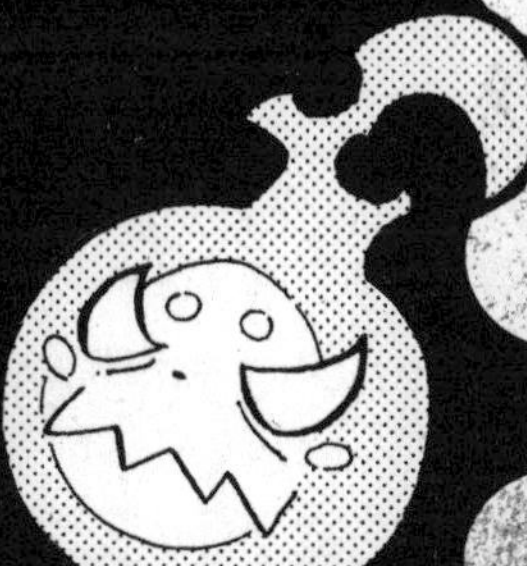
our
our
burns to

FIRE FORCE

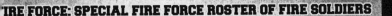

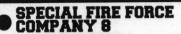

SPECIAL FIRE FORCE COMPANY 8

SECOND CLASS FIRE SOLDIER
(THIRD GENERATION PYROKINETIC)

ARTHUR BOYLE

Trained at the academy with Shinra. He follows his own personal code of chivalry as the self-proclaimed Knight King. He's a blockhead who is so bad at mental exercise that, if he does it for too long, he starts to die. But girls love him. He creates a fire sword with a blade that can cut through almost anything.

CAPTAIN
(NON-POWERED)

AKITARU ŌBI

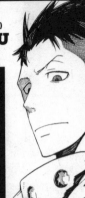

The popular and charismatic leader of the newly established Company 8. His goal is to investigate the other companies and uncover the truth about spontaneous human combustion. He has no powers, but uses his finely-honed muscles as a weapon in a battle style that's on even par with Benimaru's. Loves bodybuilding to an almost creepy extent.

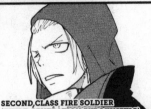

WATCHES OUT FOR

TRUSTS

IDIOT!!

WATCHES OUT FOR

TRUSTS

STRONG BOND

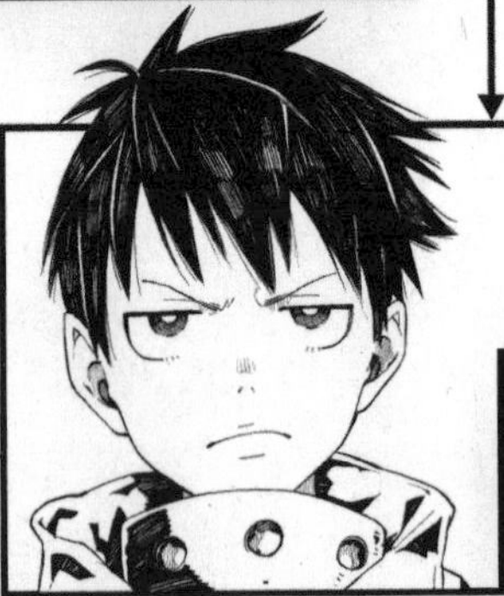

SECOND CLASS FIRE SOLDIER
(THIRD GENERATION PYROKINETIC)

SHINRA KUSAKABE

The bizarre smile that shows on his face when he gets nervous has earned him the derisive nickname of "devil." As he searches for his long-lost brother, he aims to be a hero who saves humanity from spontaneous combustion! In addition to his fiery kick, he appears to have a special flame known as the adolla burst...

A NICE GIRL

LOOKS AWESOME ON THE JOB

A TOUGH BUT WEIRD LADY

HANG IN THERE, ROOKIE!

TERRIFIED

STRICT DISCIPLINARIAN

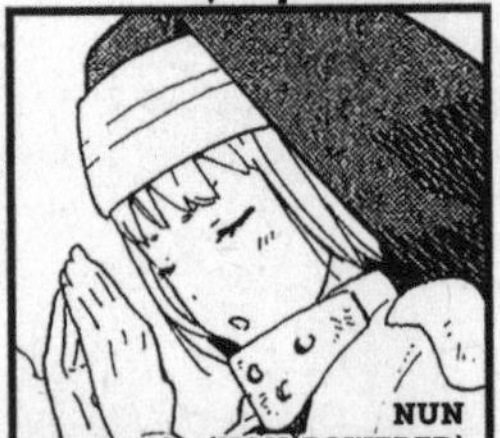

NUN
(NON-POWERED)

IRIS

A sister of the Holy Sol Temple, her prayers are an indispensable part of extinguishing Infernals. Personality-wise, she is no less than an angel. Her boobs are big. Very big. Since reconciling with Captain Hibana from Company 5, they have been as close as real sisters.

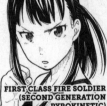

FIRST CLASS FIRE SOLDIER
(SECOND GENERATION PYROKINETIC)

MAKI OZE

A former member of the military, she is an excellent fighter who controls fire. She's a cool lady, but is mad about love stories, and her beauty is overshadowed by her "head full of flowers and wedding bells." She's friendly, but goes berserk when anyone comments on her muscles. Apparently she used to be slender.

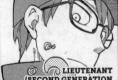

LIEUTENANT
(SECOND GENERATION PYROKINETIC)

TAKEHISA HINAWA

A dry, unemotional ex-military man, whose stern discipline is feared among the new recruits. He helped Ōbi to found Company 8. He never allows the soldiers to play with fire. The gun he uses is a cherished memento from his friend who became an Infernal.

THE GIRLS' CLUB

RESPECTS

● SPECIAL FIRE FORCE COMPANY 7

An unorthodox company made up of former vigilante corps members?!

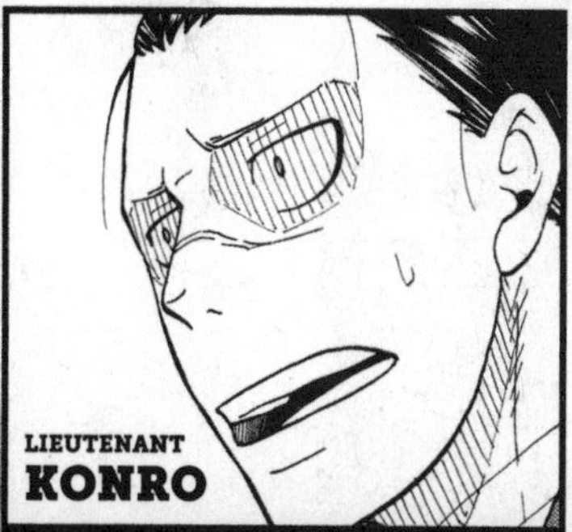

LIEUTENANT
KONRO

The man who is always found at Benimaru's side, addressing him as "Waka." One of Konro's duties is to rein in the combative Benimaru. The reason part of his body has turned to charcoal is...?

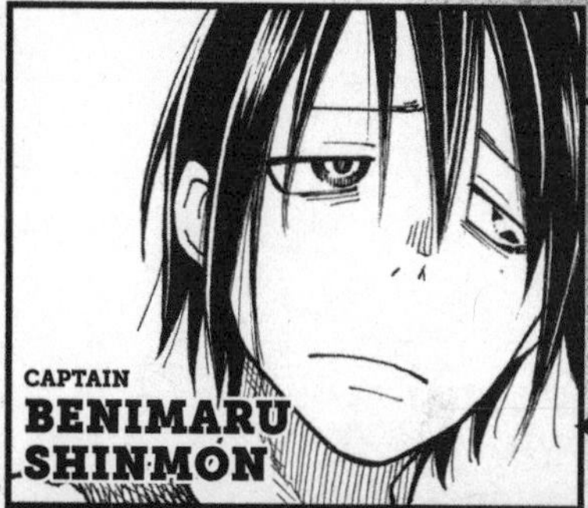

CAPTAIN
BENIMARU SHINMON

A composite fire soldier, with the powers of a second gen and a third gen pyrokinetic. The leader of the rough-and-tumble Company 7, there are whispered rumors that he is the toughest soldier on the force. He has little faith in the Great Sun God, and is a proto-nationalist opposed to the reign of the Holy Sol Temple.

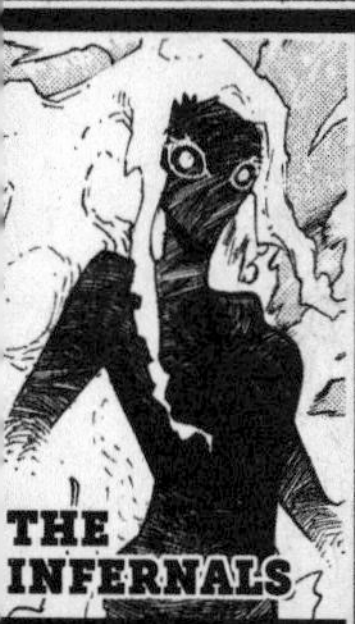

THE INFERNALS

Born from the cryptogenic phenomenon of spontaneous human combustion (SHC), they have no self-awareness, and only wreak havoc until their lives burn out.

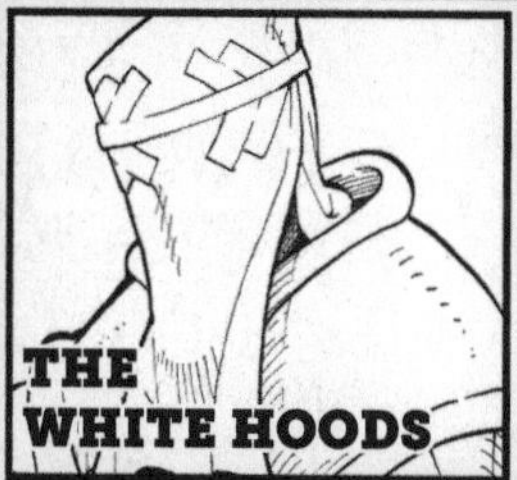

THE WHITE HOODS

An esoteric group that uses bugs to artificially ignite Infernals in their mission to carry out the Evangelist's precepts. They appear to have high-level fighting powers, but there are many aspects of their objective that remain unclear.

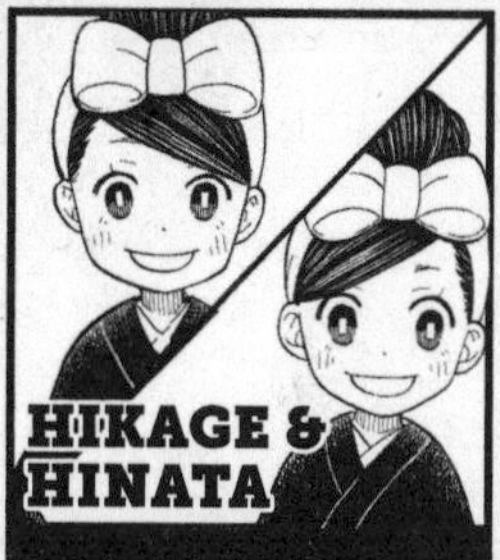

HIKAGE & HINATA

Cute twins, each with a sweet tooth, who have unfortunately picked up Benimaru's rude speech habits. They've taken quite a shine to Shinra.

SUMMARY...

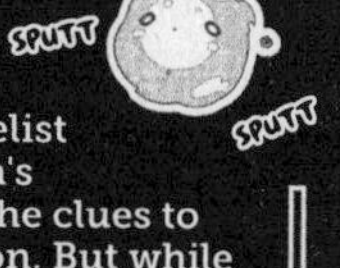
SPUTT
SPUTT

Company 8 has decided to trust Joker's information for now, and to search for the Evangelist under the assumption that Shinra's brother is still alive. They follow the clues to Asakusa—Company 7's jurisdiction. But while there, they run into another Infernal outbreak. Benimaru suspects Ōbi and Hinawa of causing the combustion, and they have no choice but to fight a duel with the most powerful soldier on the force! What will be the outcome of this epic Captain-to-Captain battle?!

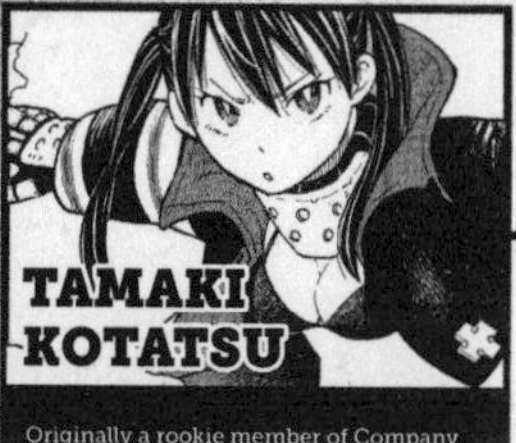

TAMAKI KOTATSU

Originally a rookie member of Company 1, she was caught up in the treasonous plot of her superior officer Hoshimiya, and is currently being disciplined under Company 8's watch. A girl with an unfortunate "lucky lecher lure" condition, she nevertheless has a pure heart.

FIRE FORCE 06
CONTENTS

FIRE FORCE

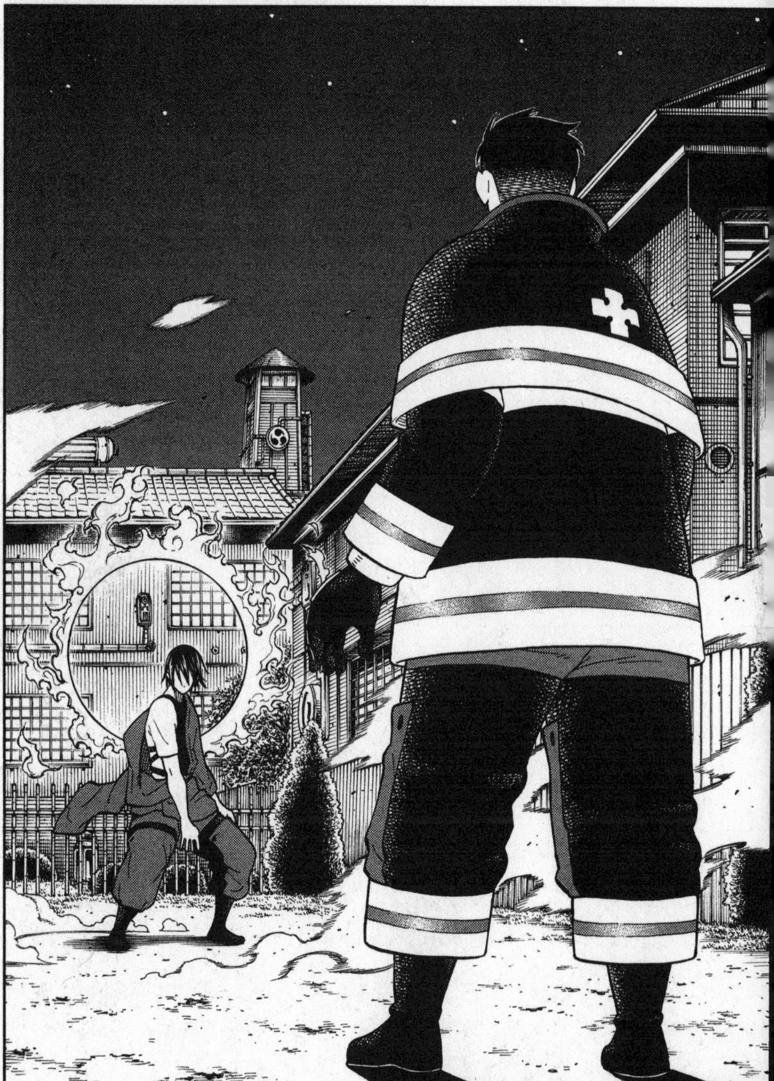

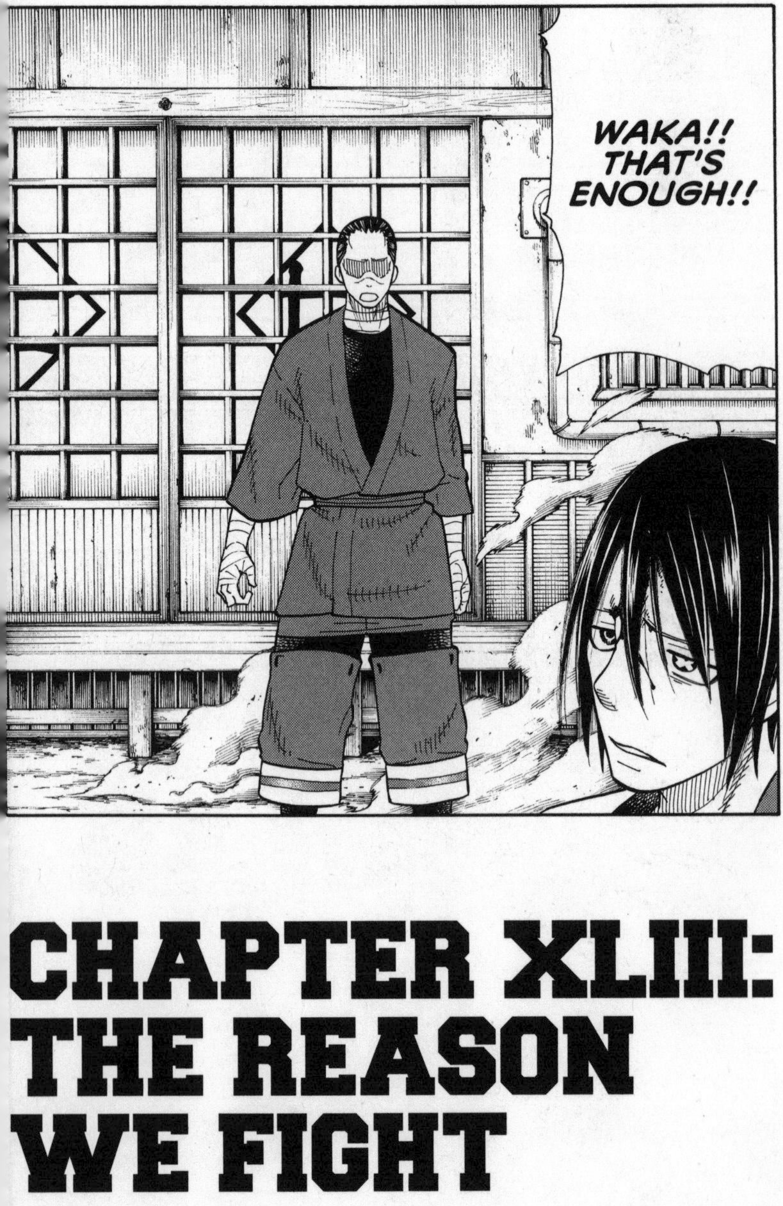
WAKA!! THAT'S ENOUGH!!

CHAPTER XLIII: THE REASON WE FIGHT

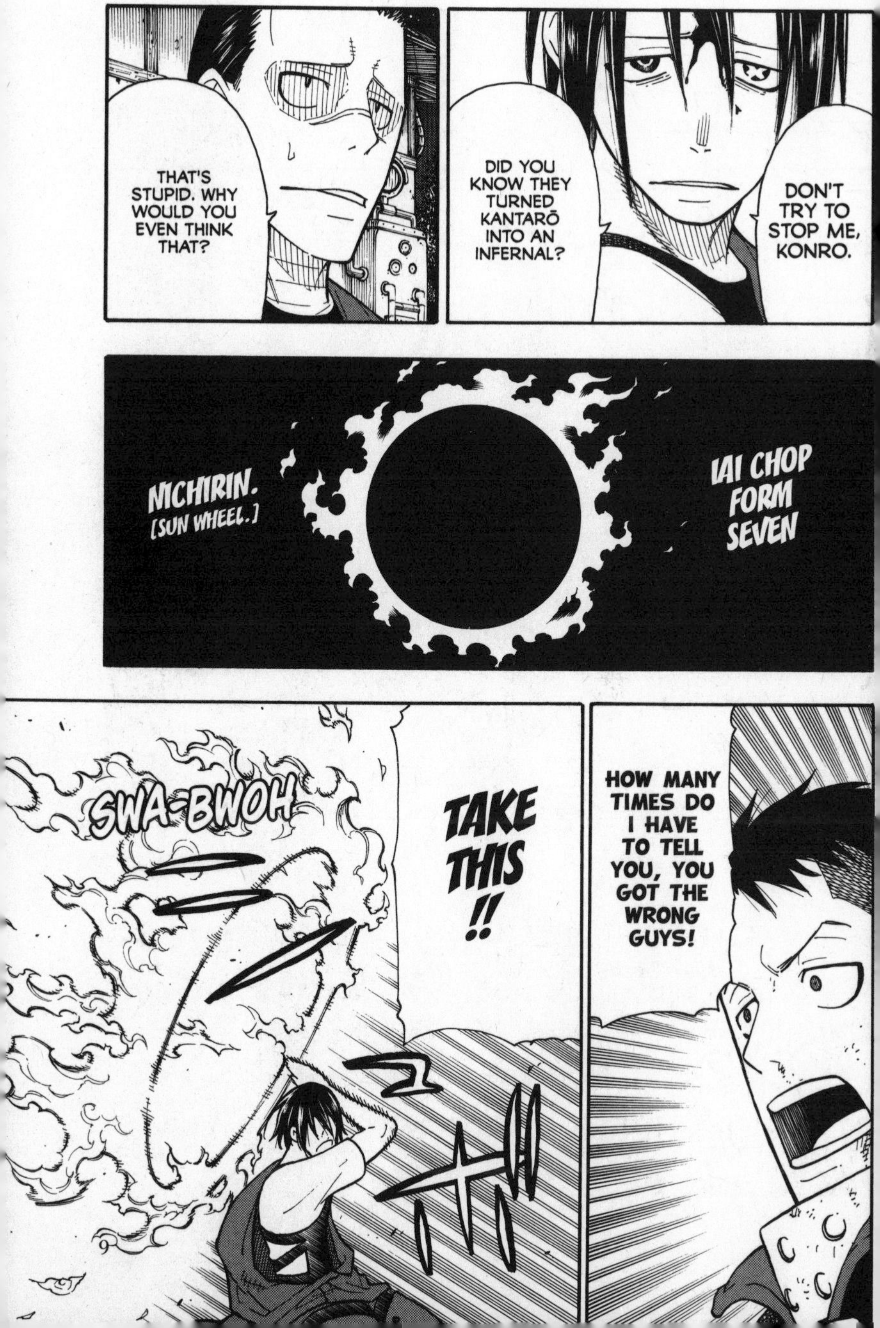
DON'T TRY TO STOP ME, KONRO.
DID YOU KNOW THEY TURNED KANTARŌ INTO AN INFERNAL?
THAT'S STUPID. WHY WOULD YOU EVEN THINK THAT?
IAI CHOP FORM SEVEN
NICHIRIN. [SUN WHEEL.]
HOW MANY TIMES DO I HAVE TO TELL YOU, YOU GOT THE WRONG GUYS!
TAKE THIS!!
SWA-BWOH

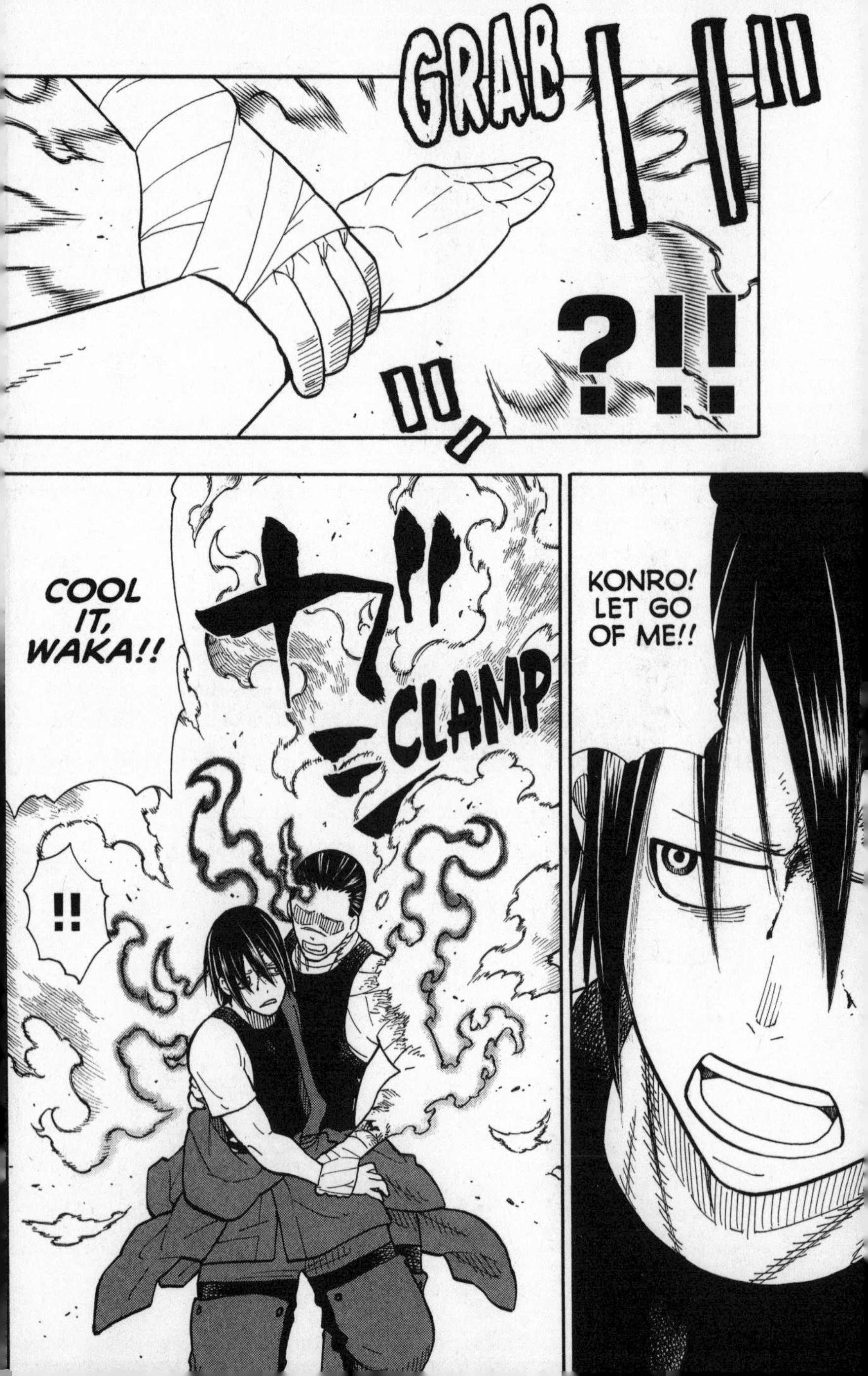
GRAB
?!!
KONRO! LET GO OF ME!!
COOL IT, WAKA!!
CLAMP
!!

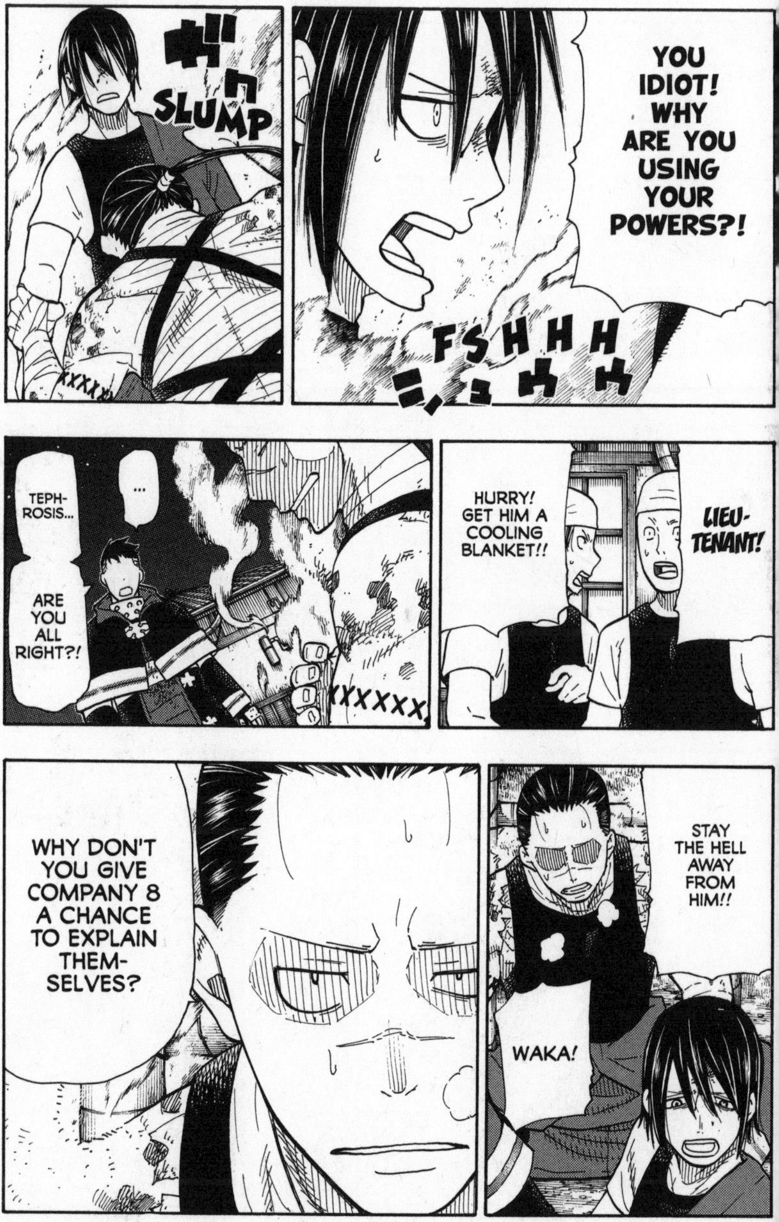
YOU IDIOT! WHY ARE YOU USING YOUR POWERS?!
FSHHHH
SLUMP
LIEU-TENANT!
HURRY! GET HIM A COOLING BLANKET!!
...
TEPH-ROSIS...
ARE YOU ALL RIGHT?!
STAY THE HELL AWAY FROM HIM!!
WAKA!
WHY DON'T YOU GIVE COMPANY 8 A CHANCE TO EXPLAIN THEM-SELVES?

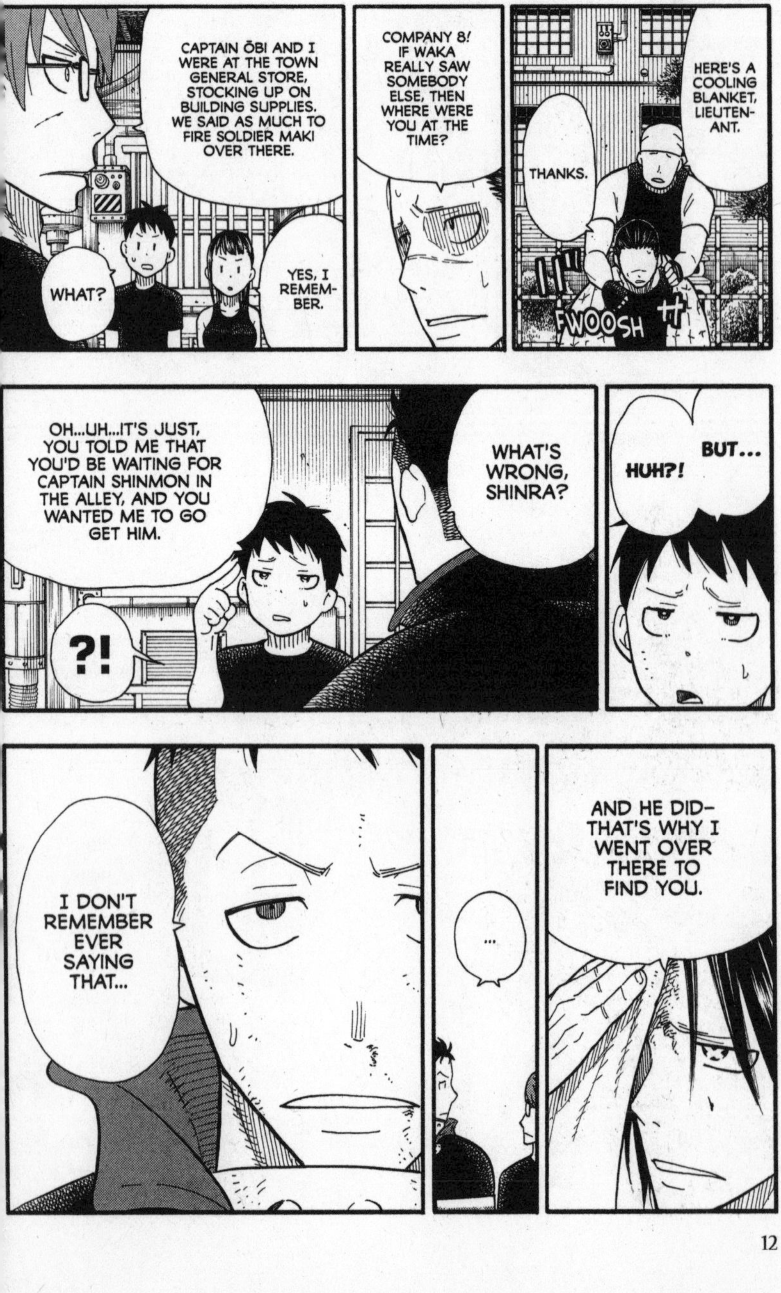
HERE'S A COOLING BLANKET, LIEUTEN-ANT.
THANKS.
FWOOSH
COMPANY 8! IF WAKA REALLY SAW SOMEBODY ELSE, THEN WHERE WERE YOU AT THE TIME?
CAPTAIN ŌBI AND I WERE AT THE TOWN GENERAL STORE, STOCKING UP ON BUILDING SUPPLIES. WE SAID AS MUCH TO FIRE SOLDIER MAKI OVER THERE.
YES, I REMEM-BER.
WHAT?
BUT...
HUH?!
WHAT'S WRONG, SHINRA?
OH...UH...IT'S JUST, YOU TOLD ME THAT YOU'D BE WAITING FOR CAPTAIN SHINMON IN THE ALLEY, AND YOU WANTED ME TO GO GET HIM.
?!
AND HE DID—THAT'S WHY I WENT OVER THERE TO FIND YOU.
...
I DON'T REMEMBER EVER SAYING THAT...

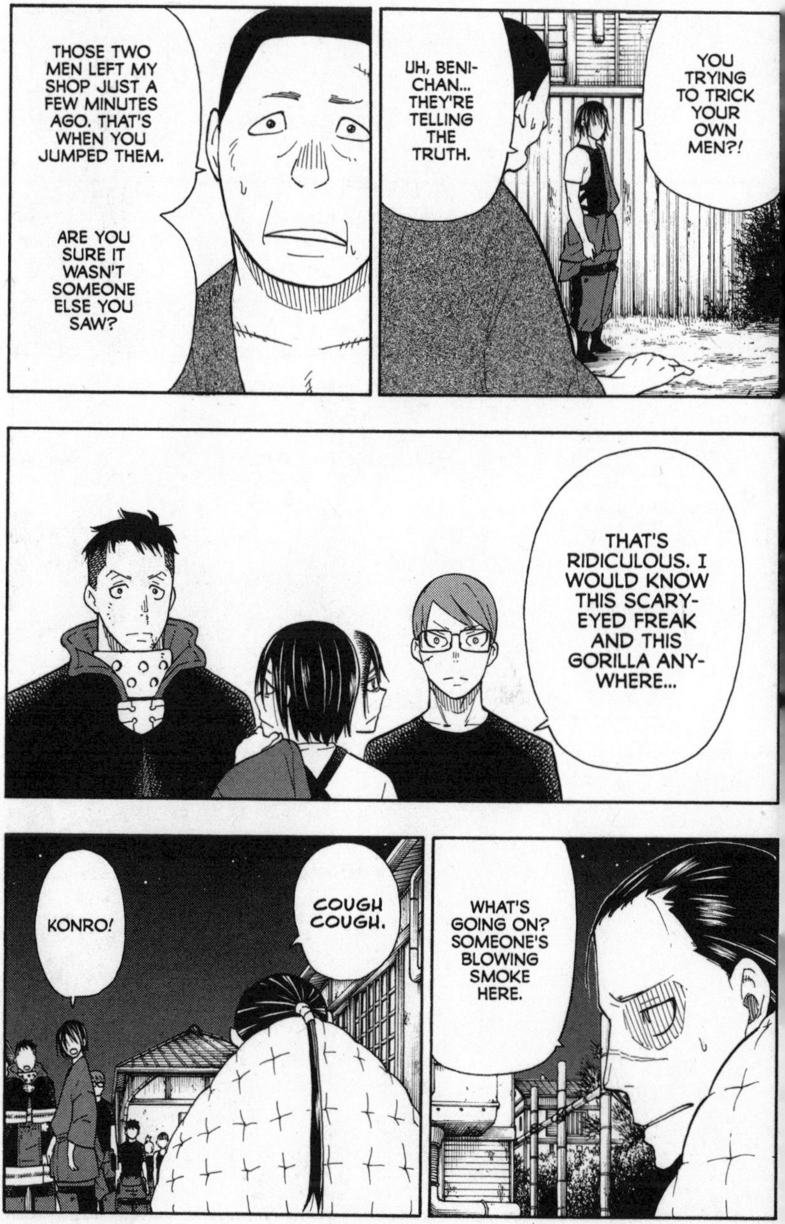
YOU TRYING TO TRICK YOUR OWN MEN?!
UH, BENI-CHAN... THEY'RE TELLING THE TRUTH.
THOSE TWO MEN LEFT MY SHOP JUST A FEW MINUTES AGO. THAT'S WHEN YOU JUMPED THEM.
ARE YOU SURE IT WASN'T SOMEONE ELSE YOU SAW?
THAT'S RIDICULOUS. I WOULD KNOW THIS SCARY-EYED FREAK AND THIS GORILLA ANY-WHERE...
WHAT'S GOING ON? SOMEONE'S BLOWING SMOKE HERE.
COUGH COUGH.
KONRO!

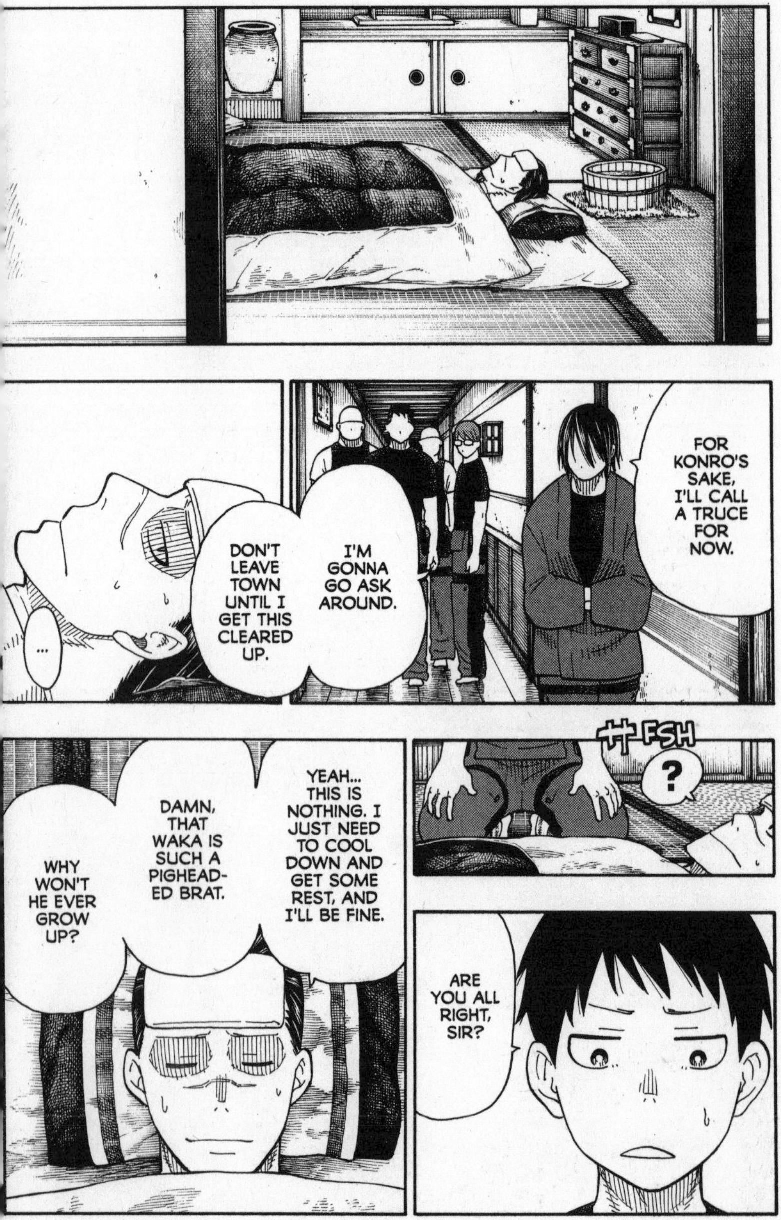
FOR KONRO'S SAKE, I'LL CALL A TRUCE FOR NOW.
I'M GONNA GO ASK AROUND.
DON'T LEAVE TOWN UNTIL I GET THIS CLEARED UP.
...
FSH
?
ARE YOU ALL RIGHT, SIR?
YEAH... THIS IS NOTHING. I JUST NEED TO COOL DOWN AND GET SOME REST, AND I'LL BE FINE.
DAMN, THAT WAKA IS SUCH A PIGHEAD-ED BRAT.
WHY WON'T HE EVER GROW UP?

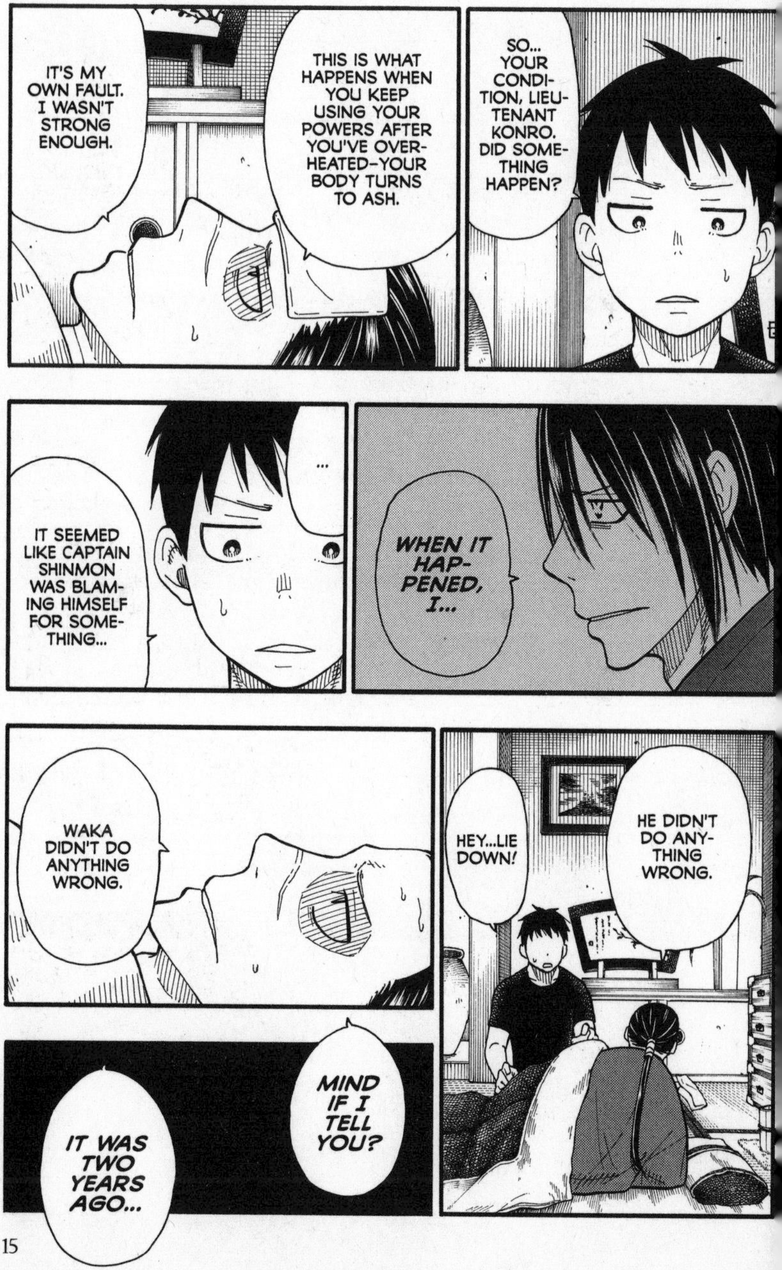
SO... YOUR CONDITION, LIEUTENANT KONRO. DID SOMETHING HAPPEN?
THIS IS WHAT HAPPENS WHEN YOU KEEP USING YOUR POWERS AFTER YOU'VE OVERHEATED–YOUR BODY TURNS TO ASH.
IT'S MY OWN FAULT. I WASN'T STRONG ENOUGH.
WHEN IT HAPPENED, I...
...
IT SEEMED LIKE CAPTAIN SHINMON WAS BLAMING HIMSELF FOR SOMETHING...
HE DIDN'T DO ANYTHING WRONG.
HEY...LIE DOWN!
WAKA DIDN'T DO ANYTHING WRONG.
MIND IF I TELL YOU?
IT WAS TWO YEARS AGO...

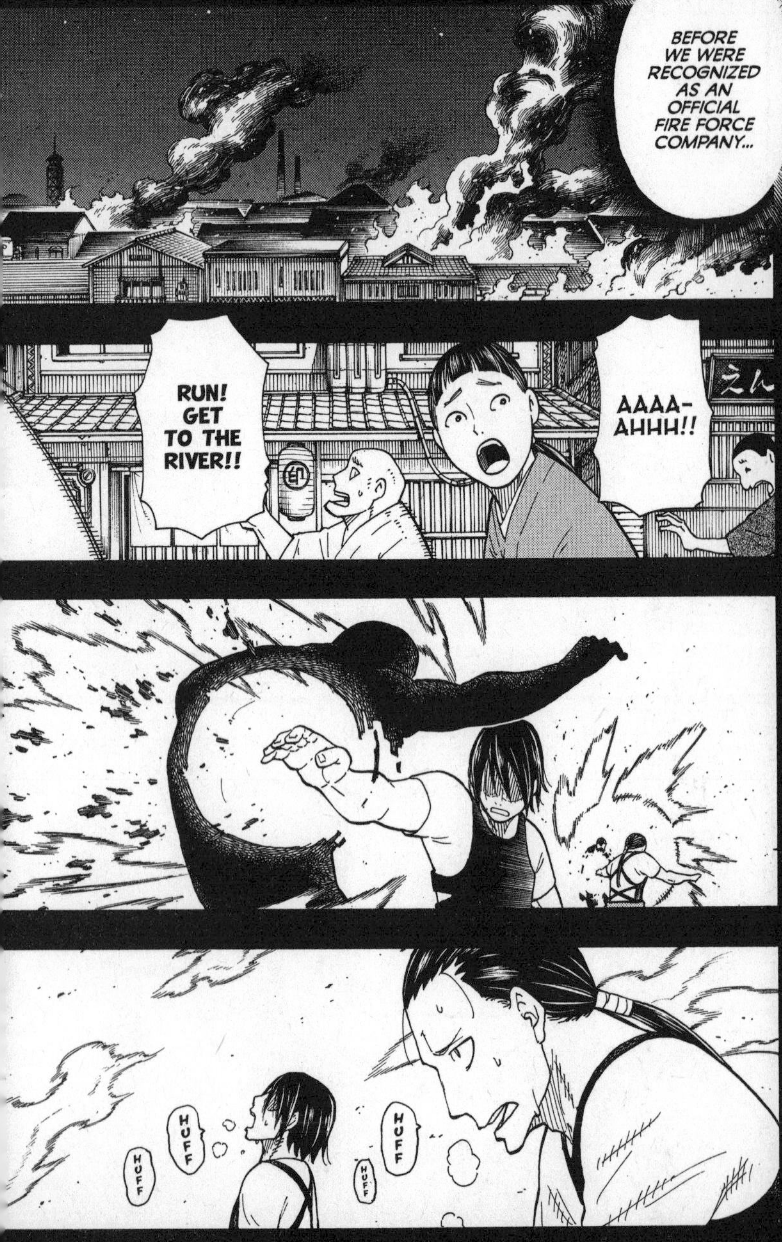
BEFORE WE WERE RECOGNIZED AS AN OFFICIAL FIRE FORCE COMPANY...
AAAA-AHHH!!
RUN! GET TO THE RIVER!!
HUFF
HUFF
HUFF
HUFF

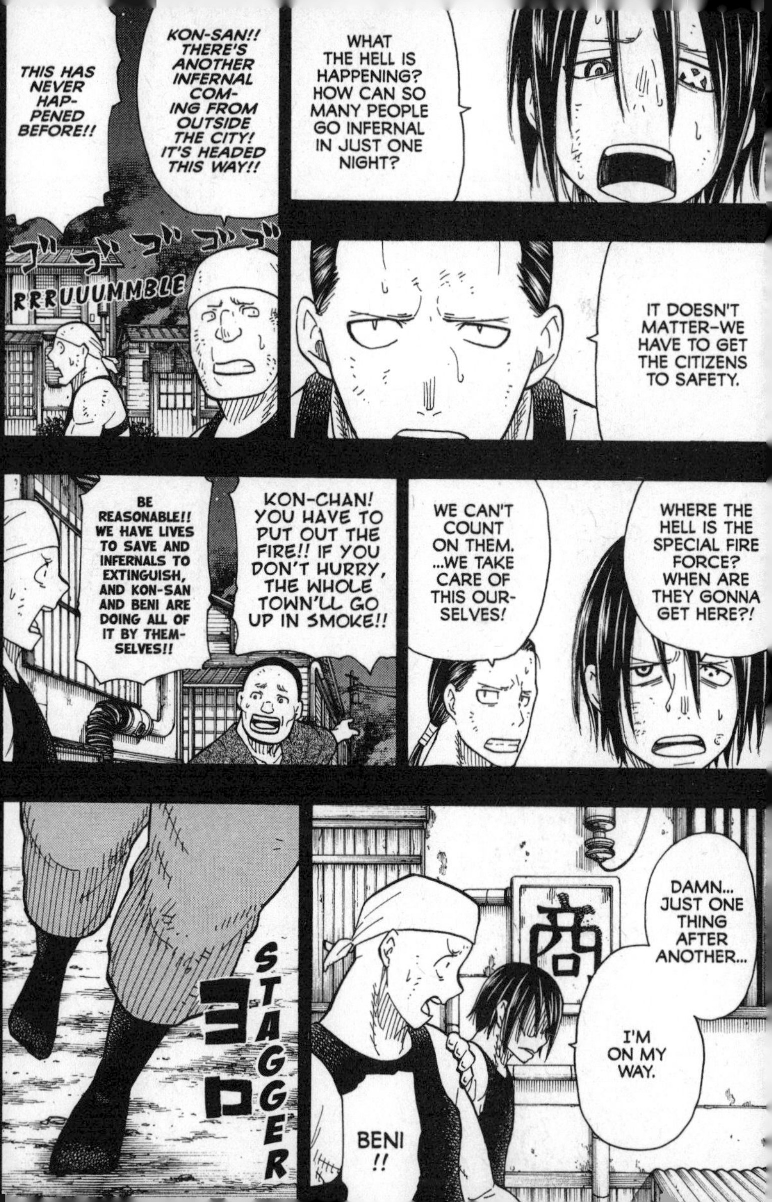
WHAT THE HELL IS HAPPENING? HOW CAN SO MANY PEOPLE GO INFERNAL IN JUST ONE NIGHT?
IT DOESN'T MATTER—WE HAVE TO GET THE CITIZENS TO SAFETY.
KON-SAN!! THERE'S ANOTHER INFERNAL COMING FROM OUTSIDE THE CITY! IT'S HEADED THIS WAY!!
THIS HAS NEVER HAPPENED BEFORE!!
ゴゴゴゴゴ
RRRUUUMMBLE
WHERE THE HELL IS THE SPECIAL FIRE FORCE? WHEN ARE THEY GONNA GET HERE?!
WE CAN'T COUNT ON THEM. ...WE TAKE CARE OF THIS OURSELVES!
KON-CHAN! YOU HAVE TO PUT OUT THE FIRE!! IF YOU DON'T HURRY, THE WHOLE TOWN'LL GO UP IN SMOKE!!
BE REASONABLE!! WE HAVE LIVES TO SAVE AND INFERNALS TO EXTINGUISH, AND KON-SAN AND BENI ARE DOING ALL OF IT BY THEMSELVES!!
DAMN... JUST ONE THING AFTER ANOTHER...
I'M ON MY WAY.
BENI!!
ヨロ
STAGGER

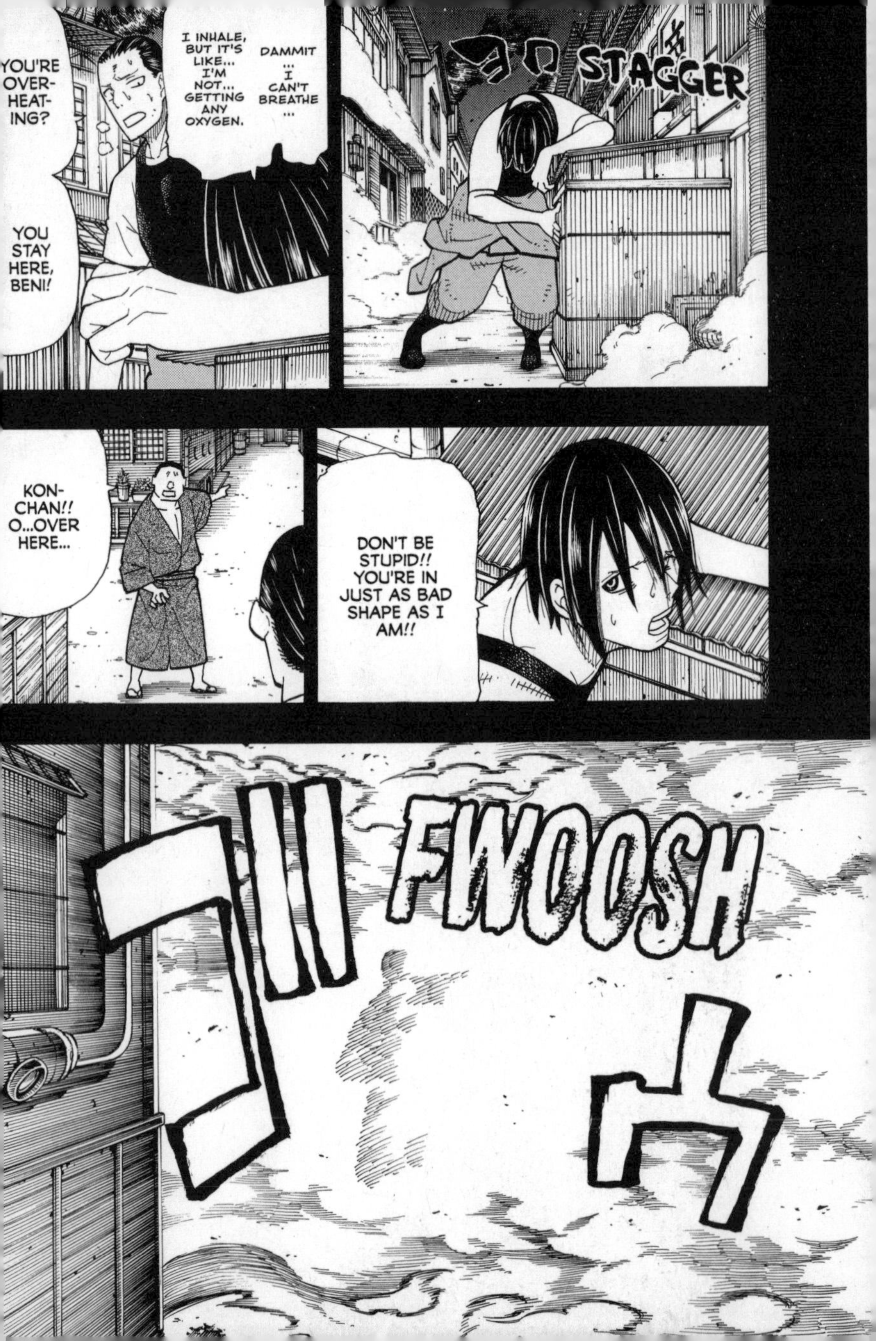
STAGGER
DAMMIT... I CAN'T BREATHE...
I INHALE, BUT IT'S LIKE... I'M NOT... GETTING ANY OXYGEN.
YOU'RE OVER-HEATING?
YOU STAY HERE, BENI!
DON'T BE STUPID!! YOU'RE IN JUST AS BAD SHAPE AS I AM!!
KON-CHAN!! O...OVER HERE...
FWOOSH

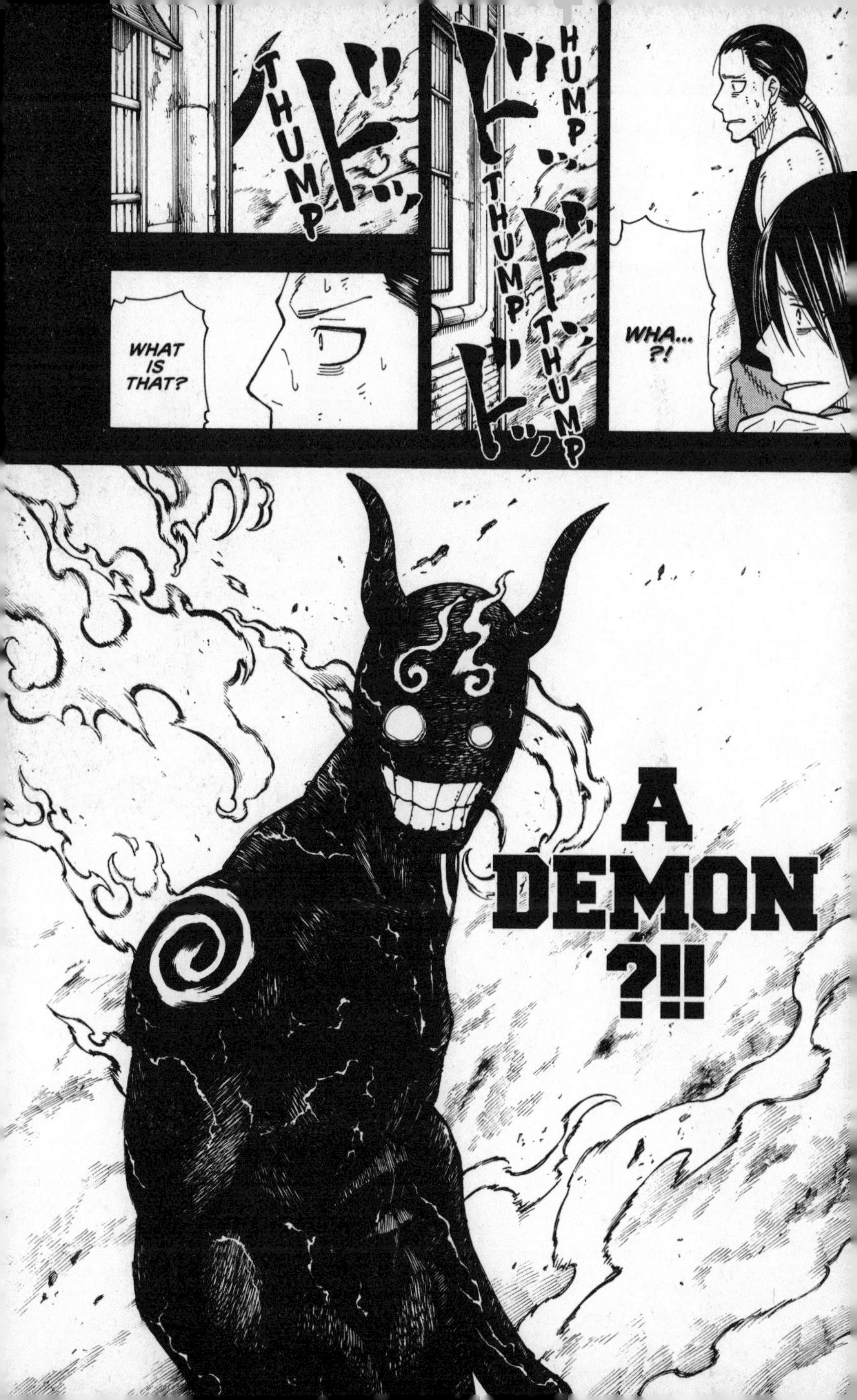

WHA... ?!
HUMP
THUMP
THUMP
THUMP
WHAT IS THAT?
A DEMON ?!!

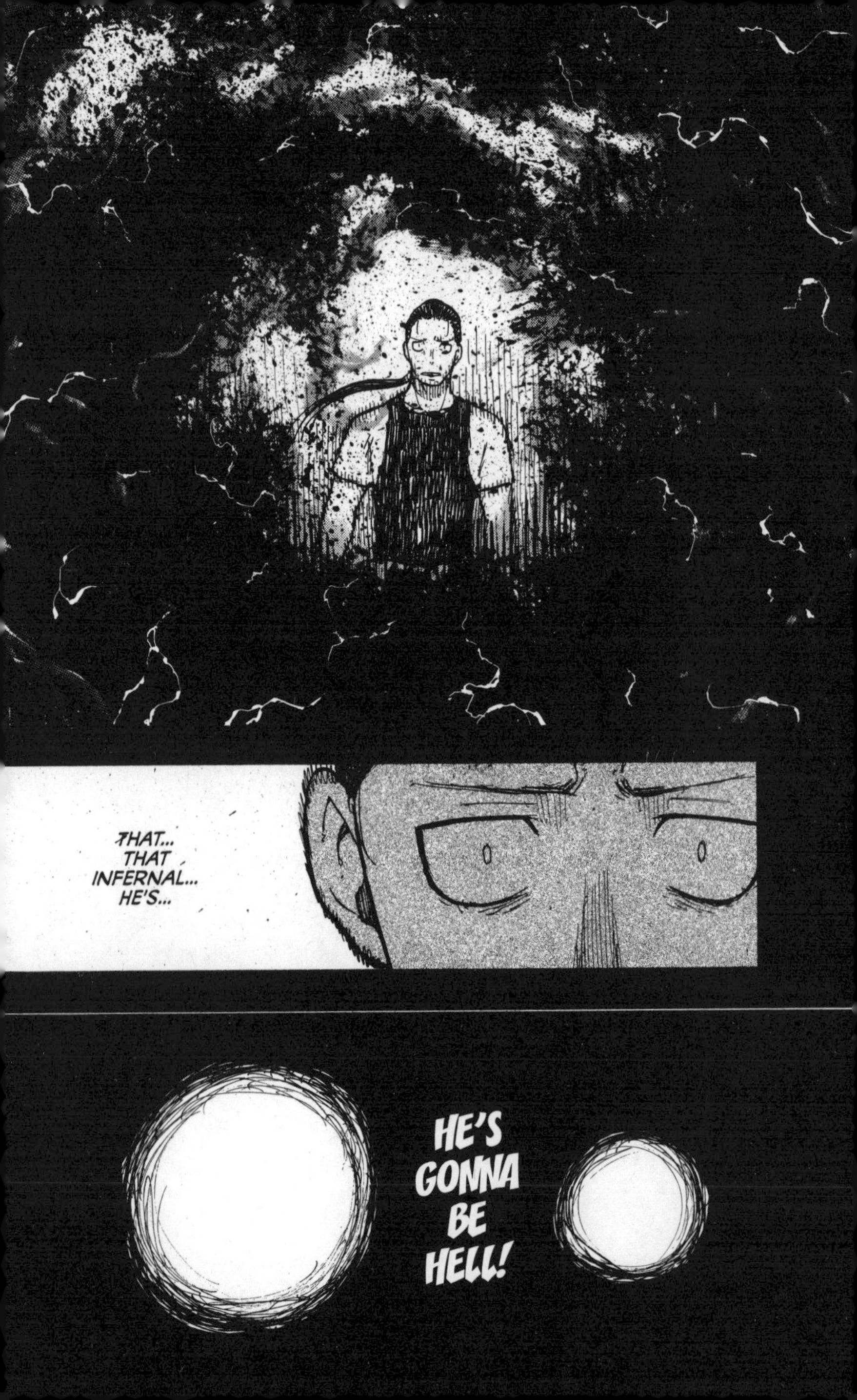
THAT... THAT INFERNAL... HE'S...
HE'S GONNA BE HELL!

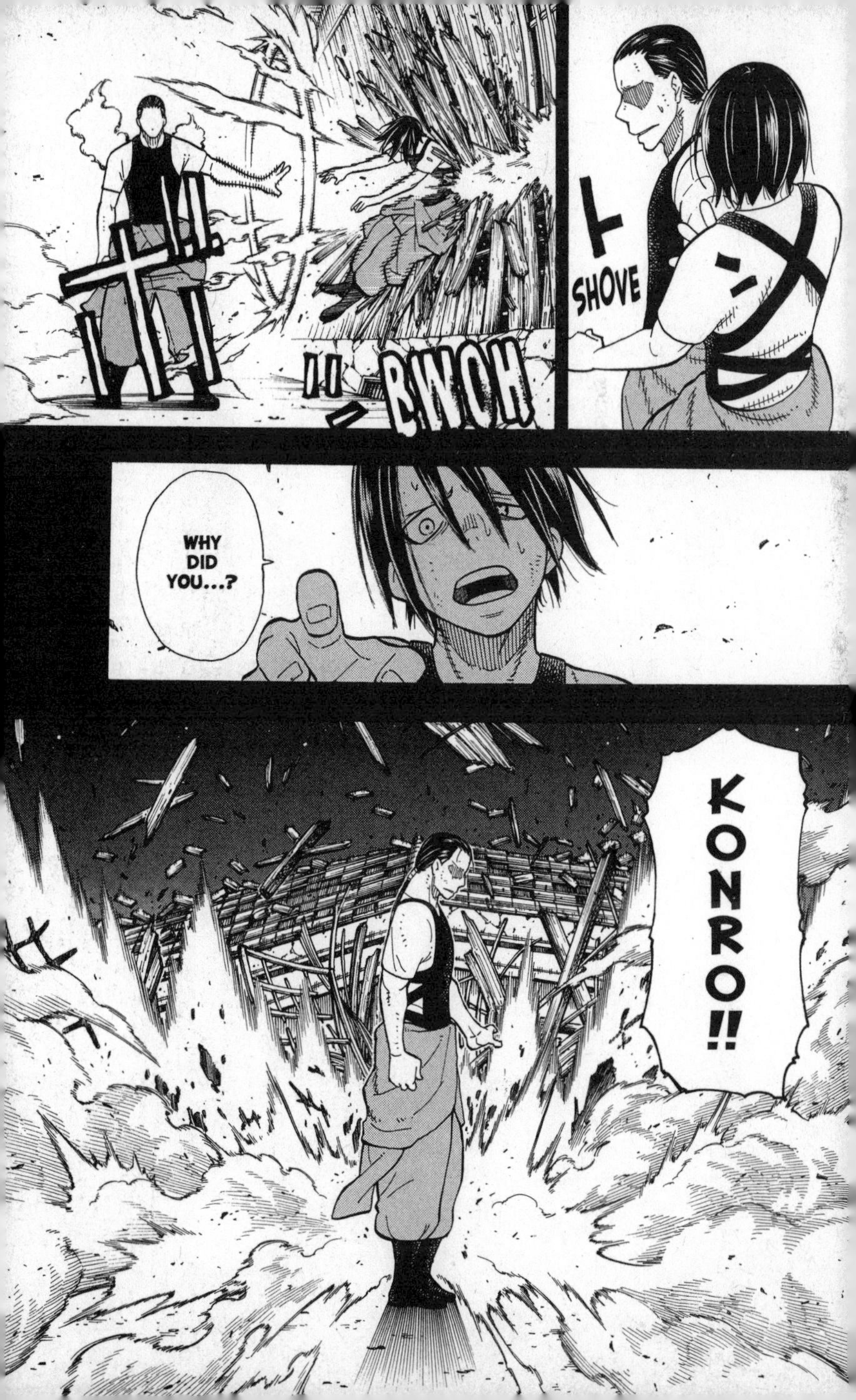
SHOVE
BWOH
WHY DID YOU...?
KONRO!!

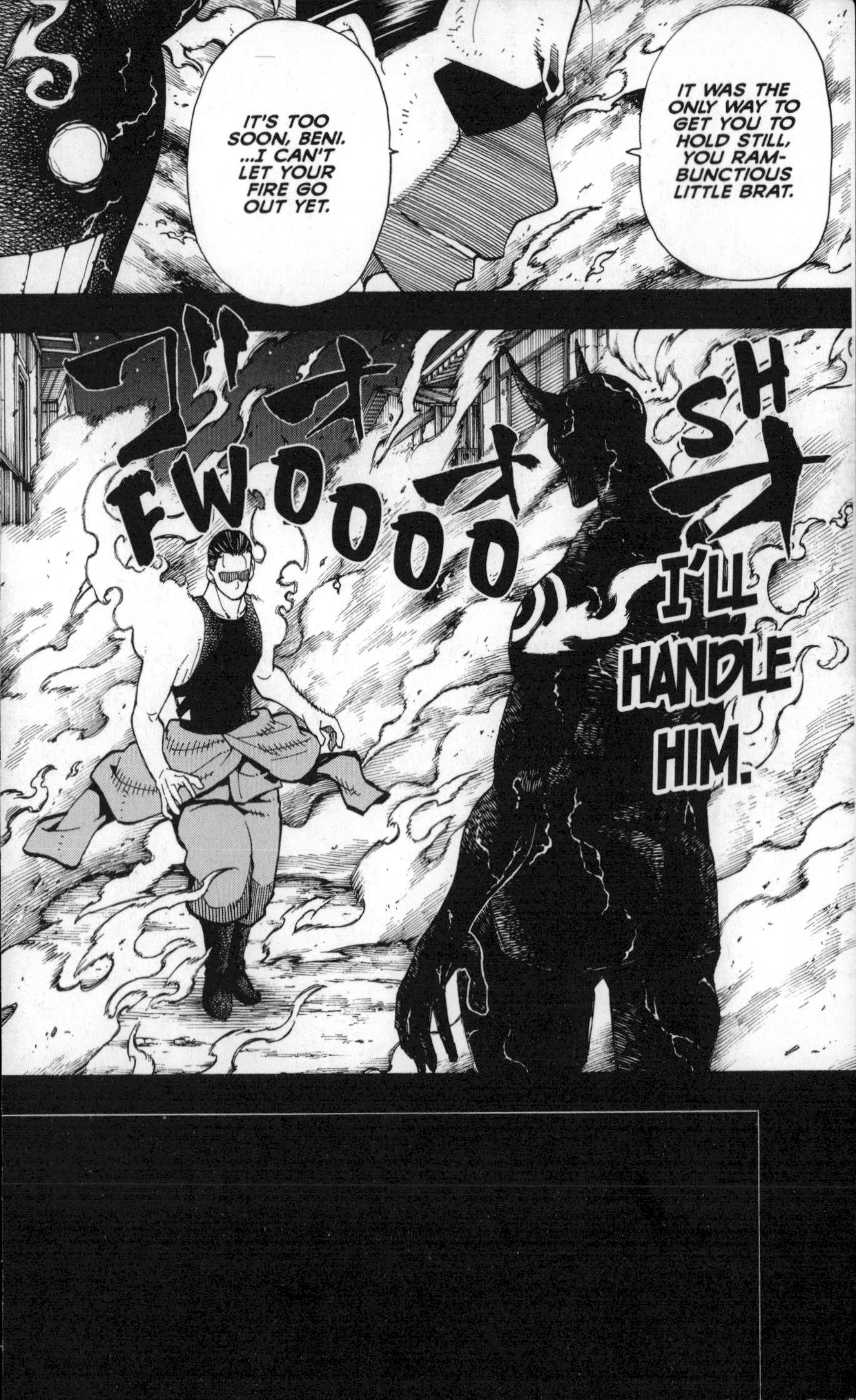
IT WAS THE ONLY WAY TO GET YOU TO HOLD STILL, YOU RAM-BUNCTIOUS LITTLE BRAT.
IT'S TOO SOON, BENI. ...I CAN'T LET YOUR FIRE GO OUT YET.
I'LL HANDLE HIM.
FWOOOOOSH

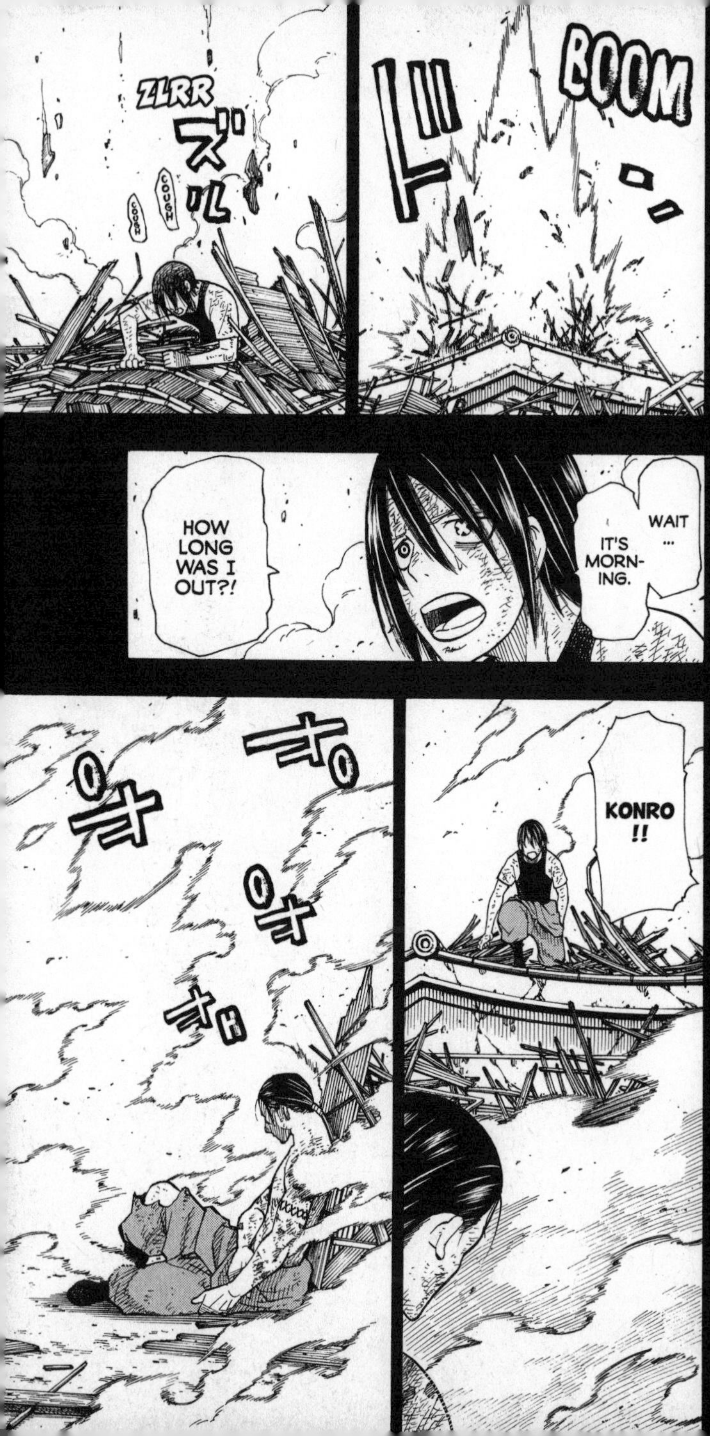
BOOM
ZLRR
COUGH
COUGH
WAIT ... IT'S MORNING.
HOW LONG WAS I OUT?!
KONRO !!

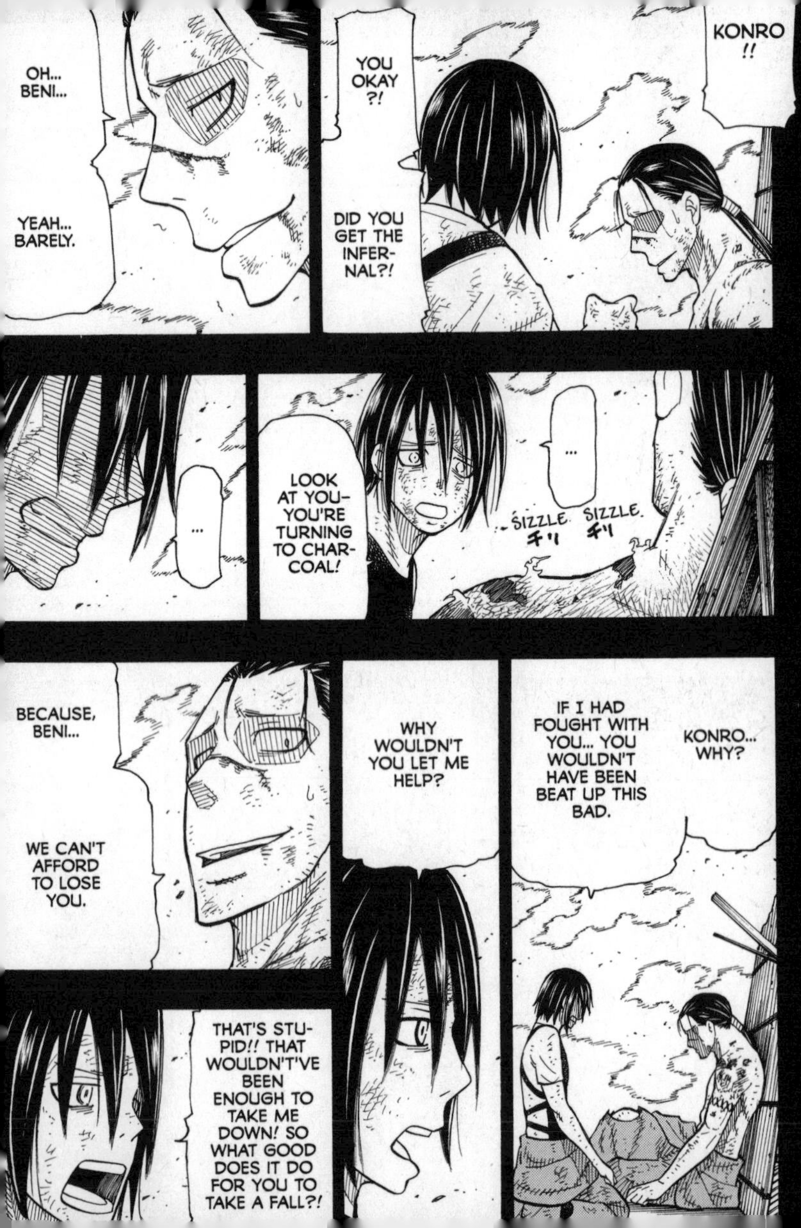
KONRO !!
YOU OKAY ?!
DID YOU GET THE INFER-NAL?!
OH... BENI...
YEAH... BARELY.
...
SIZZLE チリ SIZZLE チリ
LOOK AT YOU-YOU'RE TURNING TO CHAR-COAL!
...
KONRO... WHY?
IF I HAD FOUGHT WITH YOU... YOU WOULDN'T HAVE BEEN BEAT UP THIS BAD.
WHY WOULDN'T YOU LET ME HELP?
BECAUSE, BENI...
WE CAN'T AFFORD TO LOSE YOU.
THAT'S STU-PID!! THAT WOULDN'T'VE BEEN ENOUGH TO TAKE ME DOWN! SO WHAT GOOD DOES IT DO FOR YOU TO TAKE A FALL?!

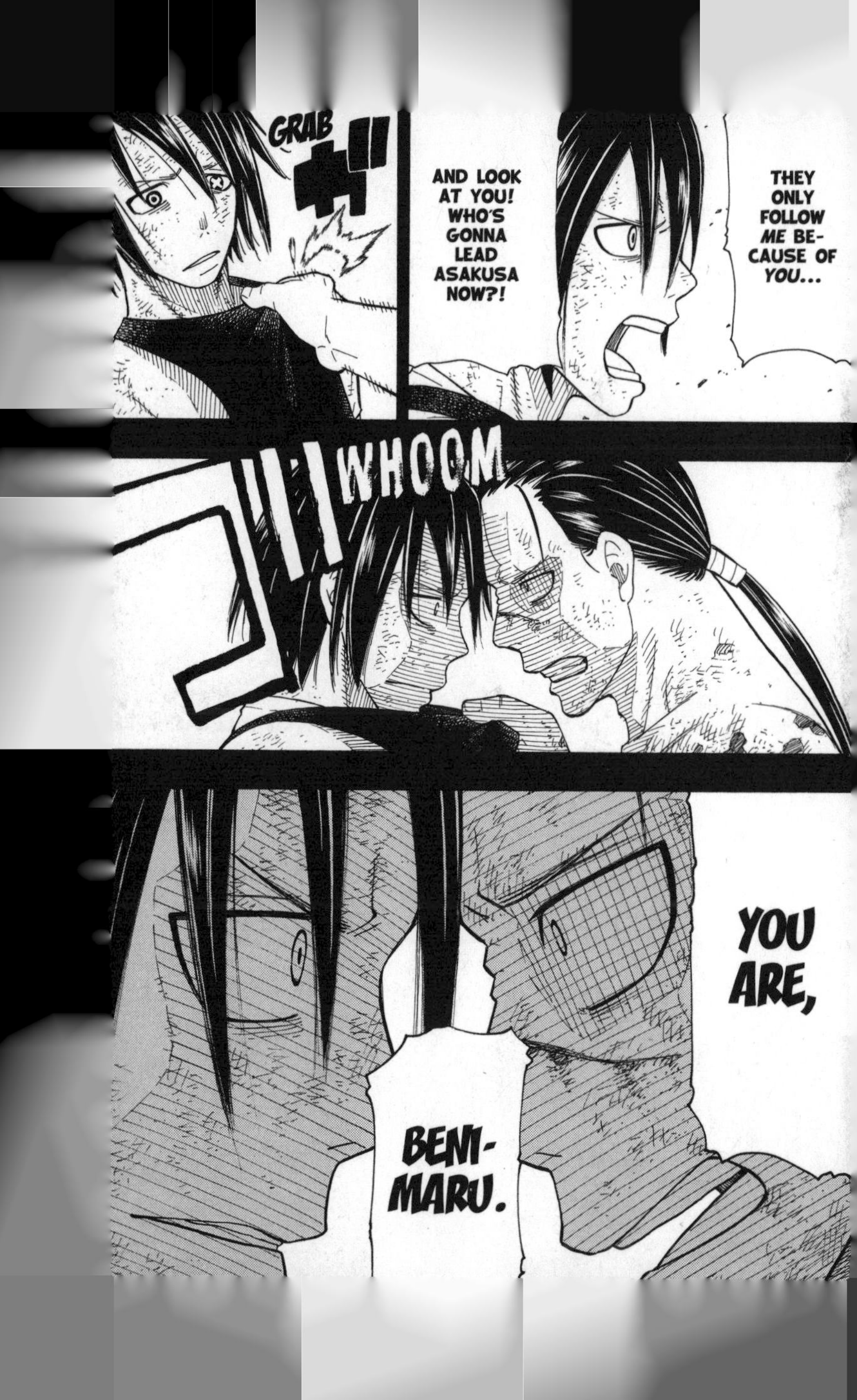

THEY ONLY FOLLOW *ME* BECAUSE OF *YOU*...
AND LOOK AT YOU! WHO'S GONNA LEAD ASAKUSA NOW?!
GRAB
WHOOM
YOU ARE,
BENIMARU.

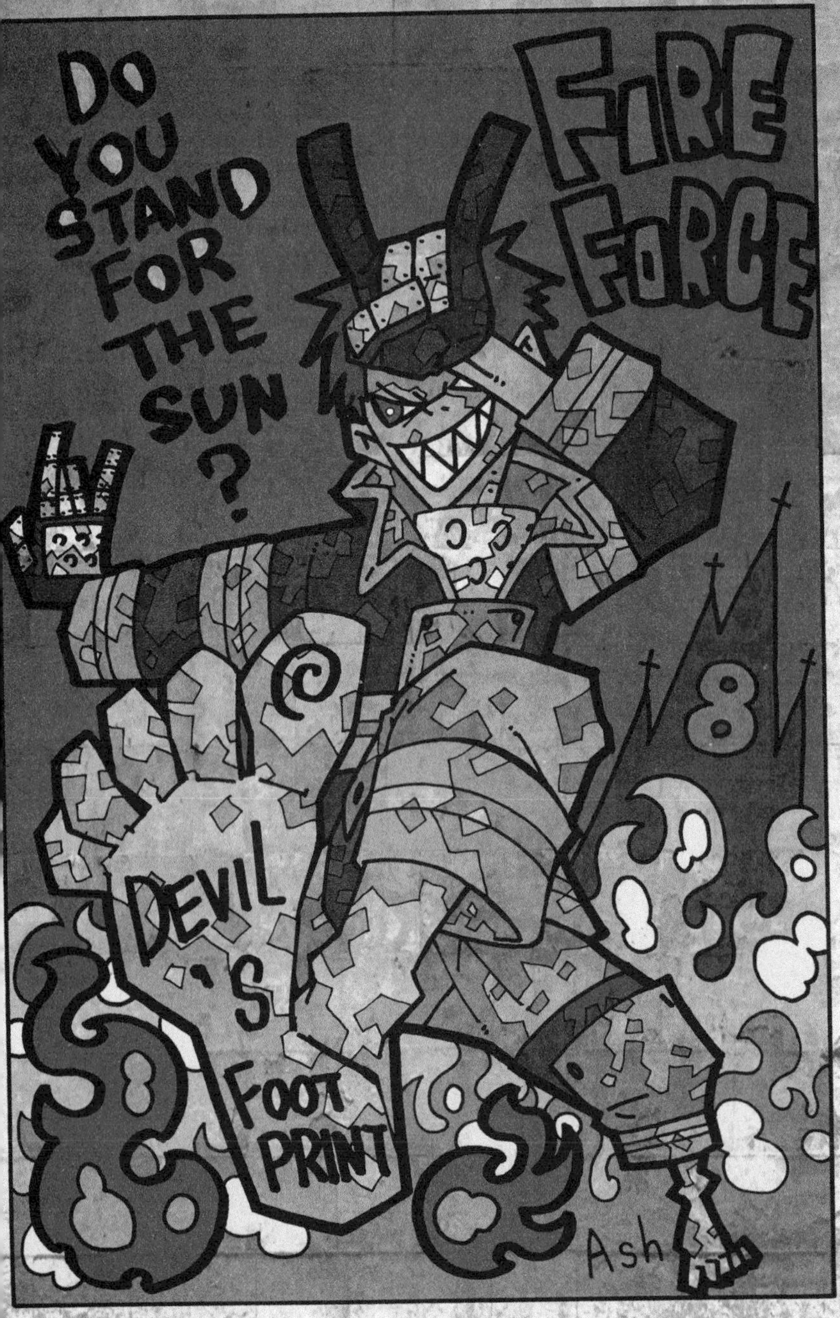
DO YOU STAND FOR THE SUN ?
FIRE FORCE
8
DEVIL 'S FOOT PRINT
Ash

CHAPTER XLIV: COMPANY 7 IS BORN

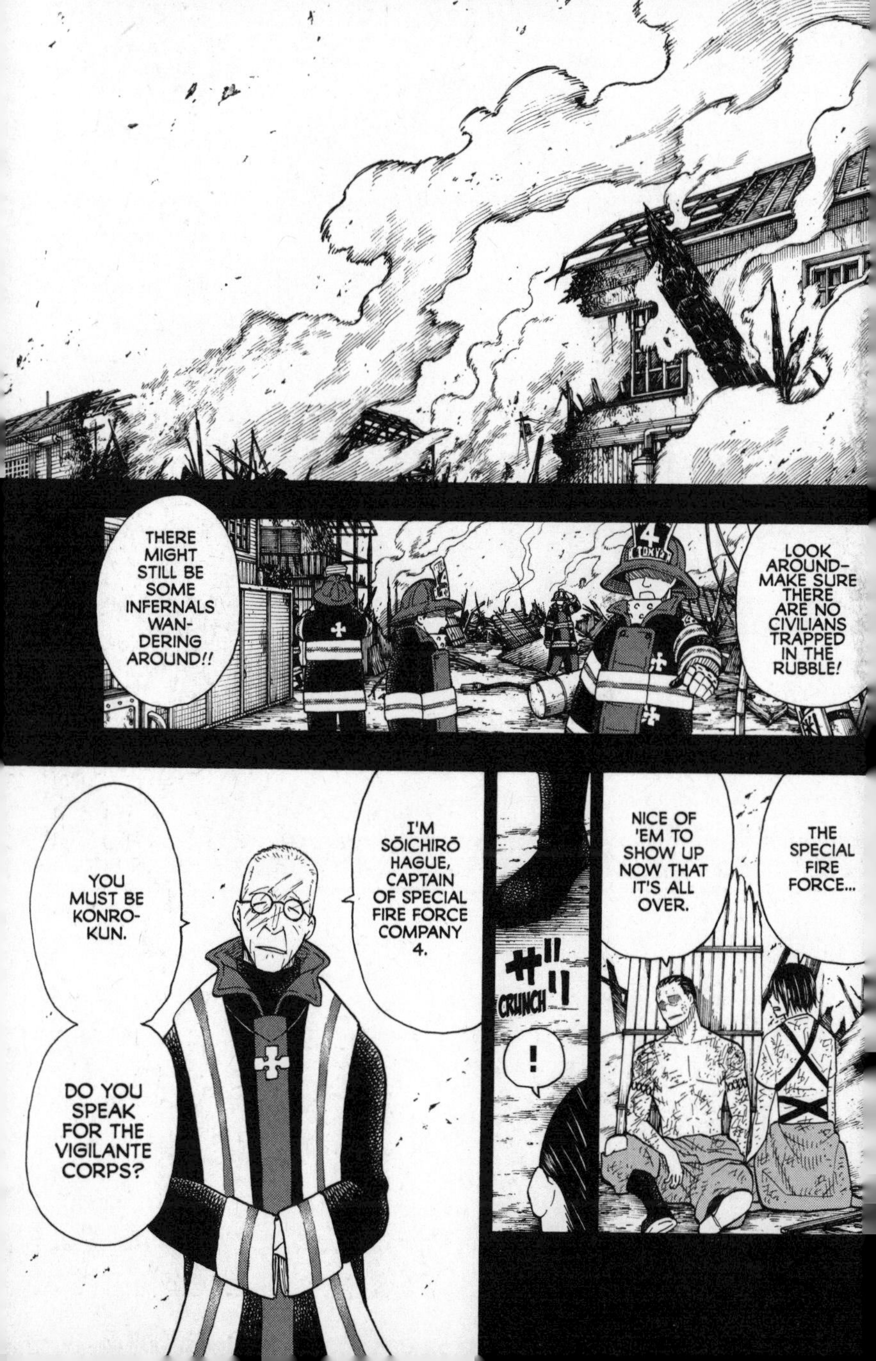
LOOK AROUND—MAKE SURE THERE ARE NO CIVILIANS TRAPPED IN THE RUBBLE!
THERE MIGHT STILL BE SOME INFERNALS WAN-DERING AROUND!!
THE SPECIAL FIRE FORCE...
NICE OF 'EM TO SHOW UP NOW THAT IT'S ALL OVER.
CRUNCH
!
I'M SŌICHIRŌ HAGUE, CAPTAIN OF SPECIAL FIRE FORCE COMPANY 4.
YOU MUST BE KONRO-KUN.
DO YOU SPEAK FOR THE VIGILANTE CORPS?

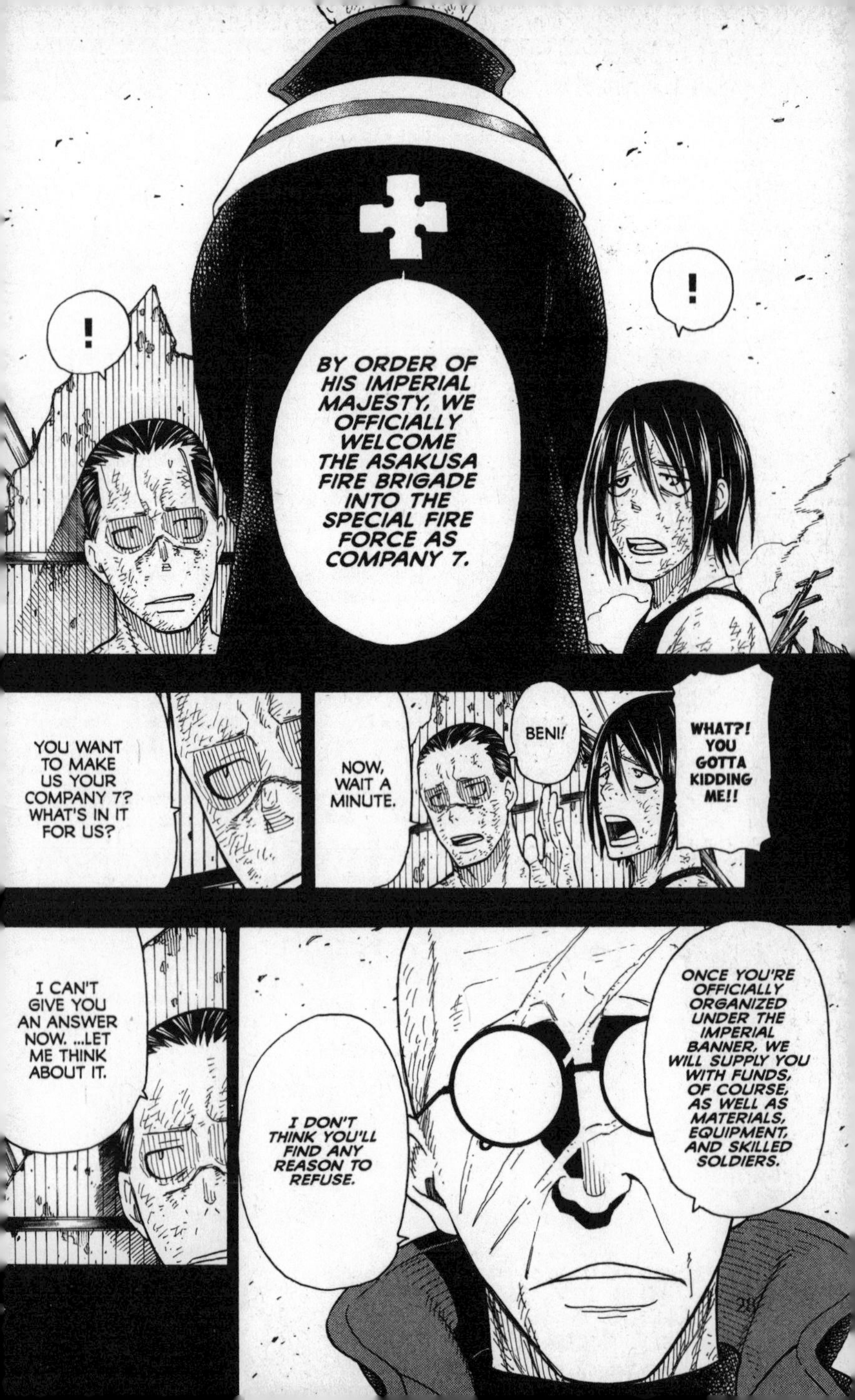
!
BY ORDER OF HIS IMPERIAL MAJESTY, WE OFFICIALLY WELCOME THE ASAKUSA FIRE BRIGADE INTO THE SPECIAL FIRE FORCE AS COMPANY 7.
!
WHAT?! YOU GOTTA KIDDING ME!!
BENI!
NOW, WAIT A MINUTE.
YOU WANT TO MAKE US YOUR COMPANY 7? WHAT'S IN IT FOR US?
ONCE YOU'RE OFFICIALLY ORGANIZED UNDER THE IMPERIAL BANNER, WE WILL SUPPLY YOU WITH FUNDS, OF COURSE, AS WELL AS MATERIALS, EQUIPMENT, AND SKILLED SOLDIERS.
I DON'T THINK YOU'LL FIND ANY REASON TO REFUSE.
I CAN'T GIVE YOU AN ANSWER NOW. ...LET ME THINK ABOUT IT.

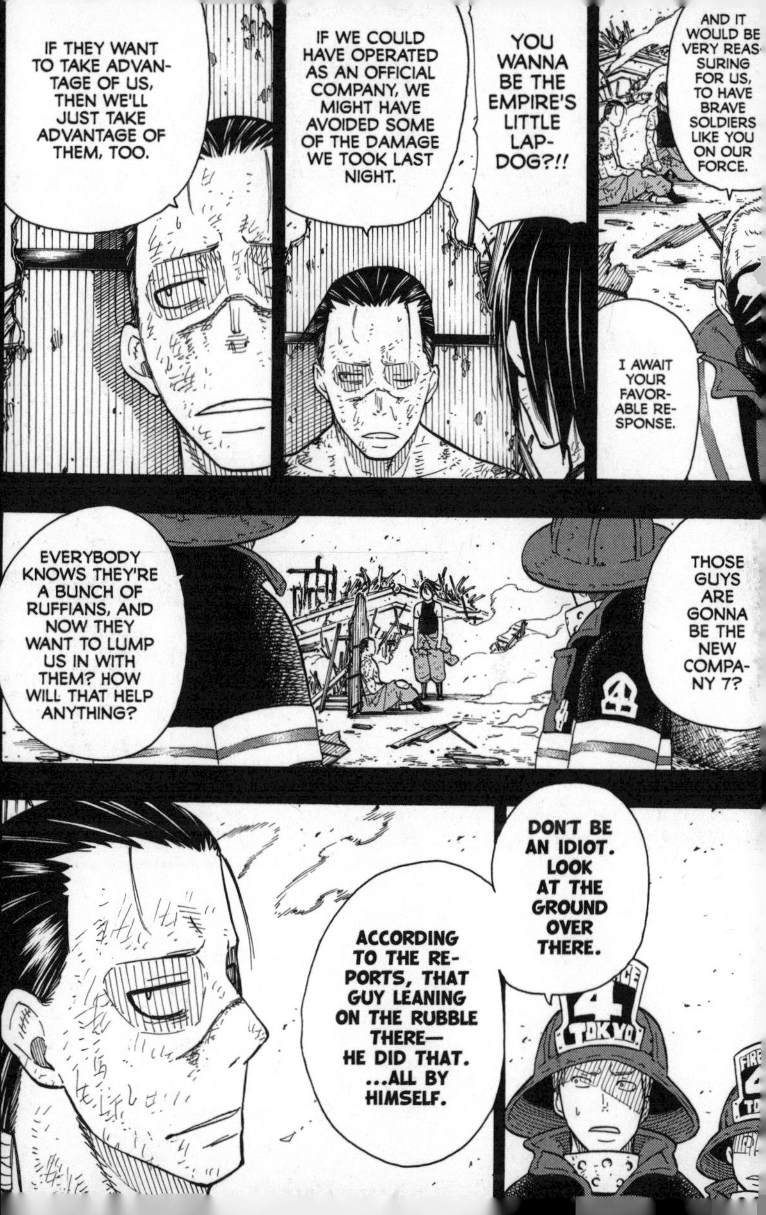
AND IT WOULD BE VERY REASSURING FOR US, TO HAVE BRAVE SOLDIERS LIKE YOU ON OUR FORCE.
I AWAIT YOUR FAVORABLE RESPONSE.
YOU WANNA BE THE EMPIRE'S LITTLE LAP-DOG?!!
IF WE COULD HAVE OPERATED AS AN OFFICIAL COMPANY, WE MIGHT HAVE AVOIDED SOME OF THE DAMAGE WE TOOK LAST NIGHT.
IF THEY WANT TO TAKE ADVANTAGE OF US, THEN WE'LL JUST TAKE ADVANTAGE OF THEM, TOO.
THOSE GUYS ARE GONNA BE THE NEW COMPANY 7?
EVERYBODY KNOWS THEY'RE A BUNCH OF RUFFIANS, AND NOW THEY WANT TO LUMP US IN WITH THEM? HOW WILL THAT HELP ANYTHING?
DON'T BE AN IDIOT. LOOK AT THE GROUND OVER THERE.
ACCORDING TO THE REPORTS, THAT GUY LEANING ON THE RUBBLE THERE—HE DID THAT. ...ALL BY HIMSELF.
TOKYO

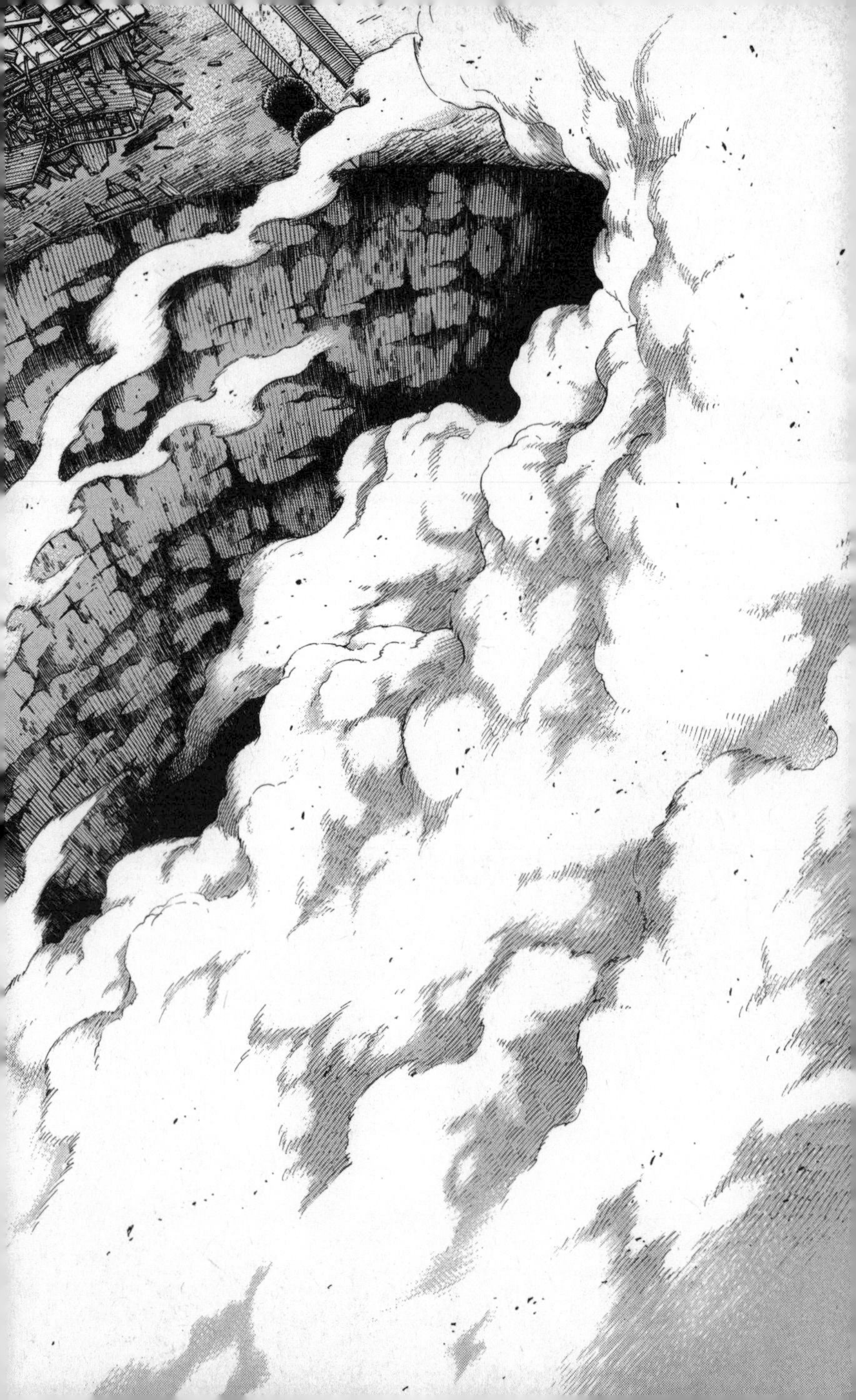

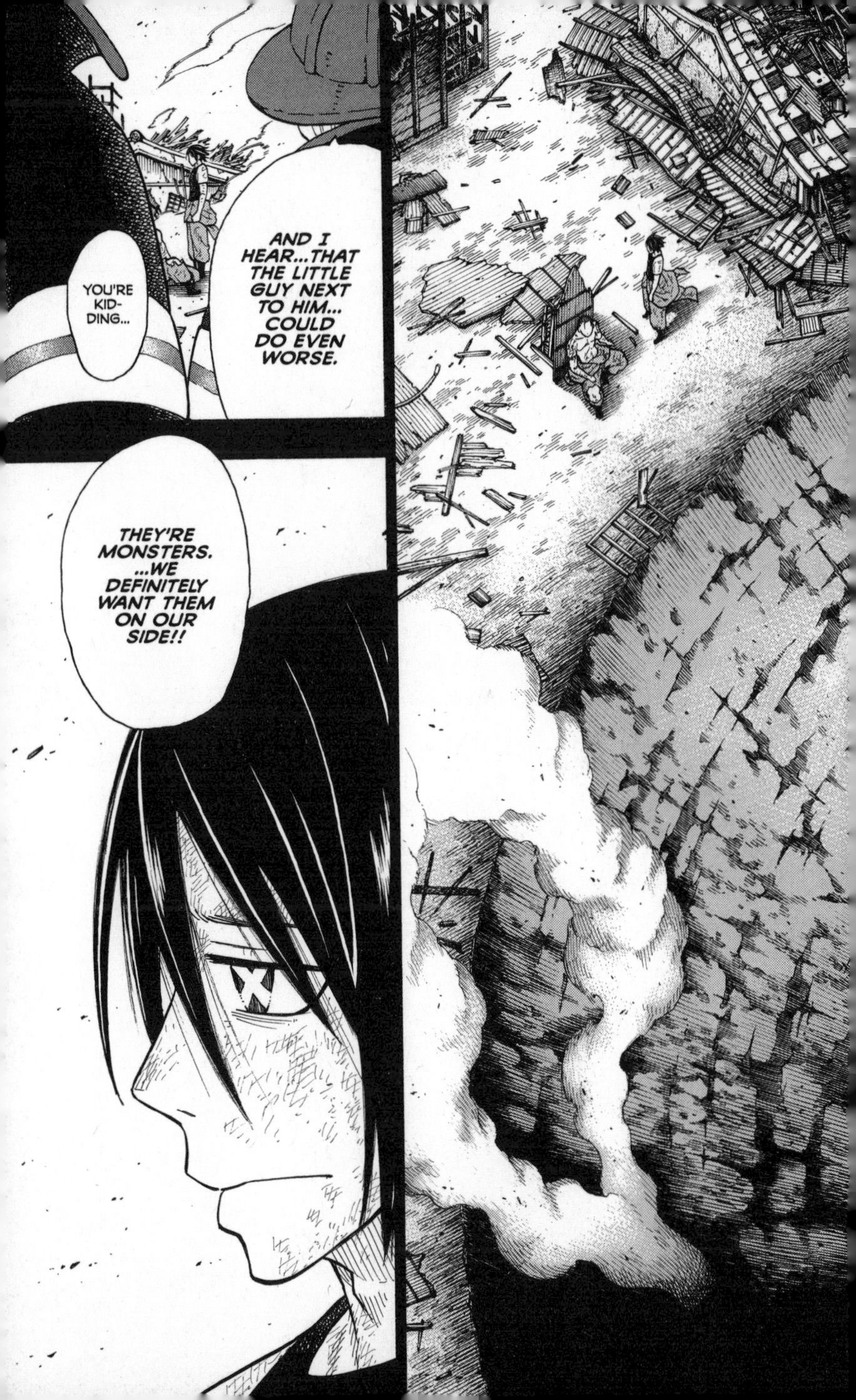
AND I HEAR...THAT THE LITTLE GUY NEXT TO HIM... COULD DO EVEN WORSE.
YOU'RE KID-DING...
THEY'RE MONSTERS. ...WE DEFINITELY WANT THEM ON OUR SIDE!!

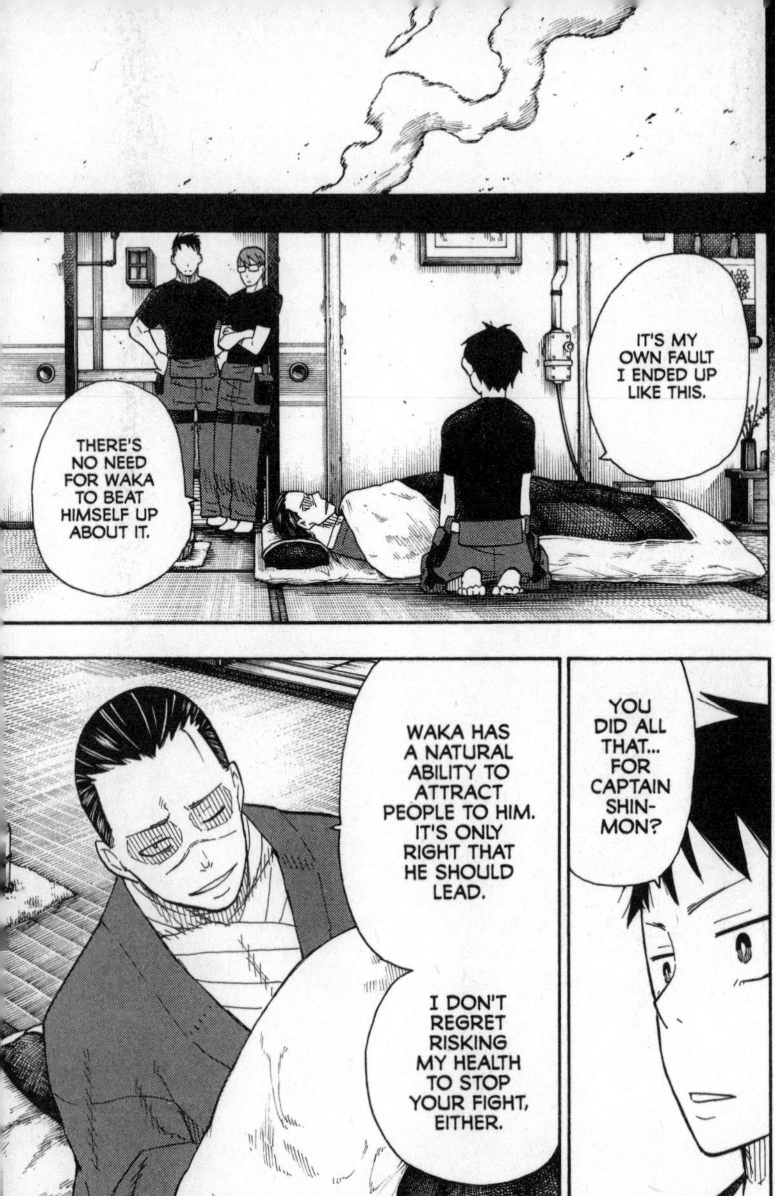
IT'S MY OWN FAULT I ENDED UP LIKE THIS.
THERE'S NO NEED FOR WAKA TO BEAT HIMSELF UP ABOUT IT.
YOU DID ALL THAT... FOR CAPTAIN SHIN-MON?
WAKA HAS A NATURAL ABILITY TO ATTRACT PEOPLE TO HIM. IT'S ONLY RIGHT THAT HE SHOULD LEAD.
I DON'T REGRET RISKING MY HEALTH TO STOP YOUR FIGHT, EITHER.

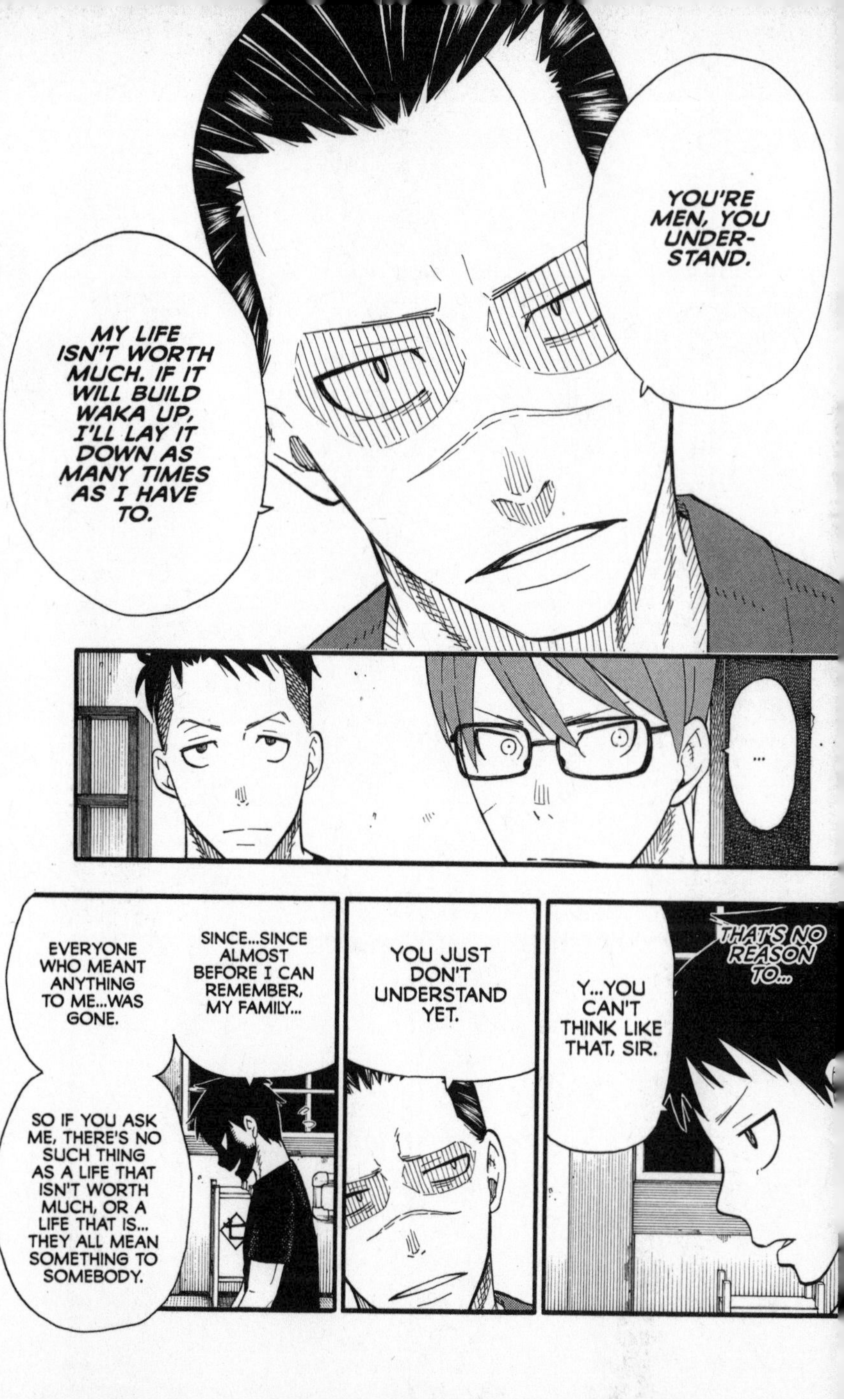
YOU'RE MEN, YOU UNDER-STAND.
MY LIFE ISN'T WORTH MUCH. IF IT WILL BUILD WAKA UP, I'LL LAY IT DOWN AS MANY TIMES AS I HAVE TO.
...
THAT'S NO REASON TO...
Y...YOU CAN'T THINK LIKE THAT, SIR.
YOU JUST DON'T UNDERSTAND YET.
SINCE...SINCE ALMOST BEFORE I CAN REMEMBER, MY FAMILY...
EVERYONE WHO MEANT ANYTHING TO ME...WAS GONE.
SO IF YOU ASK ME, THERE'S NO SUCH THING AS A LIFE THAT ISN'T WORTH MUCH, OR A LIFE THAT IS... THEY ALL MEAN SOMETHING TO SOMEBODY.

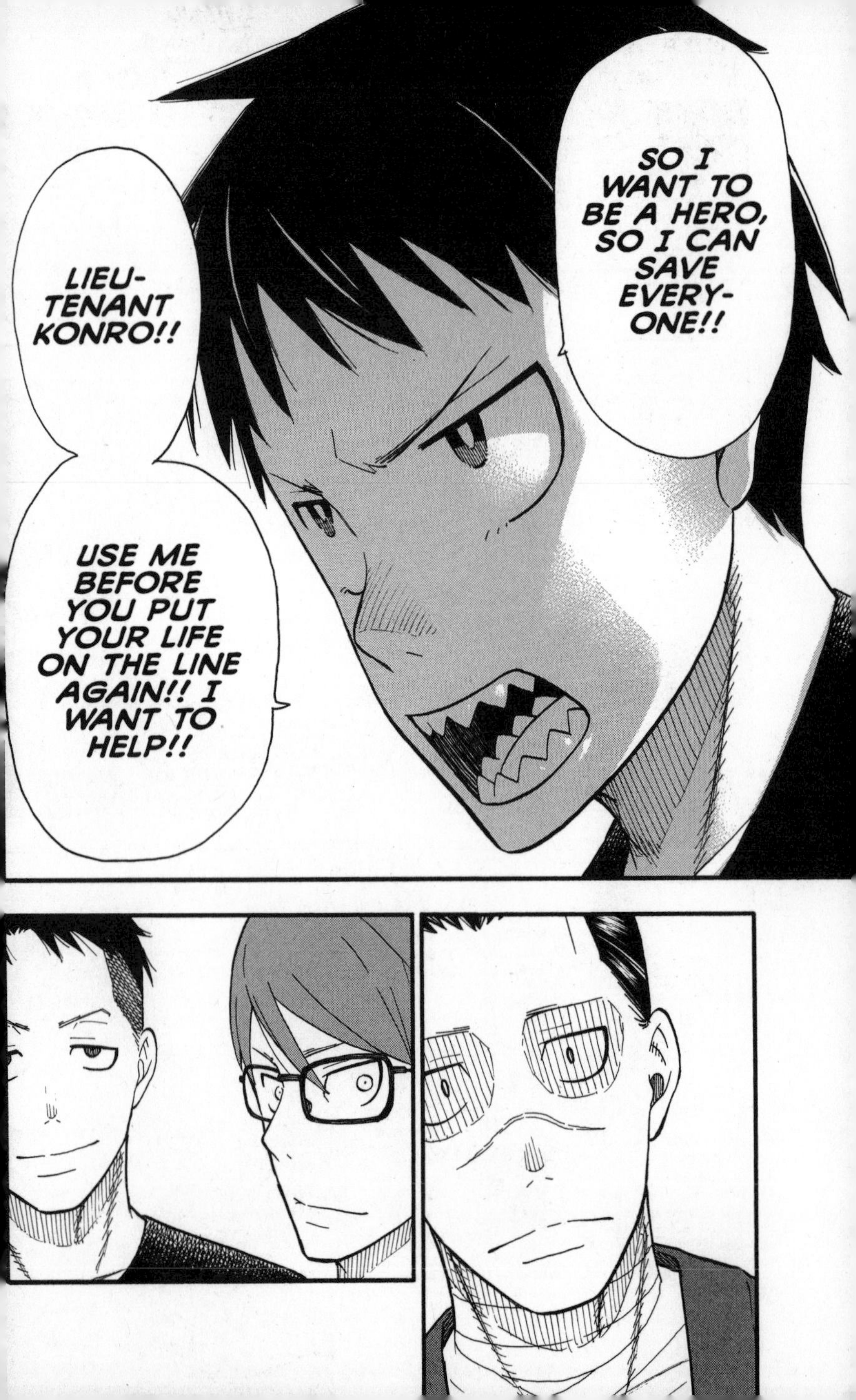
SO I WANT TO BE A HERO, SO I CAN SAVE EVERY-ONE!!
LIEU-TENANT KONRO!!
USE ME BEFORE YOU PUT YOUR LIFE ON THE LINE AGAIN!! I WANT TO HELP!!

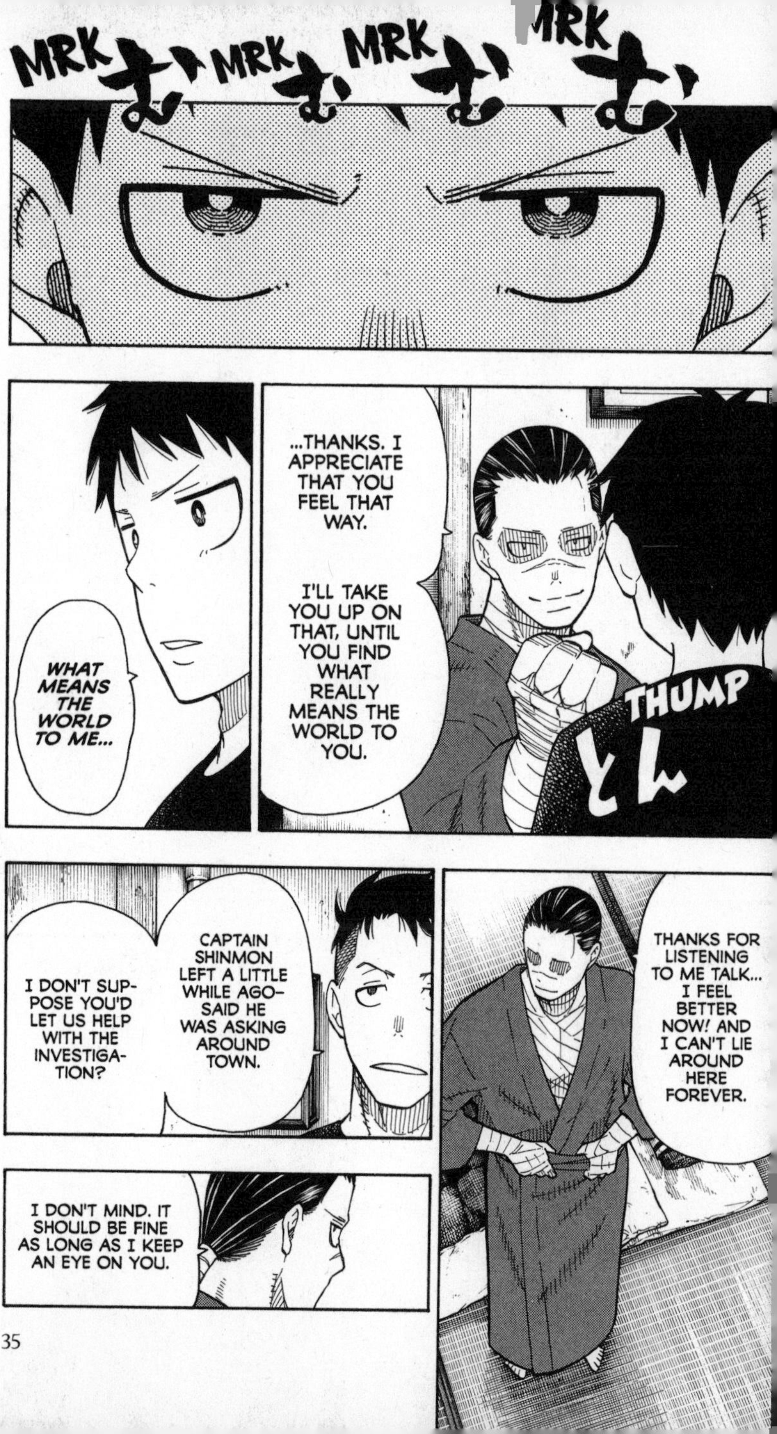
MRK むMRK むMRK むMRK む
...THANKS. I APPRECIATE THAT YOU FEEL THAT WAY.
I'LL TAKE YOU UP ON THAT, UNTIL YOU FIND WHAT REALLY MEANS THE WORLD TO YOU.
THUMP とん
WHAT MEANS THE WORLD TO ME...
THANKS FOR LISTENING TO ME TALK... I FEEL BETTER NOW! AND I CAN'T LIE AROUND HERE FOREVER.
CAPTAIN SHINMON LEFT A LITTLE WHILE AGO–SAID HE WAS ASKING AROUND TOWN.
I DON'T SUPPOSE YOU'D LET US HELP WITH THE INVESTIGATION?
I DON'T MIND. IT SHOULD BE FINE AS LONG AS I KEEP AN EYE ON YOU.

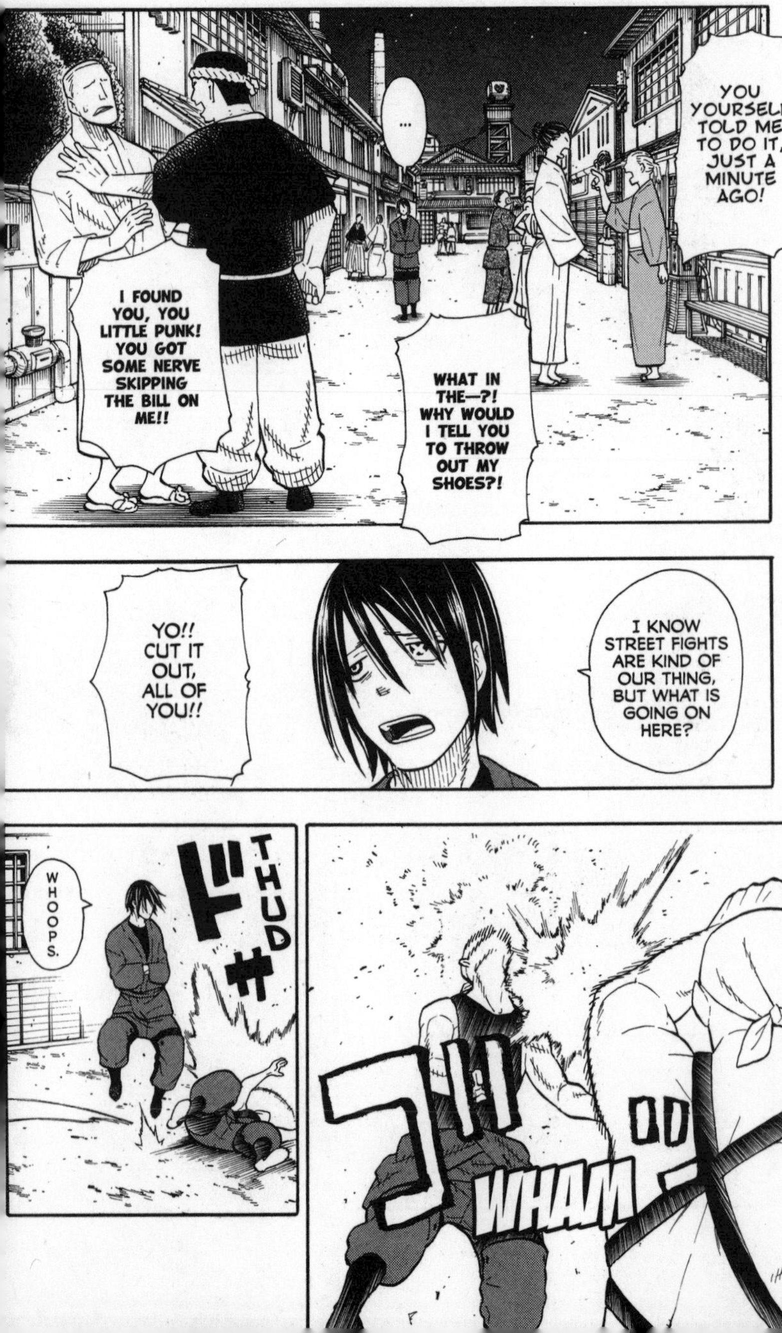
YOU YOURSELF TOLD ME TO DO IT, JUST A MINUTE AGO!
...
WHAT IN THE—?! WHY WOULD I TELL YOU TO THROW OUT MY SHOES?!
I FOUND YOU, YOU LITTLE PUNK! YOU GOT SOME NERVE SKIPPING THE BILL ON ME!!
I KNOW STREET FIGHTS ARE KIND OF OUR THING, BUT WHAT IS GOING ON HERE?
YO!! CUT IT OUT, ALL OF YOU!!
ゴッ
WHAM
ドサ
THUD
WHOOPS.

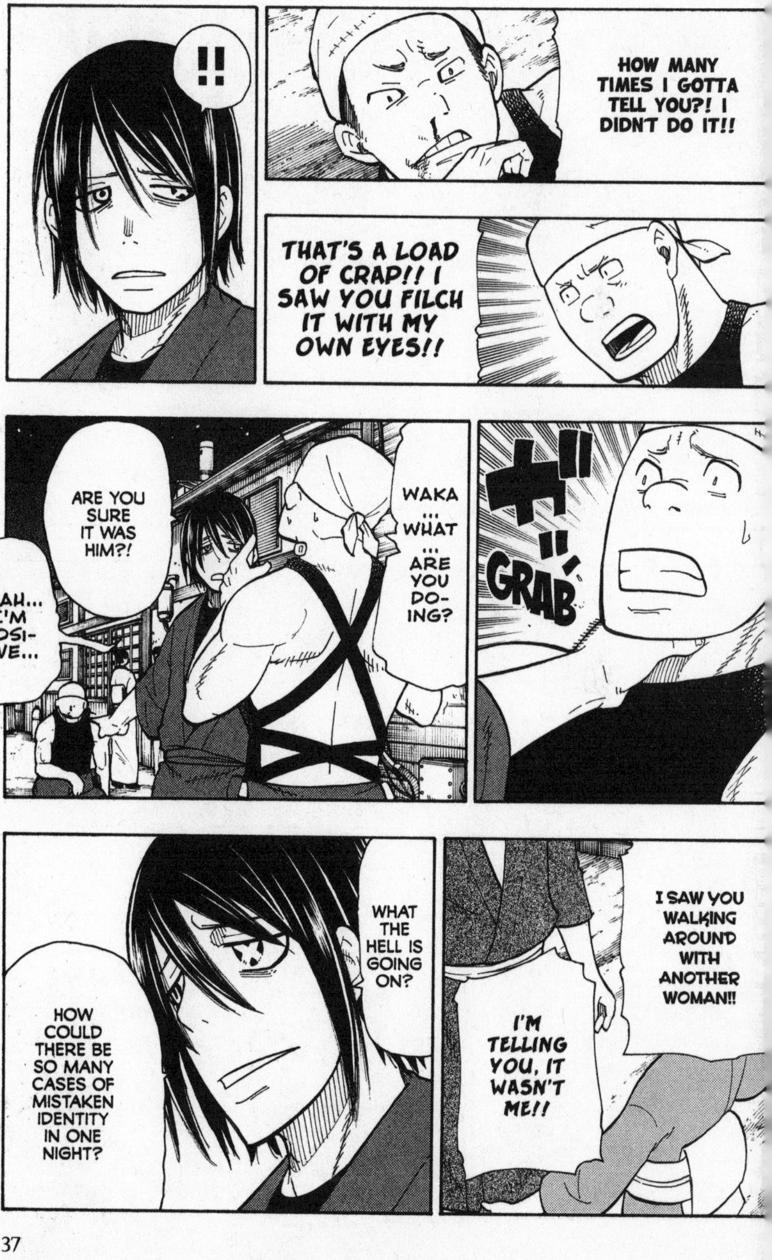
HOW MANY TIMES I GOTTA TELL YOU?! I DIDN'T DO IT!!
THAT'S A LOAD OF CRAP!! I SAW YOU FILCH IT WITH MY OWN EYES!!
!!
GRAB
WAKA ... WHAT ... ARE YOU DO-ING?
ARE YOU SURE IT WAS HIM?!
YEAH... I'M POSI-TIVE...
I SAW YOU WALKING AROUND WITH ANOTHER WOMAN!!
I'M TELLING YOU, IT WASN'T ME!!
WHAT THE HELL IS GOING ON?
HOW COULD THERE BE SO MANY CASES OF MISTAKEN IDENTITY IN ONE NIGHT?

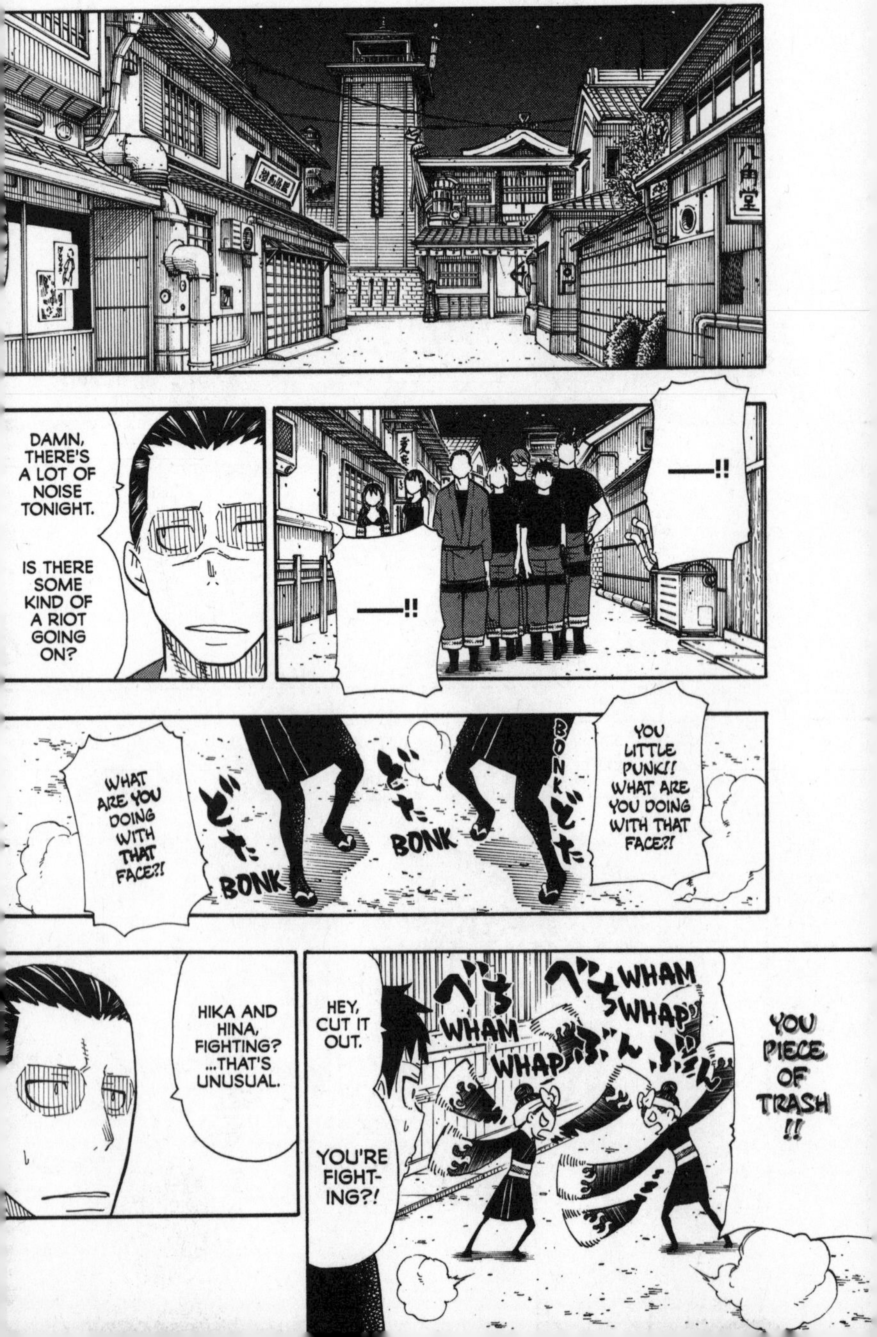
——!!
——!!
DAMN, THERE'S A LOT OF NOISE TONIGHT.
IS THERE SOME KIND OF A RIOT GOING ON?
YOU LITTLE PUNK!! WHAT ARE YOU DOING WITH THAT FACE?!
BONK
BONK
BONK
WHAT ARE YOU DOING WITH THAT FACE?!
YOU PIECE OF TRASH!!
WHAM
WHAP
WHAM
WHAP
HEY, CUT IT OUT.
YOU'RE FIGHTING?!
HIKA AND HINA, FIGHTING? ...THAT'S UNUSUAL.

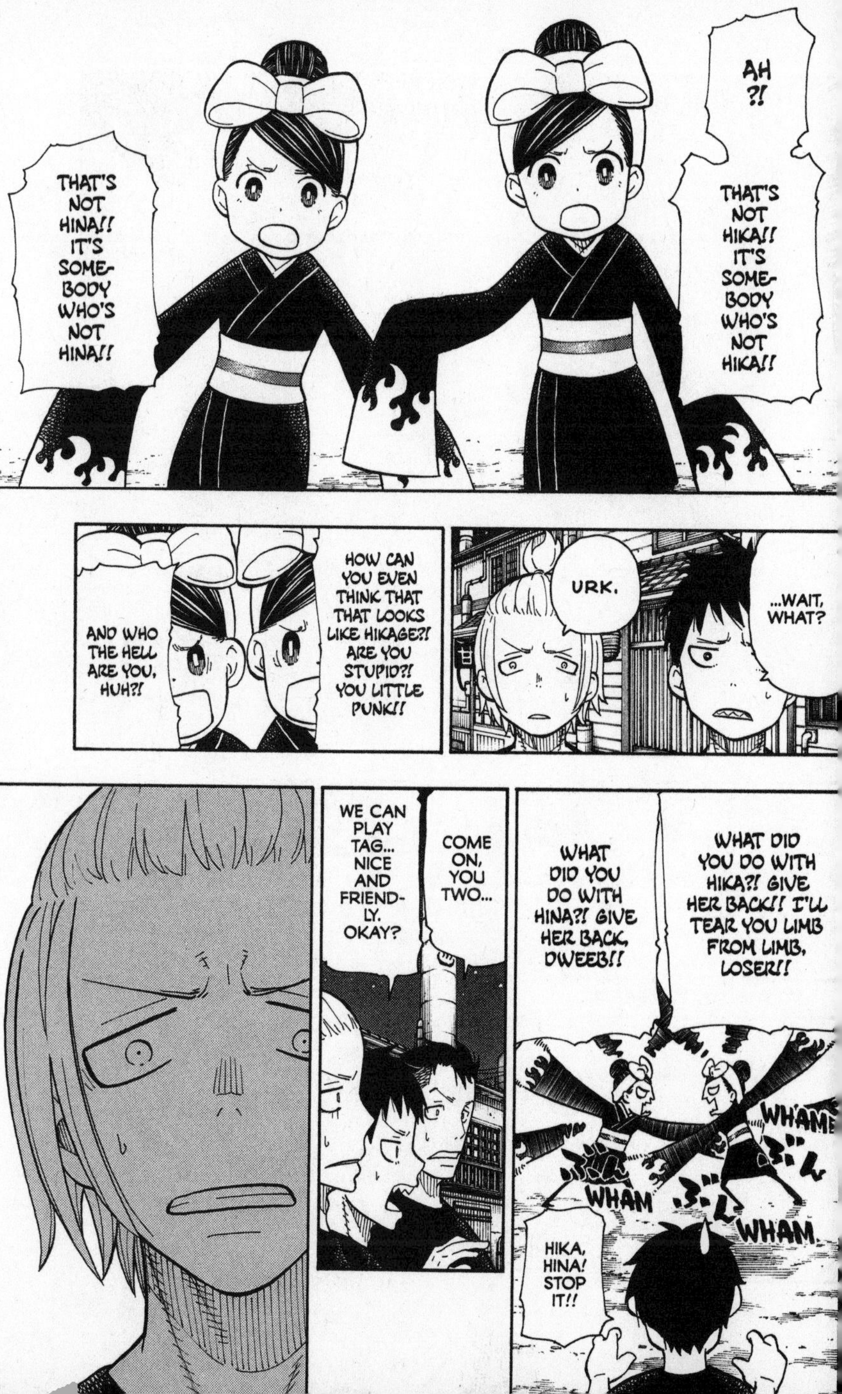
AH?!
THAT'S NOT HIKA!! IT'S SOMEBODY WHO'S NOT HIKA!!
THAT'S NOT HINA!! IT'S SOMEBODY WHO'S NOT HINA!!
...WAIT, WHAT?
URK.
HOW CAN YOU EVEN THINK THAT THAT LOOKS LIKE HIKAGE?! ARE YOU STUPID?! YOU LITTLE PUNK!!
AND WHO THE HELL ARE YOU, HUH?!
WHAT DID YOU DO WITH HIKA?! GIVE HER BACK!! I'LL TEAR YOU LIMB FROM LIMB, LOSER!!
WHAT DID YOU DO WITH HINA?! GIVE HER BACK, DWEEB!!
WHAM
WHAM
WHAM
HIKA, HINA! STOP IT!!
COME ON, YOU TWO...
WE CAN PLAY TAG... NICE AND FRIENDLY. OKAY?

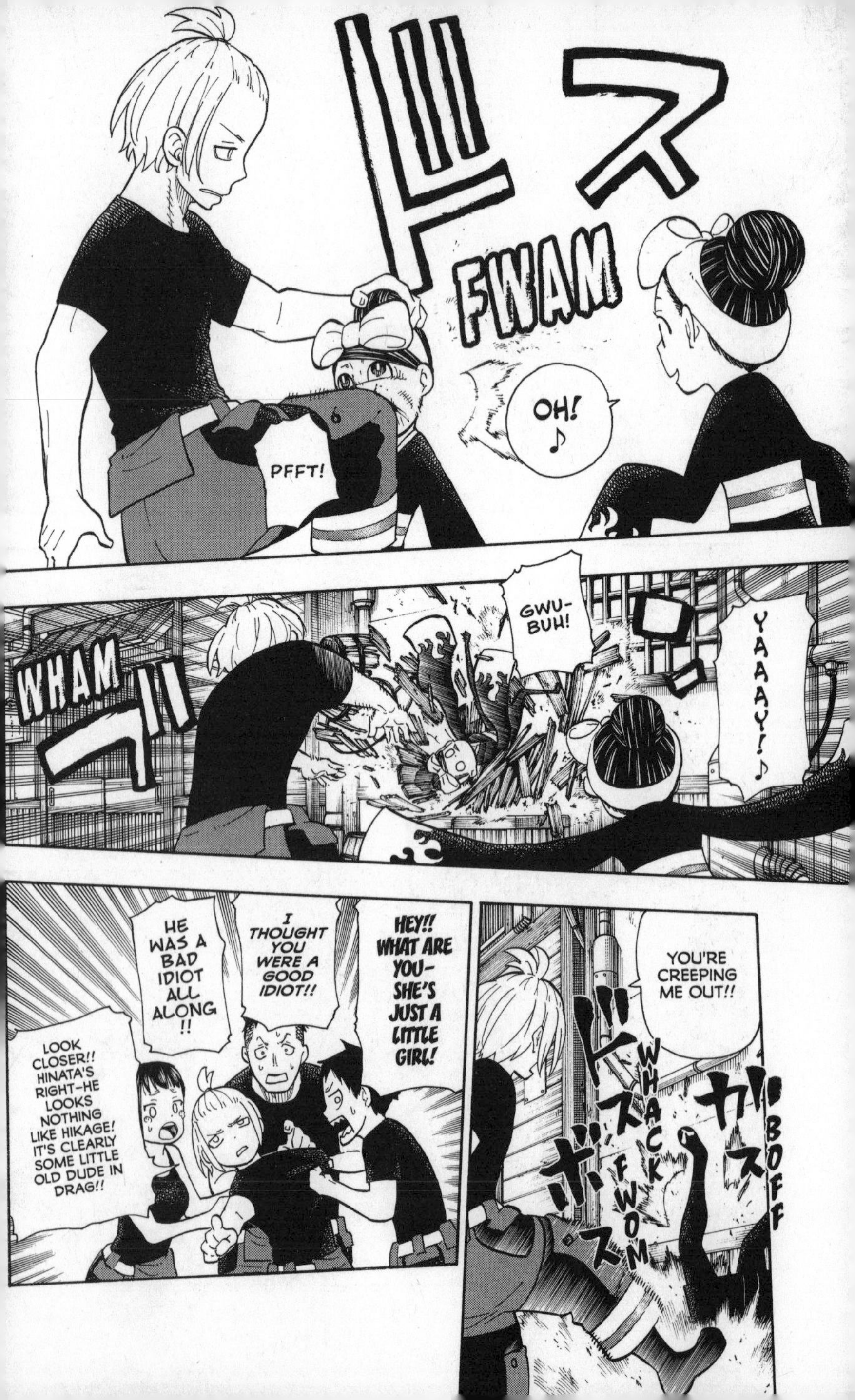

ドス
FWAM
OH! ♪
PFFT!
YAAAAY!♪
GWU-BUH!
WHAM
YOU'RE CREEPING ME OUT!!
カス
BOFF
ドス
WHACK
ザス
FWOM
HEY!! WHAT ARE YOU— SHE'S JUST A LITTLE GIRL!
I THOUGHT YOU WERE A GOOD IDIOT!!
HE WAS A BAD IDIOT ALL ALONG!!
LOOK CLOSER!! HINATA'S RIGHT—HE LOOKS NOTHING LIKE HIKAGE! IT'S CLEARLY SOME LITTLE OLD DUDE IN DRAG!!

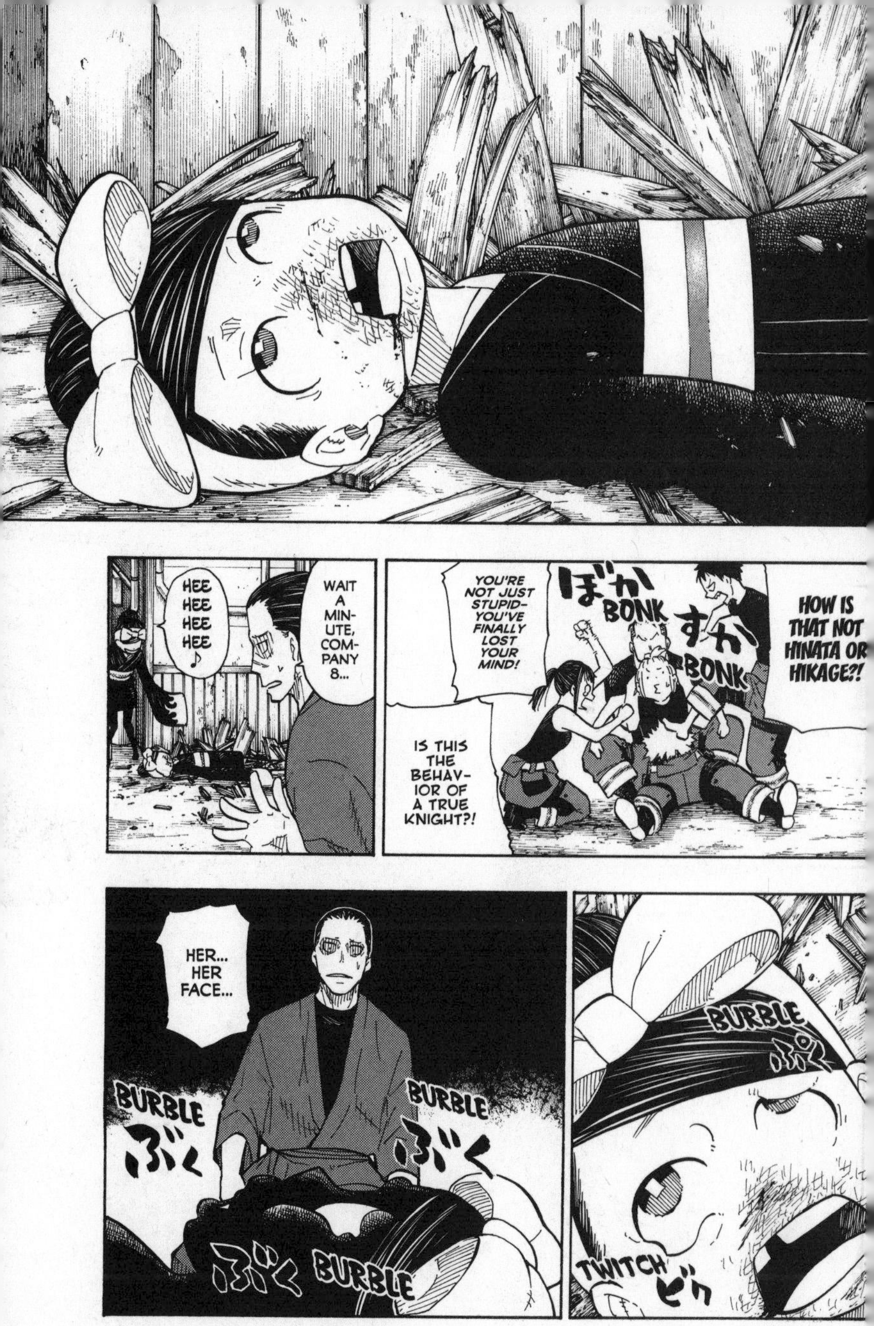
HOW IS THAT NOT HINATA OR HIKAGE?!
YOU'RE NOT JUST STUPID-YOU'VE FINALLY LOST YOUR MIND!
ぼか BONK
すか BONK
IS THIS THE BEHAVIOR OF A TRUE KNIGHT?!
WAIT A MINUTE, COMPANY 8...
HEE HEE HEE HEE ♪
BURBLE ぷく
TWITCH ピク
HER... HER FACE...
BURBLE ぶく
BURBLE ぶく
ぶく BURBLE

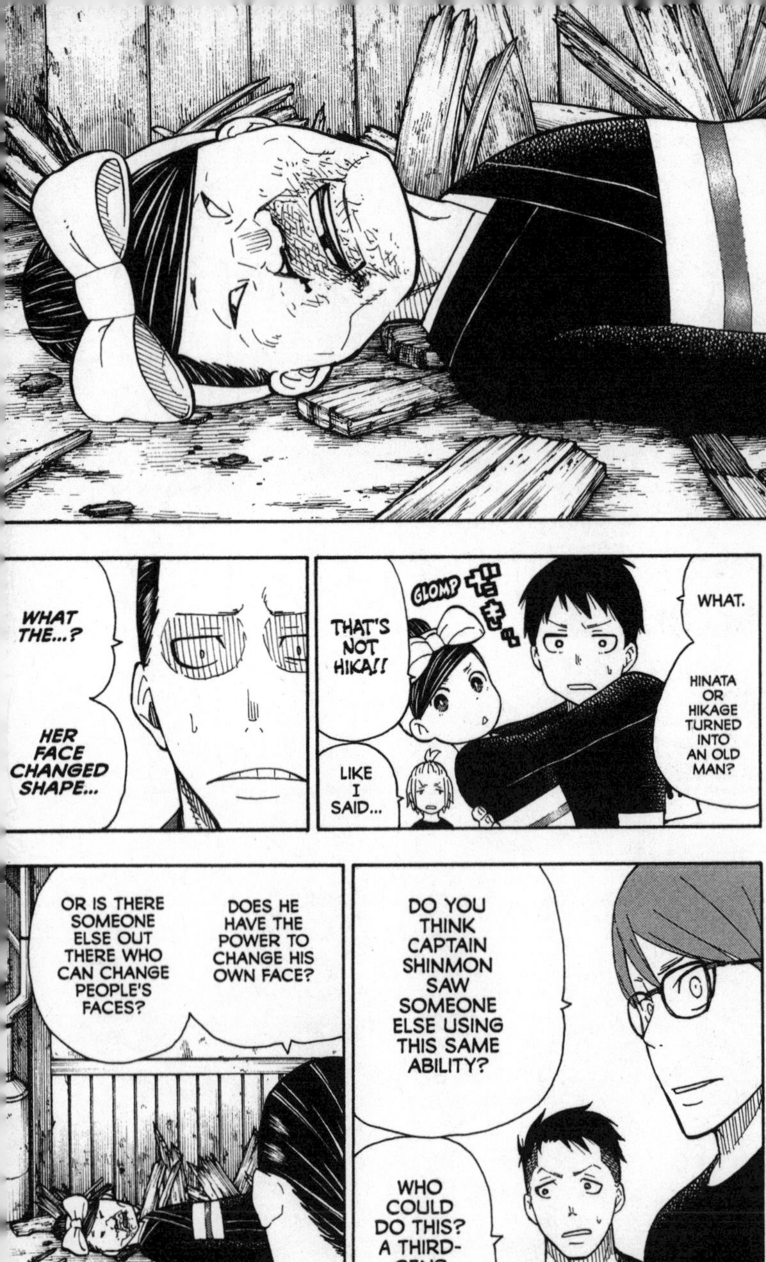
WHAT.
HINATA OR HIKAGE TURNED INTO AN OLD MAN?
GLOMP
THAT'S NOT HIKA!!
LIKE I SAID...
WHAT THE...?
HER FACE CHANGED SHAPE...
DO YOU THINK CAPTAIN SHINMON SAW SOMEONE ELSE USING THIS SAME ABILITY?
WHO COULD DO THIS? A THIRD-GEN?
DOES HE HAVE THE POWER TO CHANGE HIS OWN FACE?
OR IS THERE SOMEONE ELSE OUT THERE WHO CAN CHANGE PEOPLE'S FACES?

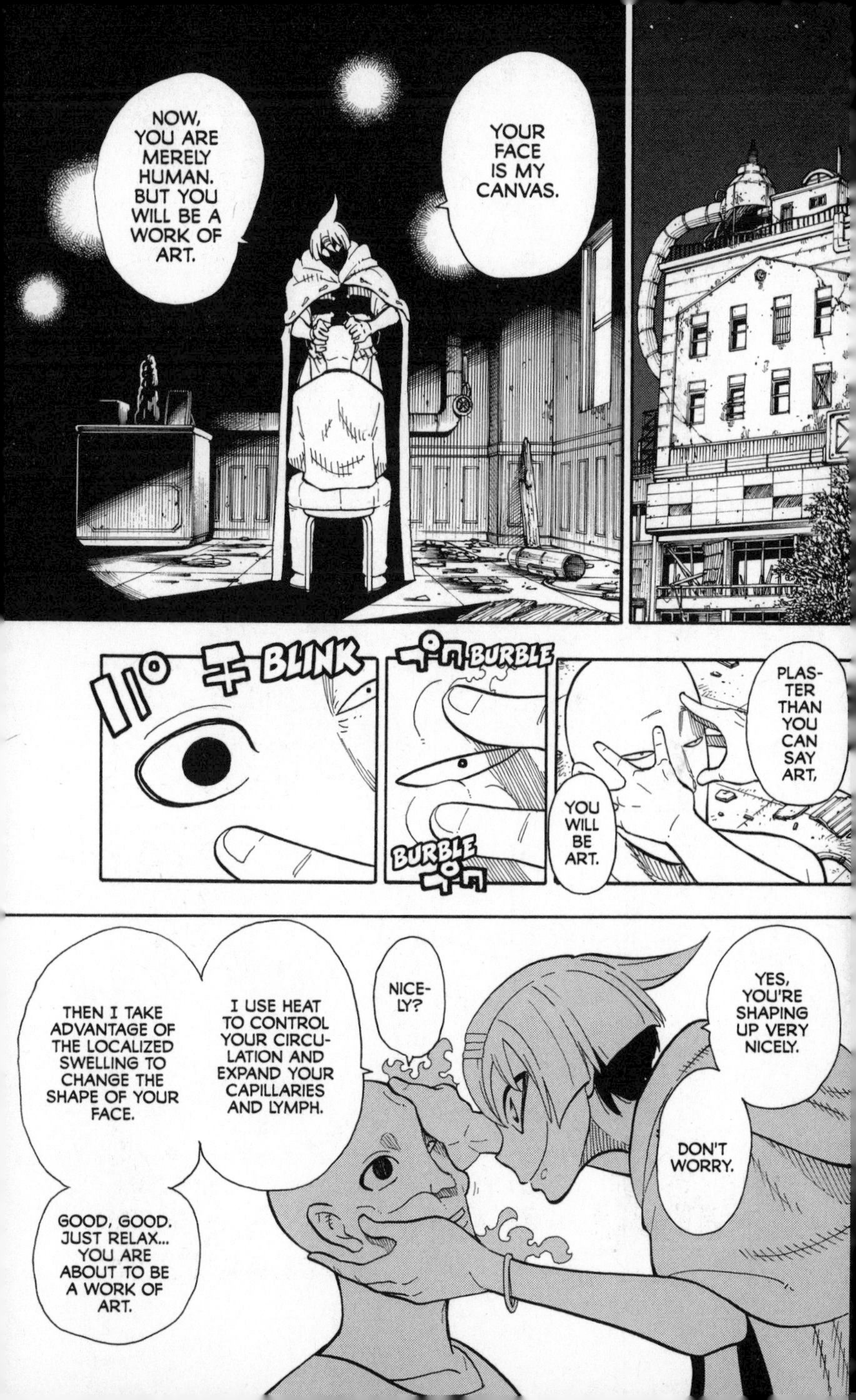
YOUR FACE IS MY CANVAS.
NOW, YOU ARE MERELY HUMAN. BUT YOU WILL BE A WORK OF ART.
PLAS-TER THAN YOU CAN SAY ART,
YOU WILL BE ART.
BURBLE
BURBLE
BLINK
YES, YOU'RE SHAPING UP VERY NICELY.
DON'T WORRY.
NICE-LY?
I USE HEAT TO CONTROL YOUR CIRCU-LATION AND EXPAND YOUR CAPILLARIES AND LYMPH.
THEN I TAKE ADVANTAGE OF THE LOCALIZED SWELLING TO CHANGE THE SHAPE OF YOUR FACE.
GOOD, GOOD. JUST RELAX... YOU ARE ABOUT TO BE A WORK OF ART.

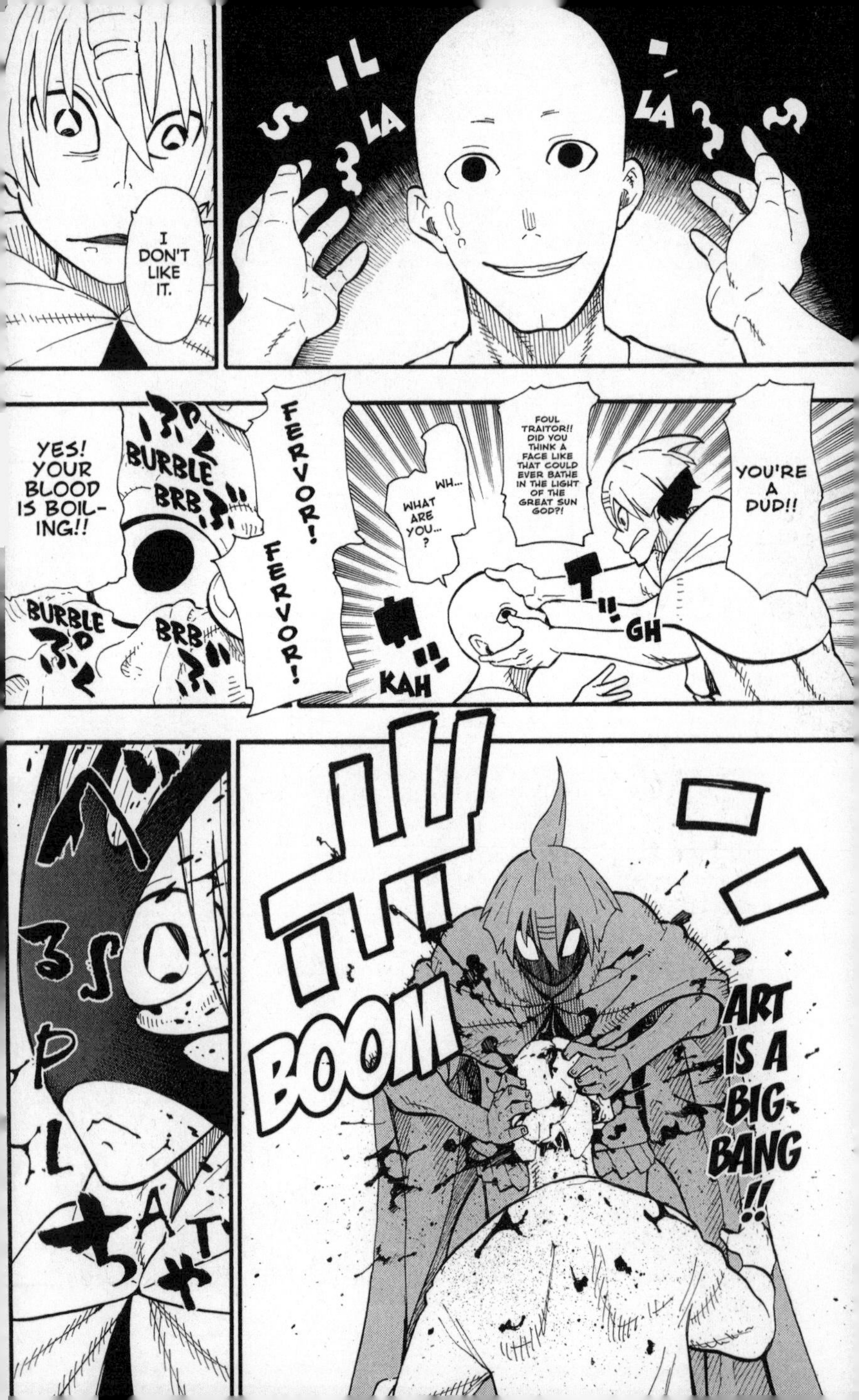
IL
LA
LA
I DON'T LIKE IT.
YOU'RE A DUD!!
FOUL TRAITOR!! DID YOU THINK A FACE LIKE THAT COULD EVER BATHE IN THE LIGHT OF THE GREAT SUN GOD?!
GH
WH... WHAT ARE YOU... ?
KAH
FERVOR! FERVOR!
BURBLE
BRB
YES! YOUR BLOOD IS BOILING!!
BURBLE
BRB
ART IS A BIG BANG!!
BOOM

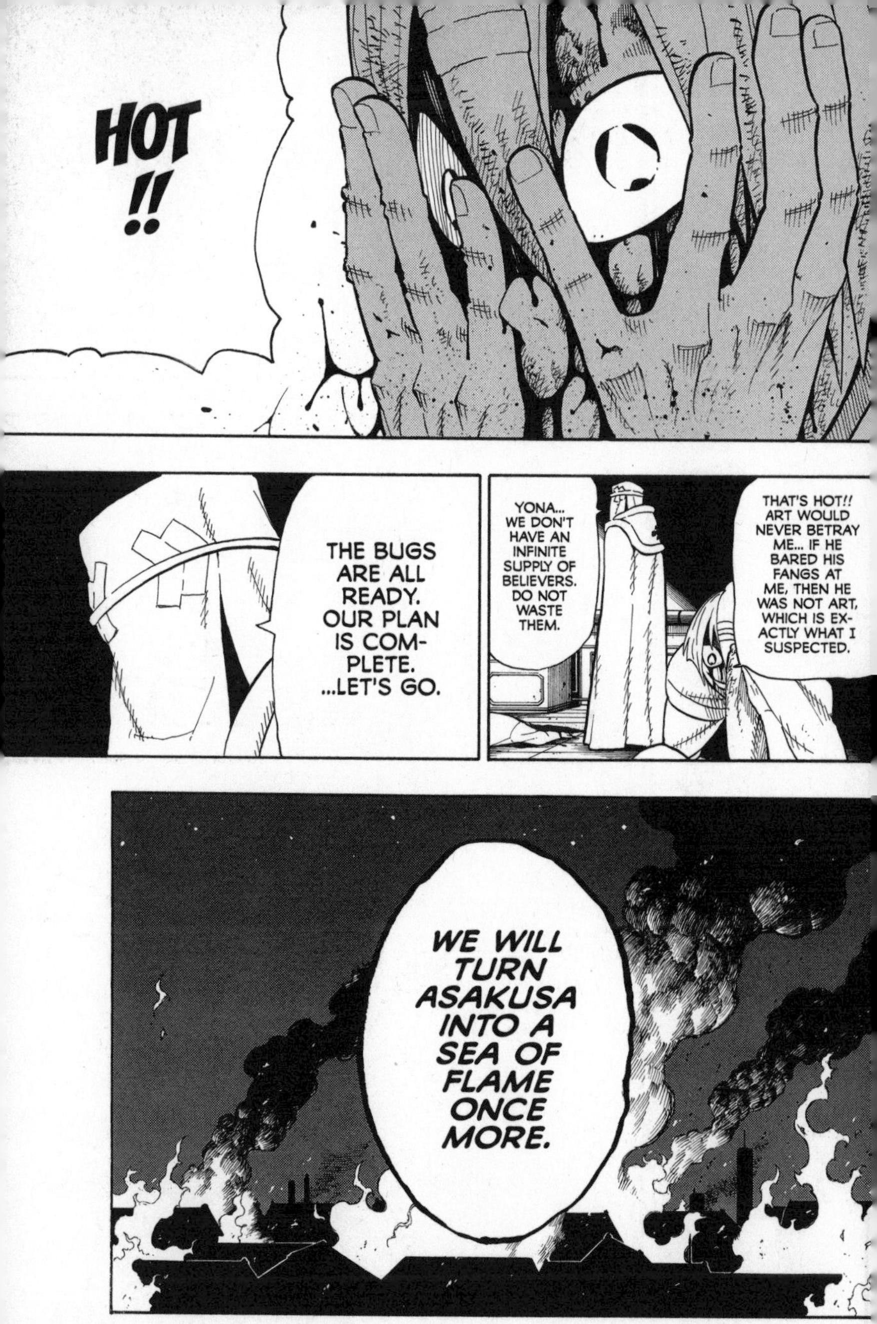
HOT!!
THAT'S HOT!! ART WOULD NEVER BETRAY ME... IF HE BARED HIS FANGS AT ME, THEN HE WAS NOT ART, WHICH IS EXACTLY WHAT I SUSPECTED.
YONA... WE DON'T HAVE AN INFINITE SUPPLY OF BELIEVERS. DO NOT WASTE THEM.
THE BUGS ARE ALL READY. OUR PLAN IS COMPLETE. ...LET'S GO.
WE WILL TURN ASAKUSA INTO A SEA OF FLAME ONCE MORE.

FIRE FORCE

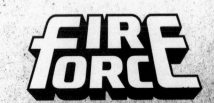

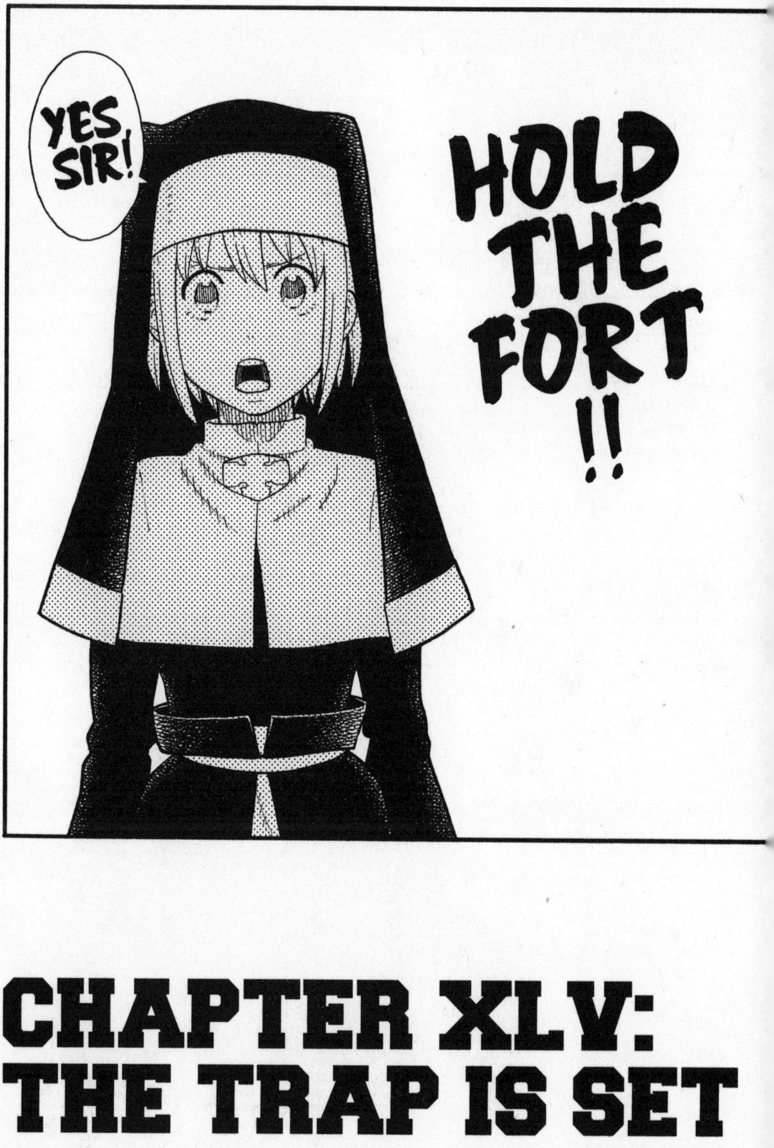
YES SIR!
HOLD THE FORT!!

CHAPTER XLV: THE TRAP IS SET

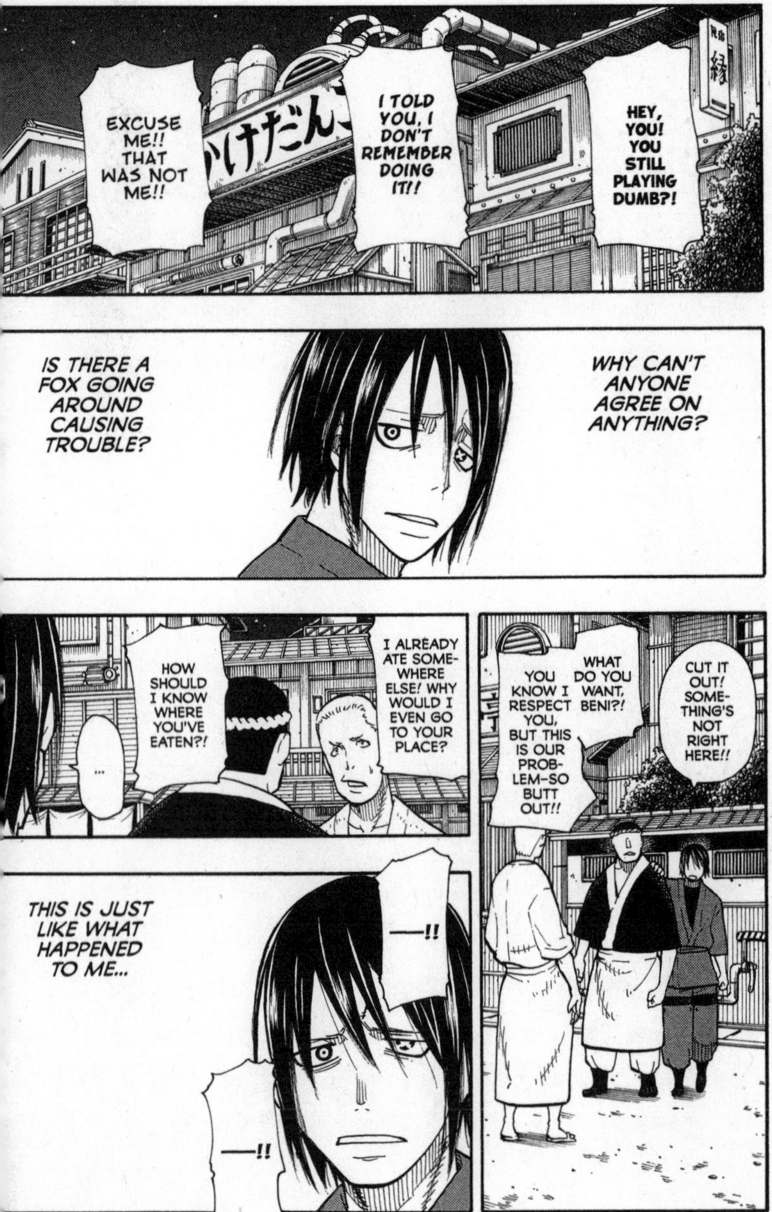

HEY, YOU! YOU STILL PLAYING DUMB?!
I TOLD YOU, I DON'T REMEMBER DOING IT!!
EXCUSE ME!! THAT WAS NOT ME!!
WHY CAN'T ANYONE AGREE ON ANYTHING?
IS THERE A FOX GOING AROUND CAUSING TROUBLE?
CUT IT OUT! SOME-THING'S NOT RIGHT HERE!!
WHAT DO YOU WANT, BENI?!
YOU KNOW I RESPECT YOU, BUT THIS IS OUR PROB-LEM—SO BUTT OUT!!
I ALREADY ATE SOME-WHERE ELSE! WHY WOULD I EVEN GO TO YOUR PLACE?
HOW SHOULD I KNOW WHERE YOU'VE EATEN?!
...
—!!
THIS IS JUST LIKE WHAT HAPPENED TO ME...
—!!

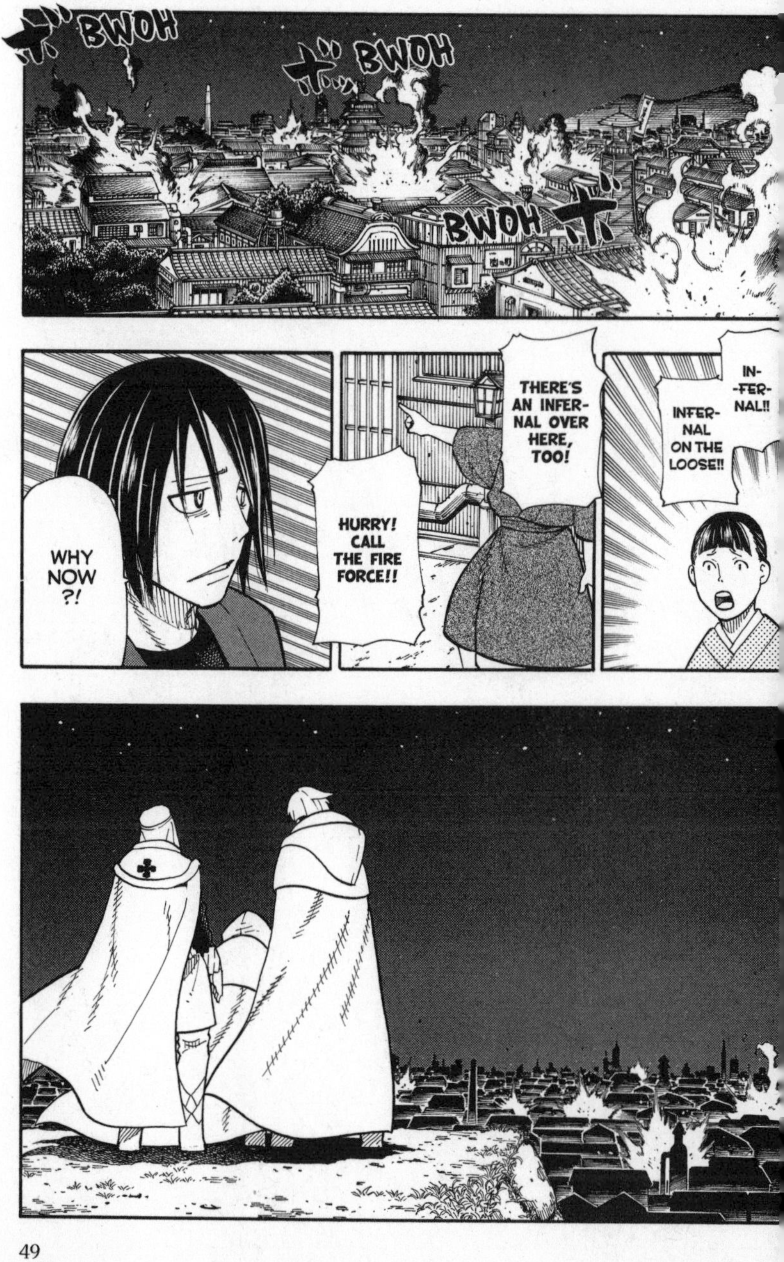
BWOH
BWOH
BWOH
IN- -FER- NAL!!
INFER- NAL ON THE LOOSE!!
THERE'S AN INFER- NAL OVER HERE, TOO!
HURRY! CALL THE FIRE FORCE!!
WHY NOW ?!

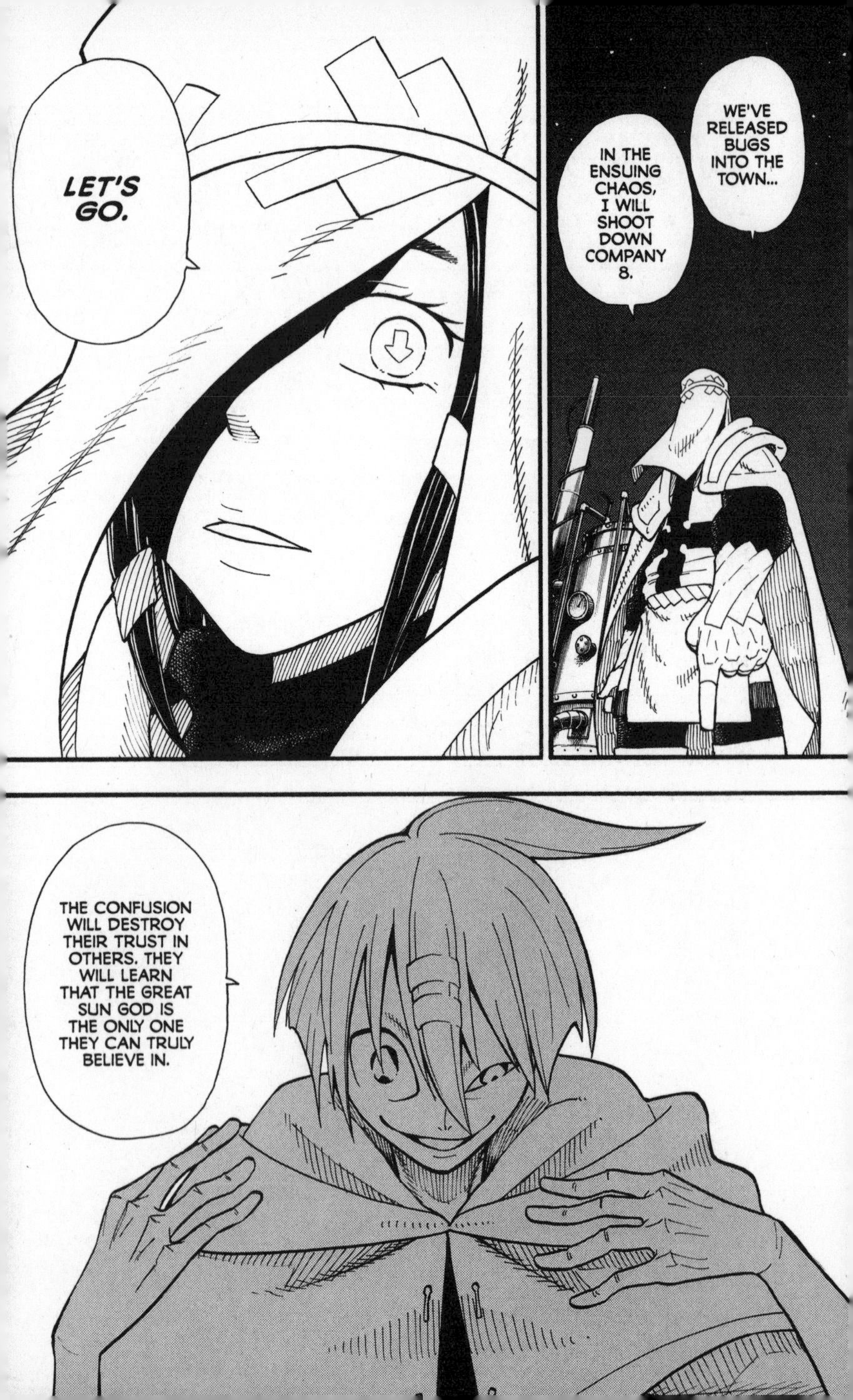
WE'VE RELEASED BUGS INTO THE TOWN...
IN THE ENSUING CHAOS, I WILL SHOOT DOWN COMPANY 8.
LET'S GO.
THE CONFUSION WILL DESTROY THEIR TRUST IN OTHERS. THEY WILL LEARN THAT THE GREAT SUN GOD IS THE ONLY ONE THEY CAN TRULY BELIEVE IN.

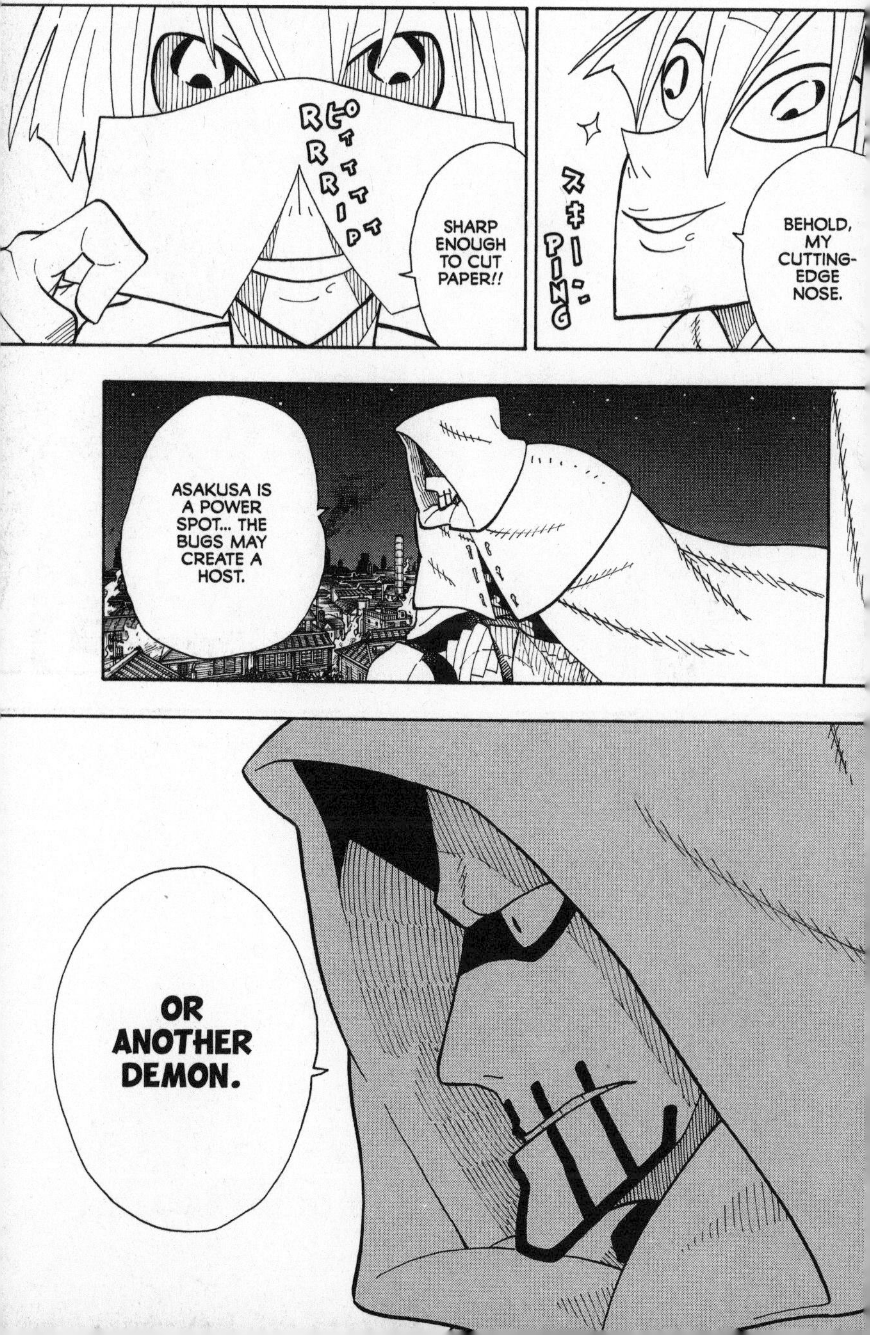

PING
BEHOLD, MY CUTTING-EDGE NOSE.
RRRIP
SHARP ENOUGH TO CUT PAPER!!
ASAKUSA IS A POWER SPOT... THE BUGS MAY CREATE A HOST.
OR ANOTHER DEMON.

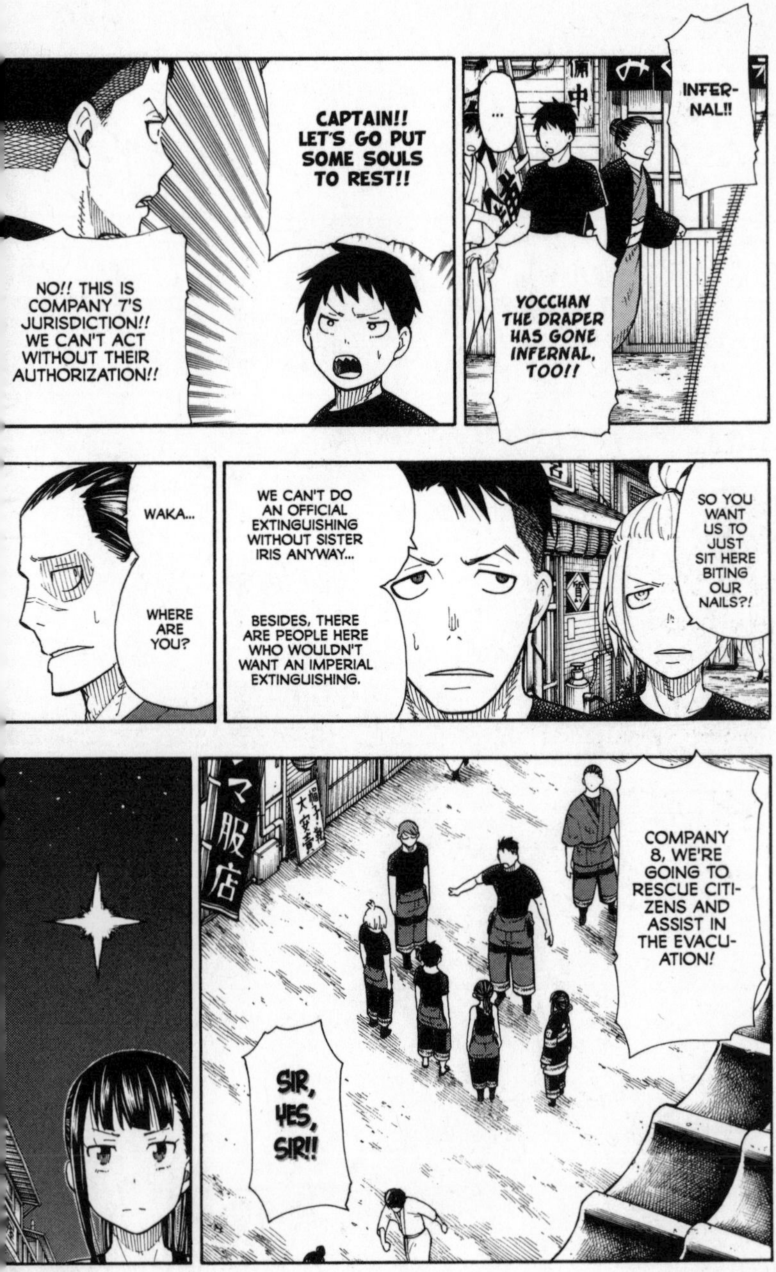
INFER-NAL!!
...
YOCCHAN THE DRAPER HAS GONE INFERNAL, TOO!!
CAPTAIN!! LET'S GO PUT SOME SOULS TO REST!!
NO!! THIS IS COMPANY 7'S JURISDICTION!! WE CAN'T ACT WITHOUT THEIR AUTHORIZATION!!
SO YOU WANT US TO JUST SIT HERE BITING OUR NAILS?!
WE CAN'T DO AN OFFICIAL EXTINGUISHING WITHOUT SISTER IRIS ANYWAY...
BESIDES, THERE ARE PEOPLE HERE WHO WOULDN'T WANT AN IMPERIAL EXTINGUISHING.
WAKA...
WHERE ARE YOU?
COMPANY 8, WE'RE GOING TO RESCUE CITI-ZENS AND ASSIST IN THE EVACU-ATION!
SIR, YES, SIR!!

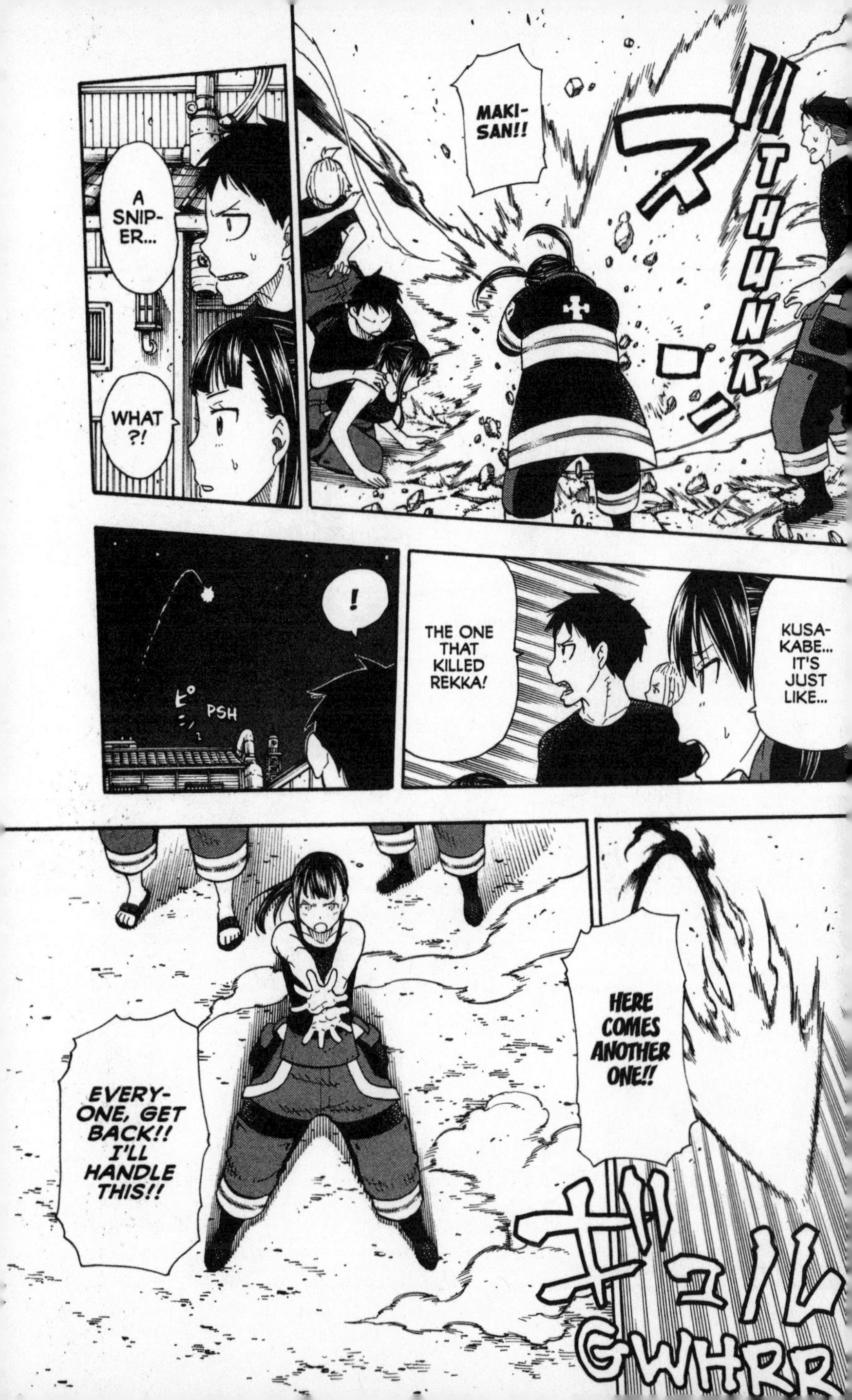
THUNK
MAKI-SAN!!
A SNIPER...
WHAT?!
KUSA-KABE... IT'S JUST LIKE...
THE ONE THAT KILLED REKKA!
!
PSH
HERE COMES ANOTHER ONE!!
GWHRR
EVERY-ONE, GET BACK!! I'LL HANDLE THIS!!

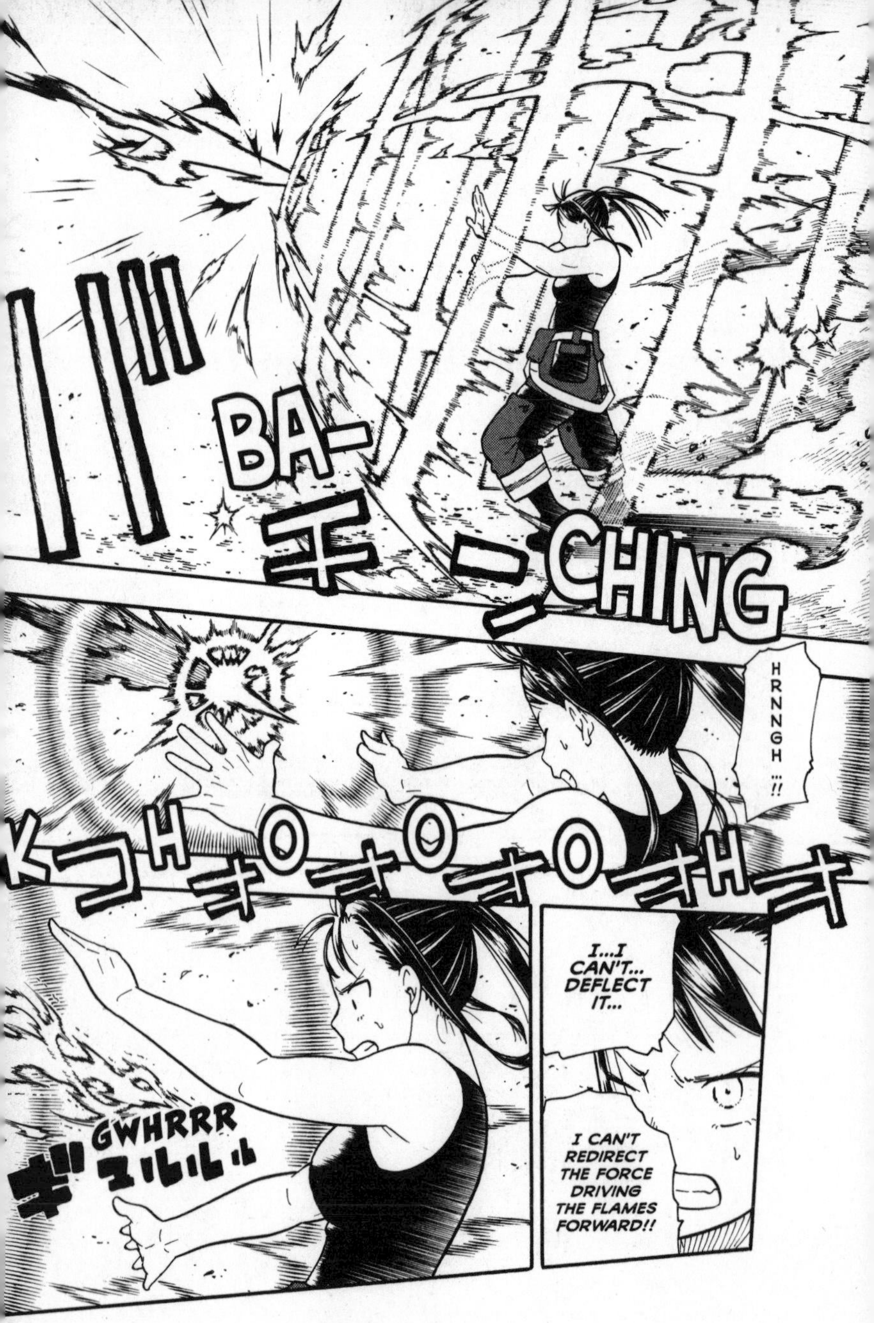
BA-CHING
HRNNGH!!
KHOOOH
I...I CAN'T... DEFLECT IT...
I CAN'T REDIRECT THE FORCE DRIVING THE FLAMES FORWARD!!
GWHRRR

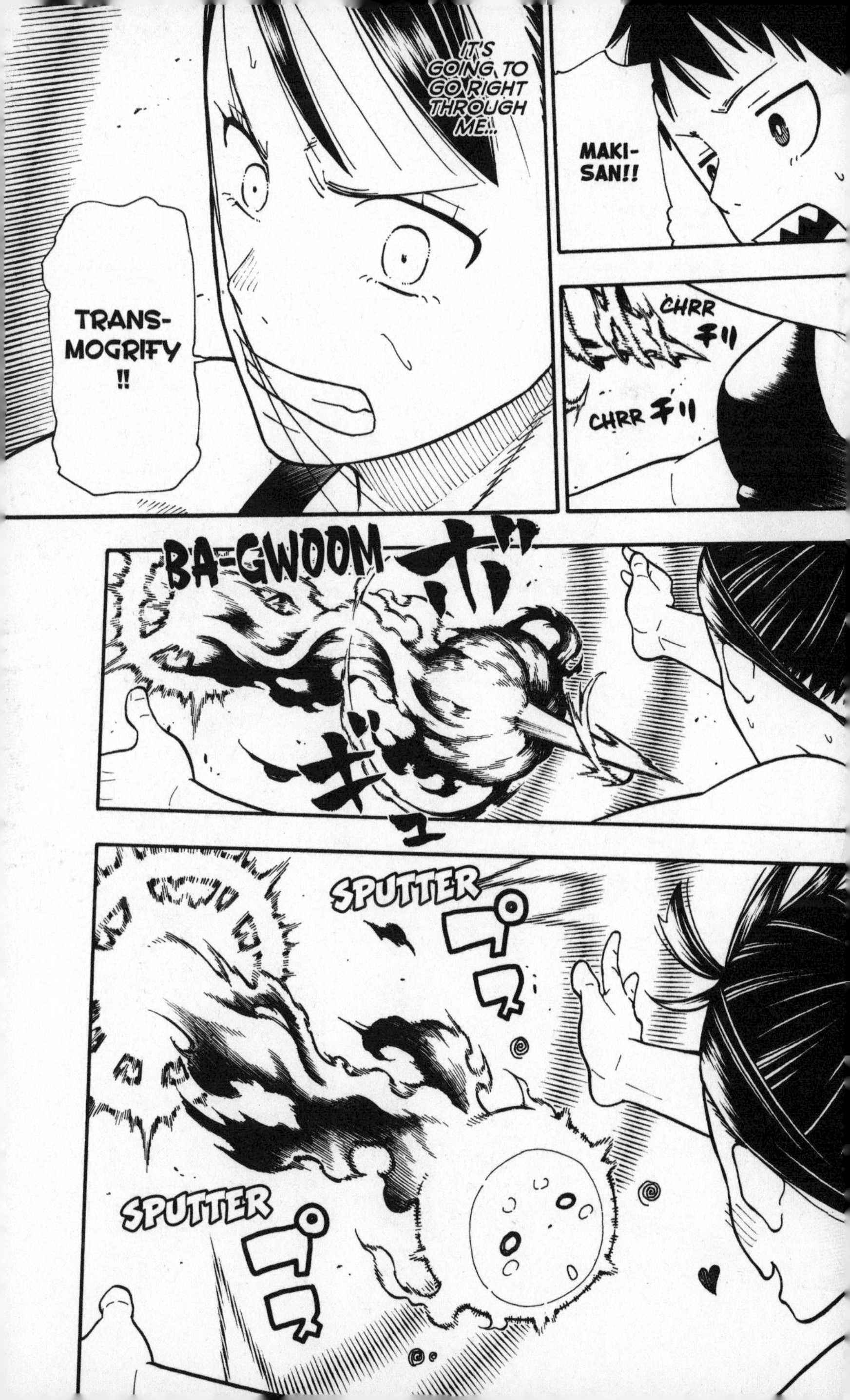
MAKI-SAN!!
CHRR チリ
CHRR チリ
IT'S GOING TO GO RIGHT THROUGH ME...
TRANS-MOGRIFY!!
BA-GWOOM
SPUTTER
SPUTTER

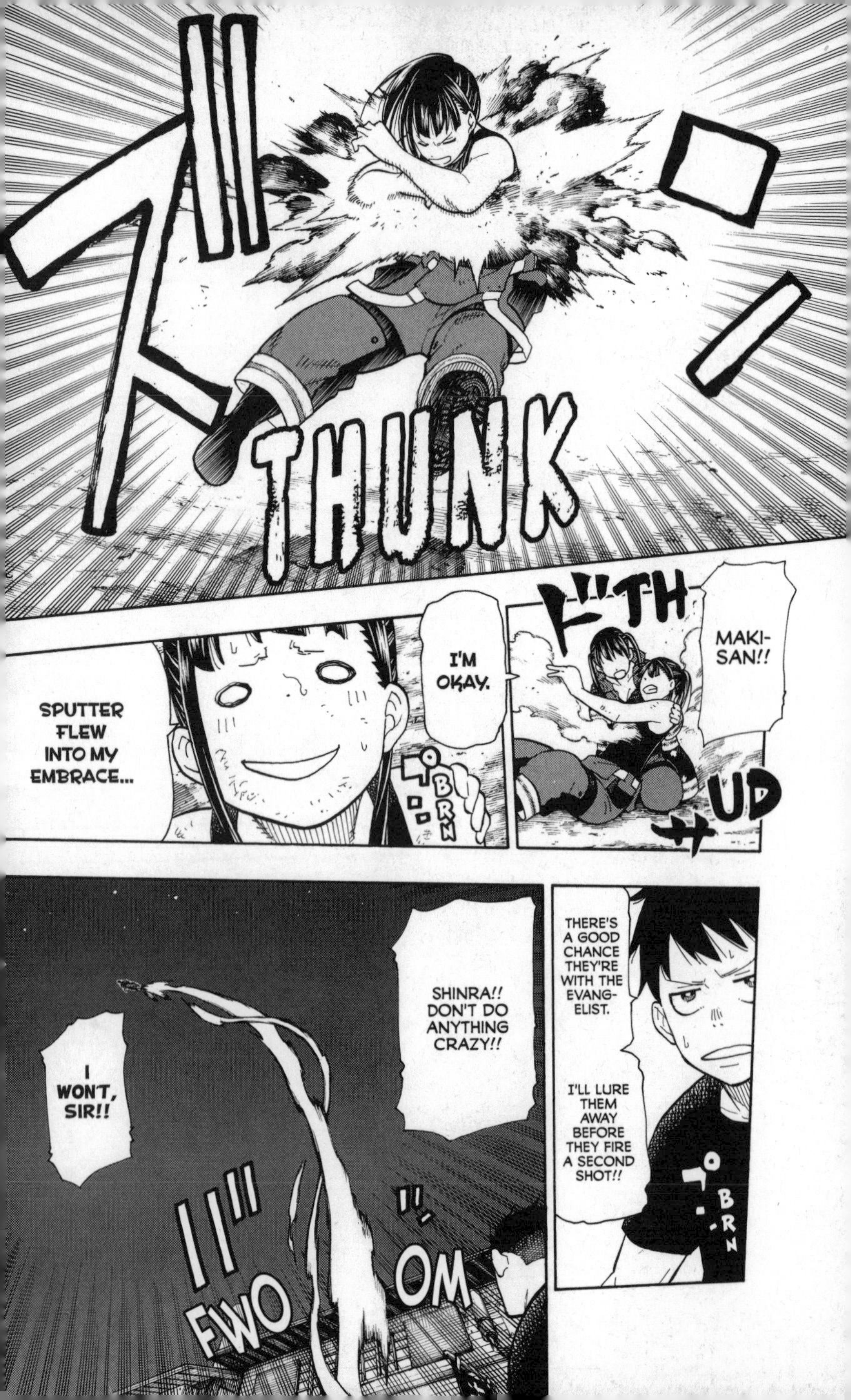
THUNK
MAKI-SAN!!
TH
UD
I'M OKAY.
BRN
SPUTTER FLEW INTO MY EMBRACE...
THERE'S A GOOD CHANCE THEY'RE WITH THE EVANG-ELIST.
I'LL LURE THEM AWAY BEFORE THEY FIRE A SECOND SHOT!!
BRN
SHINRA!! DON'T DO ANYTHING CRAZY!!
I WON'T, SIR!!
FWO
OM

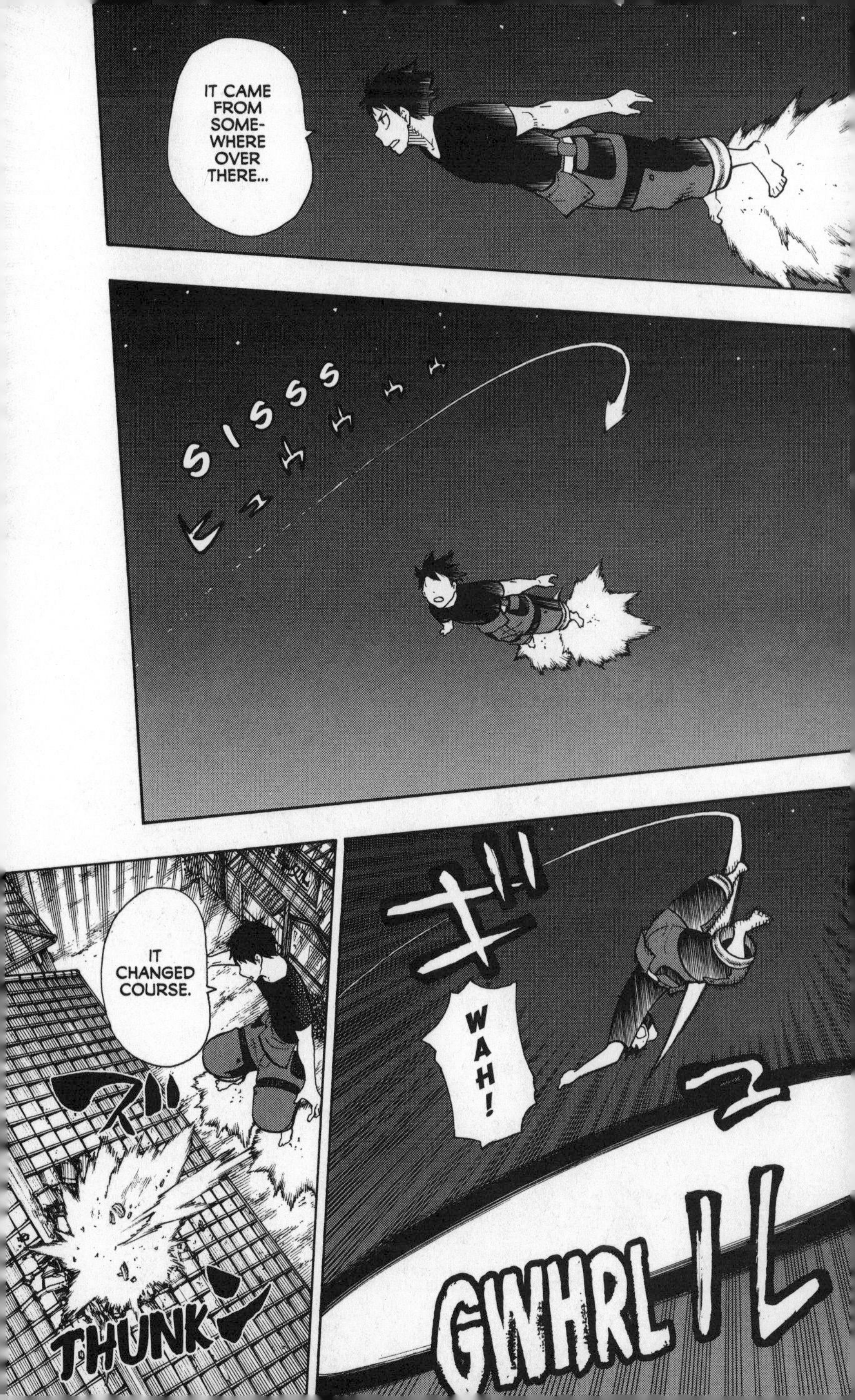
IT CAME FROM SOME-WHERE OVER THERE...
SISSSS
WAH!
GWHRL
IT CHANGED COURSE.
THUNK

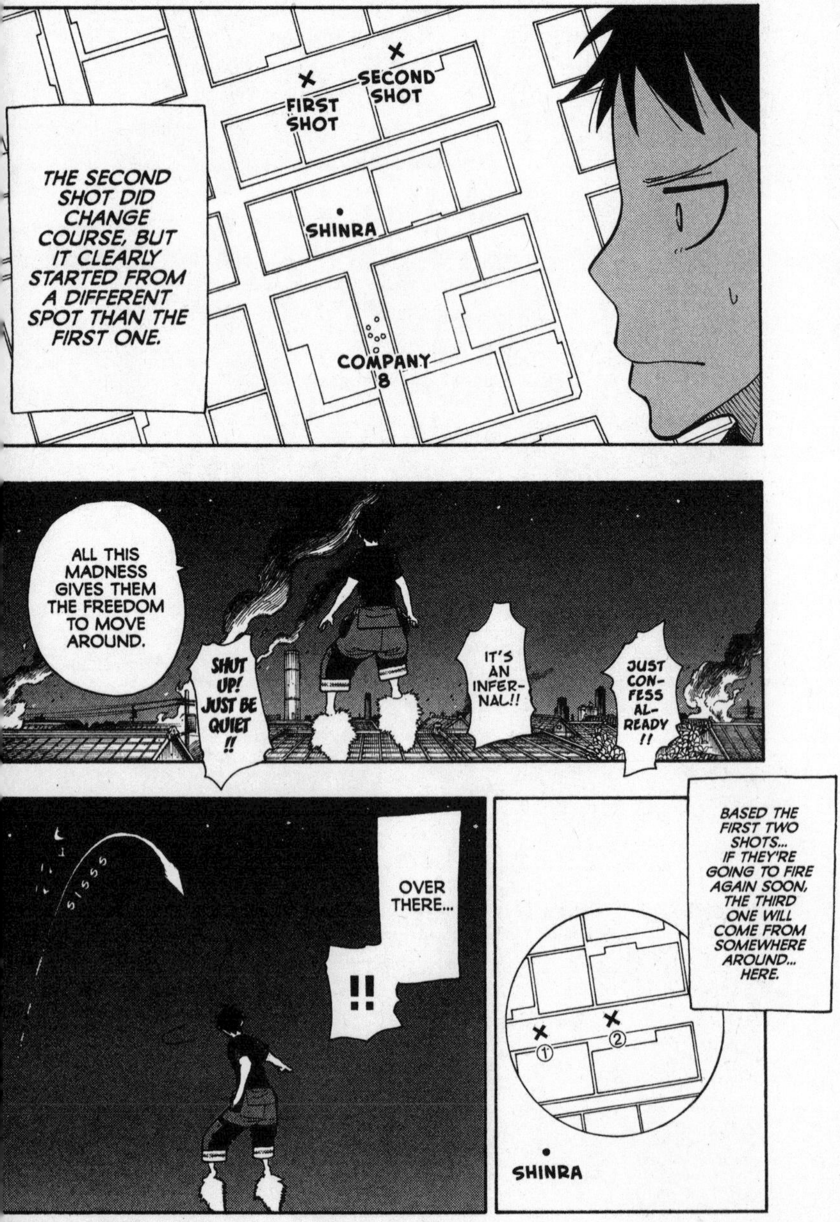
SECOND SHOT
FIRST SHOT
THE SECOND SHOT DID CHANGE COURSE, BUT IT CLEARLY STARTED FROM A DIFFERENT SPOT THAN THE FIRST ONE.
SHINRA
COMPANY 8
JUST CONFESS ALREADY!!
IT'S AN INFERNAL!!
SHUT UP! JUST BE QUIET!!
ALL THIS MADNESS GIVES THEM THE FREEDOM TO MOVE AROUND.
BASED THE FIRST TWO SHOTS... IF THEY'RE GOING TO FIRE AGAIN SOON, THE THIRD ONE WILL COME FROM SOMEWHERE AROUND... HERE.
①
②
SHINRA
OVER THERE...
!!
SISSSS

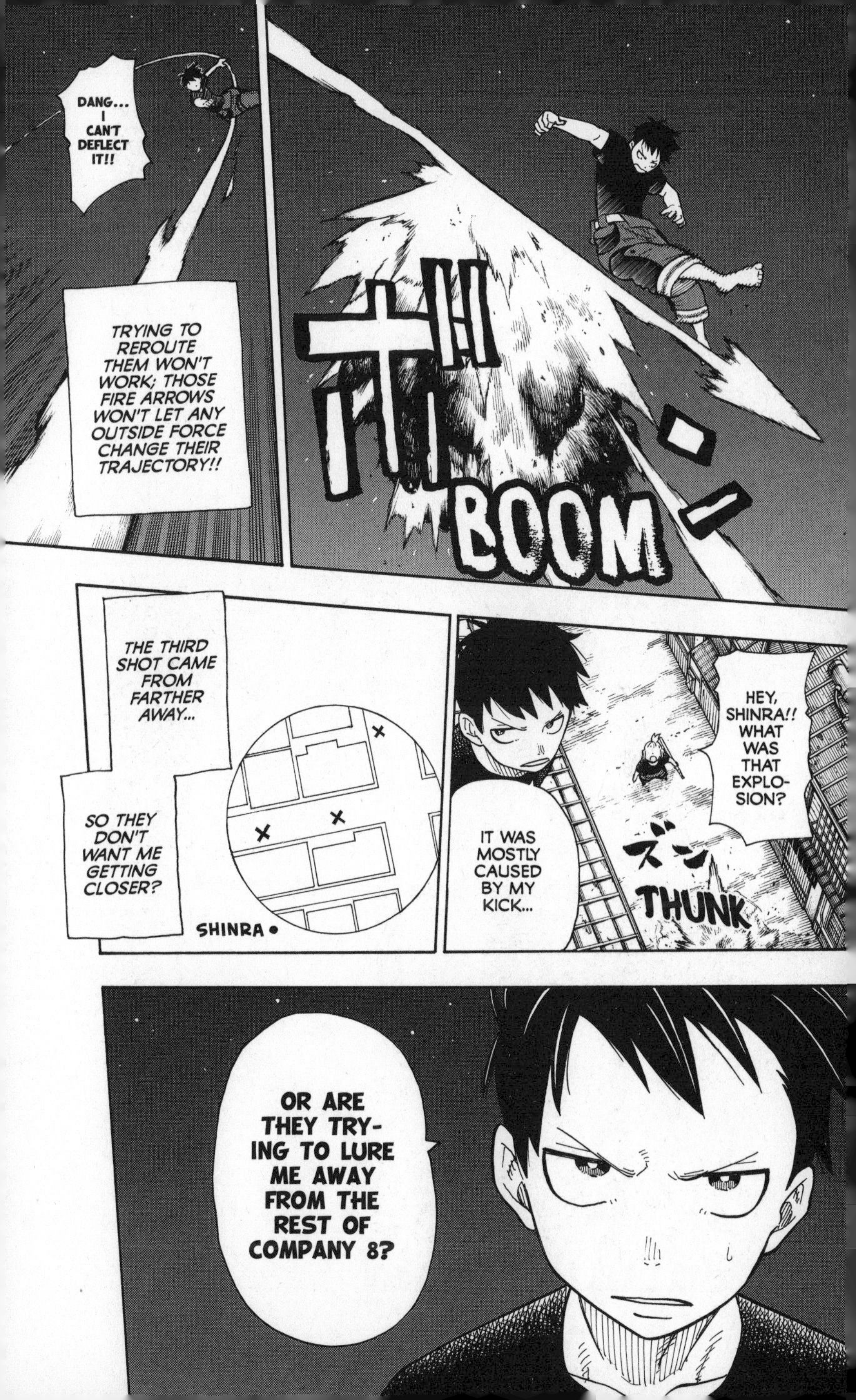
BOOM
DANG... I CAN'T DEFLECT IT!!
TRYING TO REROUTE THEM WON'T WORK; THOSE FIRE ARROWS WON'T LET ANY OUTSIDE FORCE CHANGE THEIR TRAJECTORY!!
HEY, SHINRA!! WHAT WAS THAT EXPLO-SION?
IT WAS MOSTLY CAUSED BY MY KICK...
ズン
THUNK
THE THIRD SHOT CAME FROM FARTHER AWAY...
SO THEY DON'T WANT ME GETTING CLOSER?
SHINRA
OR ARE THEY TRY-ING TO LURE ME AWAY FROM THE REST OF COMPANY 8?

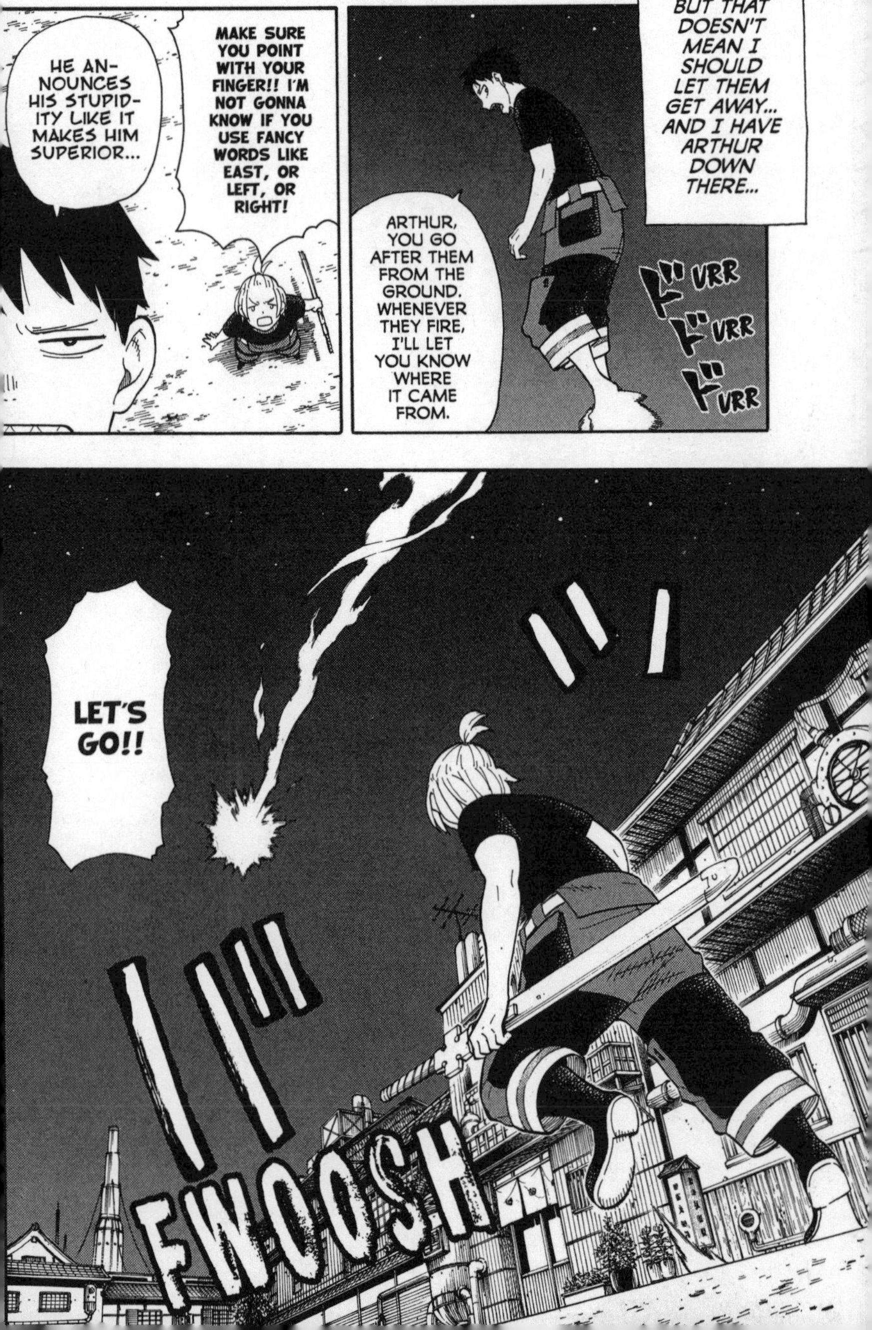
BUT THAT DOESN'T MEAN I SHOULD LET THEM GET AWAY... AND I HAVE ARTHUR DOWN THERE...
ARTHUR, YOU GO AFTER THEM FROM THE GROUND. WHENEVER THEY FIRE, I'LL LET YOU KNOW WHERE IT CAME FROM.
ドVRR
ドVRR
ドVRR
MAKE SURE YOU POINT WITH YOUR FINGER!! I'M NOT GONNA KNOW IF YOU USE FANCY WORDS LIKE EAST, OR LEFT, OR RIGHT!
HE AN-NOUNCES HIS STUPID-ITY LIKE IT MAKES HIM SUPERIOR...
LET'S GO!!
FWOOSH

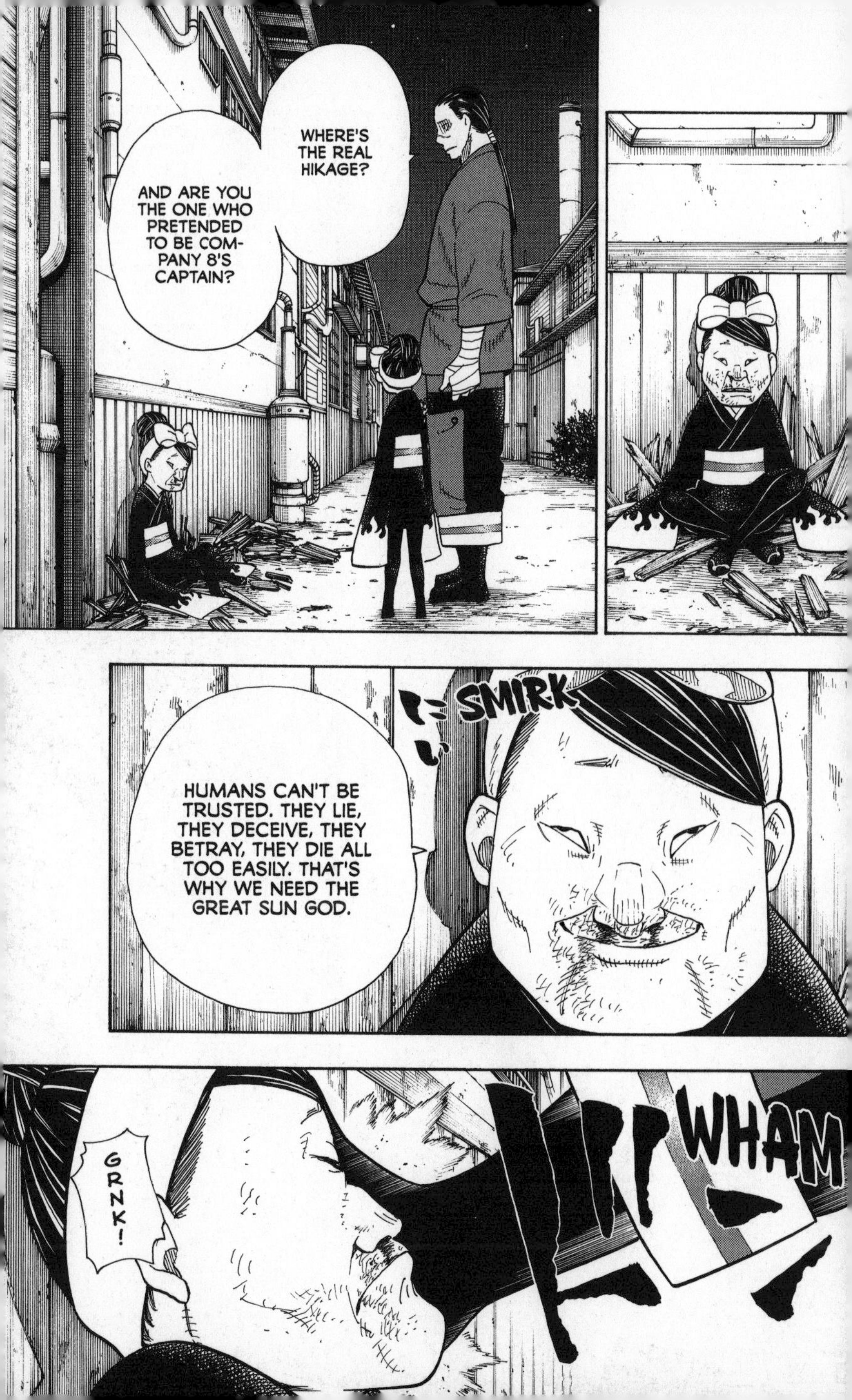
WHERE'S THE REAL HIKAGE?
AND ARE YOU THE ONE WHO PRETENDED TO BE COMPANY 8'S CAPTAIN?
SMIRK
HUMANS CAN'T BE TRUSTED. THEY LIE, THEY DECEIVE, THEY BETRAY, THEY DIE ALL TOO EASILY. THAT'S WHY WE NEED THE GREAT SUN GOD.
WHAM
GRNK!

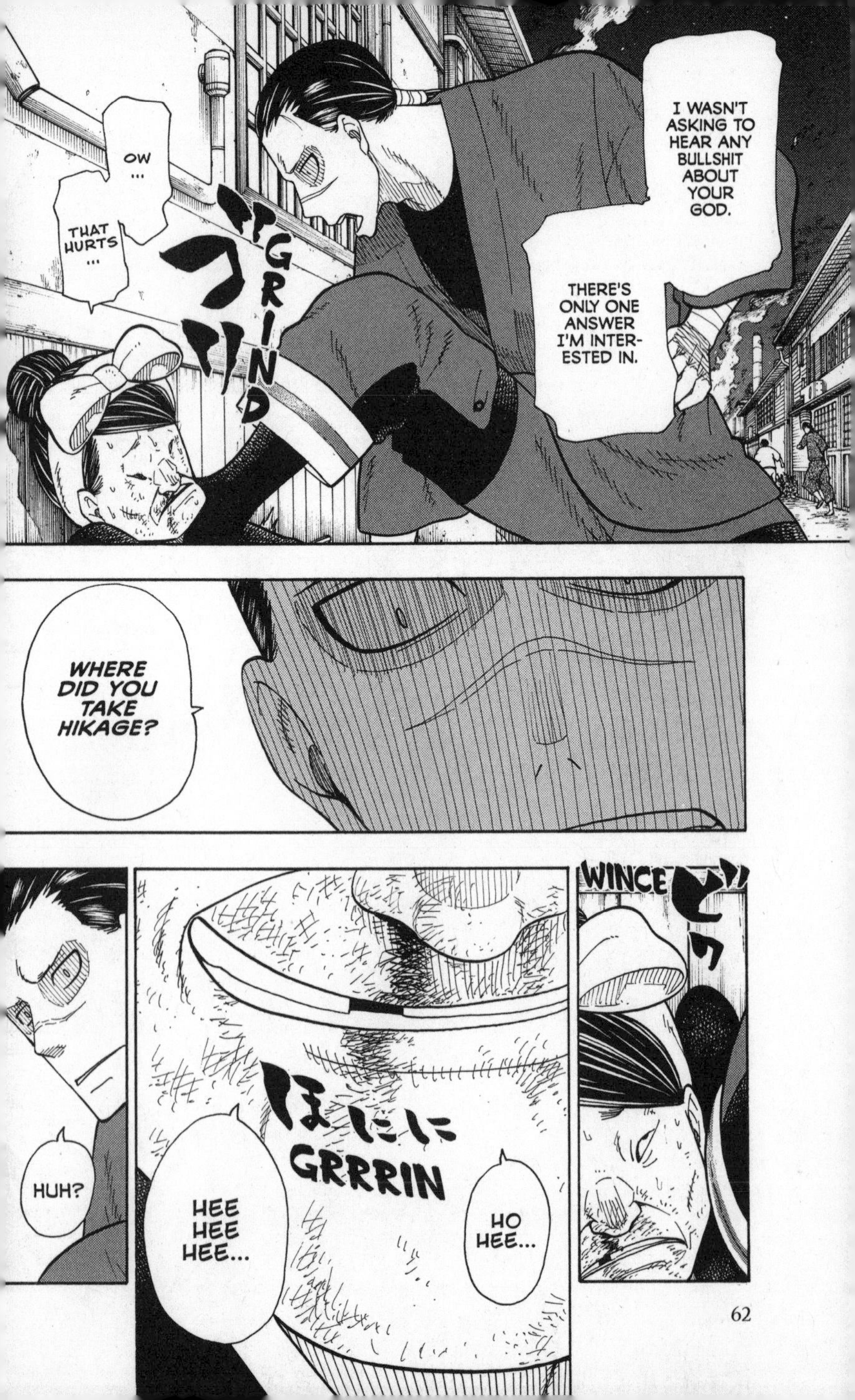
I WASN'T ASKING TO HEAR ANY BULLSHIT ABOUT YOUR GOD.
THERE'S ONLY ONE ANSWER I'M INTERESTED IN.
GRIND
OW ...
THAT HURTS ...
WHERE DID YOU TAKE HIKAGE?
WINCE
GRRRIN
HO HEE...
HEE HEE HEE...
HUH?

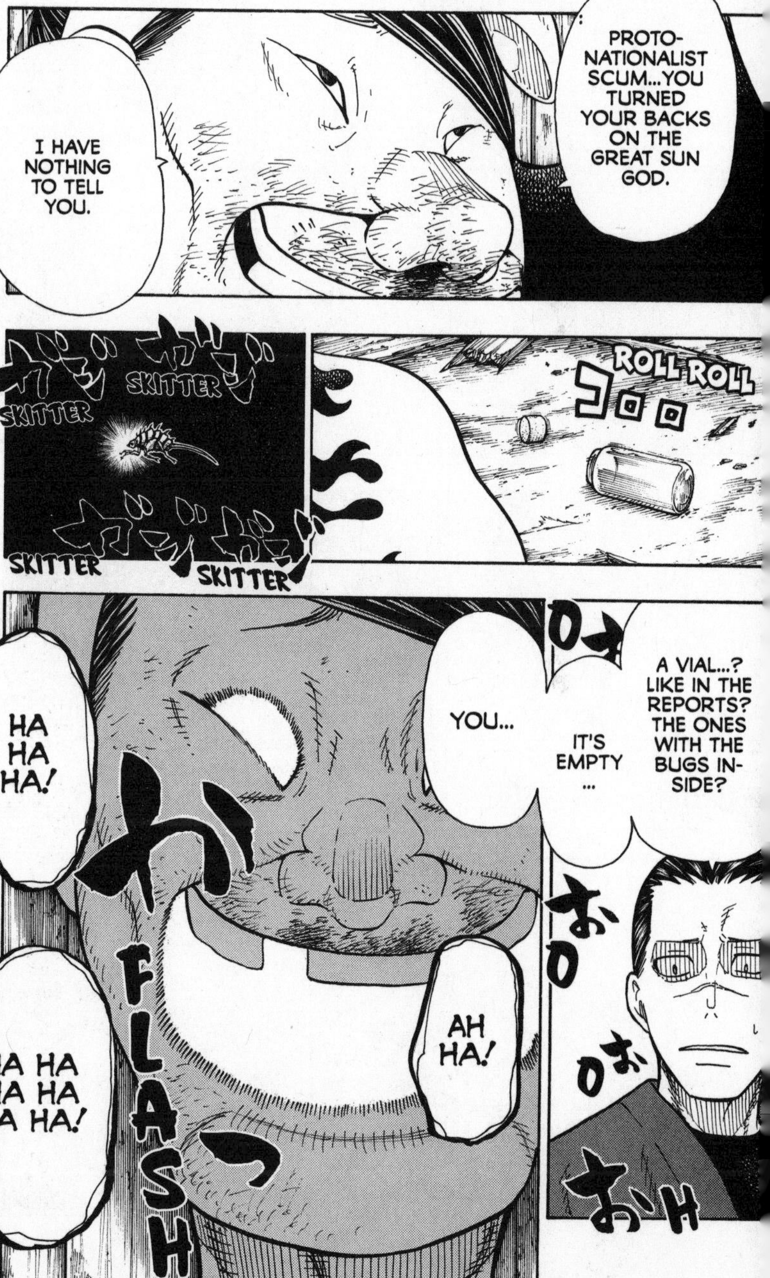
PROTO-NATIONALIST SCUM...YOU TURNED YOUR BACKS ON THE GREAT SUN GOD.
I HAVE NOTHING TO TELL YOU.
ROLL ROLL
SKITTER
SKITTER
SKITTER
SKITTER
A VIAL...? LIKE IN THE REPORTS? THE ONES WITH THE BUGS IN-SIDE?
IT'S EMPTY ...
YOU...
H
AH HA!
FLASH
HA HA HA!
HA HA HA HA HA HA!

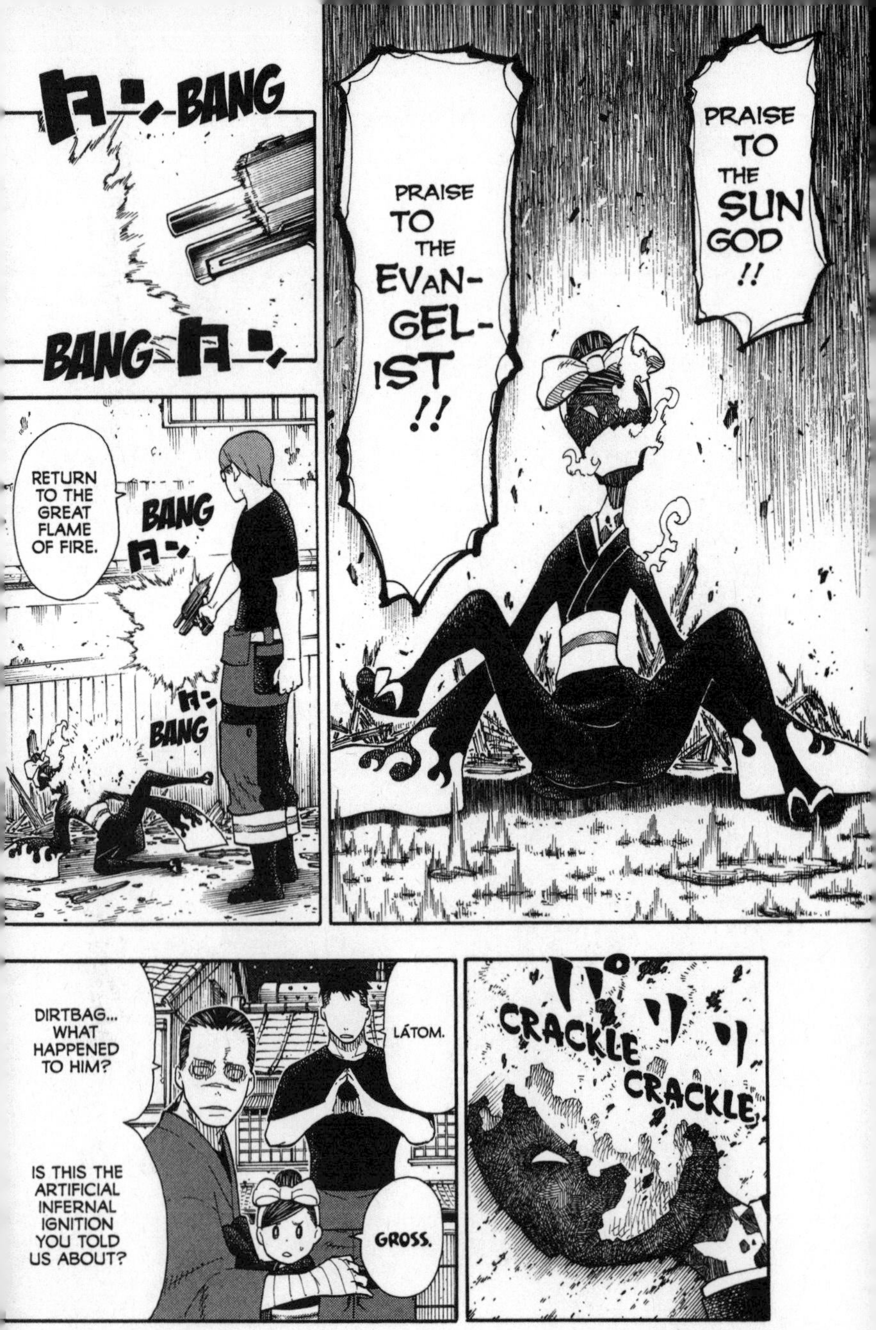
PRAISE TO THE SUN GOD!!
PRAISE TO THE EVAN-GEL-IST!!
BANG
BANG
RETURN TO THE GREAT FLAME OF FIRE.
BANG
BANG
CRACKLE
CRACKLE
LÁTOM.
DIRTBAG... WHAT HAPPENED TO HIM?
IS THIS THE ARTIFICIAL INFERNAL IGNITION YOU TOLD US ABOUT?
GROSS.

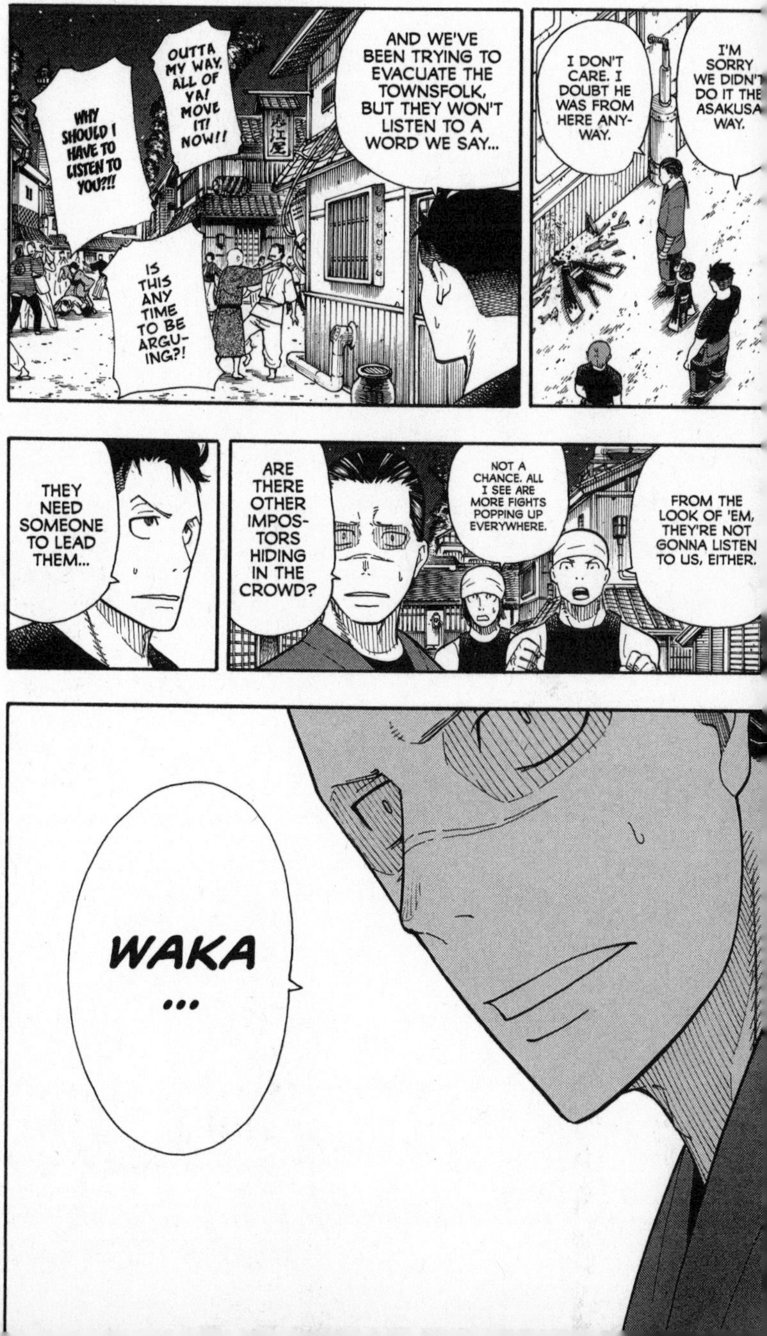
I'M SORRY WE DIDN'T DO IT THE ASAKUSA WAY.
I DON'T CARE. I DOUBT HE WAS FROM HERE ANYWAY.
AND WE'VE BEEN TRYING TO EVACUATE THE TOWNSFOLK, BUT THEY WON'T LISTEN TO A WORD WE SAY...
OUTTA MY WAY, ALL OF YA! MOVE IT! NOW!!
WHY SHOULD I HAVE TO LISTEN TO YOU?!!
IS THIS ANY TIME TO BE ARGUING?!
FROM THE LOOK OF 'EM, THEY'RE NOT GONNA LISTEN TO US, EITHER.
NOT A CHANCE. ALL I SEE ARE MORE FIGHTS POPPING UP EVERYWHERE.
ARE THERE OTHER IMPOSTORS HIDING IN THE CROWD?
THEY NEED SOMEONE TO LEAD THEM...
WAKA...

FIRE FORCE

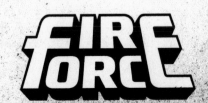

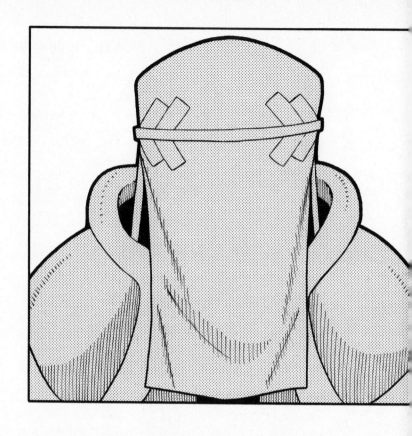

CHAPTER XLVI: AFTER THAT SNIPER!

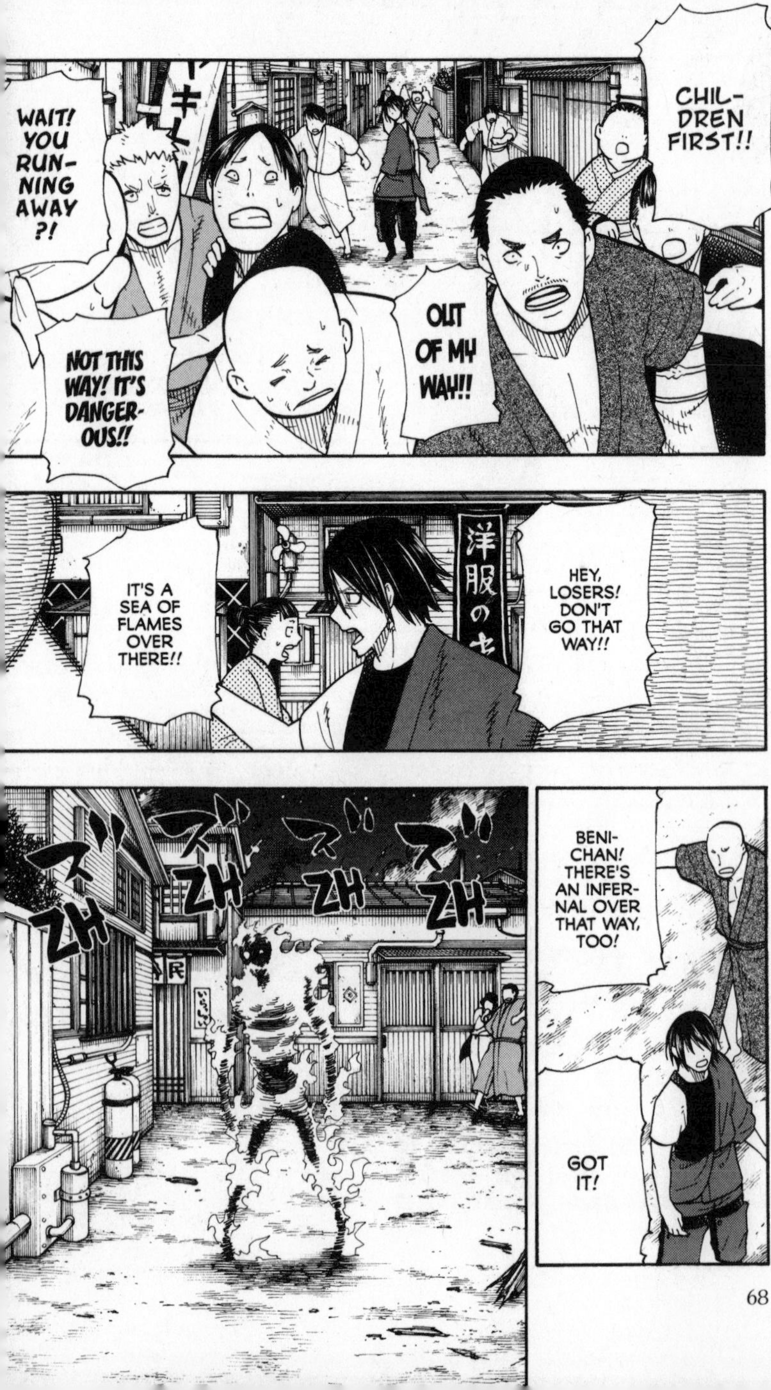
CHILDREN FIRST!!
OUT OF MY WAY!!
WAIT! YOU RUNNING AWAY?!
NOT THIS WAY! IT'S DANGEROUS!!
HEY, LOSERS! DON'T GO THAT WAY!!
IT'S A SEA OF FLAMES OVER THERE!!
BENI-CHAN! THERE'S AN INFERNAL OVER THAT WAY, TOO!
GOT IT!
ZH ZH ZH ZH

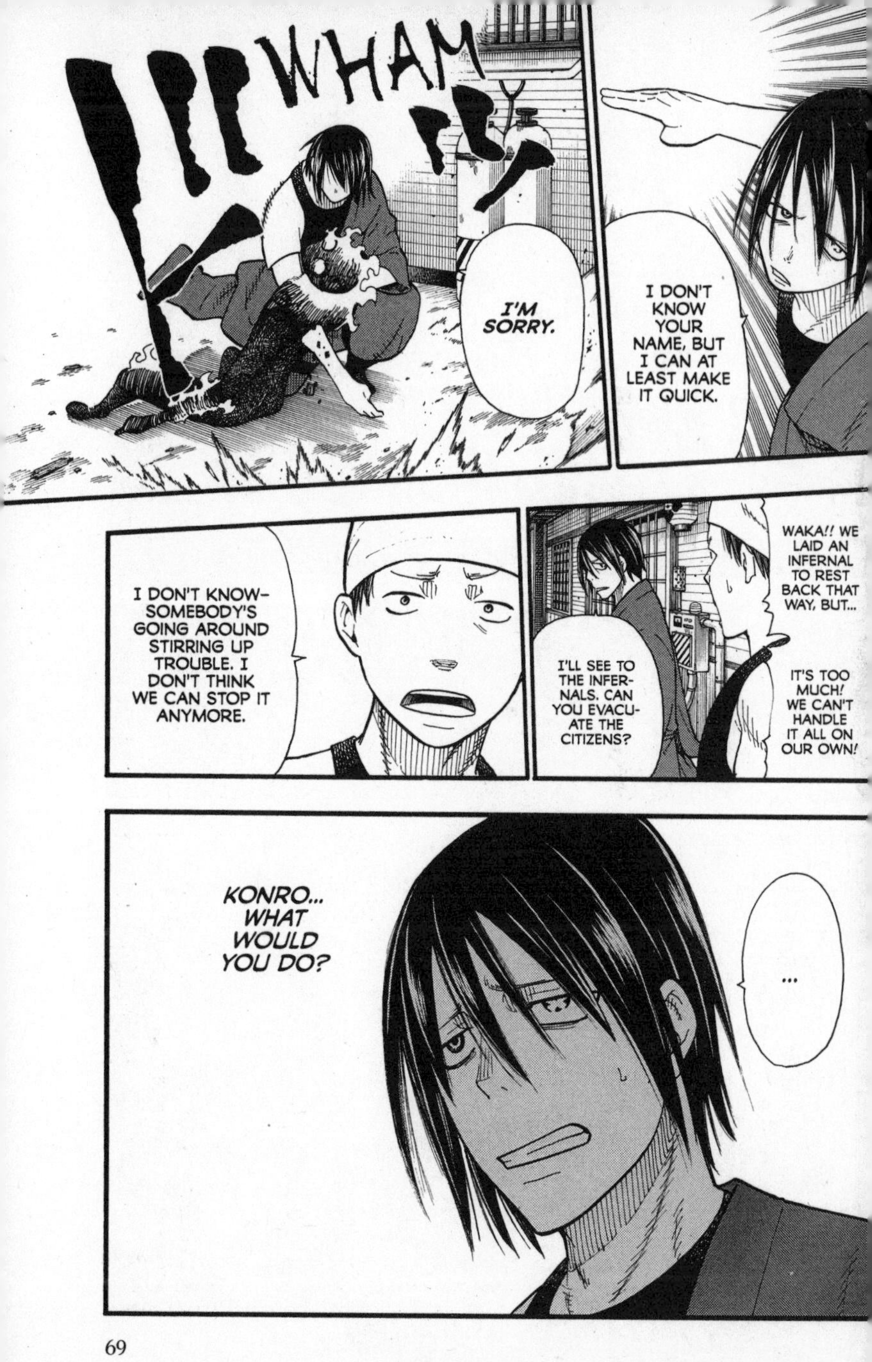
I DON'T KNOW YOUR NAME, BUT I CAN AT LEAST MAKE IT QUICK.
I'M SORRY.
WHAM
WAKA!! WE LAID AN INFERNAL TO REST BACK THAT WAY, BUT...
IT'S TOO MUCH! WE CAN'T HANDLE IT ALL ON OUR OWN!
I'LL SEE TO THE INFERNALS. CAN YOU EVACUATE THE CITIZENS?
I DON'T KNOW–SOMEBODY'S GOING AROUND STIRRING UP TROUBLE. I DON'T THINK WE CAN STOP IT ANYMORE.
...
KONRO... WHAT WOULD YOU DO?

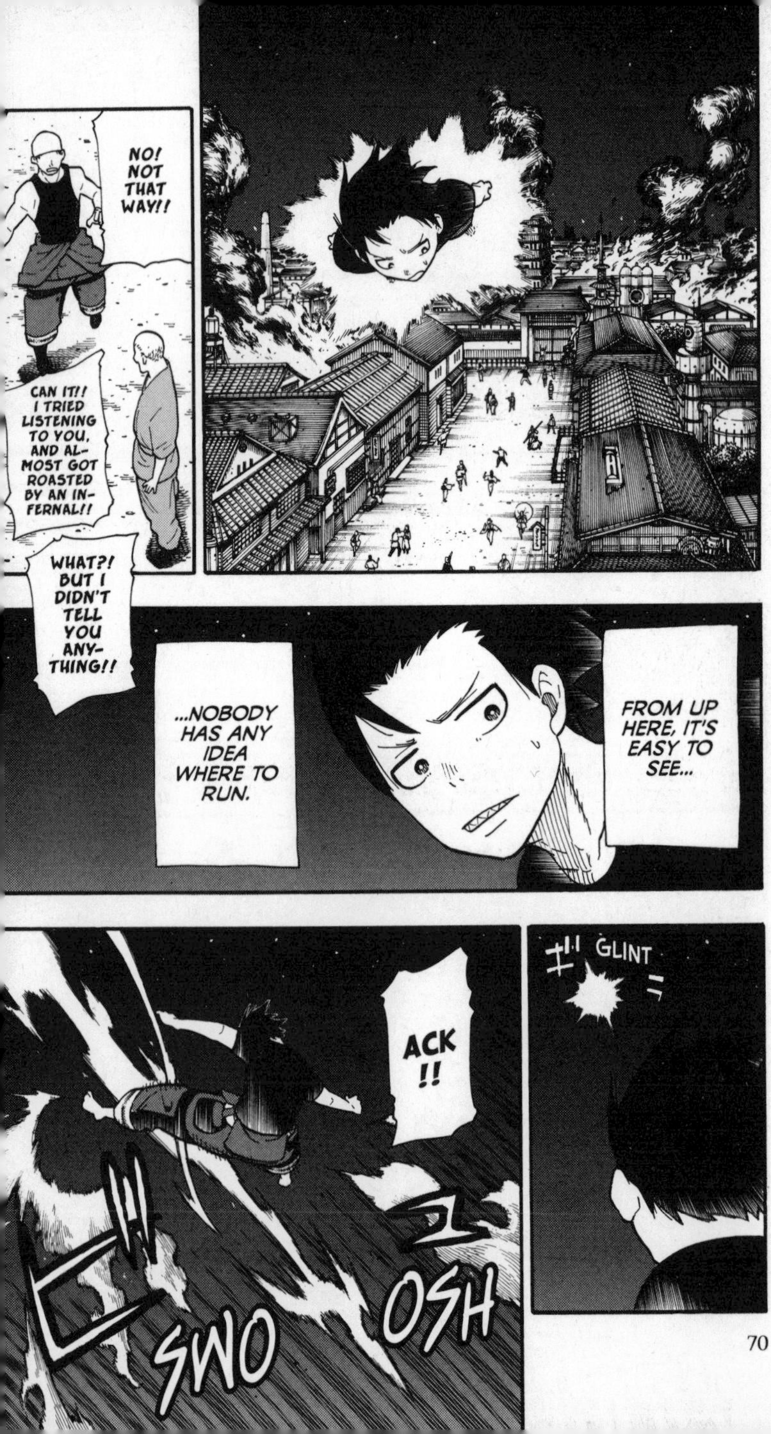
NO! NOT THAT WAY!!
CAN IT!! I TRIED LISTENING TO YOU, AND ALMOST GOT ROASTED BY AN INFERNAL!!
WHAT?! BUT I DIDN'T TELL YOU ANYTHING!!
FROM UP HERE, IT'S EASY TO SEE...
...NOBODY HAS ANY IDEA WHERE TO RUN.
GLINT
ACK !!
SWOOSH

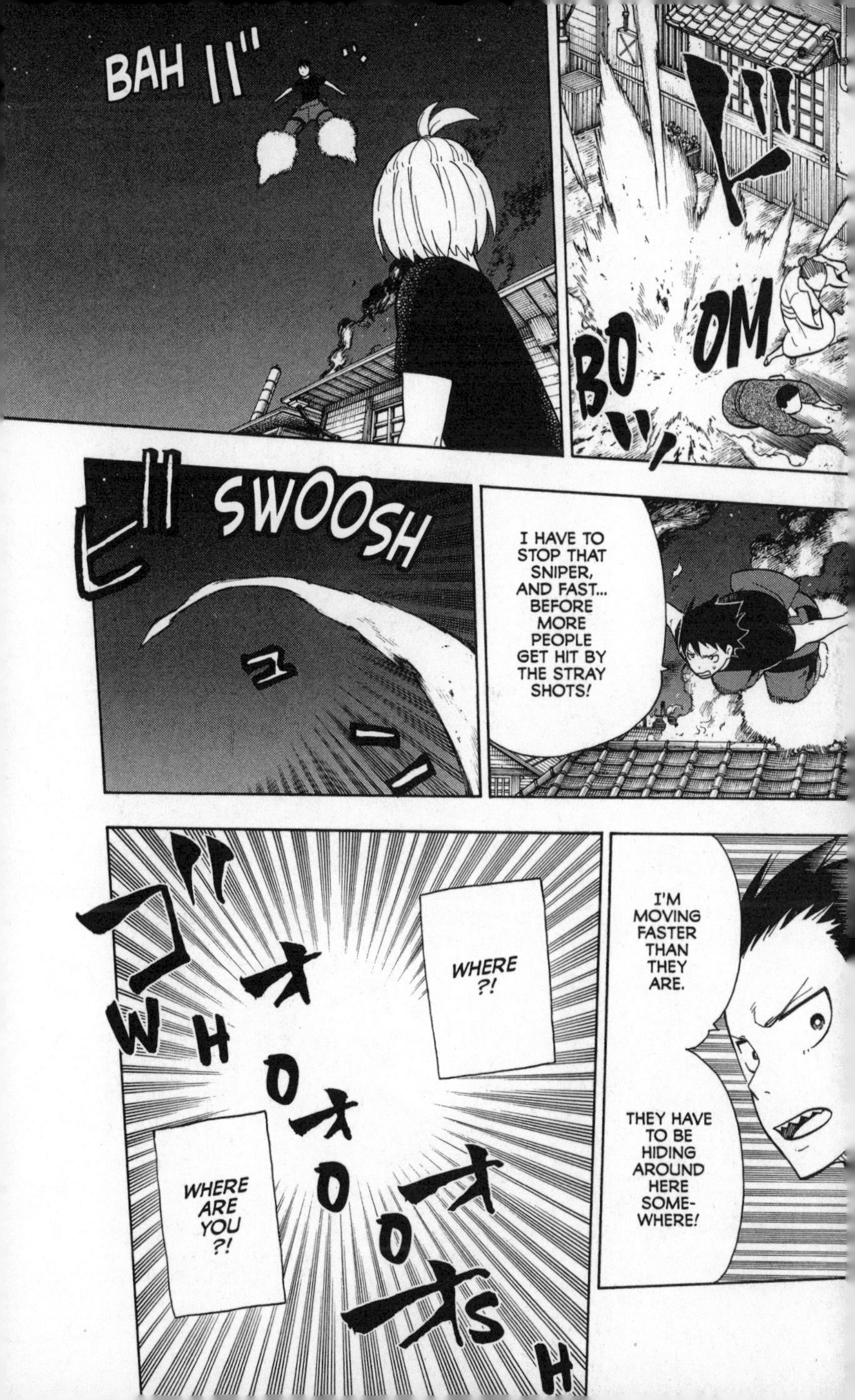
BOOM
BAH
I HAVE TO STOP THAT SNIPER, AND FAST... BEFORE MORE PEOPLE GET HIT BY THE STRAY SHOTS!
SWOOSH
I'M MOVING FASTER THAN THEY ARE.
THEY HAVE TO BE HIDING AROUND HERE SOME-WHERE!
WHERE ?!
WHERE ARE YOU ?!
WHOOOSH

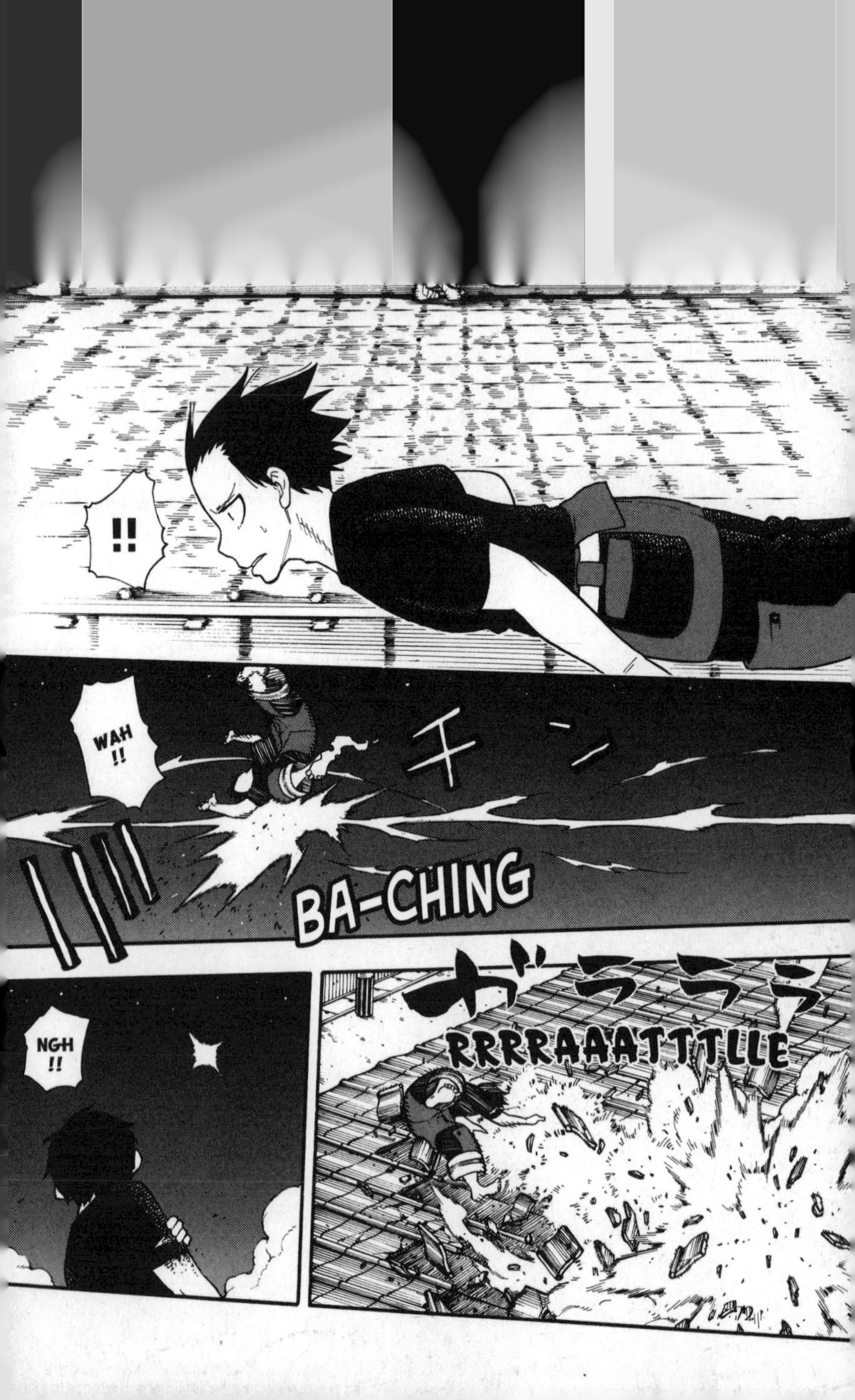
!!
WAH !!
BA-CHING
RRRRAAATTTLLE
NGH !!

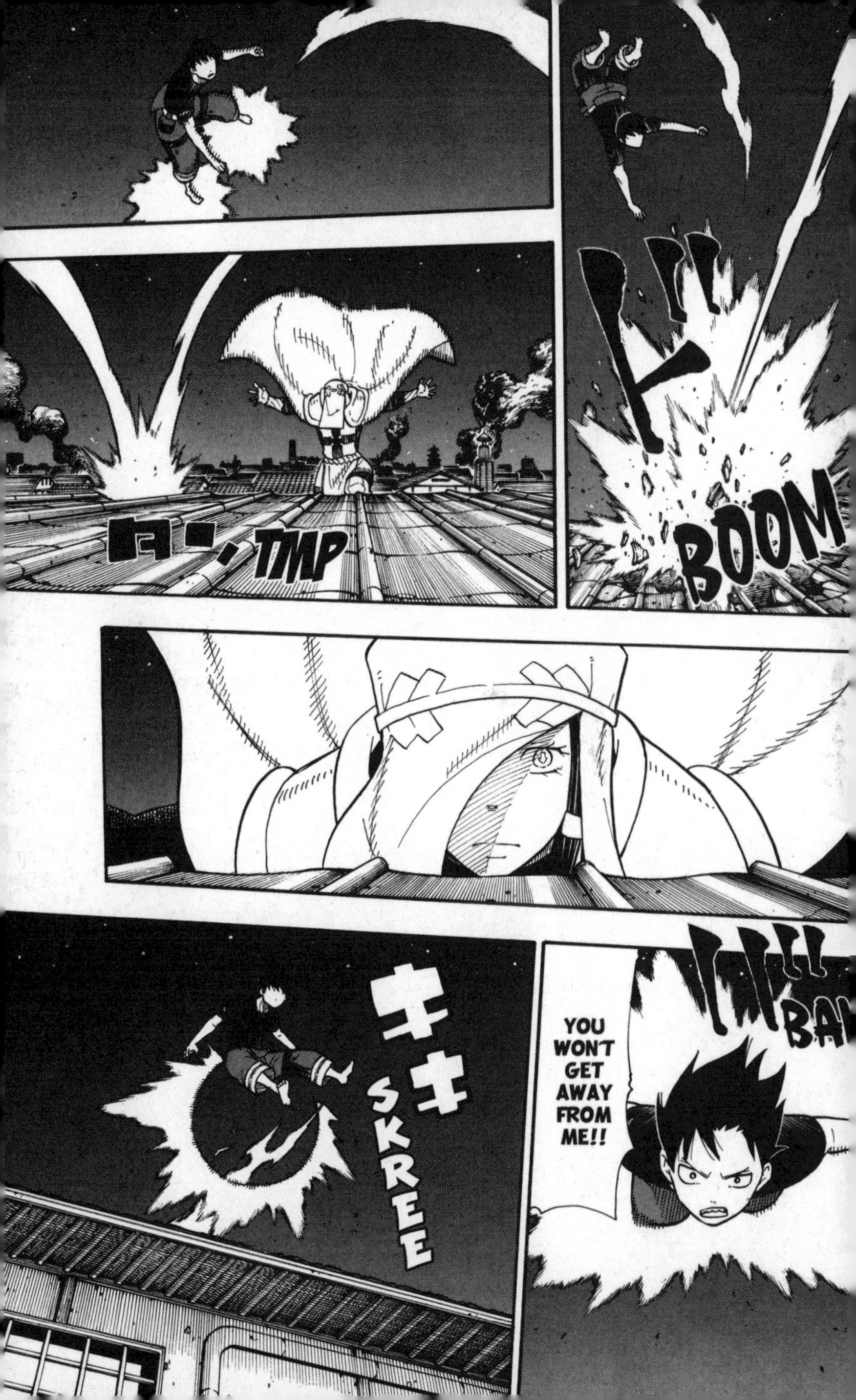
BOOM
TMP
YOU WON'T GET AWAY FROM ME!!
SKREE

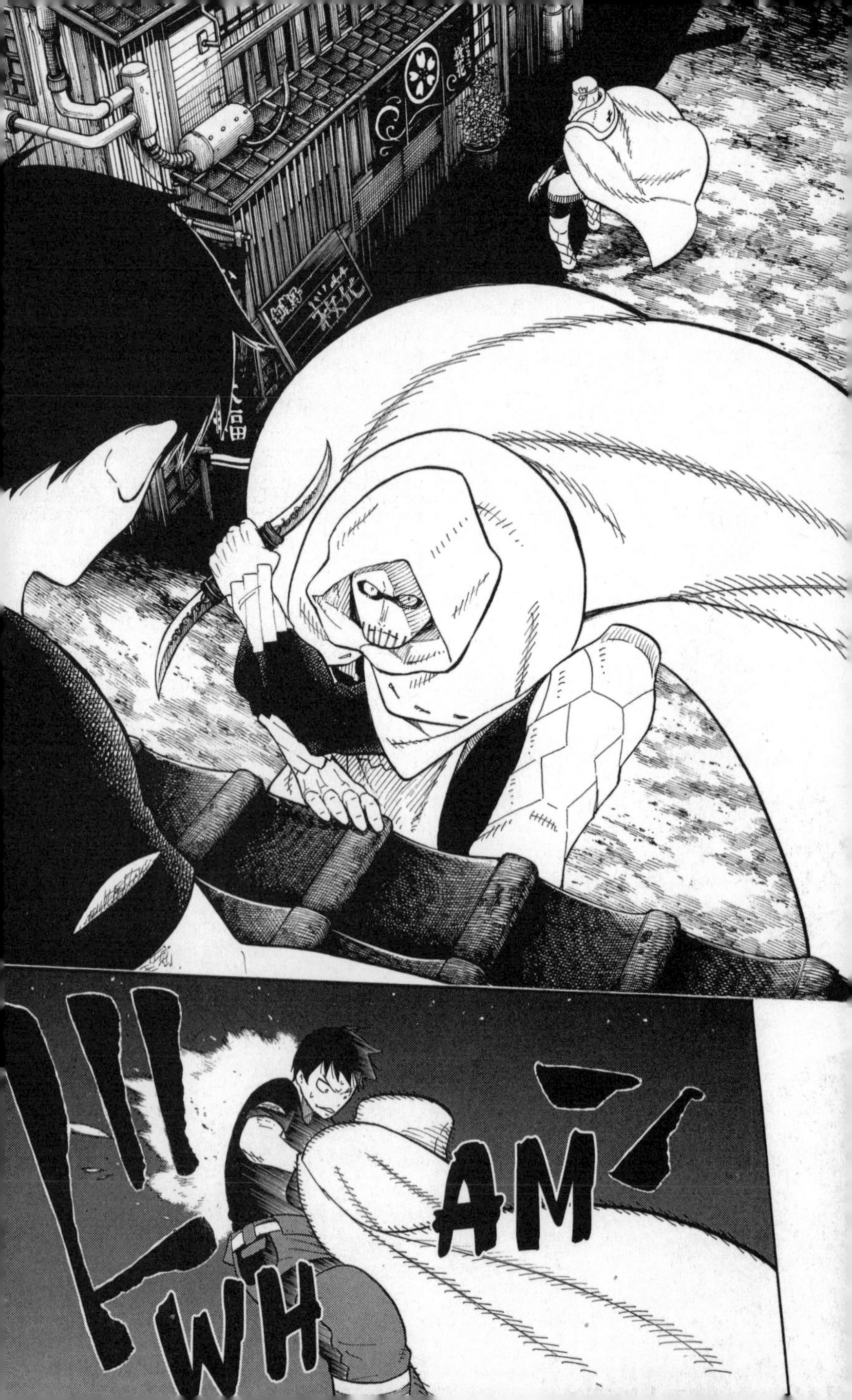
WHAM!!

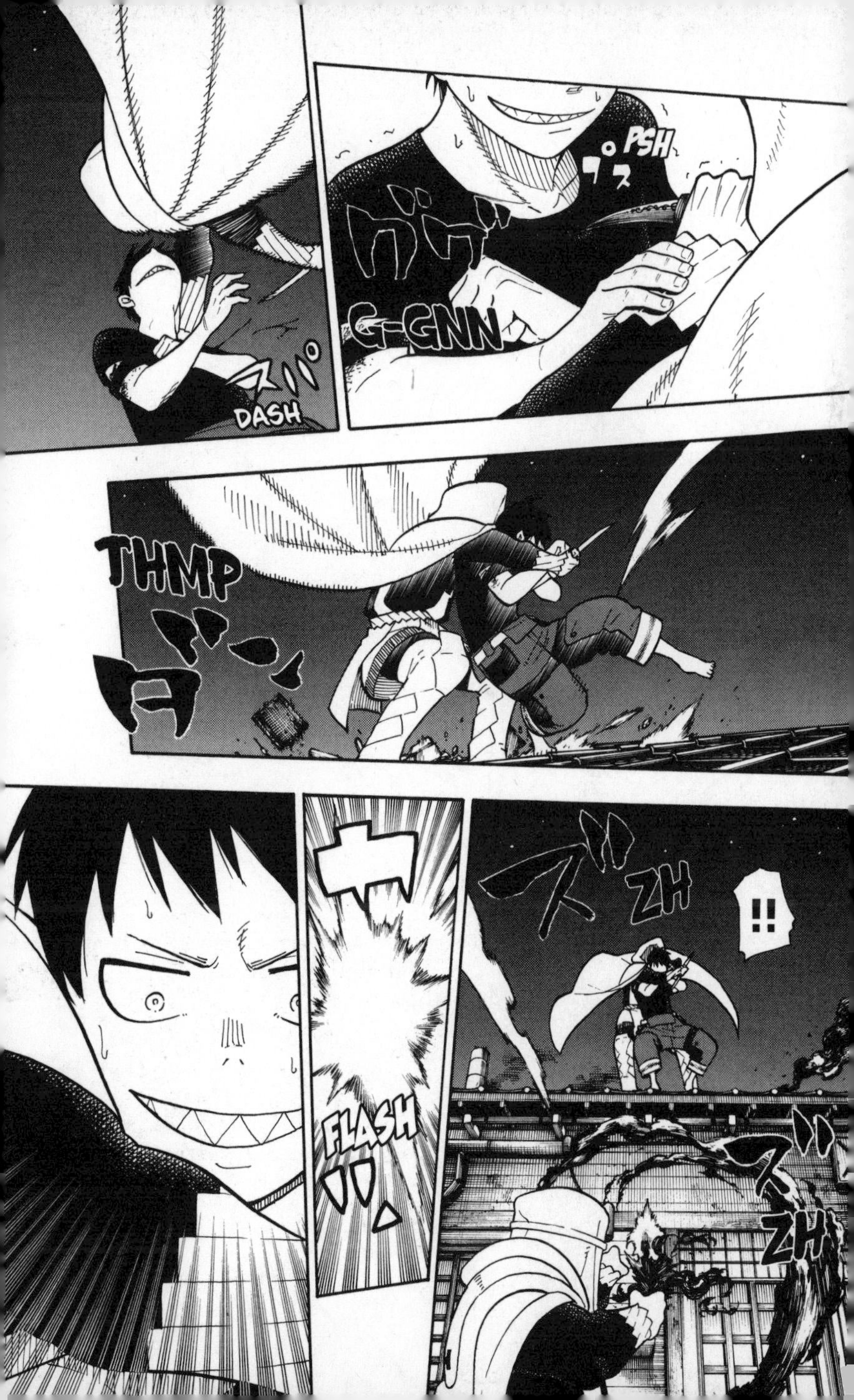
PSH
G-GNN
DASH
THMP
ZH
!!
ZH
FLASH

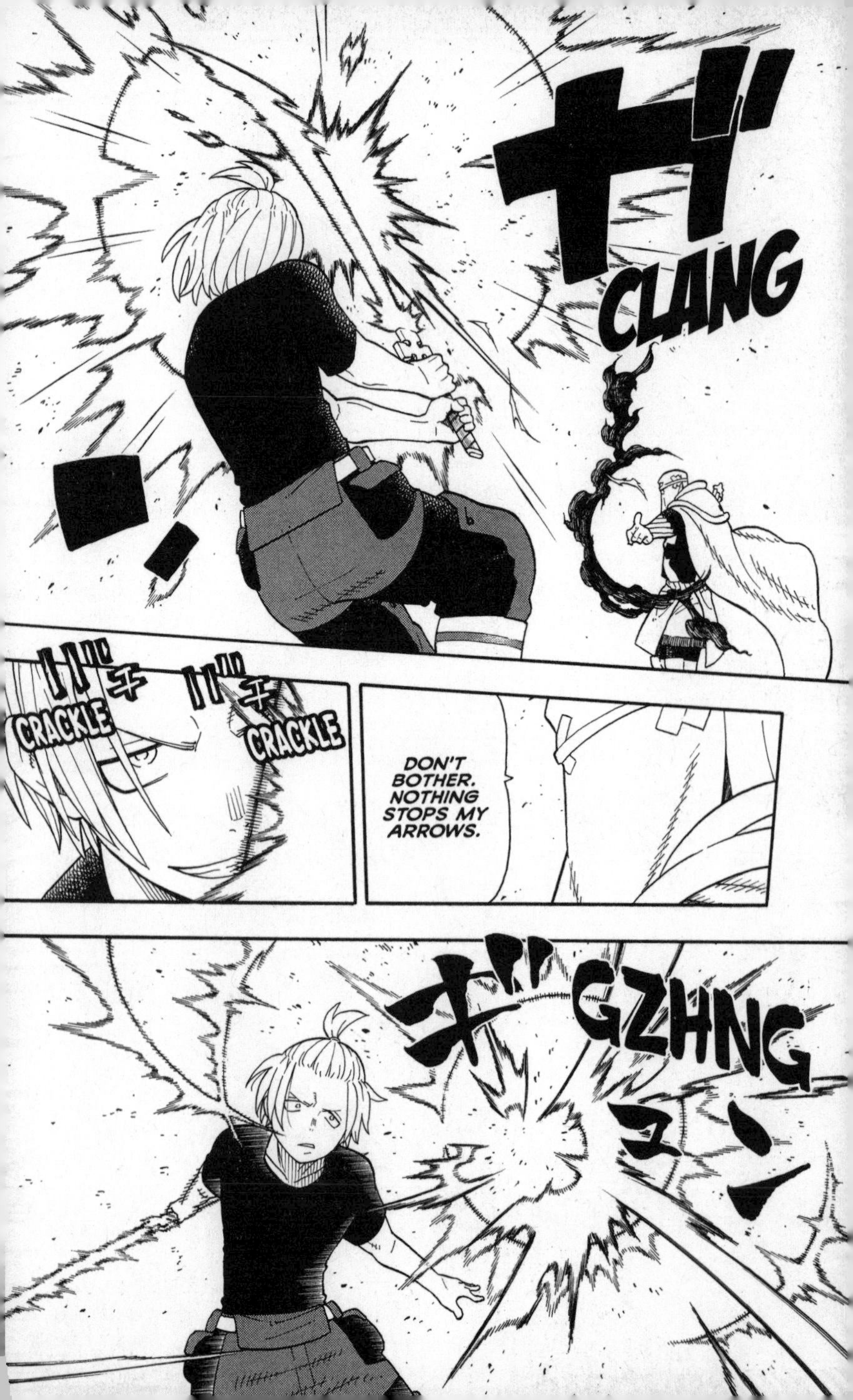

ザ
CLANG
DON'T BOTHER. NOTHING STOPS MY ARROWS.
バチ
CRACKLE
バチ
CRACKLE
ギュン
GZHNG

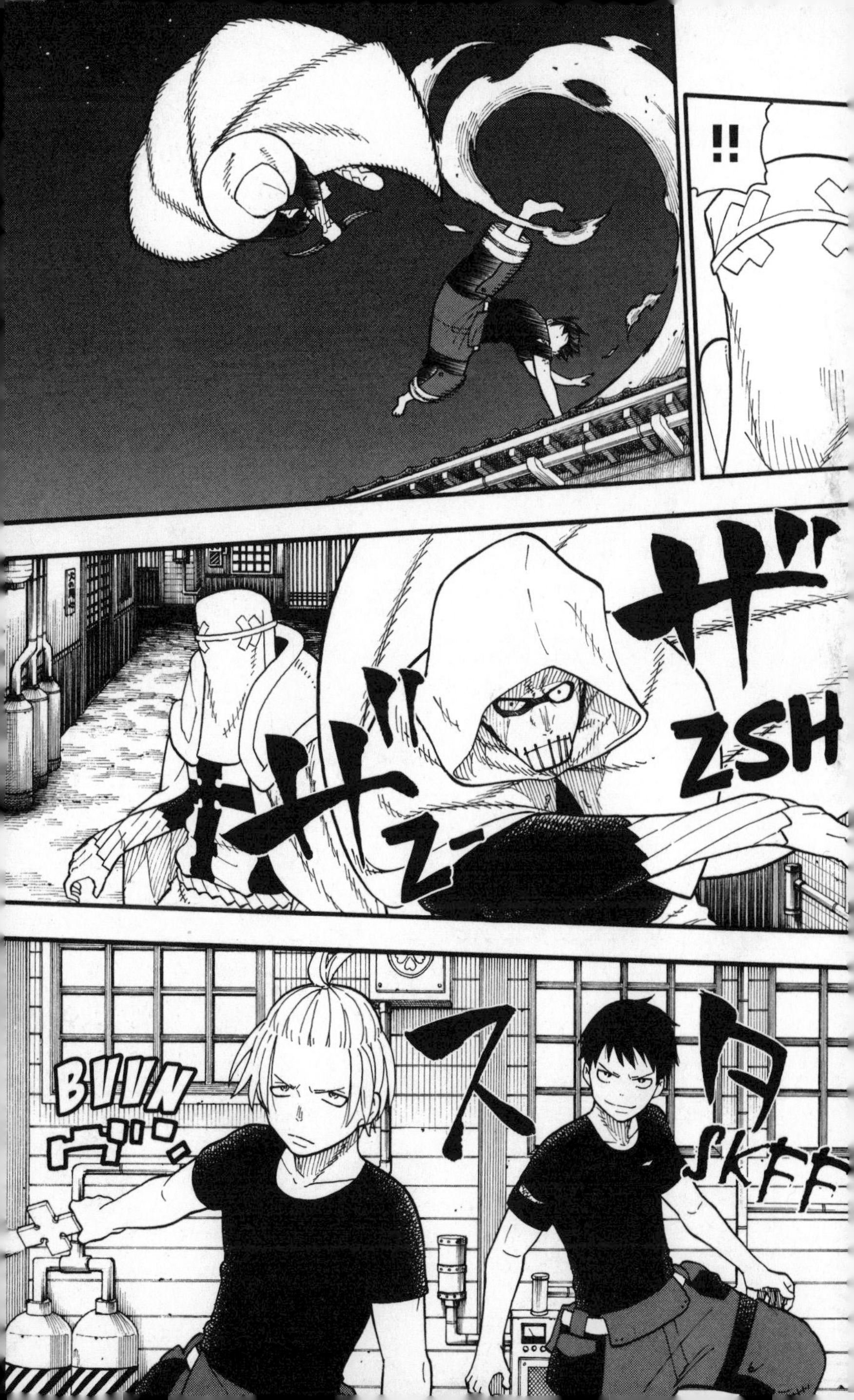
!!
ZSH
Z-
SKFF
BVVN

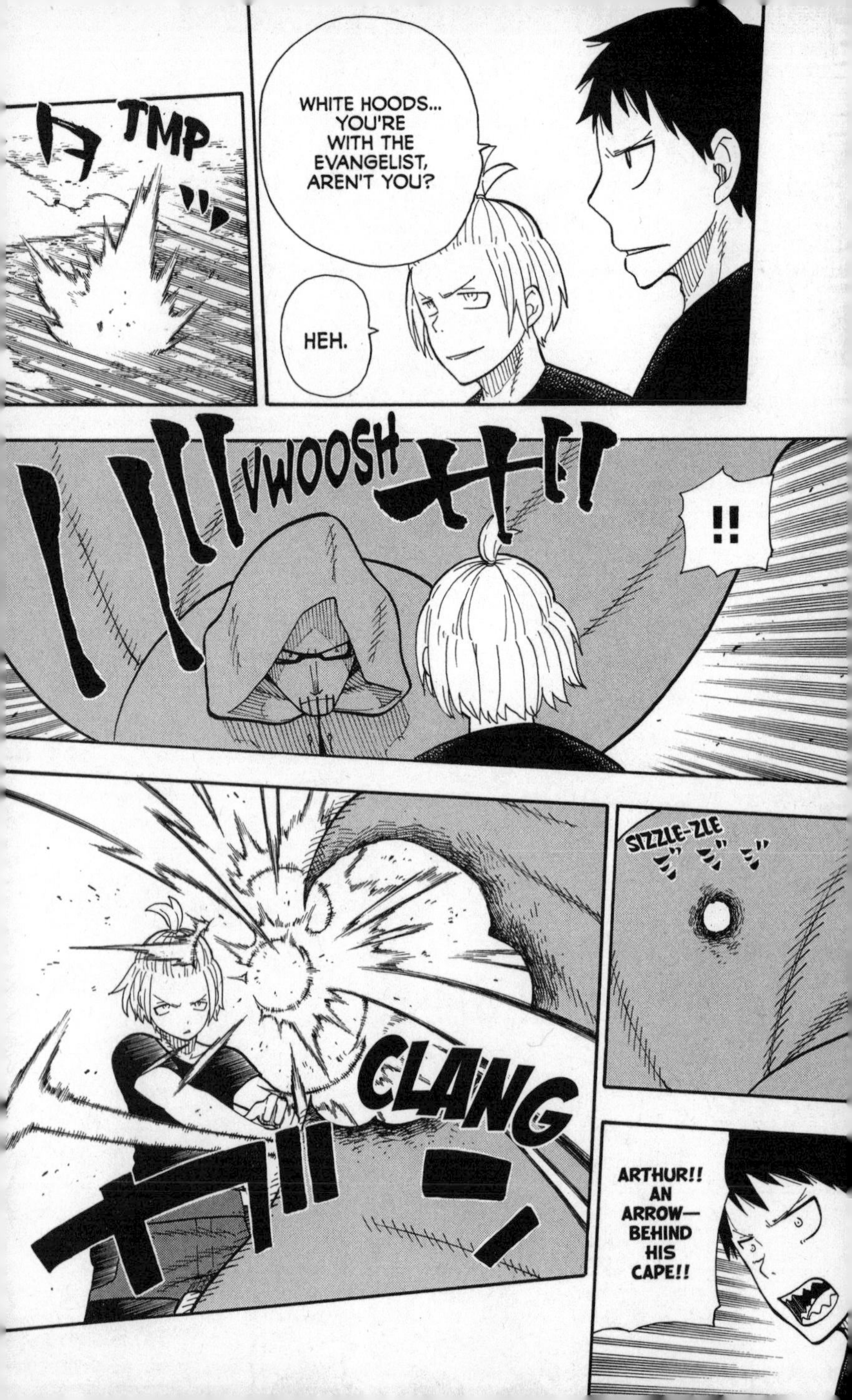

WHITE HOODS... YOU'RE WITH THE EVANGELIST, AREN'T YOU?
HEH.
TMP
VWOOSH
!!
SIZZLE-ZLE
ARTHUR!! AN ARROW— BEHIND HIS CAPE!!
CLANG

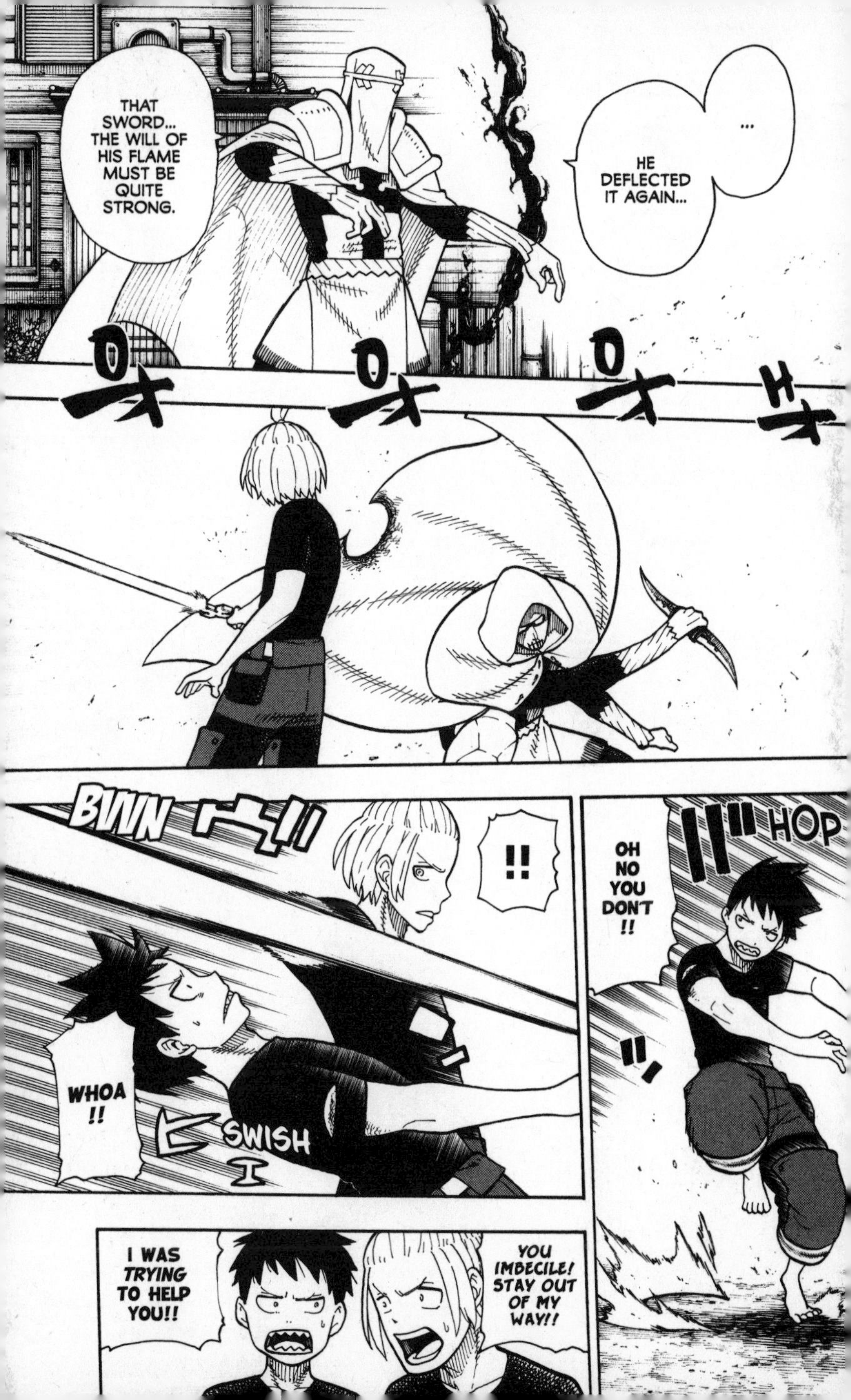
...
HE DEFLECTED IT AGAIN...
THAT SWORD... THE WILL OF HIS FLAME MUST BE QUITE STRONG.
HOOO
HOP
OH NO YOU DON'T!!
BWN
!!
WHOA!!
SWISH
YOU IMBECILE! STAY OUT OF MY WAY!!
I WAS *TRYING* TO HELP YOU!!

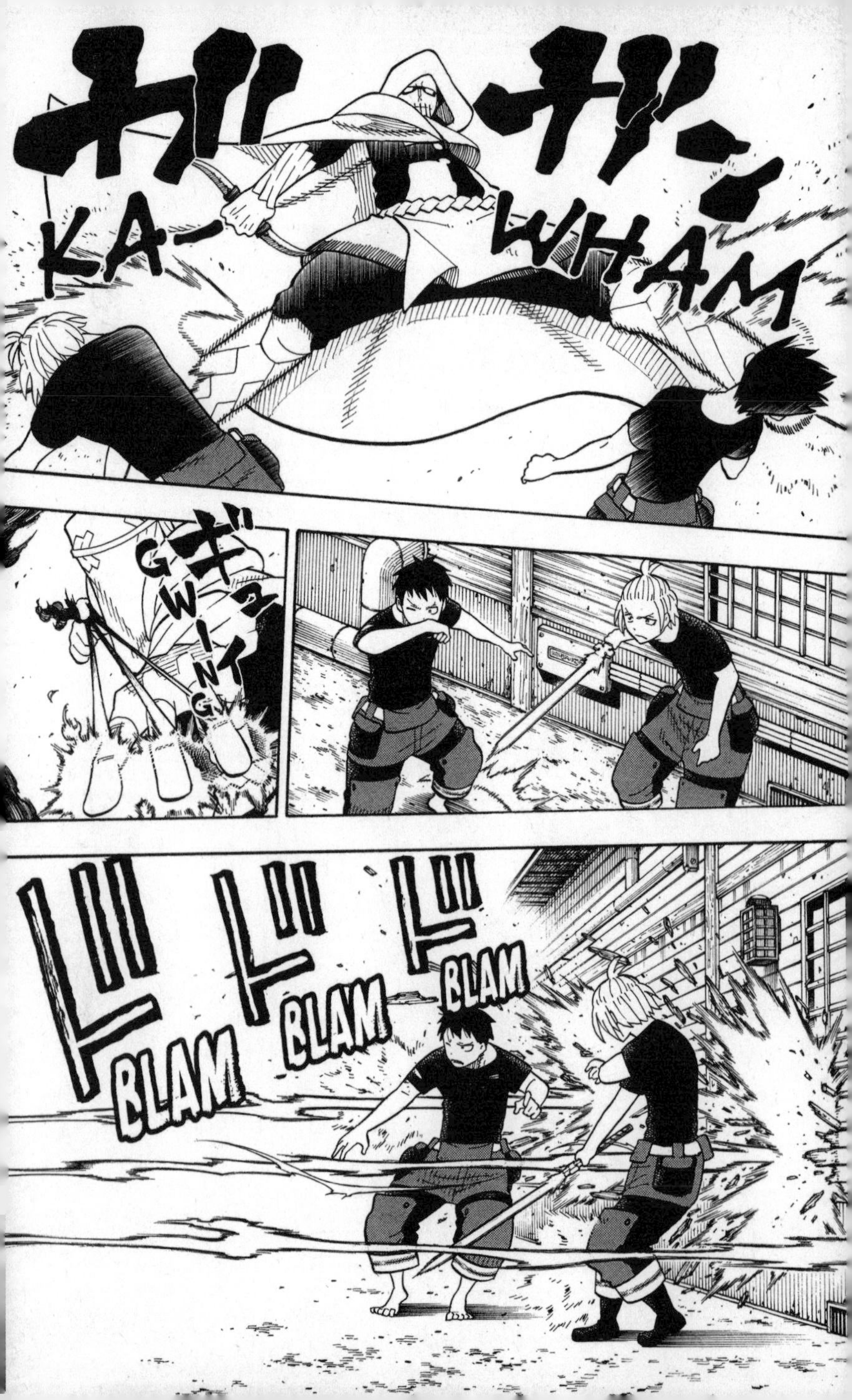
KA-WHAM
GWINNG
BLAM
BLAM
BLAM

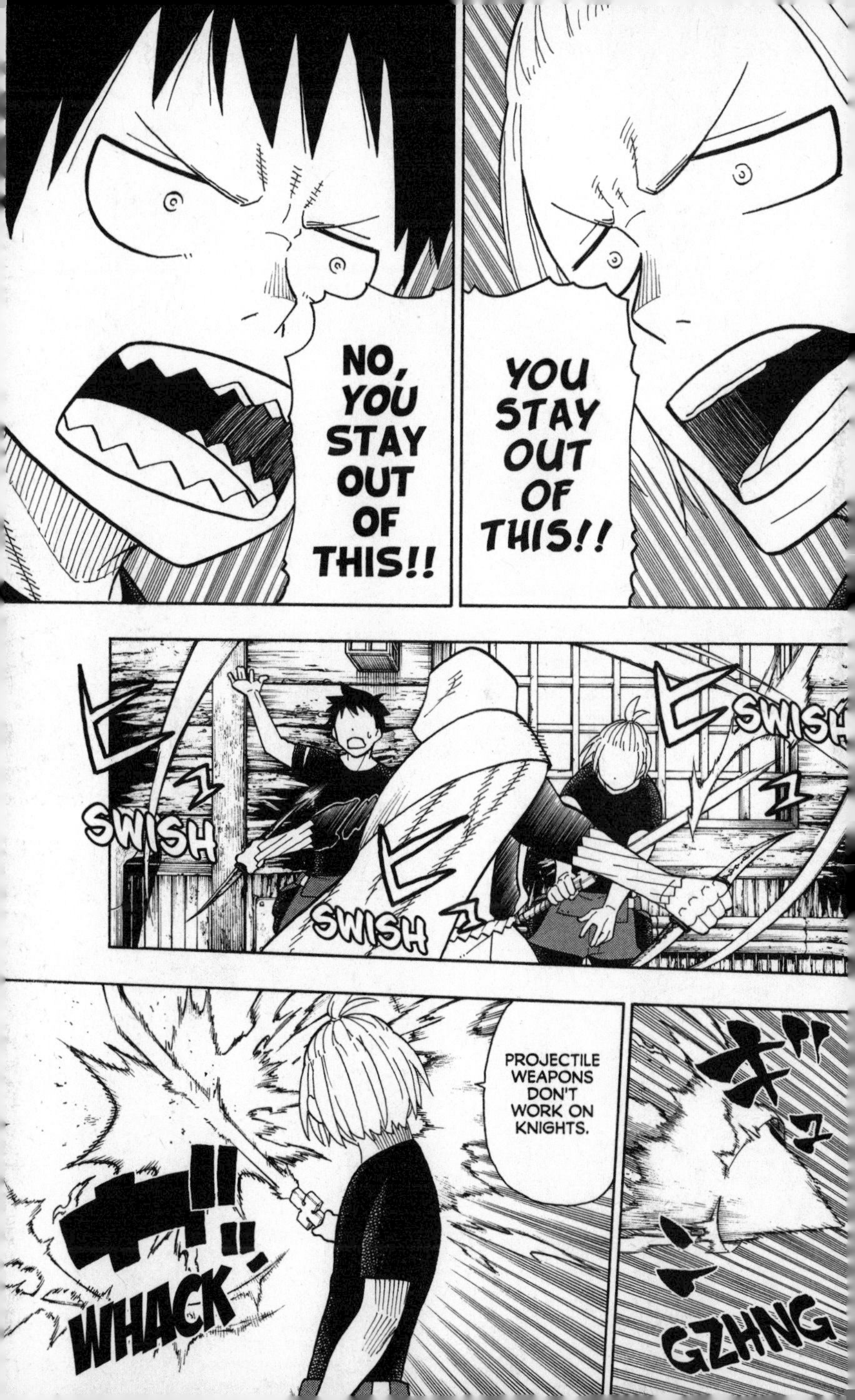
YOU STAY OUT OF THIS!!
NO, YOU STAY OUT OF THIS!!
SWISH
SWISH
SWISH
GZHNG
PROJECTILE WEAPONS DON'T WORK ON KNIGHTS.
WHACK

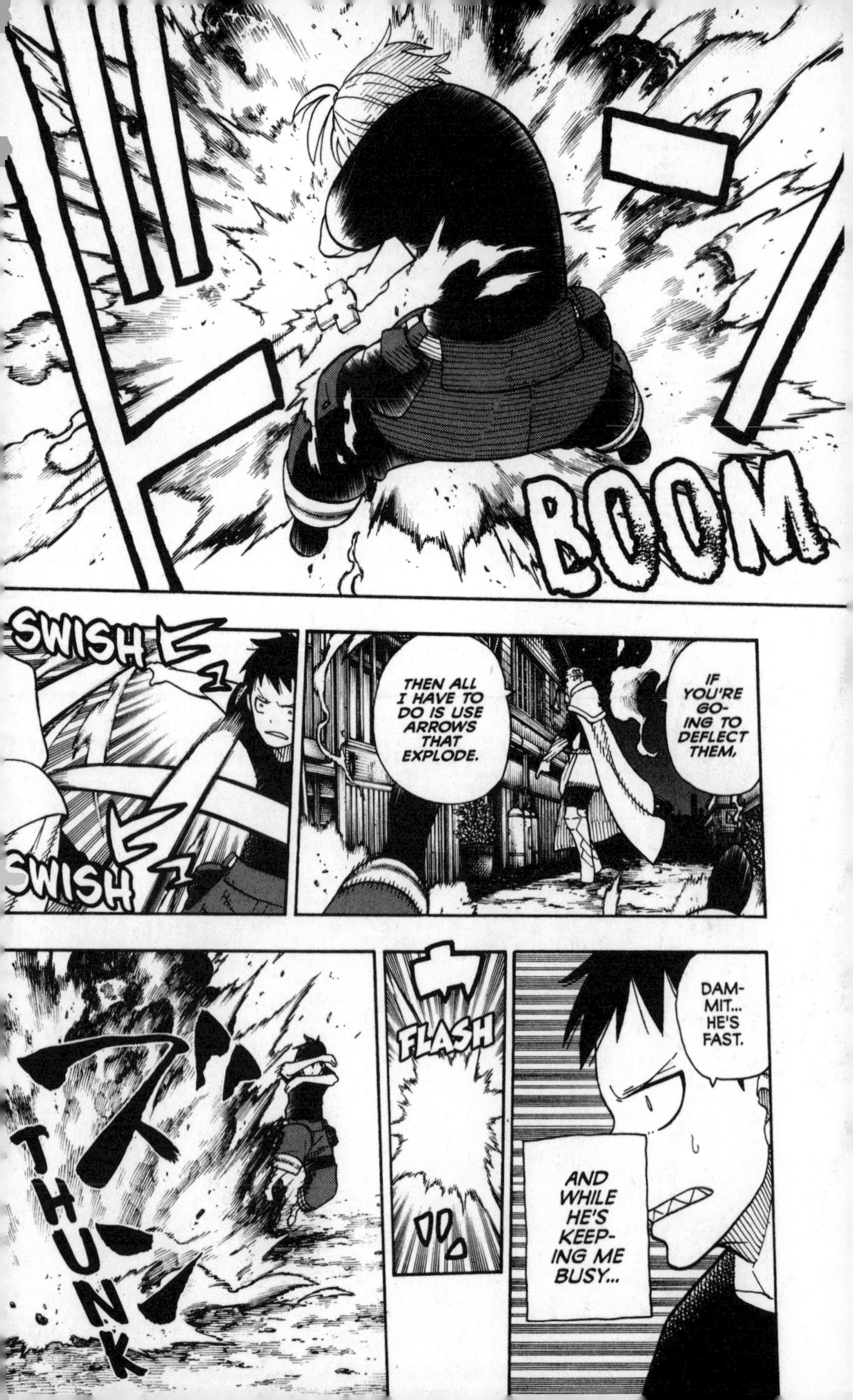
BOOM
IF YOU'RE GOING TO DEFLECT THEM,
THEN ALL I HAVE TO DO IS USE ARROWS THAT EXPLODE.
SWISH
SWISH
DAMMIT... HE'S FAST.
AND WHILE HE'S KEEPING ME BUSY...
FLASH
THUNK

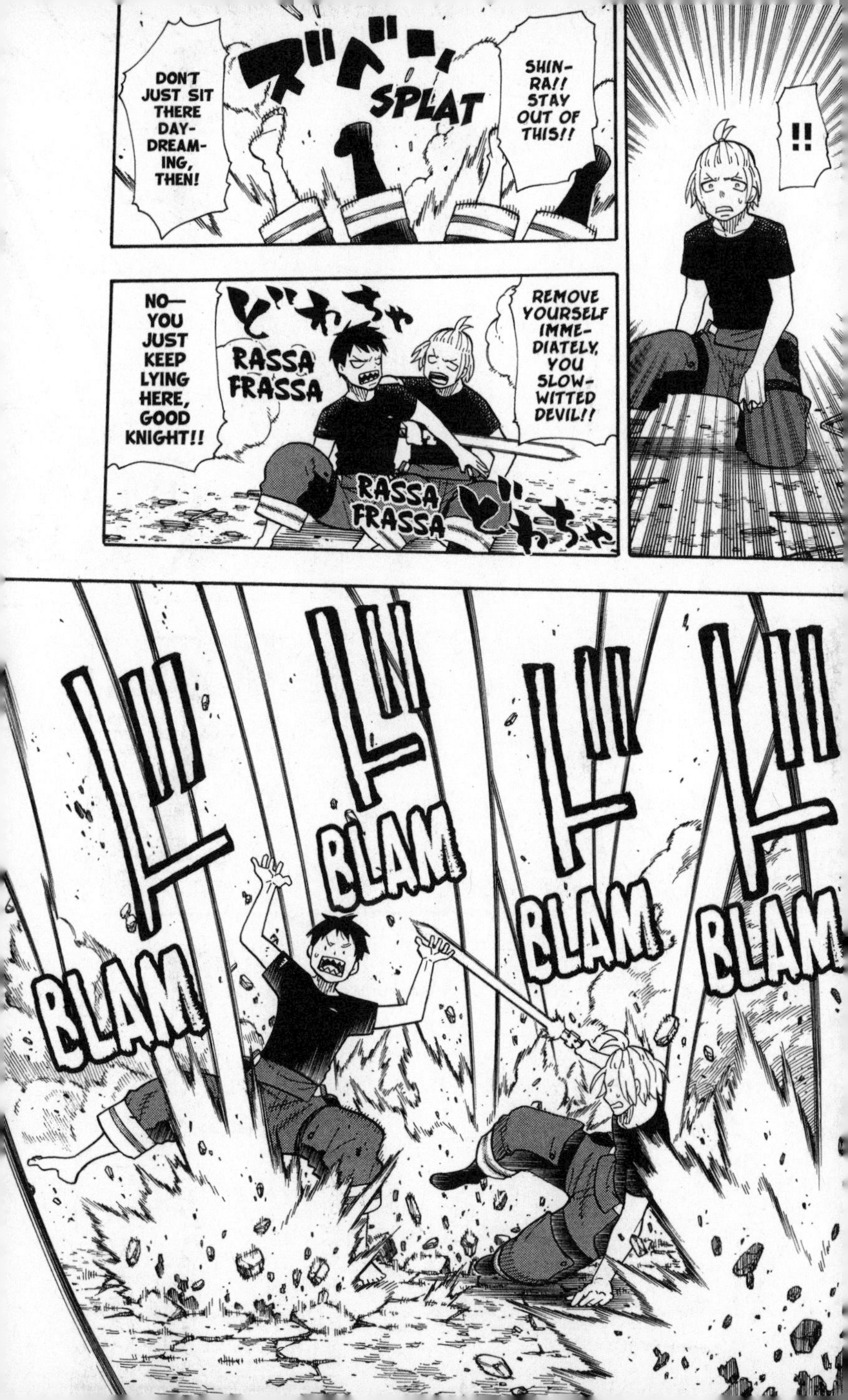
!!
SHIN-RA!! STAY OUT OF THIS!!
SPLAT
DON'T JUST SIT THERE DAY-DREAM-ING, THEN!
REMOVE YOURSELF IMME-DIATELY, YOU SLOW-WITTED DEVIL!!
RASSA FRASSA
NO— YOU JUST KEEP LYING HERE, GOOD KNIGHT!!
RASSA FRASSA
BLAM
BLAM
BLAM
BLAM

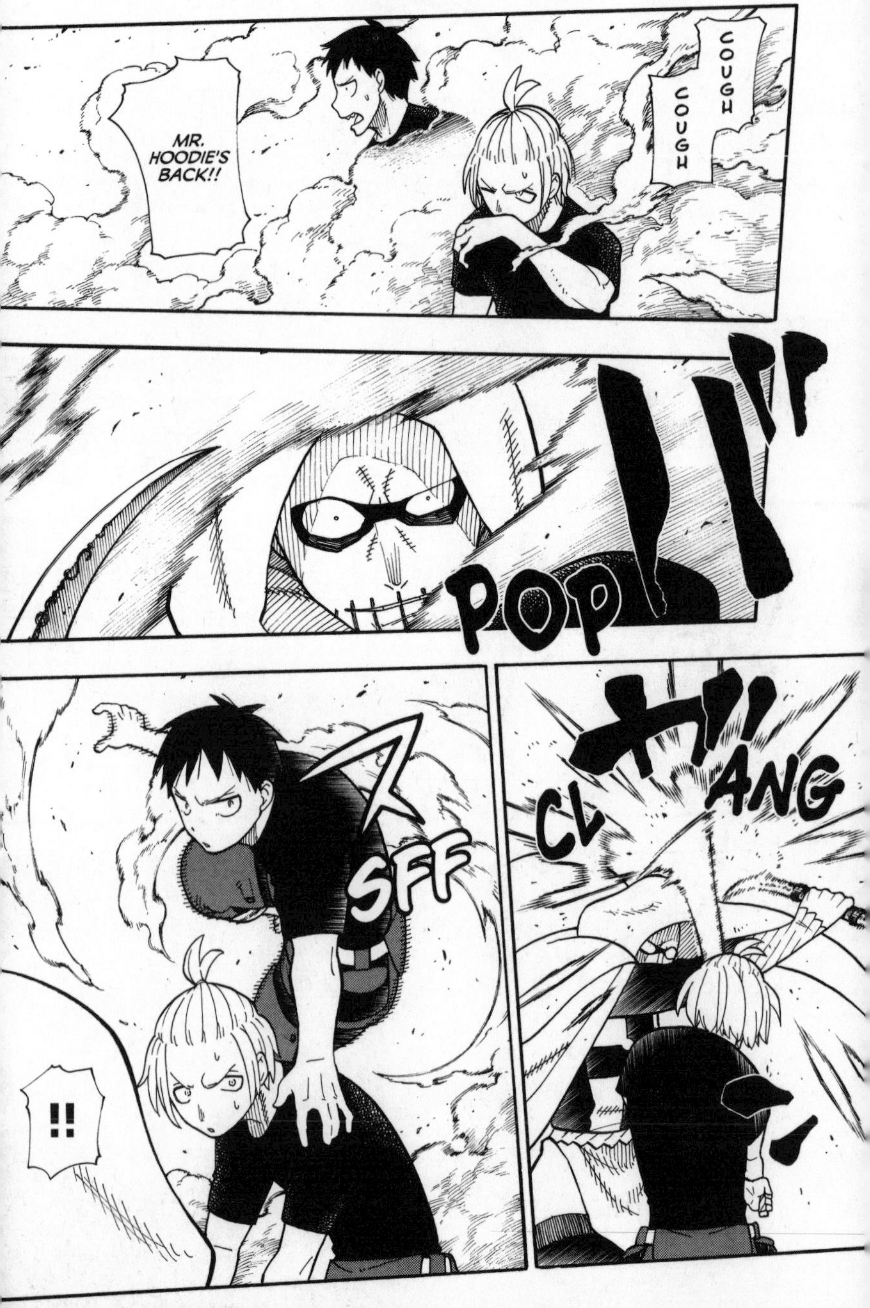
COUGH COUGH
MR. HOODIE'S BACK!!
POP
CLANG
SFF
!!

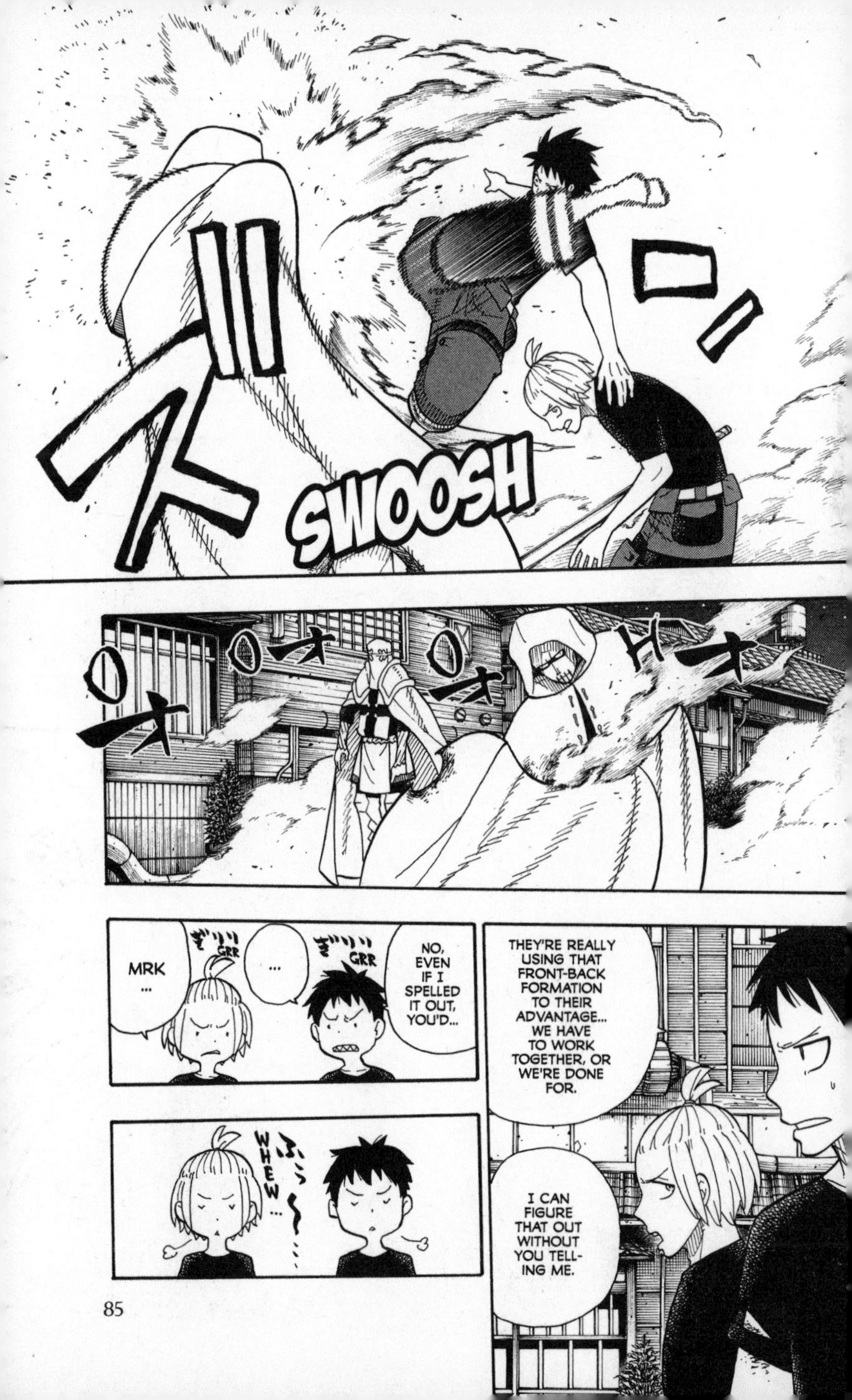
SWOOSH
THEY'RE REALLY USING THAT FRONT-BACK FORMATION TO THEIR ADVANTAGE... WE HAVE TO WORK TOGETHER, OR WE'RE DONE FOR.
I CAN FIGURE THAT OUT WITHOUT YOU TELLING ME.
NO, EVEN IF I SPELLED IT OUT, YOU'D...
GRR
...
GRR
MRK ...
WHEW...

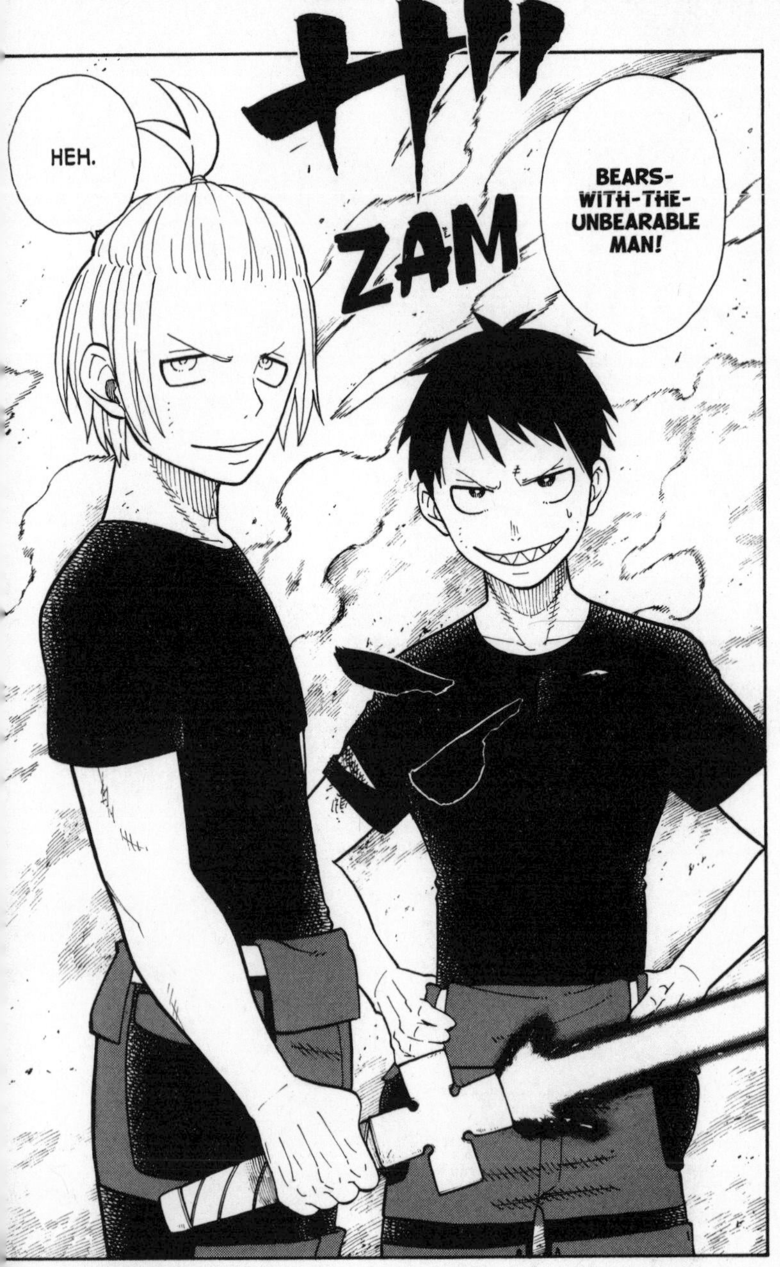
BEARS-WITH-THE-UNBEARABLE MAN!
ZAM
HEH.

FIRE FORCE

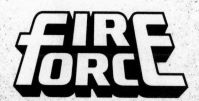

FIRE FORCE

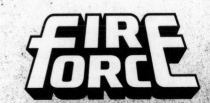

BA KA
馬鹿
BLOCK HEAD
TWI- TCH

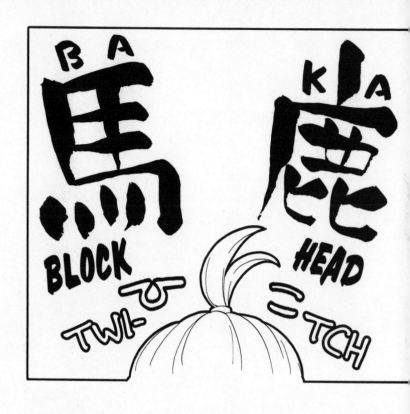

CHAPTER XLVII: TWO-ON-TWO DEATH MATCH

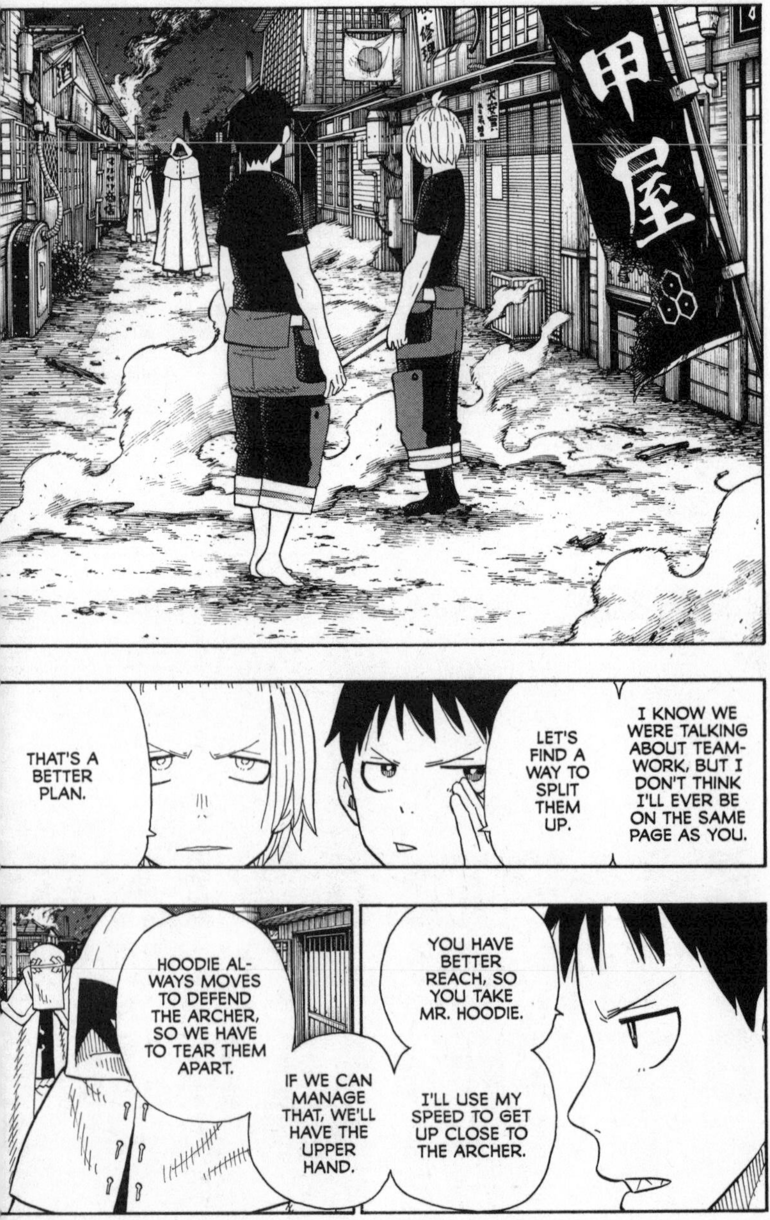
甲屋
I KNOW WE WERE TALKING ABOUT TEAM-WORK, BUT I DON'T THINK I'LL EVER BE ON THE SAME PAGE AS YOU.
LET'S FIND A WAY TO SPLIT THEM UP.
THAT'S A BETTER PLAN.
YOU HAVE BETTER REACH, SO YOU TAKE MR. HOODIE.
I'LL USE MY SPEED TO GET UP CLOSE TO THE ARCHER.
HOODIE AL-WAYS MOVES TO DEFEND THE ARCHER, SO WE HAVE TO TEAR THEM APART.
IF WE CAN MANAGE THAT, WE'LL HAVE THE UPPER HAND.

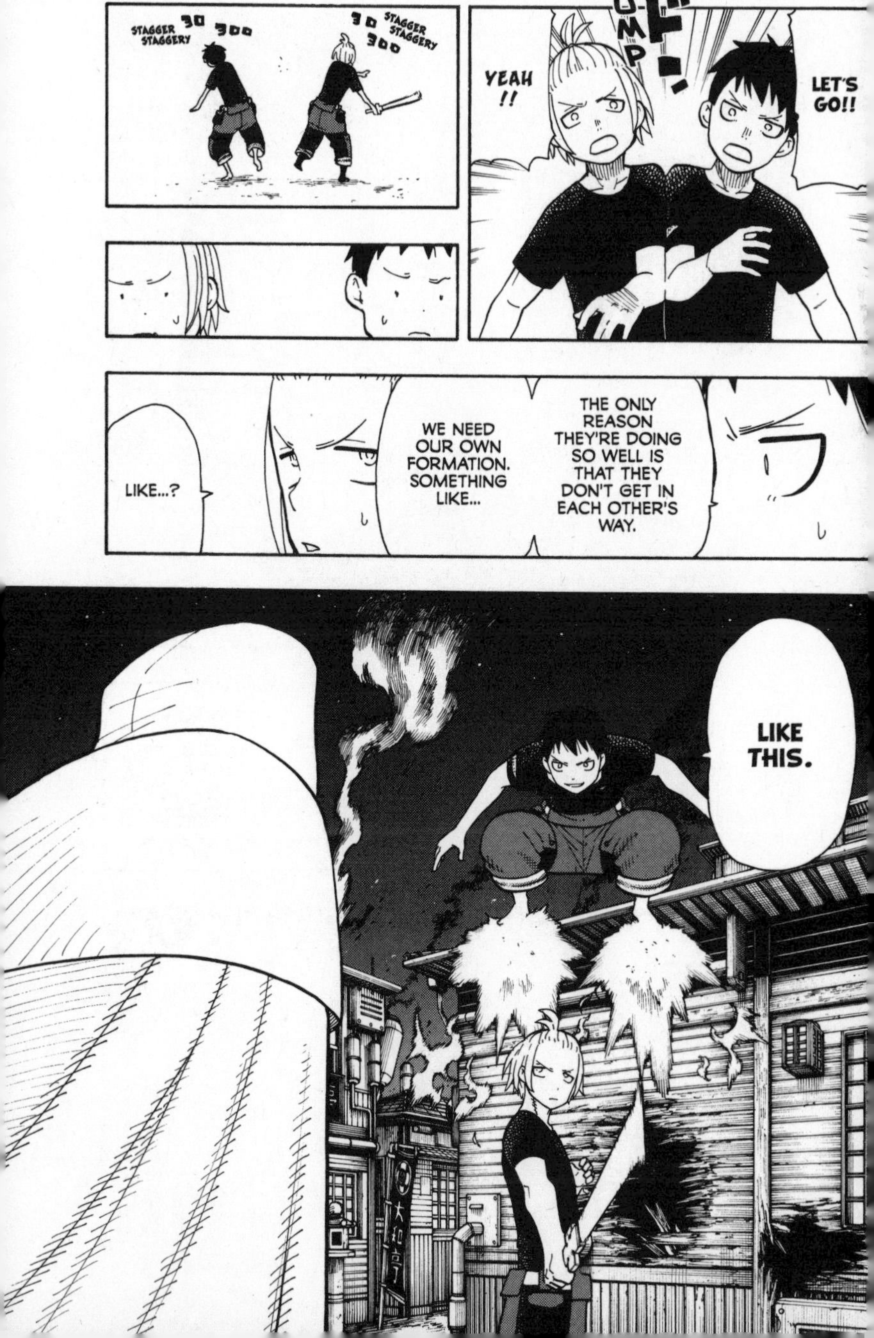
LET'S GO!!
BUMP
YEAH!!
STAGGER STAGGERY
STAGGER STAGGERY
THE ONLY REASON THEY'RE DOING SO WELL IS THAT THEY DON'T GET IN EACH OTHER'S WAY.
WE NEED OUR OWN FORMATION. SOMETHING LIKE...
LIKE...?
LIKE THIS.

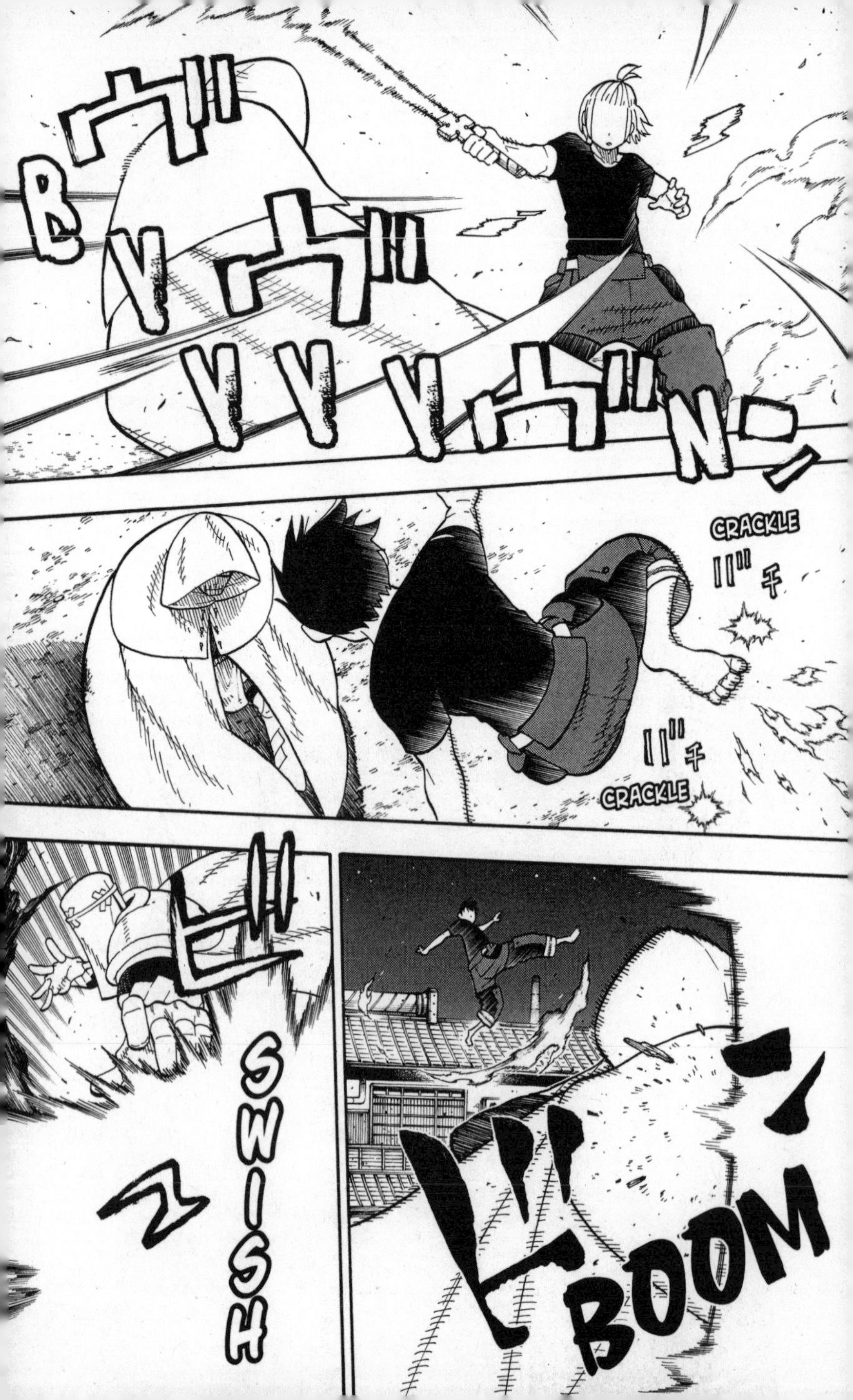
BVVVVN
ヴヴヴン
CRACKLE
バチ
バチ
CRACKLE
ドン
BOOM
ビュ
SWISH

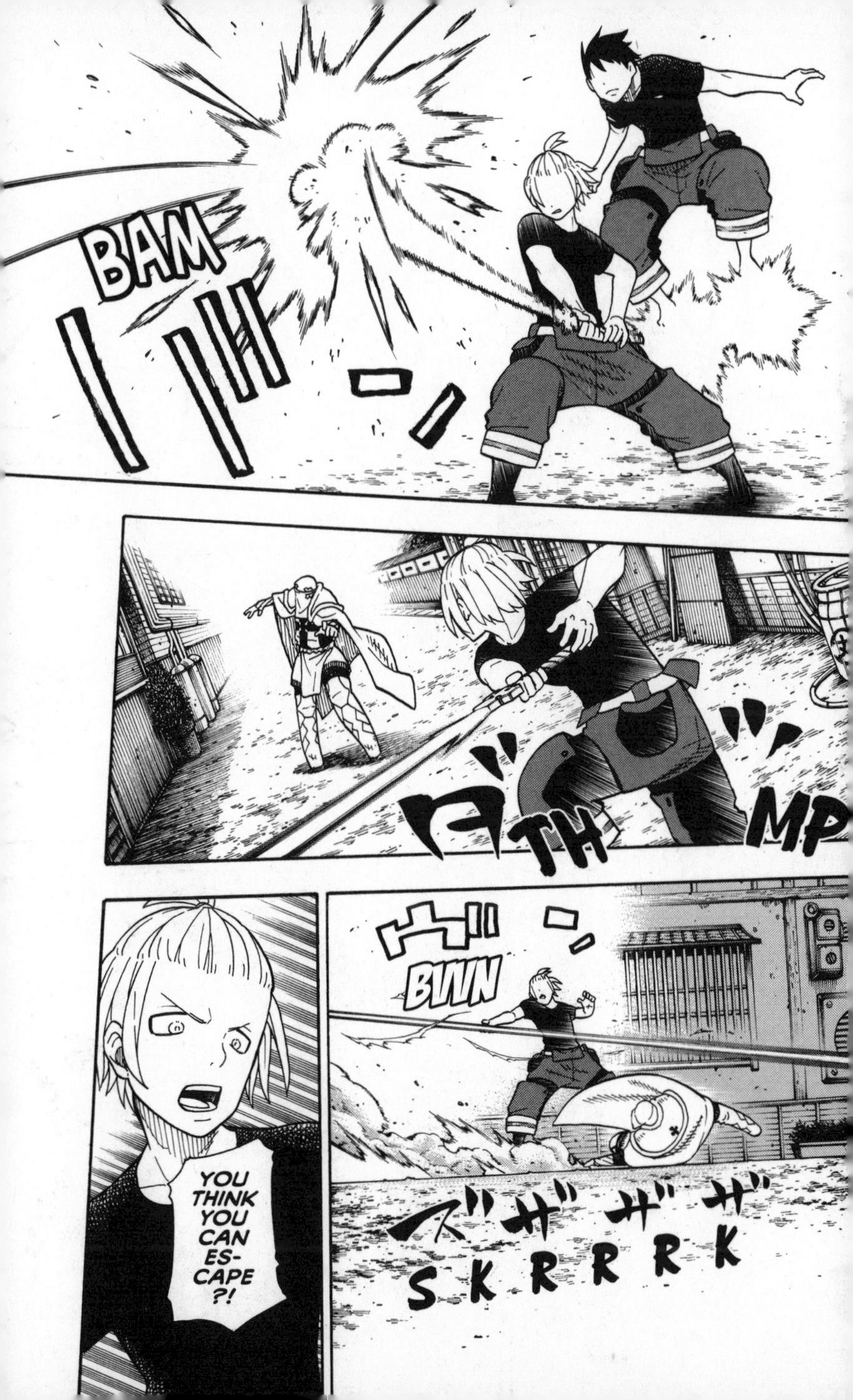
BAM
THMP
BVVN
SKRRRK
YOU THINK YOU CAN ES-CAPE?!

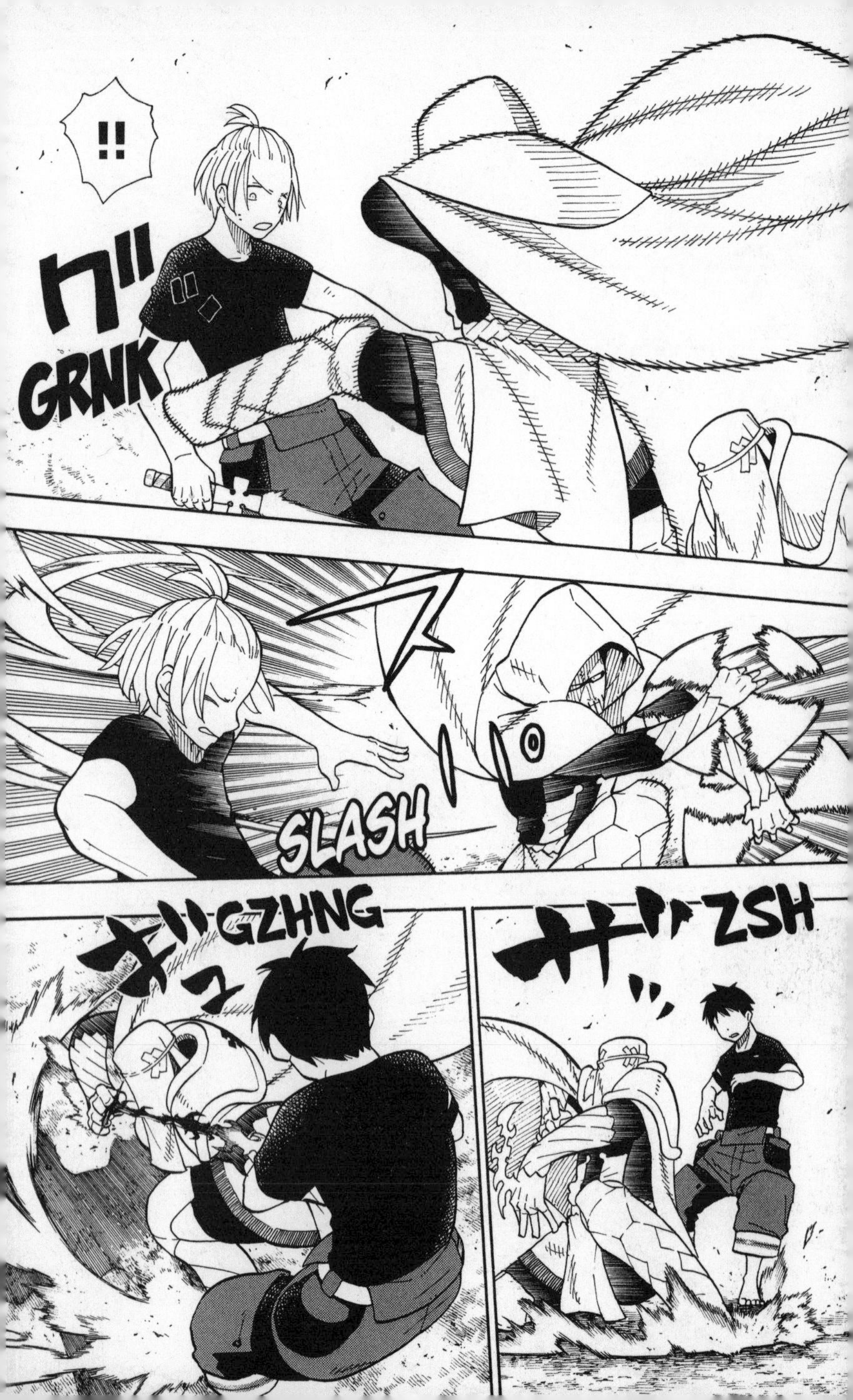
!!
GRNK
SLASH
ZSH
GZHNG

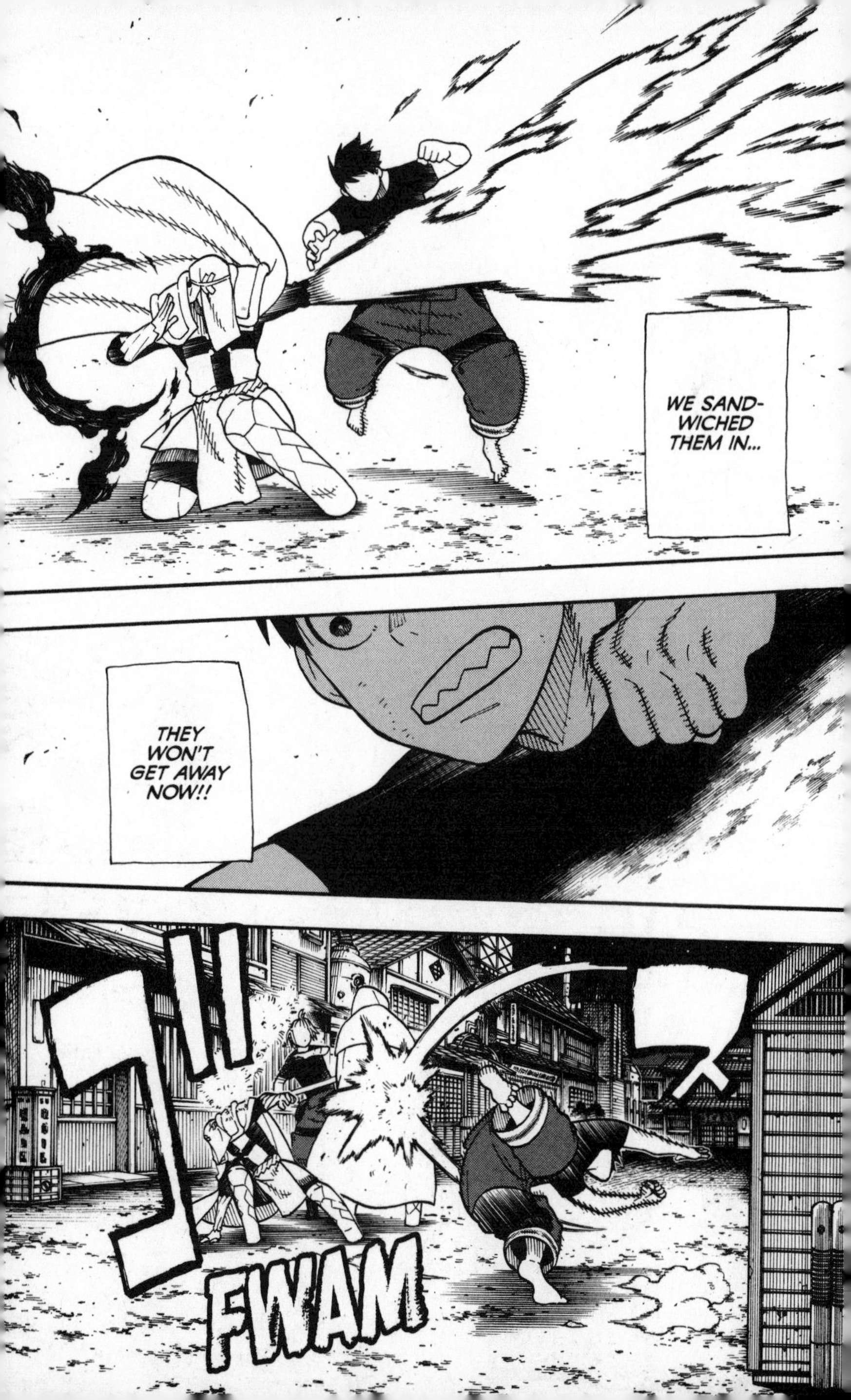
WE SAND-WICHED THEM IN...
THEY WON'T GET AWAY NOW!!
FWAM

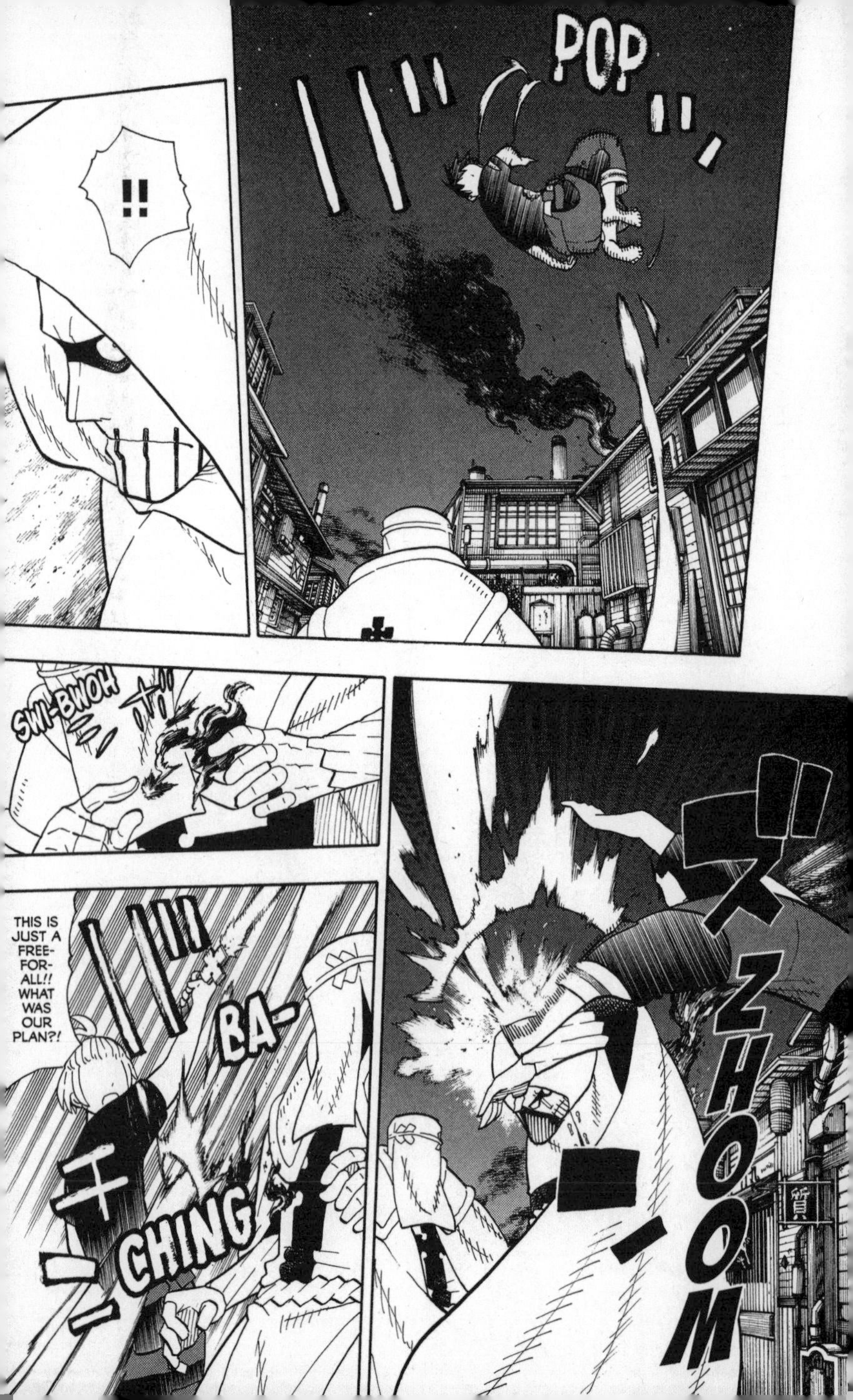
POP
!!
ZHOOM
SWI-BWOH
THIS IS JUST A FREE-FOR-ALL!! WHAT WAS OUR PLAN?!
BA-
CHING

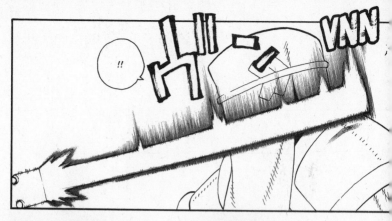

I MEAN, ACQUIT!

NOW, SUB-MIT...

CORRECT: SUBMIT

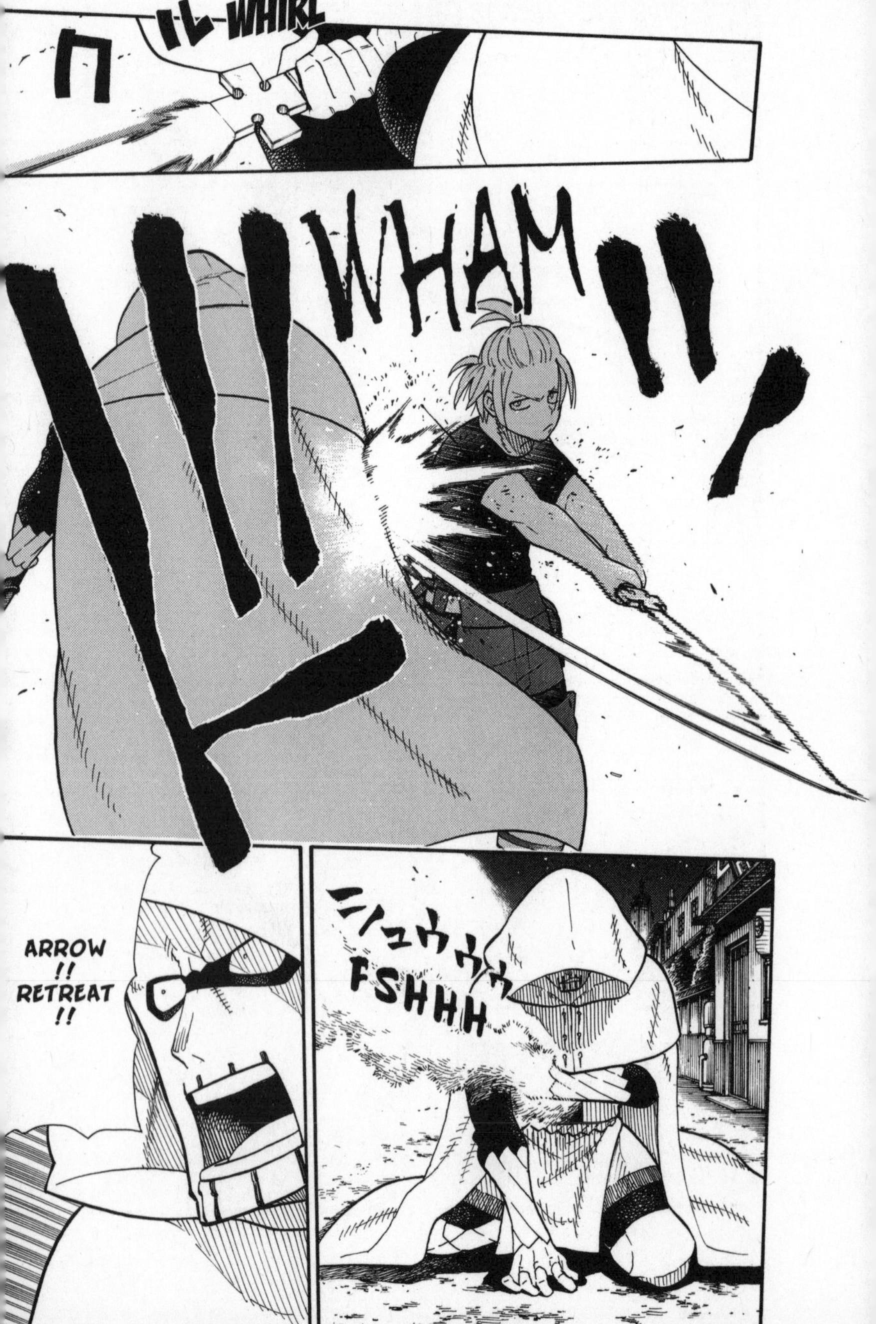
WHIRL
WHAM!!
FSHHH
ARROW!! RETREAT!!

YOU WON'T GET AWAY FROM US!!

INCH

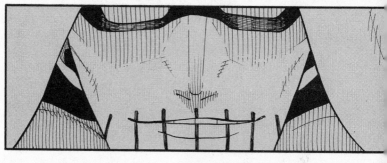

A BUG!!

!!

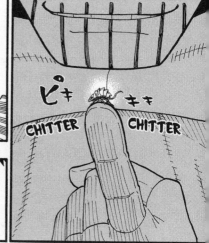

CHITTER   CHITTER

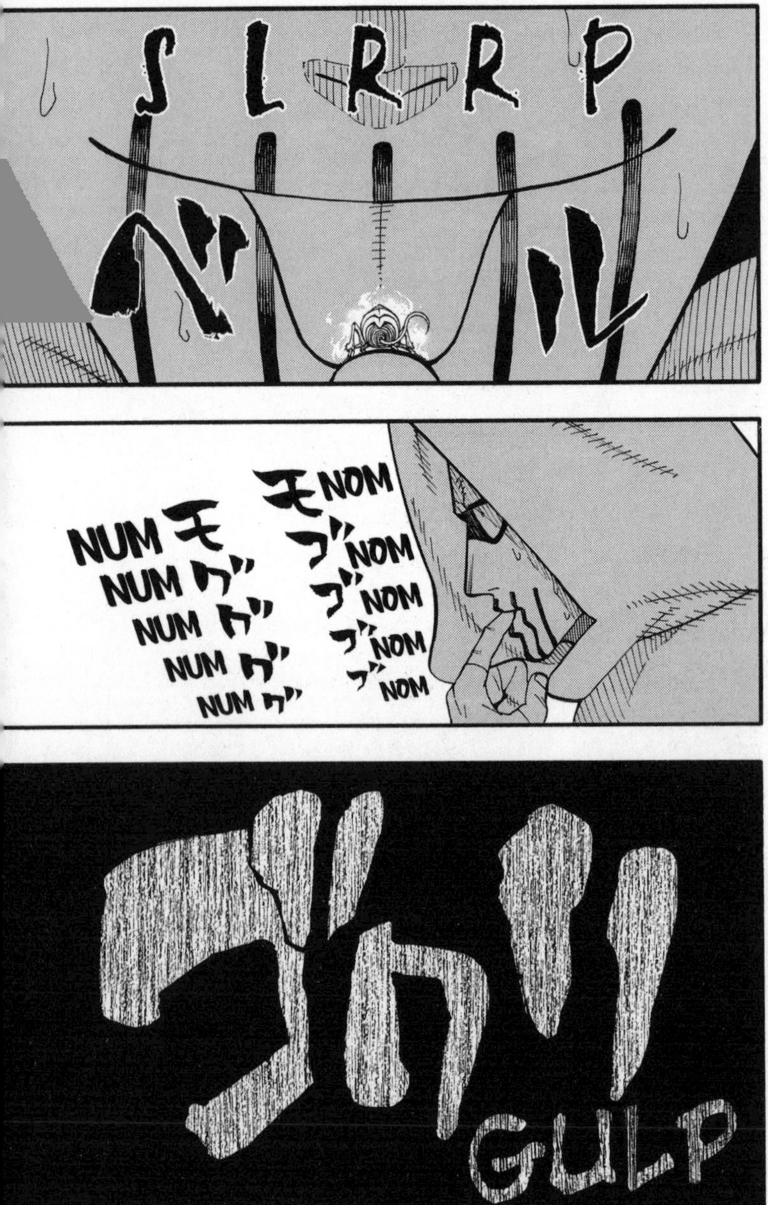
SLRRP
NOM NOM NOM NOM NOM
NUM NUM NUM NUM NUM
GULP

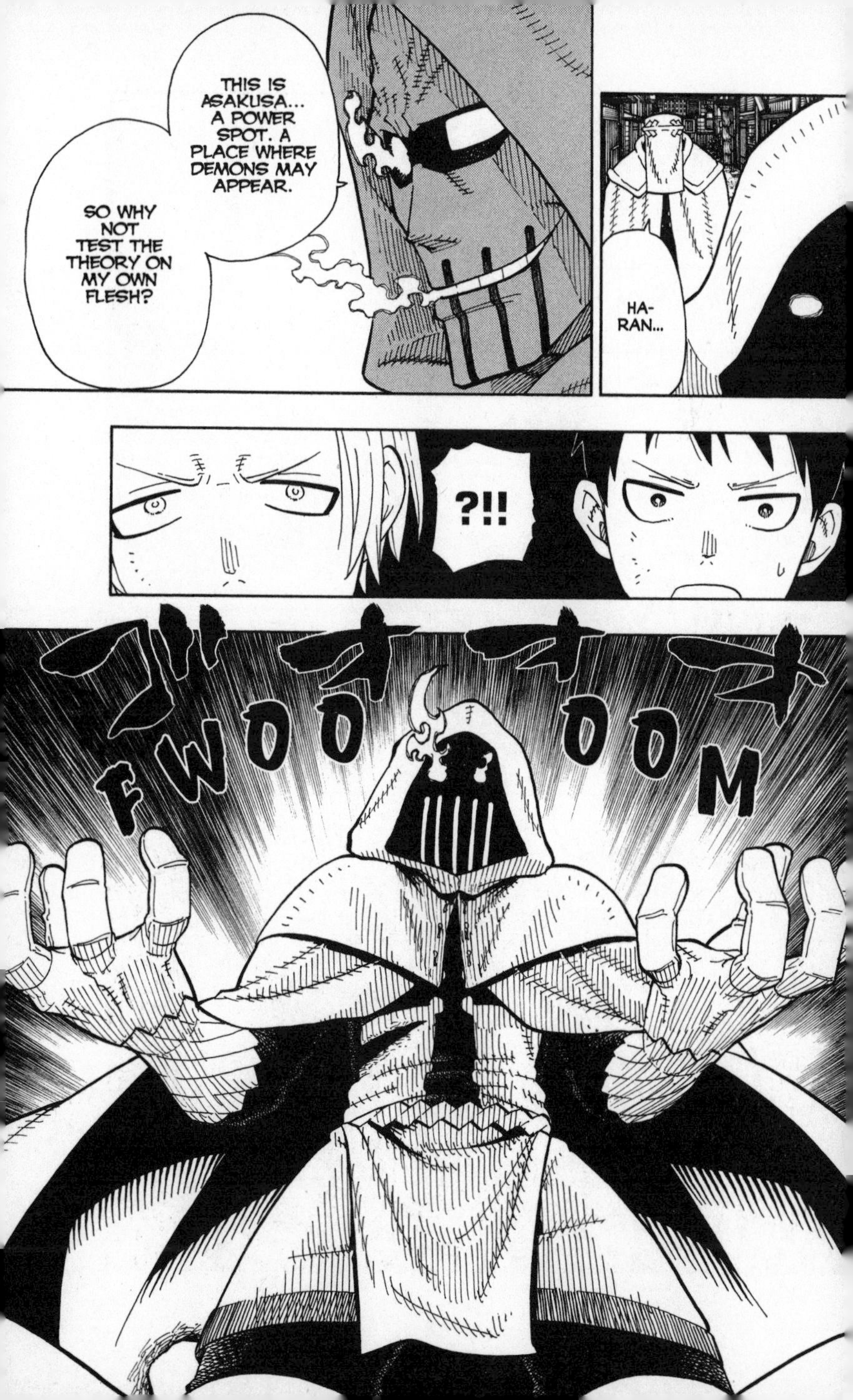

HA-RAN...
THIS IS ASAKUSA... A POWER SPOT. A PLACE WHERE DEMONS MAY APPEAR.
SO WHY NOT TEST THE THEORY ON MY OWN FLESH?
?!!
FWOOOOM

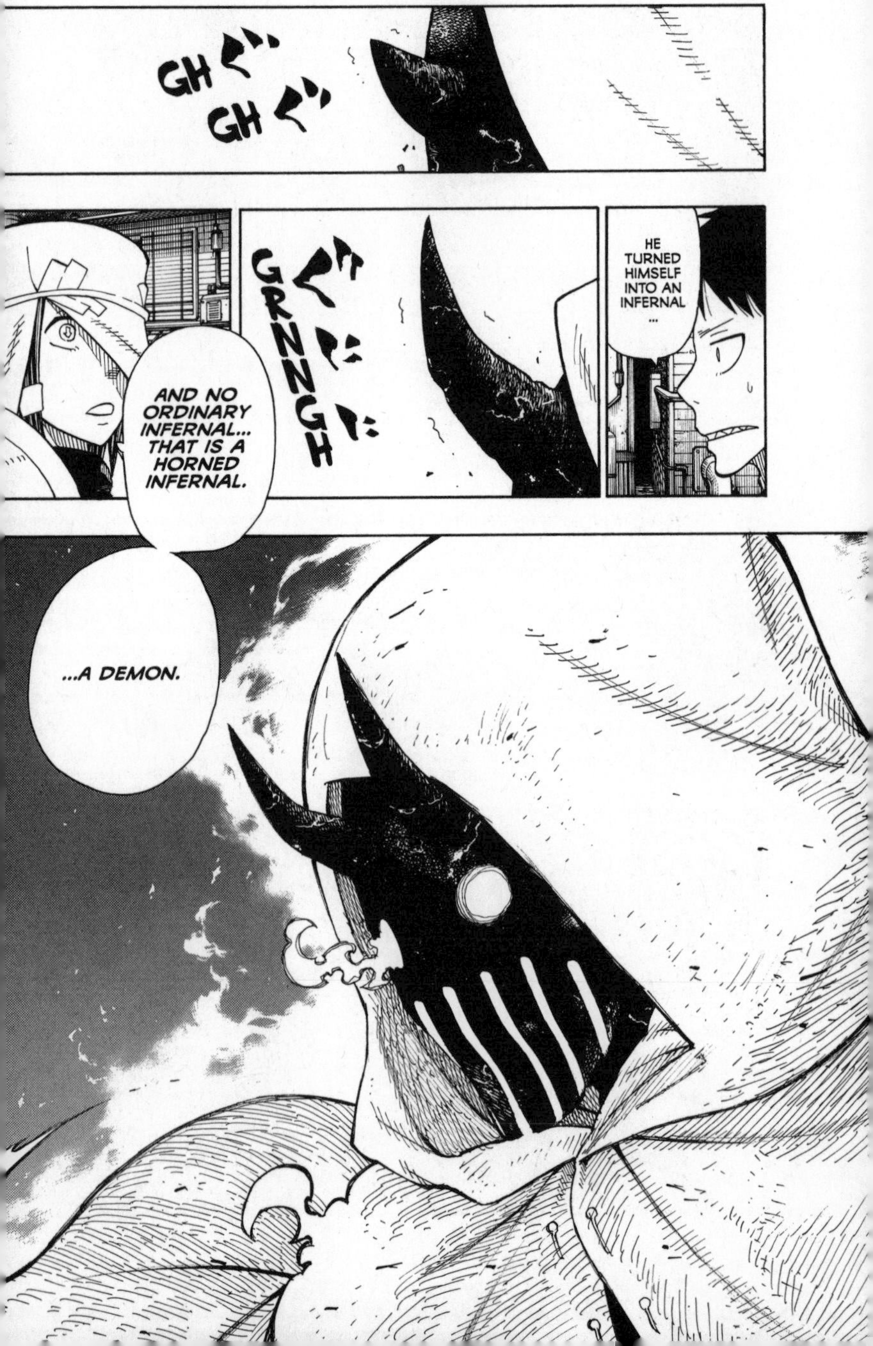
GH GH
HE TURNED HIMSELF INTO AN INFERNAL...
GRNNGH
AND NO ORDINARY INFERNAL... THAT IS A HORNED INFERNAL.
...A DEMON.

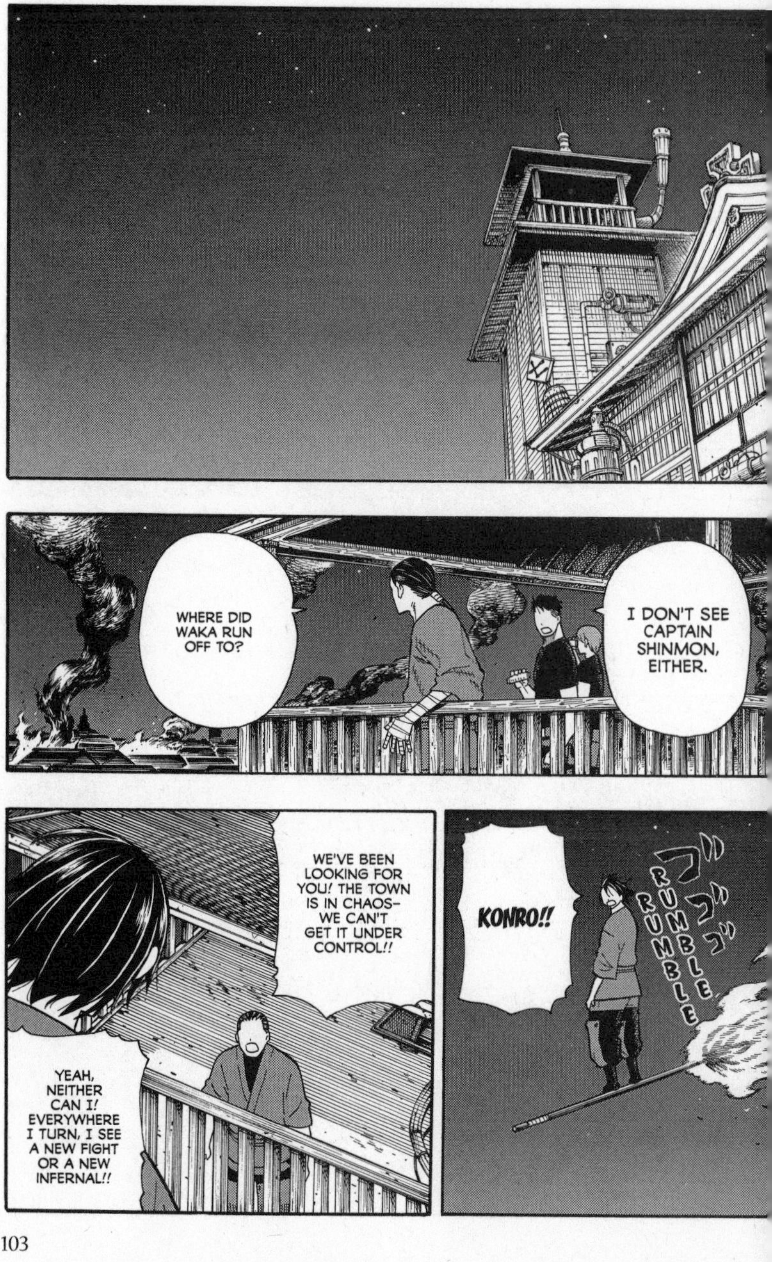
I DON'T SEE CAPTAIN SHINMON, EITHER.
WHERE DID WAKA RUN OFF TO?
KONRO!!
RUMBLE RUMBLE
WE'VE BEEN LOOKING FOR YOU! THE TOWN IS IN CHAOS— WE CAN'T GET IT UNDER CONTROL!!
YEAH, NEITHER CAN I! EVERYWHERE I TURN, I SEE A NEW FIGHT OR A NEW INFERNAL!!

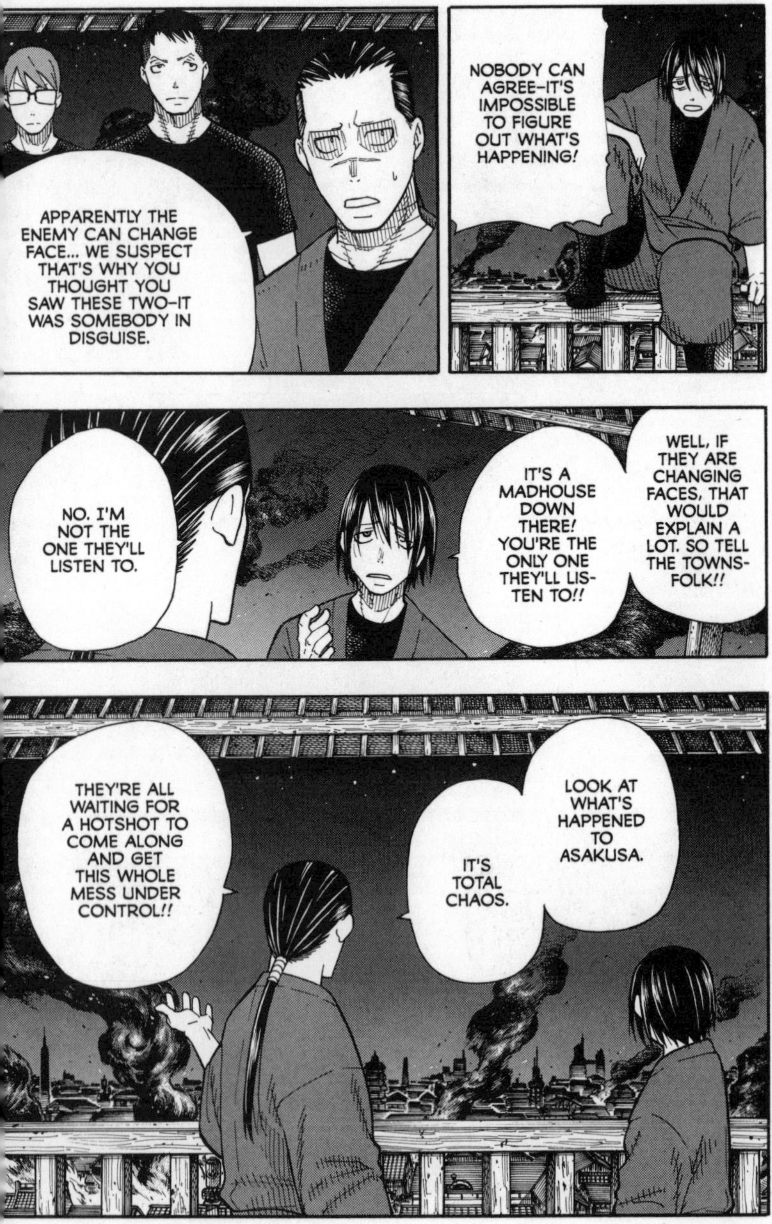
NOBODY CAN AGREE—IT'S IMPOSSIBLE TO FIGURE OUT WHAT'S HAPPENING!
APPARENTLY THE ENEMY CAN CHANGE FACE... WE SUSPECT THAT'S WHY YOU THOUGHT YOU SAW THESE TWO—IT WAS SOMEBODY IN DISGUISE.
WELL, IF THEY ARE CHANGING FACES, THAT WOULD EXPLAIN A LOT. SO TELL THE TOWNSFOLK!!
IT'S A MADHOUSE DOWN THERE! YOU'RE THE ONLY ONE THEY'LL LISTEN TO!!
NO. I'M NOT THE ONE THEY'LL LISTEN TO.
LOOK AT WHAT'S HAPPENED TO ASAKUSA.
IT'S TOTAL CHAOS.
THEY'RE ALL WAITING FOR A HOTSHOT TO COME ALONG AND GET THIS WHOLE MESS UNDER CONTROL!!

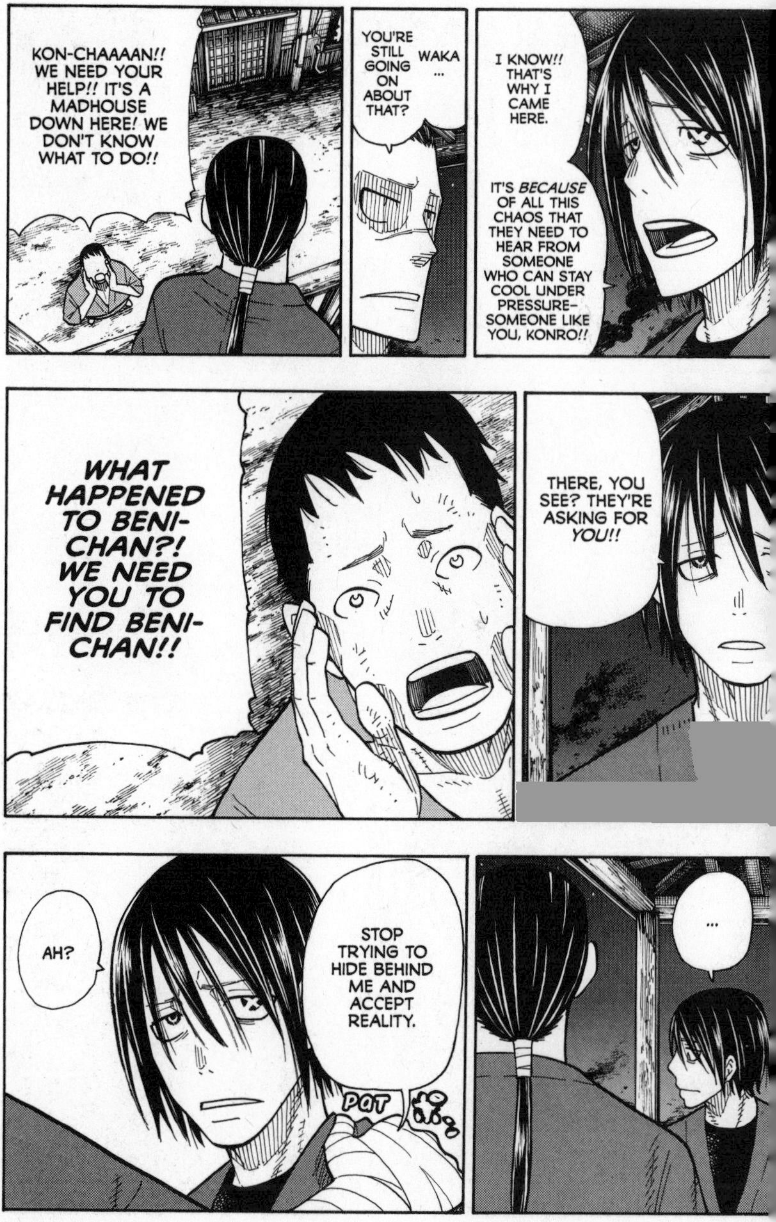
I KNOW!! THAT'S WHY I CAME HERE.
IT'S BECAUSE OF ALL THIS CHAOS THAT THEY NEED TO HEAR FROM SOMEONE WHO CAN STAY COOL UNDER PRESSURE– SOMEONE LIKE YOU, KONRO!!
WAKA ...
YOU'RE STILL GOING ON ABOUT THAT?
KON-CHAAAAN!! WE NEED YOUR HELP!! IT'S A MADHOUSE DOWN HERE! WE DON'T KNOW WHAT TO DO!!
THERE, YOU SEE? THEY'RE ASKING FOR YOU!!
WHAT HAPPENED TO BENI-CHAN?! WE NEED YOU TO FIND BENI-CHAN!!
...
STOP TRYING TO HIDE BEHIND ME AND ACCEPT REALITY.
PAT
AH?

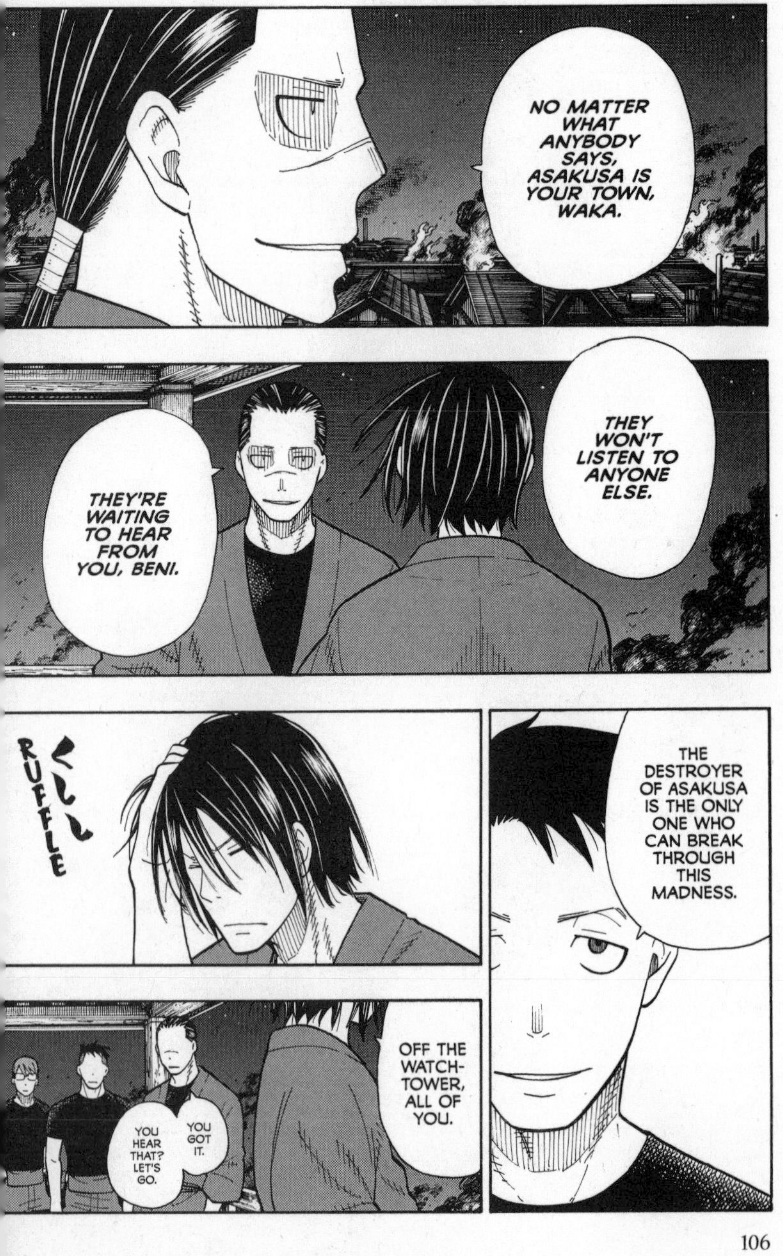

NO MATTER WHAT ANYBODY SAYS, ASAKUSA IS YOUR TOWN, WAKA.
THEY WON'T LISTEN TO ANYONE ELSE.
THEY'RE WAITING TO HEAR FROM YOU, BENI.
THE DESTROYER OF ASAKUSA IS THE ONLY ONE WHO CAN BREAK THROUGH THIS MADNESS.
RUFFLE
OFF THE WATCH-TOWER, ALL OF YOU.
YOU GOT IT.
YOU HEAR THAT? LET'S GO.

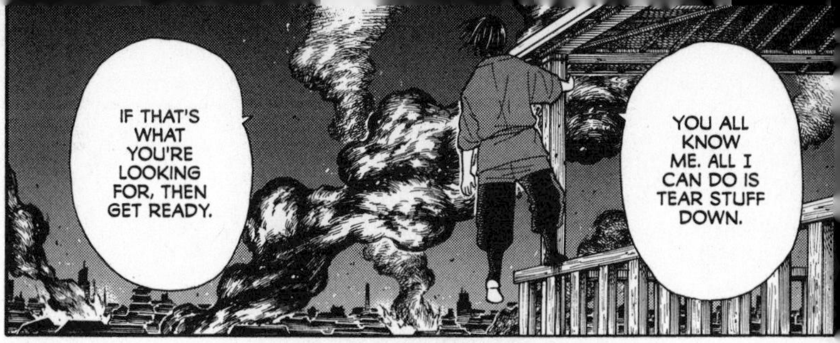
YOU ALL KNOW ME. ALL I CAN DO IS TEAR STUFF DOWN.
IF THAT'S WHAT YOU'RE LOOKING FOR, THEN GET READY.
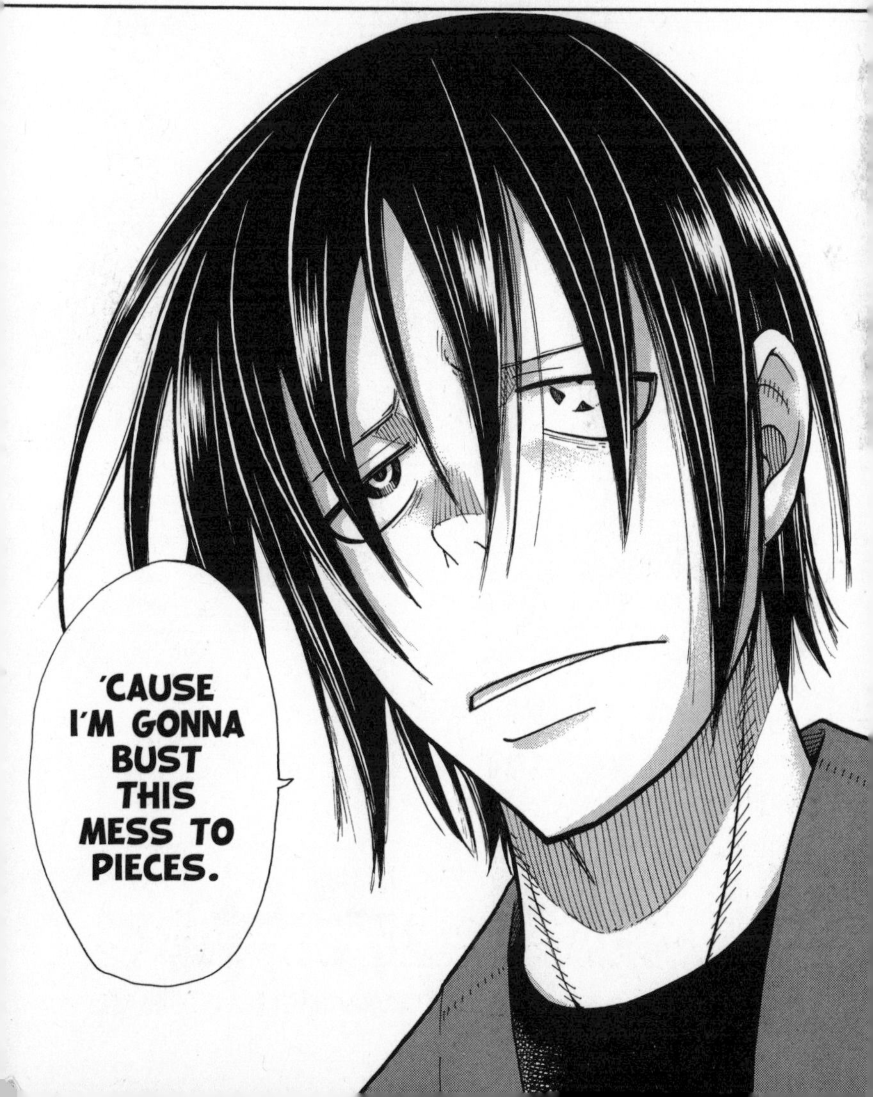
'CAUSE I'M GONNA BUST THIS MESS TO PIECES.

FIRE FORCE

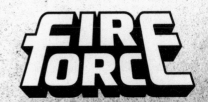

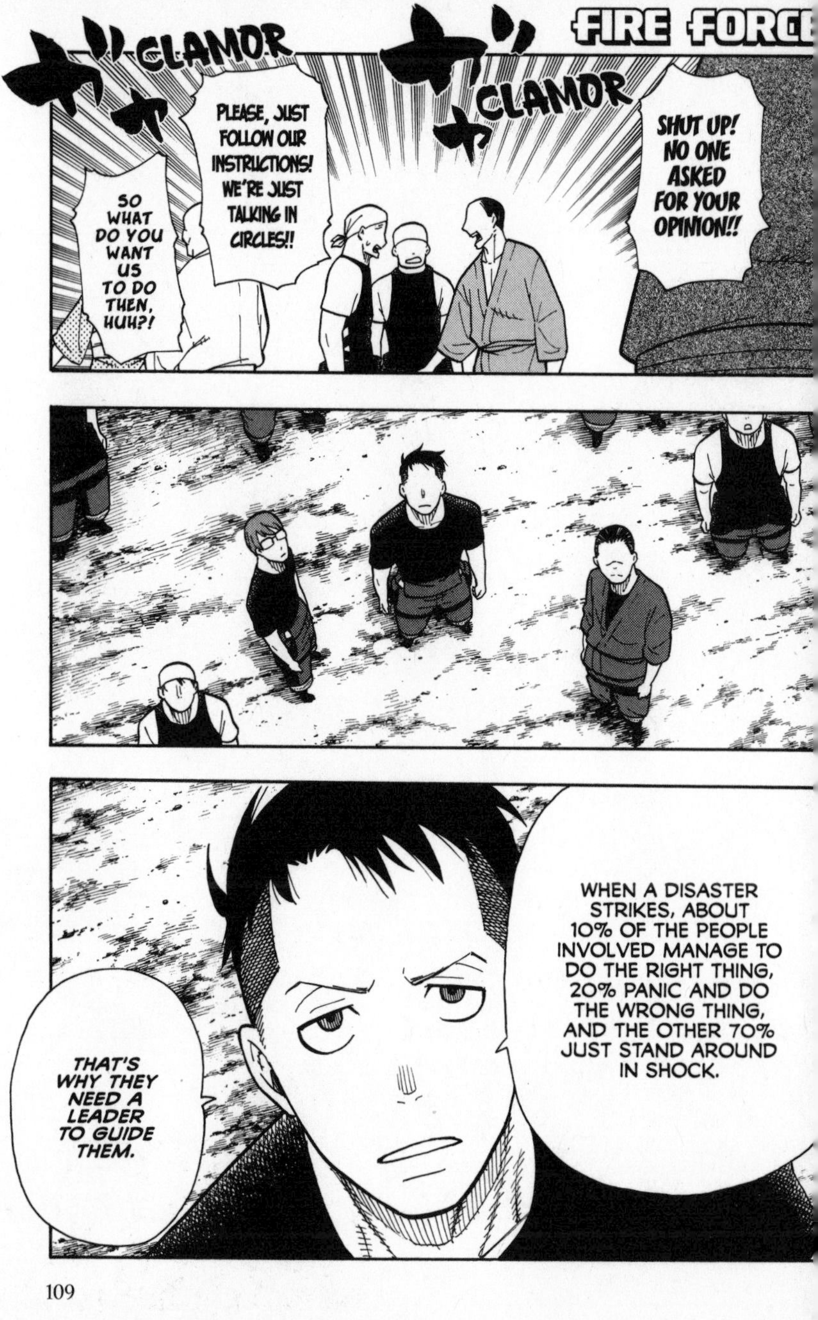
SHUT UP! NO ONE ASKED FOR YOUR OPINION!!
CLAMOR
PLEASE, JUST FOLLOW OUR INSTRUCTIONS! WE'RE JUST TALKING IN CIRCLES!!
CLAMOR
SO WHAT DO YOU WANT US TO DO THEN, HUH?!
WHEN A DISASTER STRIKES, ABOUT 10% OF THE PEOPLE INVOLVED MANAGE TO DO THE RIGHT THING, 20% PANIC AND DO THE WRONG THING, AND THE OTHER 70% JUST STAND AROUND IN SHOCK.
THAT'S WHY THEY NEED A LEADER TO GUIDE THEM.

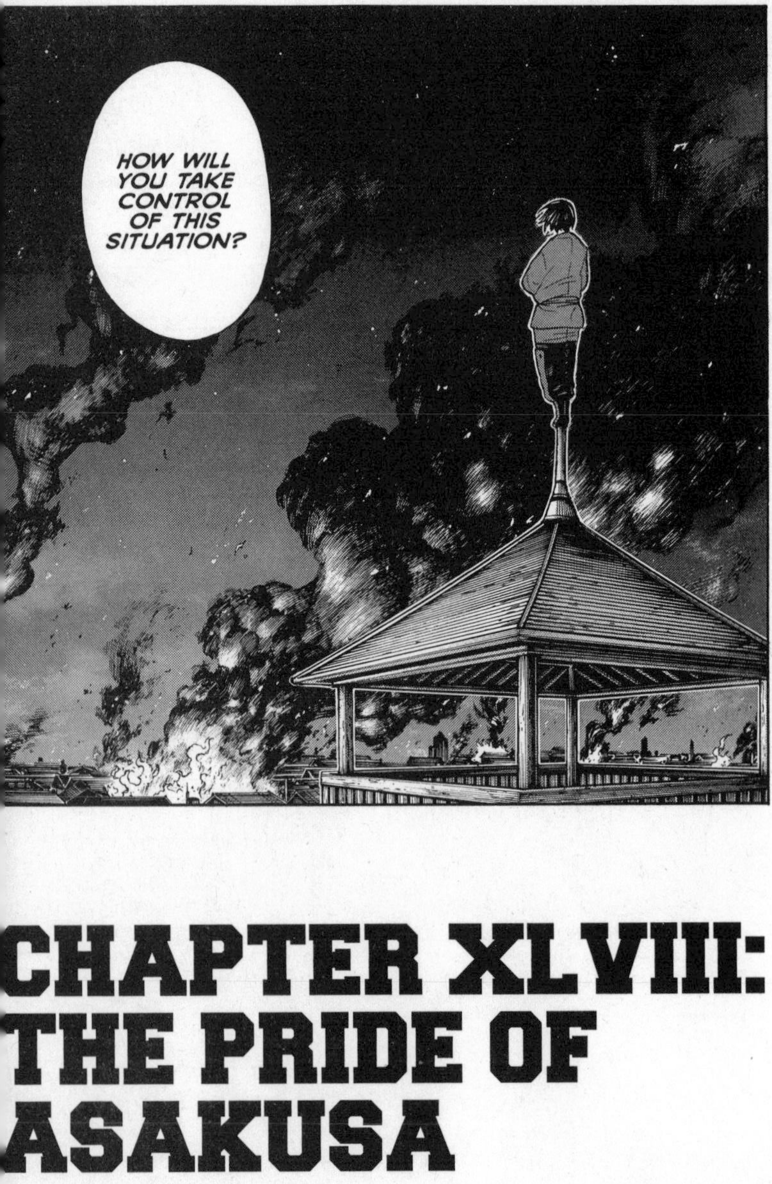
HOW WILL YOU TAKE CONTROL OF THIS SITUATION?

CHAPTER XLVIII: THE PRIDE OF ASAKUSA

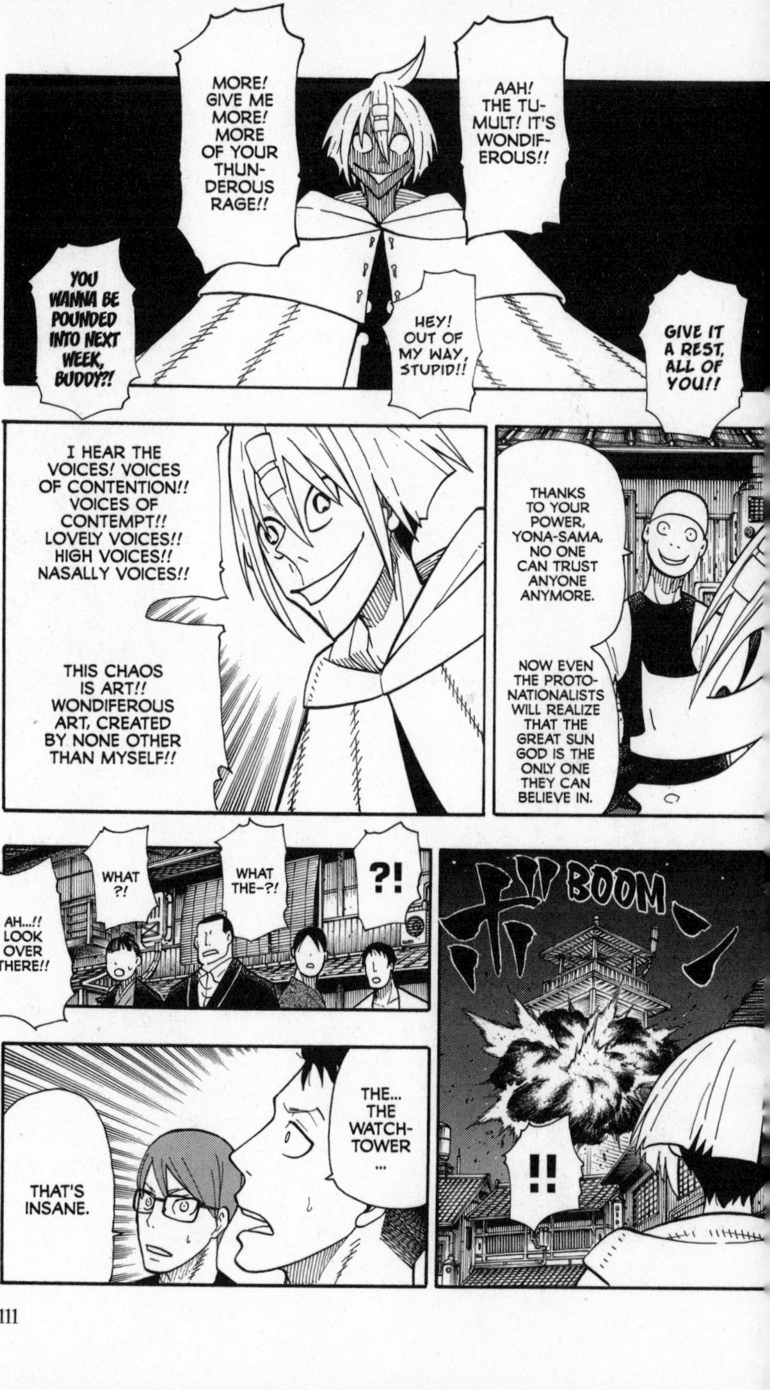

AAH! THE TUMULT! IT'S WONDIFEROUS!!
MORE! GIVE ME MORE! MORE OF YOUR THUNDEROUS RAGE!!
GIVE IT A REST, ALL OF YOU!!
HEY! OUT OF MY WAY, STUPID!!
YOU WANNA BE POUNDED INTO NEXT WEEK, BUDDY?!
THANKS TO YOUR POWER, YONA-SAMA, NO ONE CAN TRUST ANYONE ANYMORE.
NOW EVEN THE PROTO-NATIONALISTS WILL REALIZE THAT THE GREAT SUN GOD IS THE ONLY ONE THEY CAN BELIEVE IN.
I HEAR THE VOICES! VOICES OF CONTENTION!! VOICES OF CONTEMPT!! LOVELY VOICES!! HIGH VOICES!! NASALLY VOICES!!
THIS CHAOS IS ART!! WONDIFEROUS ART, CREATED BY NONE OTHER THAN MYSELF!!
BOOM
!!
?!
WHAT THE-?!
WHAT?!
AH...!! LOOK OVER THERE!!
THE... THE WATCHTOWER...
THAT'S INSANE.

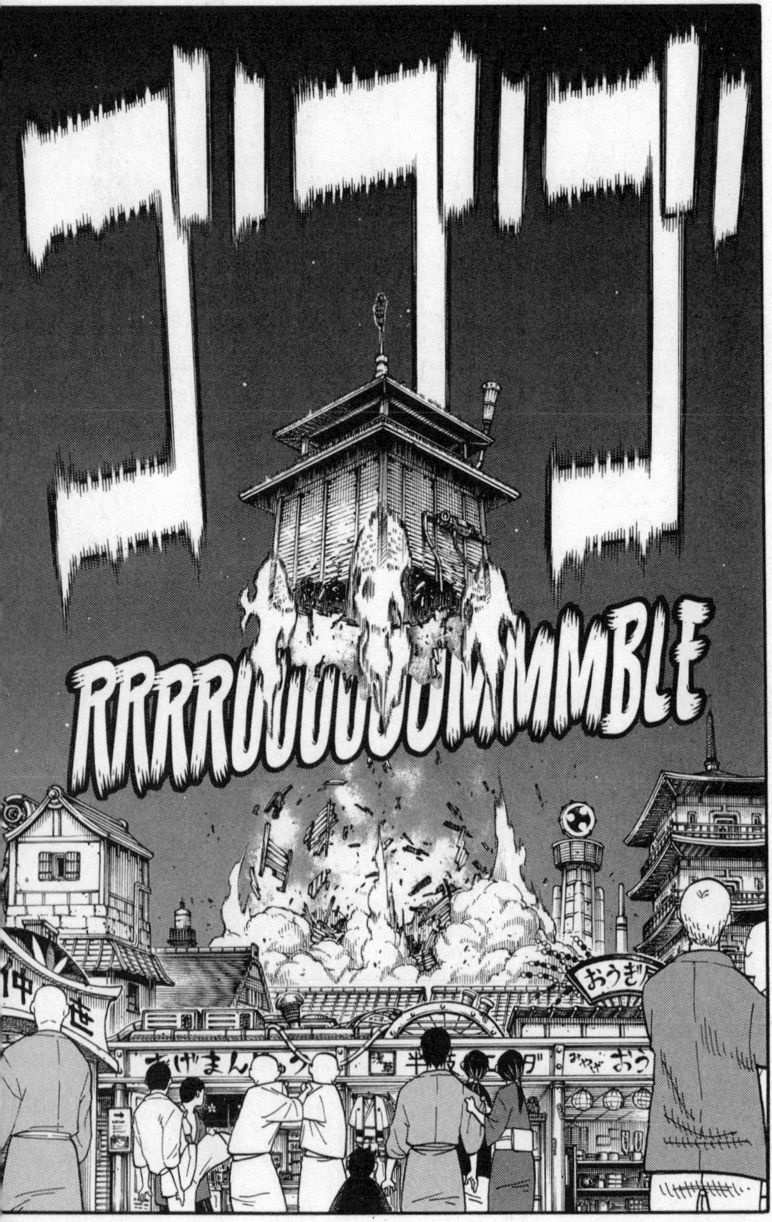
RRRROOOOOOMMMMBLE

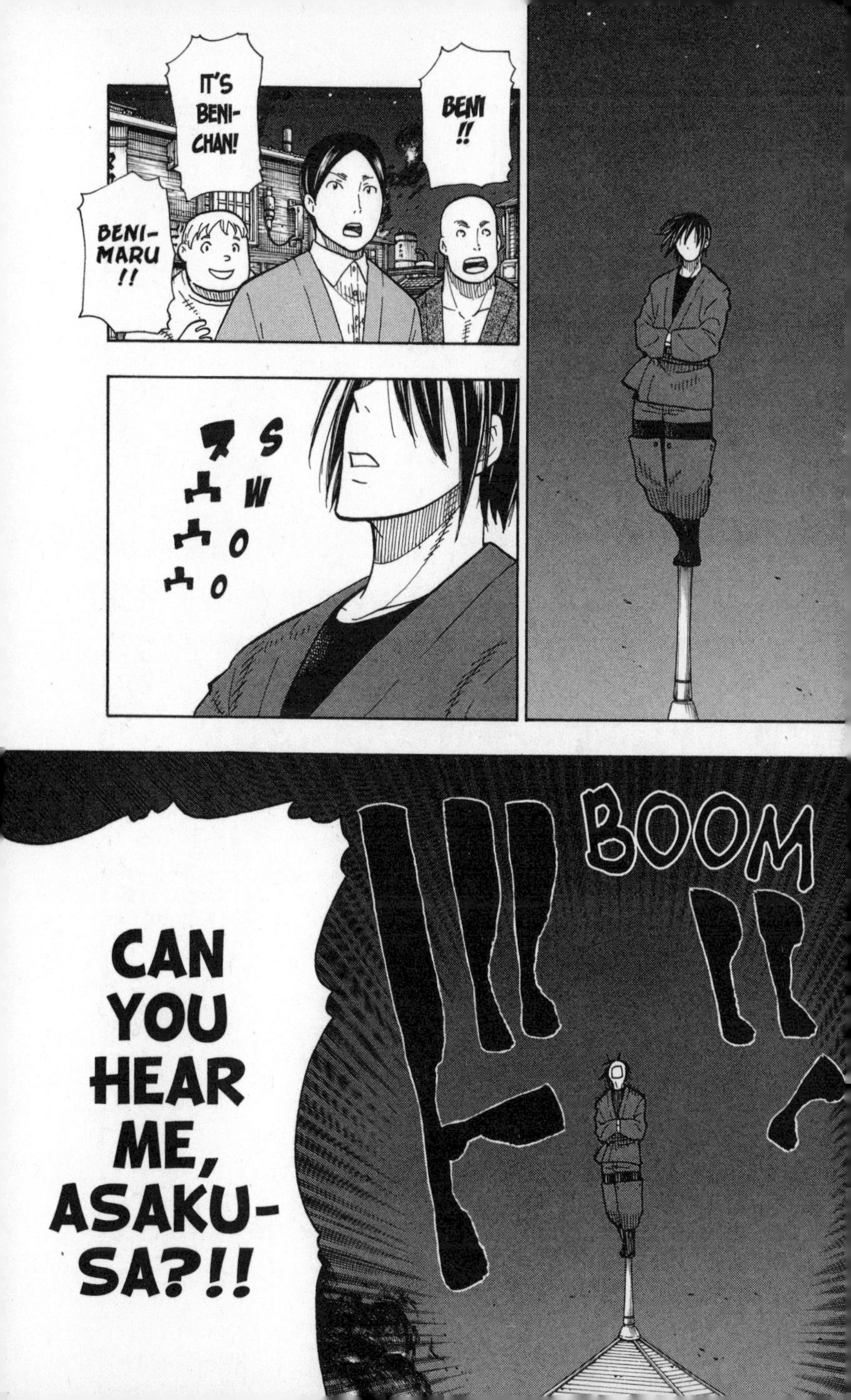
BENI!!
IT'S BENI-CHAN!
BENI-MARU!!
スーーー
SWOO
BOOM
CAN YOU HEAR ME, ASAKUSA?!!

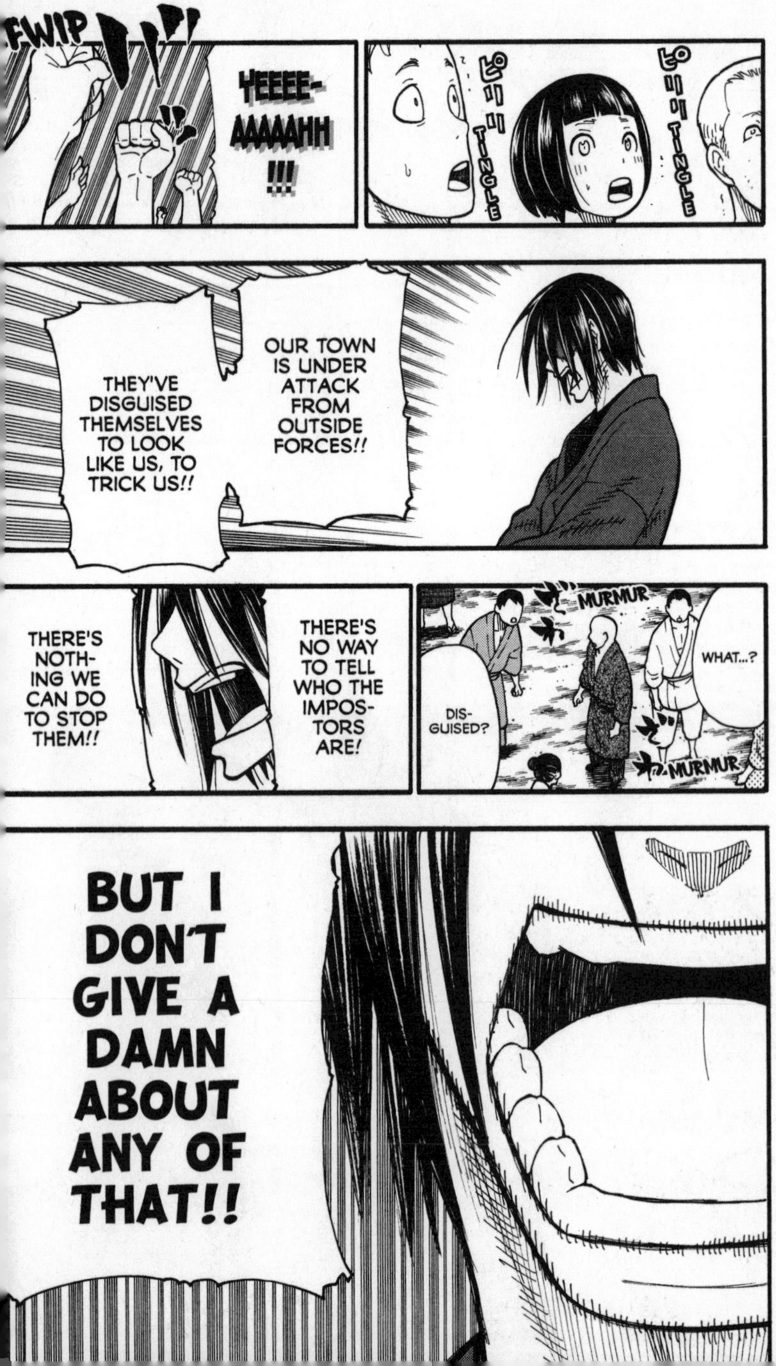
ピリリ TINGLE
ピリリ TINGLE
YEEEE-AAAAAHH!!!
FWIP
OUR TOWN IS UNDER ATTACK FROM OUTSIDE FORCES!!
THEY'VE DISGUISED THEMSELVES TO LOOK LIKE US, TO TRICK US!!
WHAT...?
MURMUR
DIS-GUISED?
MURMUR
THERE'S NO WAY TO TELL WHO THE IMPOS-TORS ARE!
THERE'S NOTH-ING WE CAN DO TO STOP THEM!!
BUT I DON'T GIVE A DAMN ABOUT ANY OF THAT!!

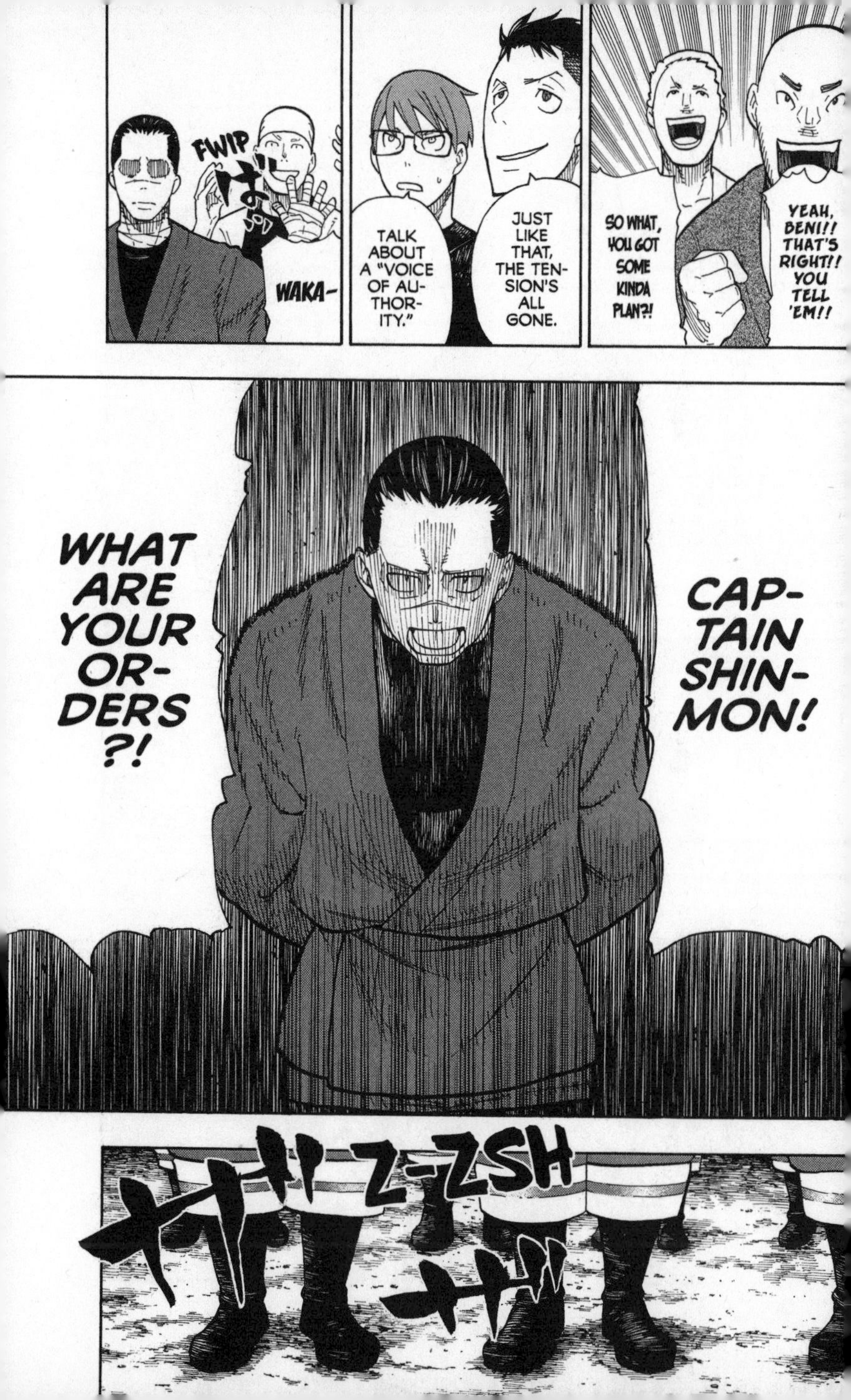
YEAH, BENI!! THAT'S RIGHT!! YOU TELL 'EM!!
SO WHAT, YOU GOT SOME KINDA PLAN?!
JUST LIKE THAT, THE TENSION'S ALL GONE.
TALK ABOUT A "VOICE OF AUTHORITY."
FWIP
WAKA-
CAPTAIN SHINMON!
WHAT ARE YOUR ORDERS?!
Z-ZSH

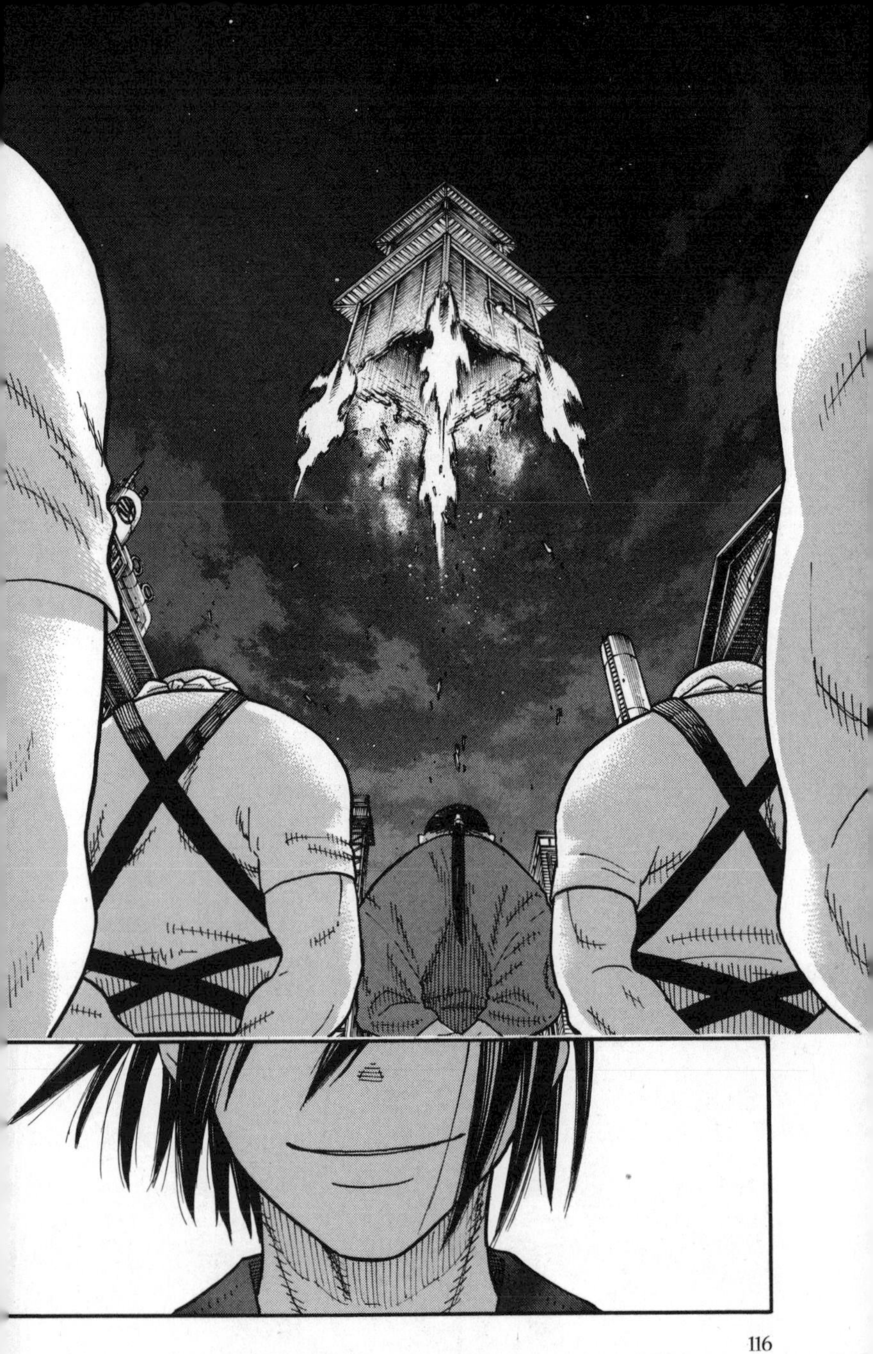

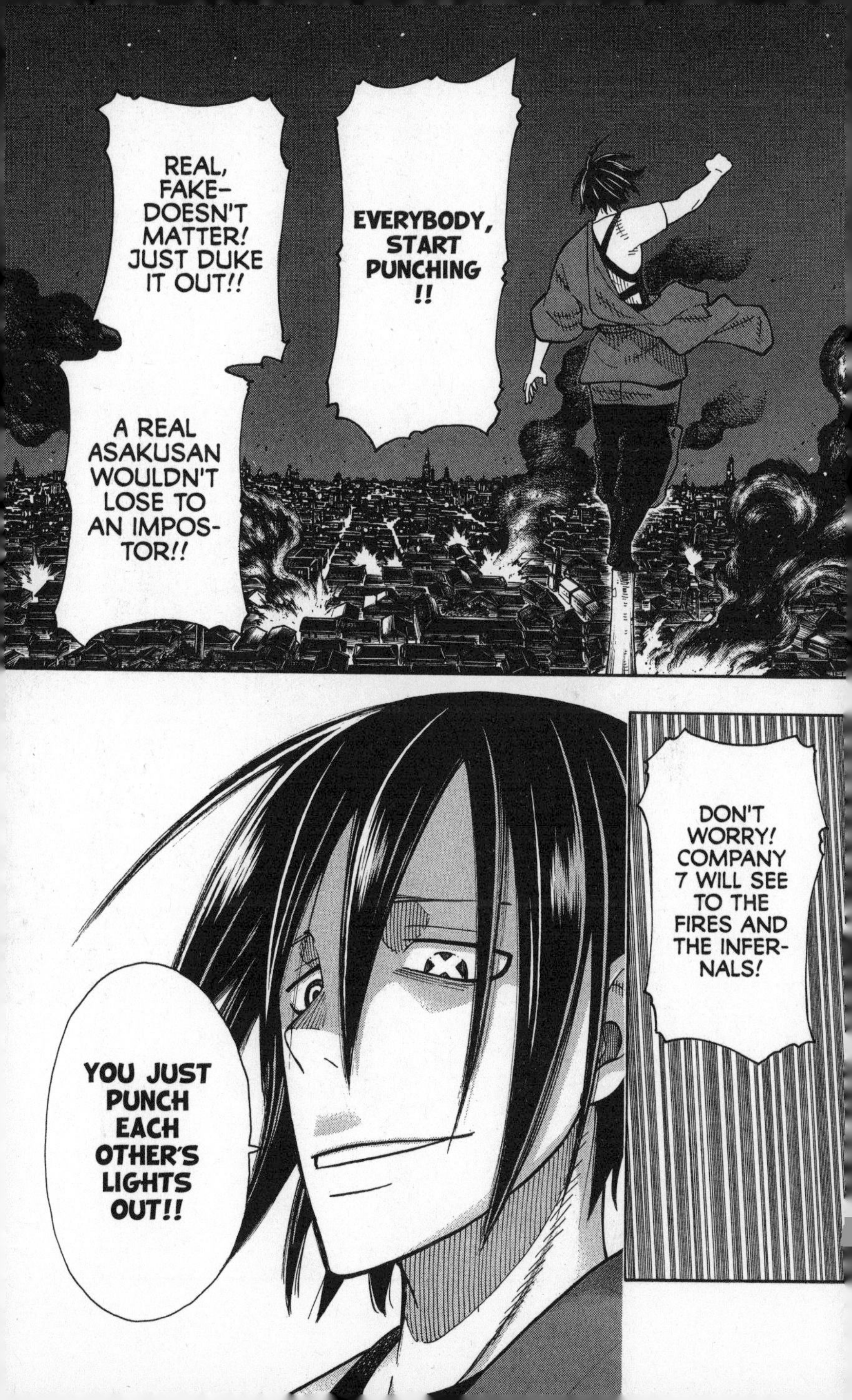
EVERYBODY, START PUNCHING!!
REAL, FAKE—DOESN'T MATTER! JUST DUKE IT OUT!!
A REAL ASAKUSAN WOULDN'T LOSE TO AN IMPOSTOR!!
DON'T WORRY! COMPANY 7 WILL SEE TO THE FIRES AND THE INFERNALS!
YOU JUST PUNCH EACH OTHER'S LIGHTS OUT!!

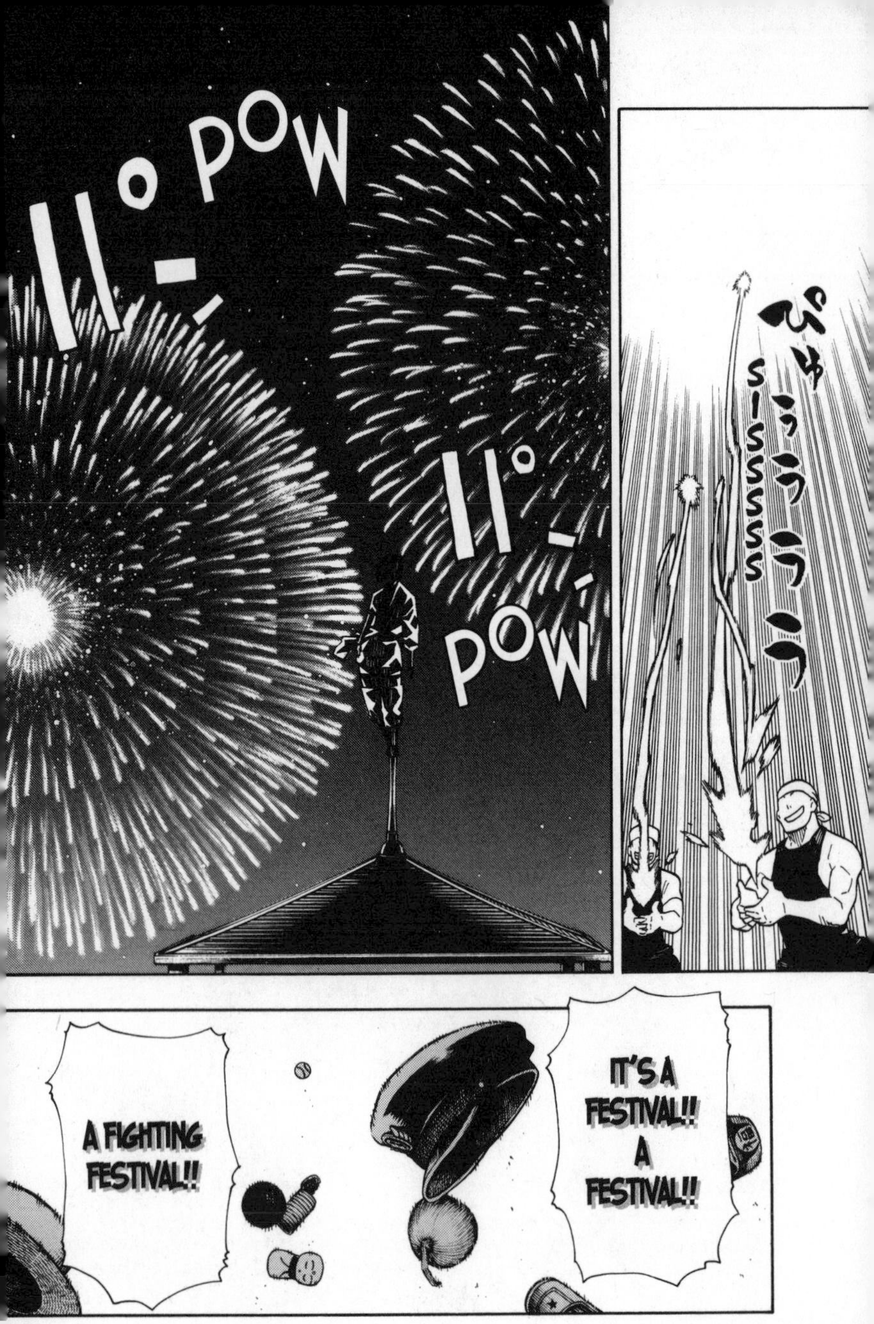
SISSSSSS
POW
POW
IT'S A FESTIVAL!! A FESTIVAL!!
A FIGHTING FESTIVAL!!

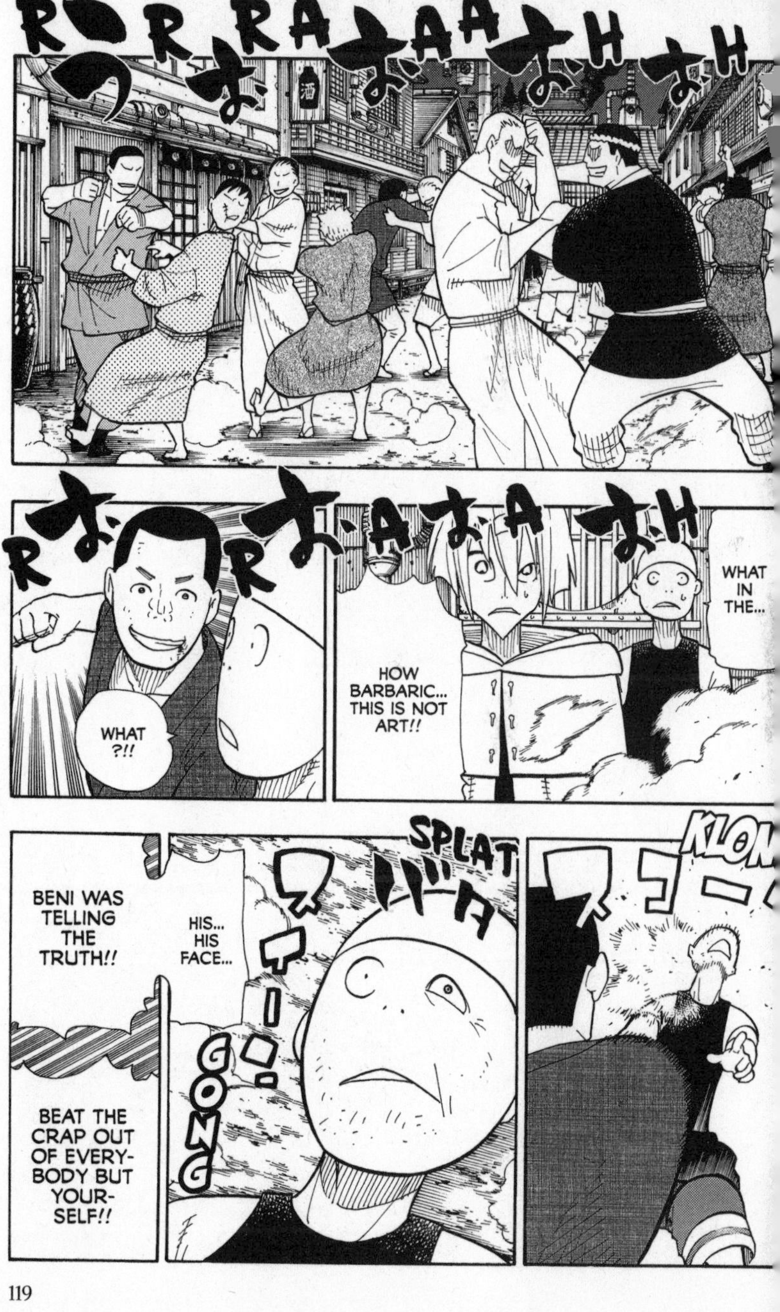
RRRAAAHH
RRAAH
WHAT IN THE...
HOW BARBARIC... THIS IS NOT ART!!
WHAT ?!!
KLON
SPLAT
HIS... HIS FACE...
GONG
BENI WAS TELLING THE TRUTH!!
BEAT THE CRAP OUT OF EVERY-BODY BUT YOUR-SELF!!

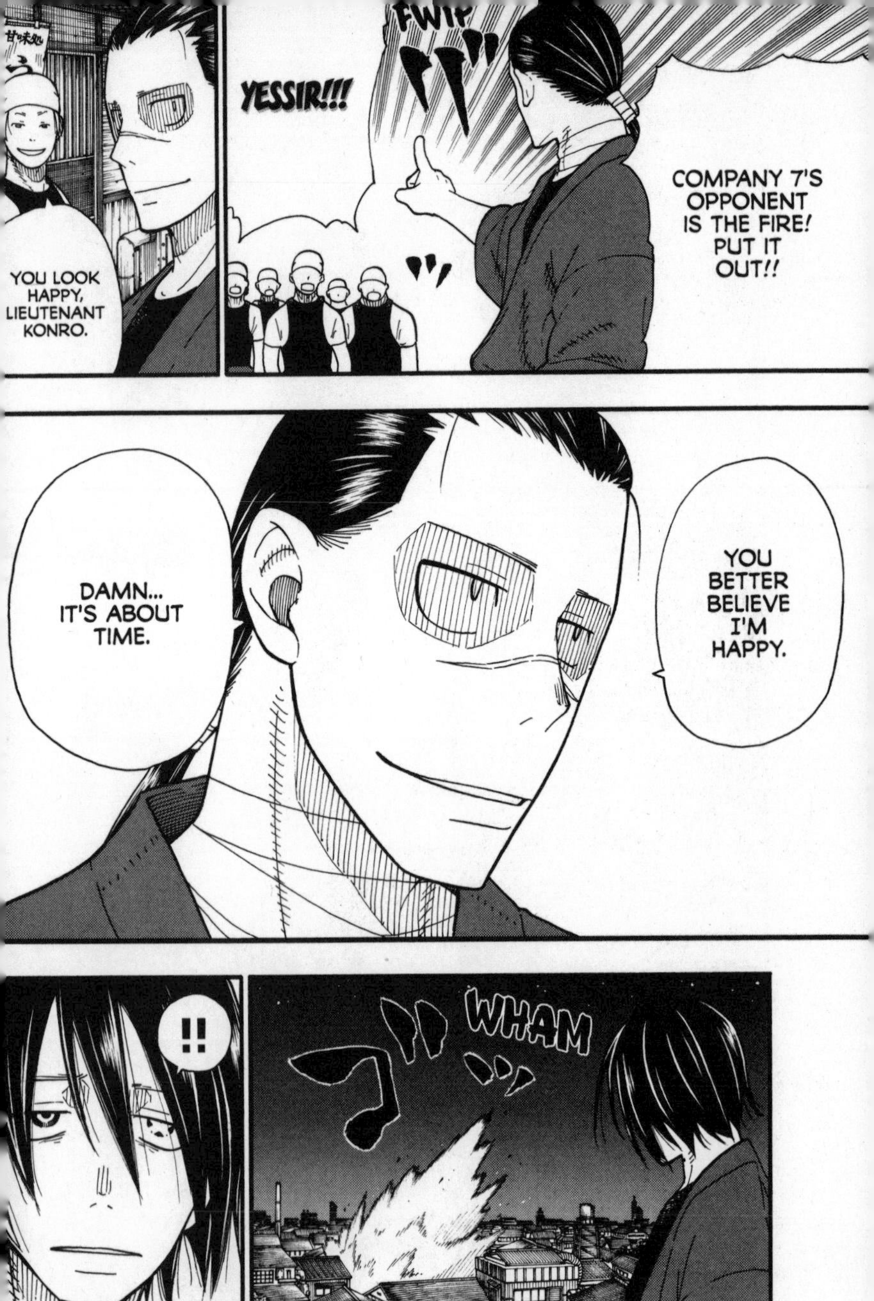
FWIP
COMPANY 7'S OPPONENT IS THE FIRE! PUT IT OUT!!
YESSIR!!!
YOU LOOK HAPPY, LIEUTENANT KONRO.
YOU BETTER BELIEVE I'M HAPPY.
DAMN... IT'S ABOUT TIME.
WHAM
!!

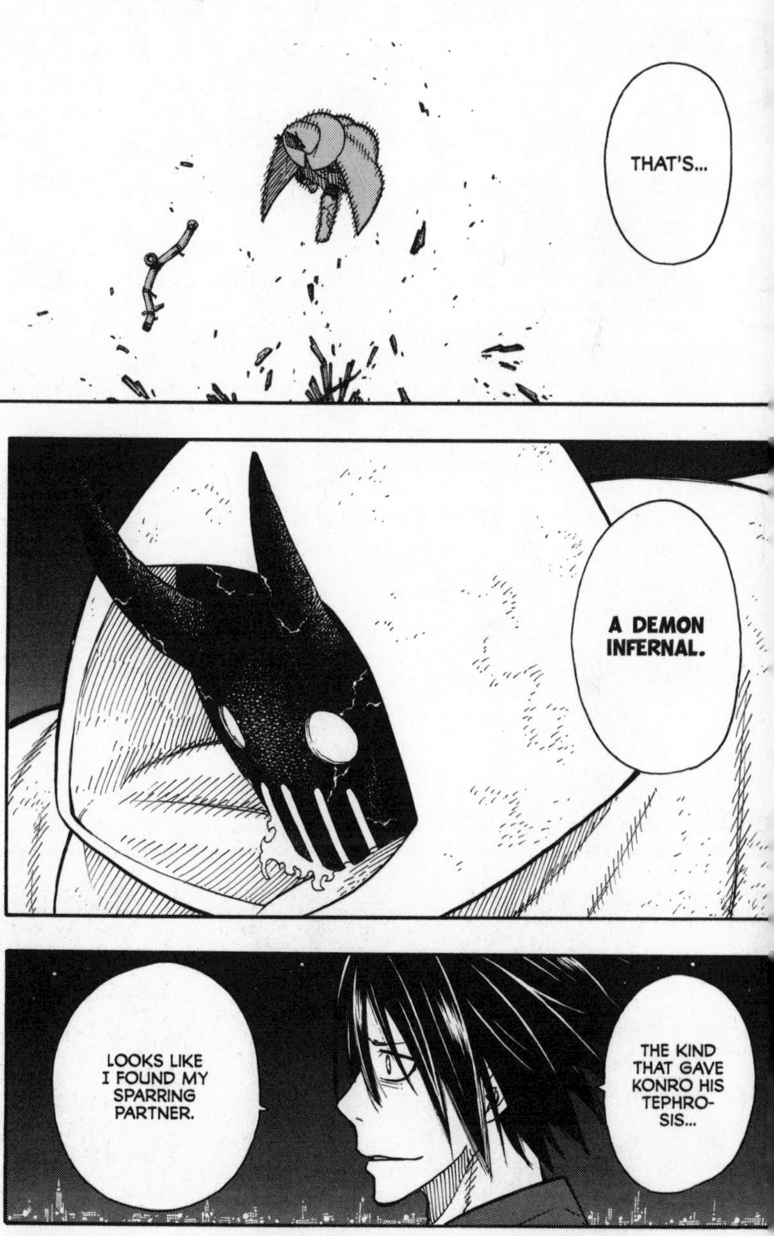
THAT'S...
A DEMON INFERNAL.
THE KIND THAT GAVE KONRO HIS TEPHROSIS...
LOOKS LIKE I FOUND MY SPARRING PARTNER.

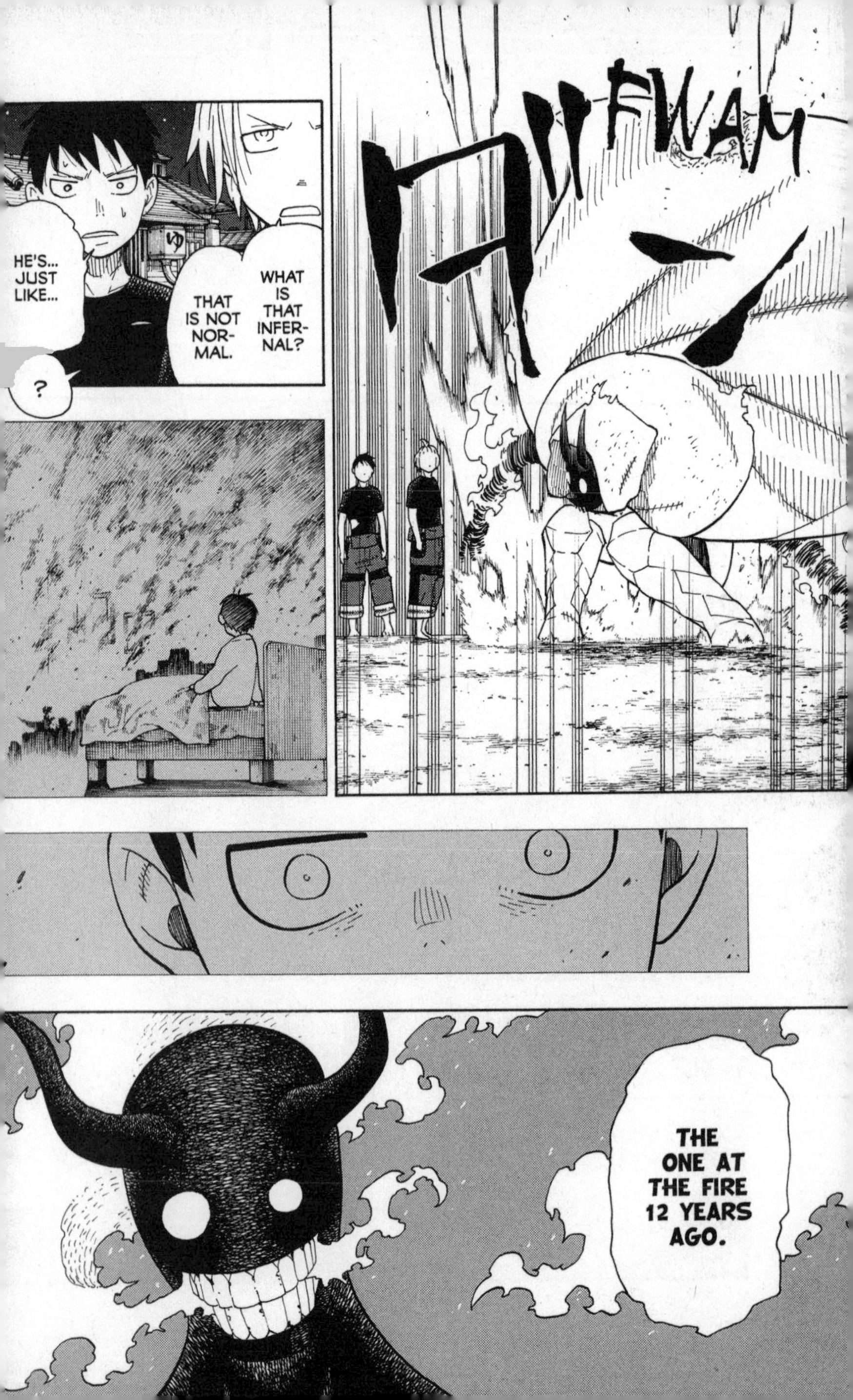
FWAM
WHAT IS THAT INFERNAL?
THAT IS NOT NORMAL.
HE'S... JUST LIKE...
?
THE ONE AT THE FIRE 12 YEARS AGO.

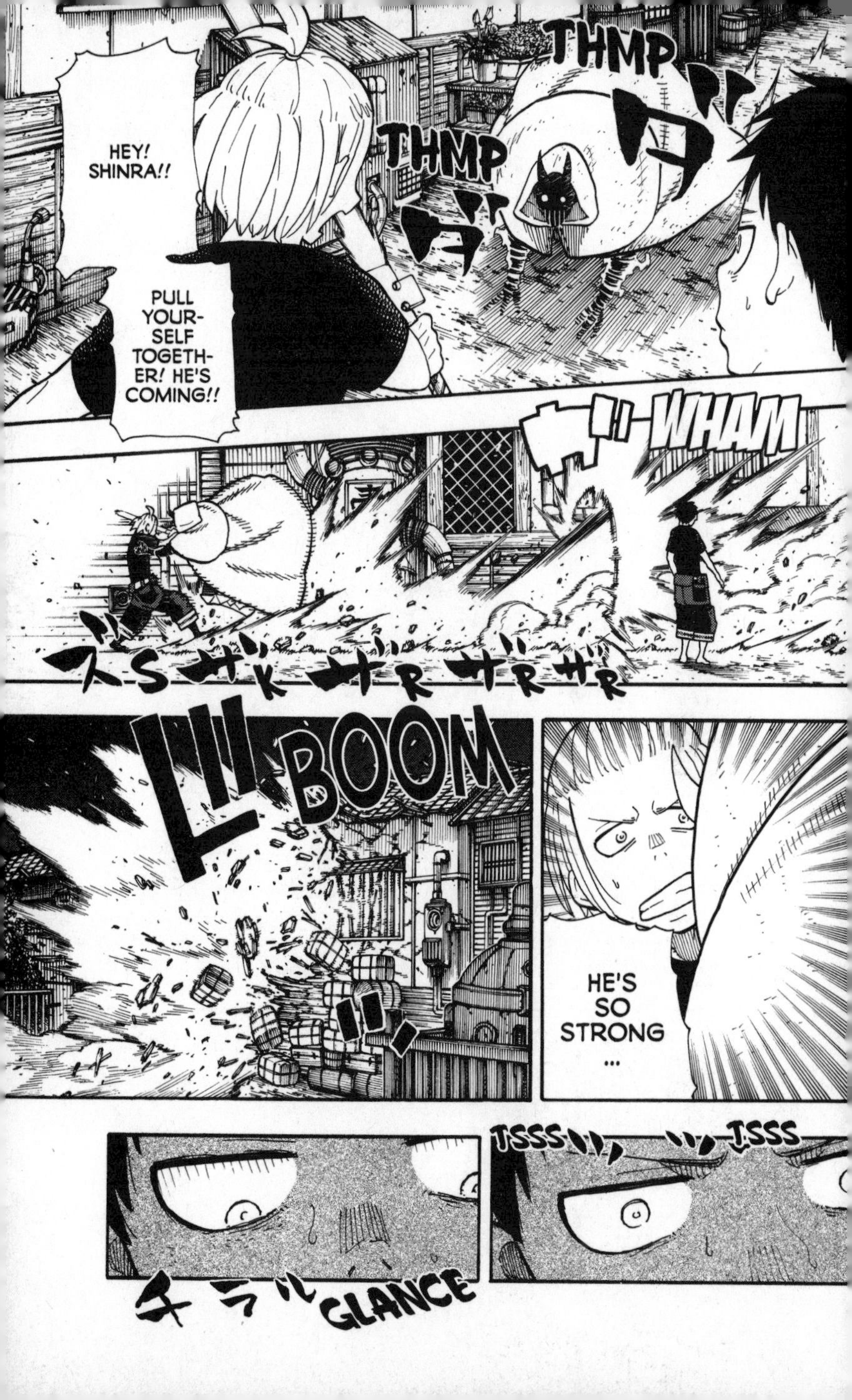
THMP
THMP
HEY! SHINRA!!
PULL YOUR-SELF TOGETH-ER! HE'S COMING!!
WHAM
SKRRR
HE'S SO STRONG ...
BOOM
TSSS
TSSS
GLANCE

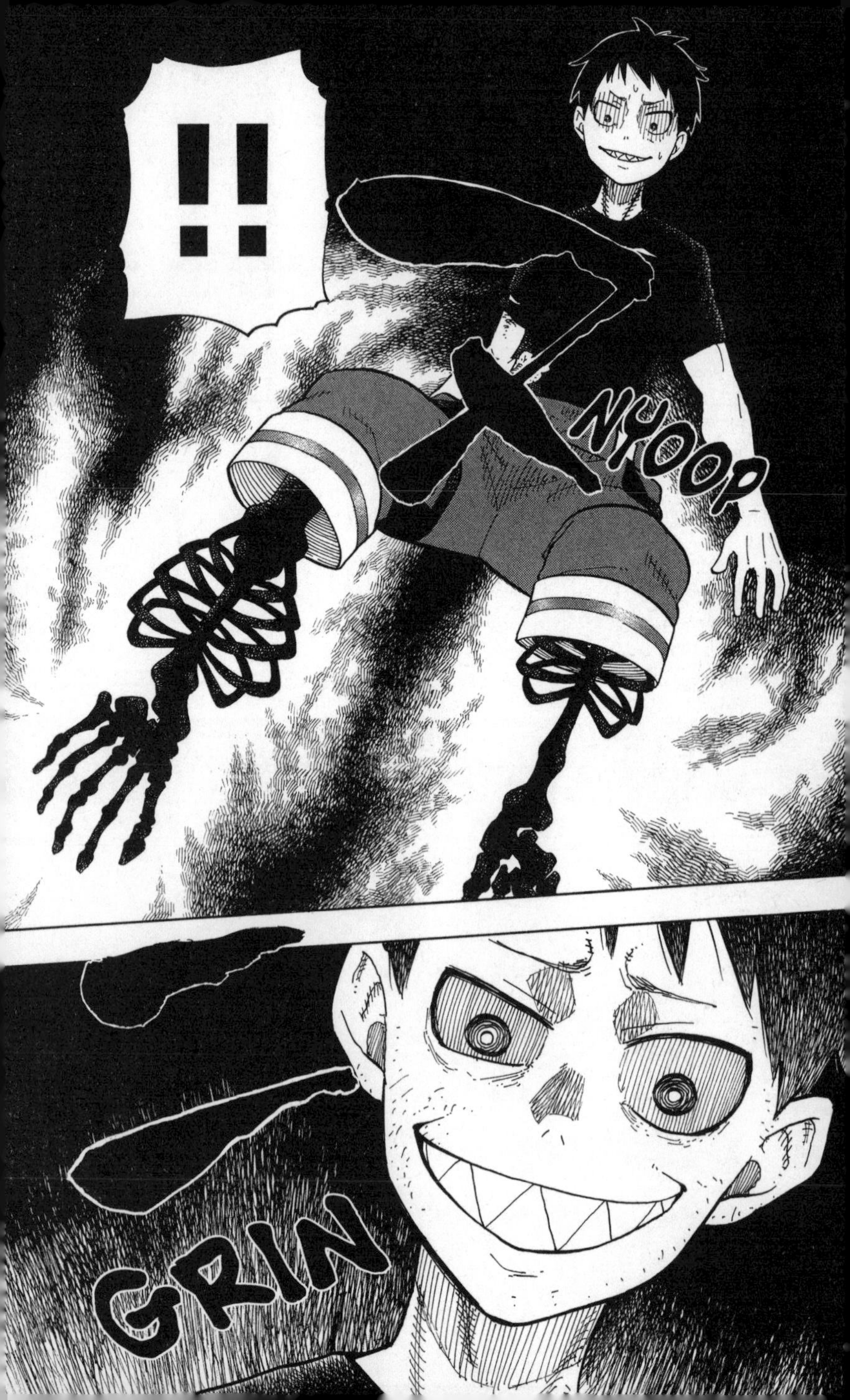
!!
NYOOP
GRIN

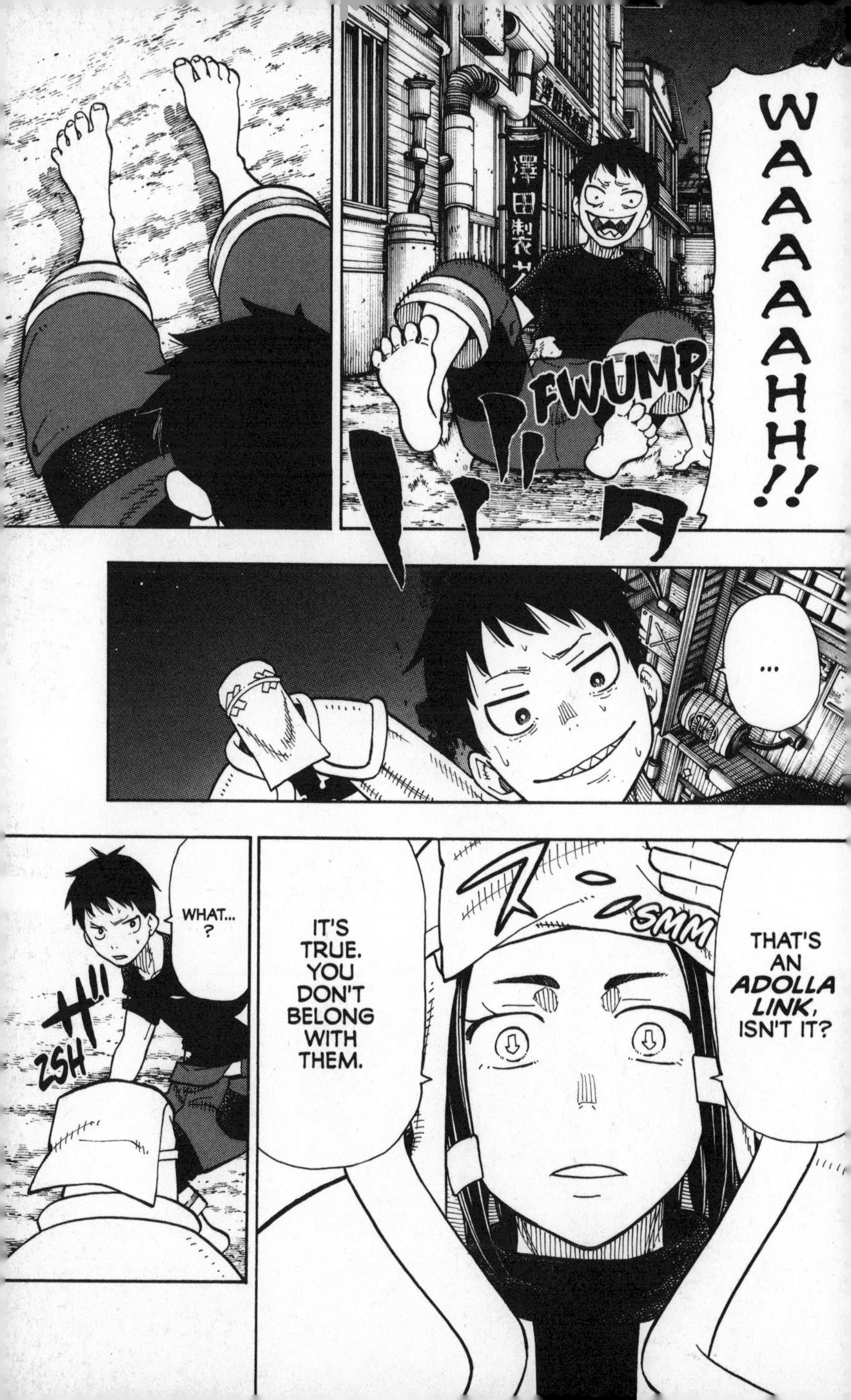
WAAAAAAHH!!
FWUMP
...
THAT'S AN *ADOLLA LINK*, ISN'T IT?
SMM
IT'S TRUE. YOU DON'T BELONG WITH THEM.
WHAT... ?
H!!
ZSH

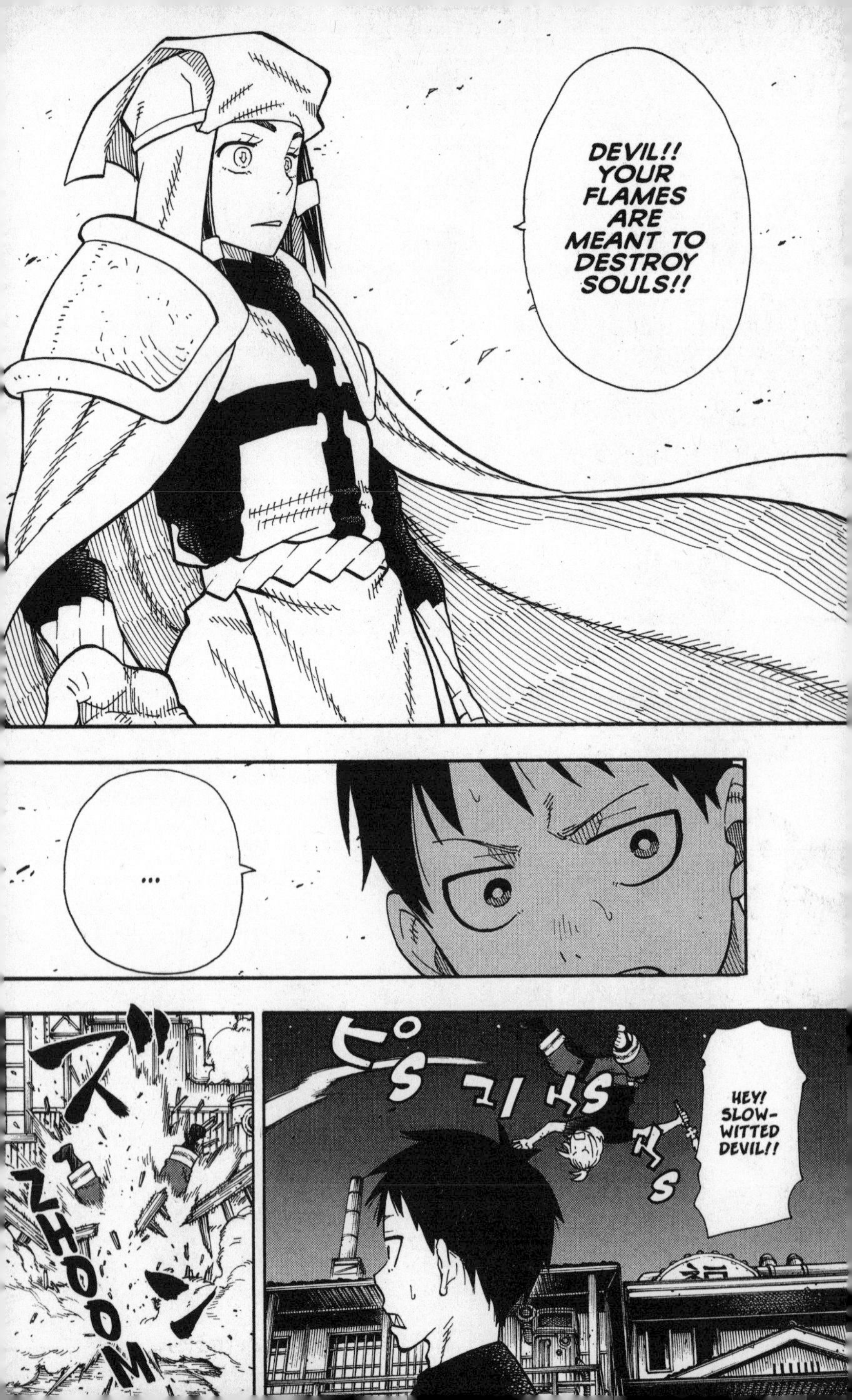
DEVIL!! YOUR FLAMES ARE MEANT TO DESTROY SOULS!!
...
HEY! SLOW-WITTED DEVIL!!
ZHOOM

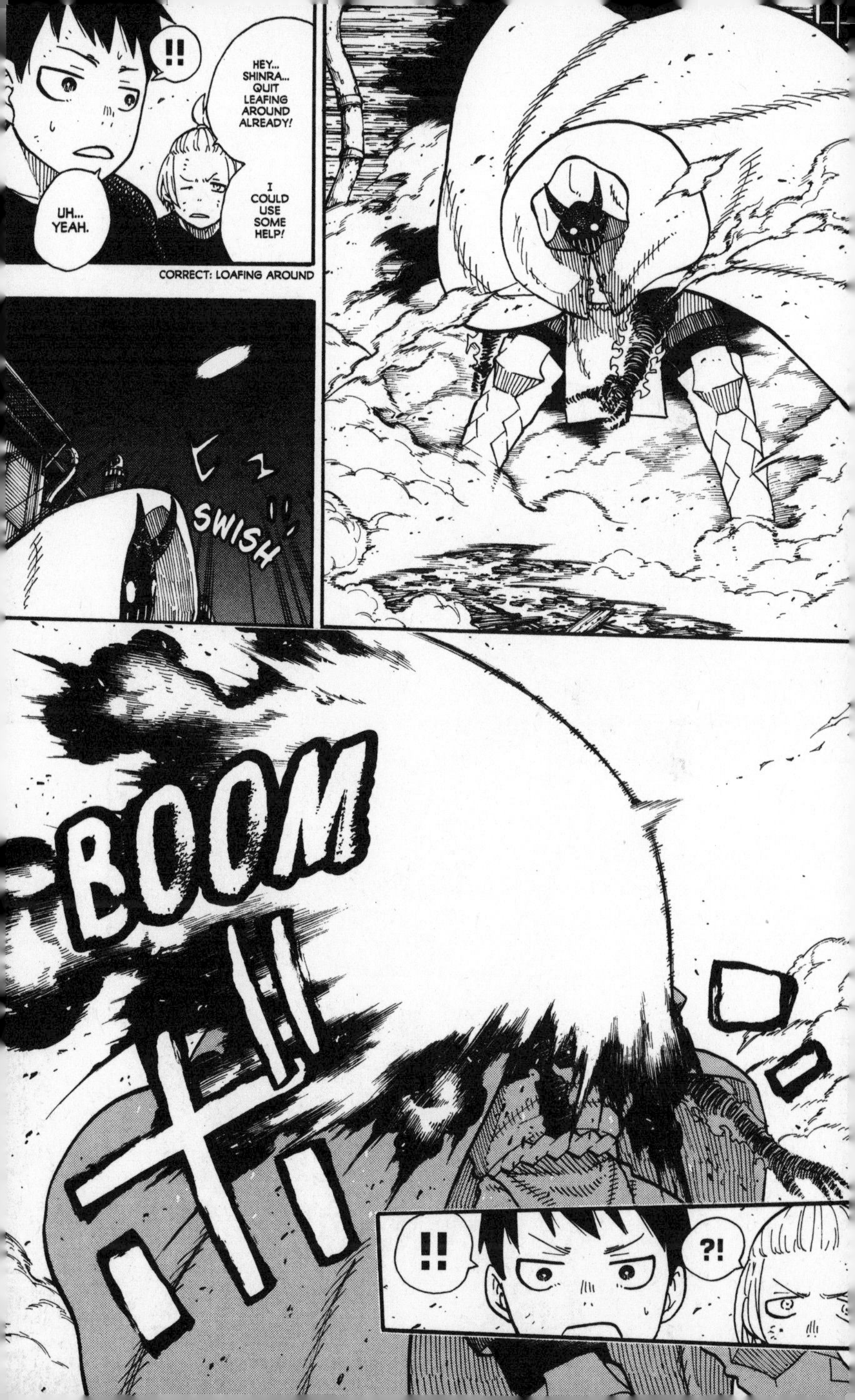
HEY... SHINRA... QUIT LEAFING AROUND ALREADY!
!!
I COULD USE SOME HELP!
UH... YEAH.
CORRECT: LOAFING AROUND
SWISH
BOOM
?!
!!

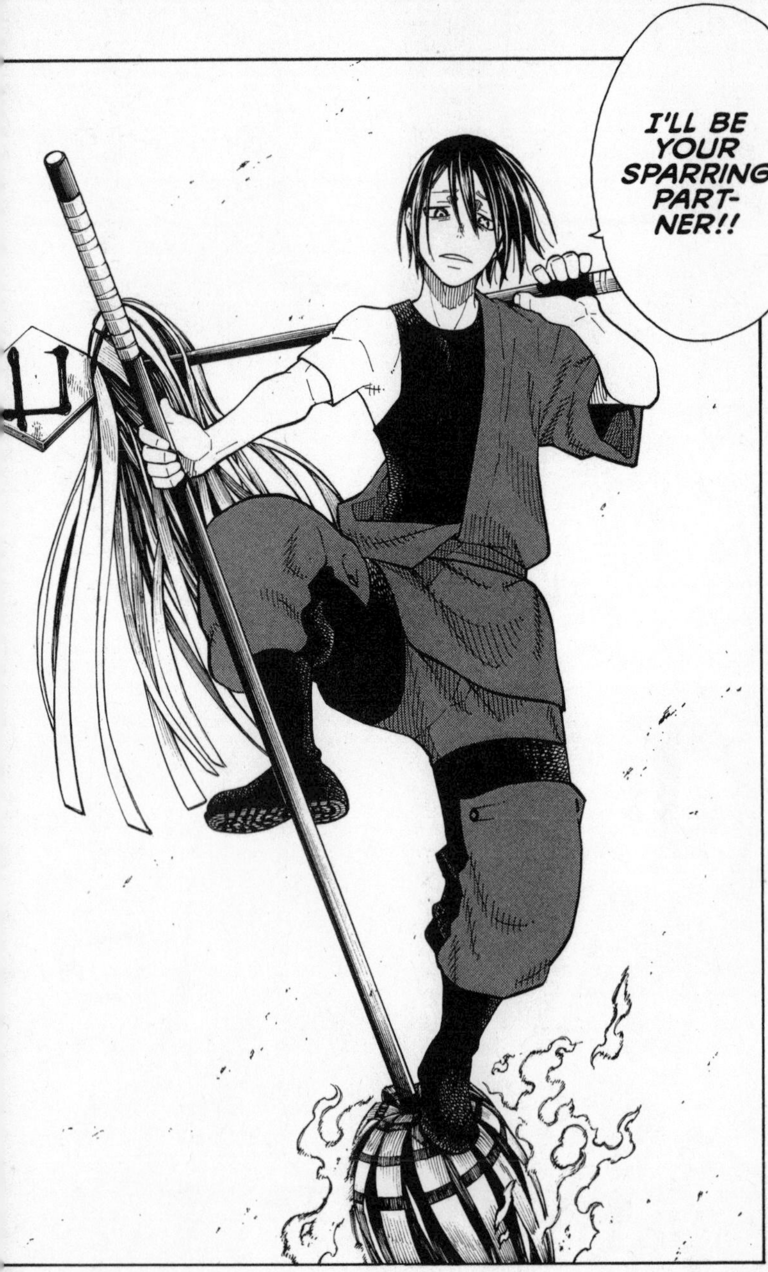
I'LL BE YOUR SPARRING PART- NER!!

FIRE FORCE

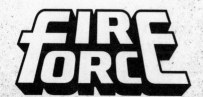

FIRE FORCE

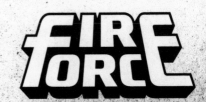

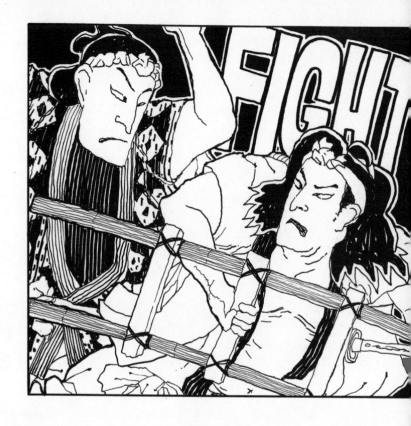

CHAPTER XLIX: FIGHTING FESTIVAL

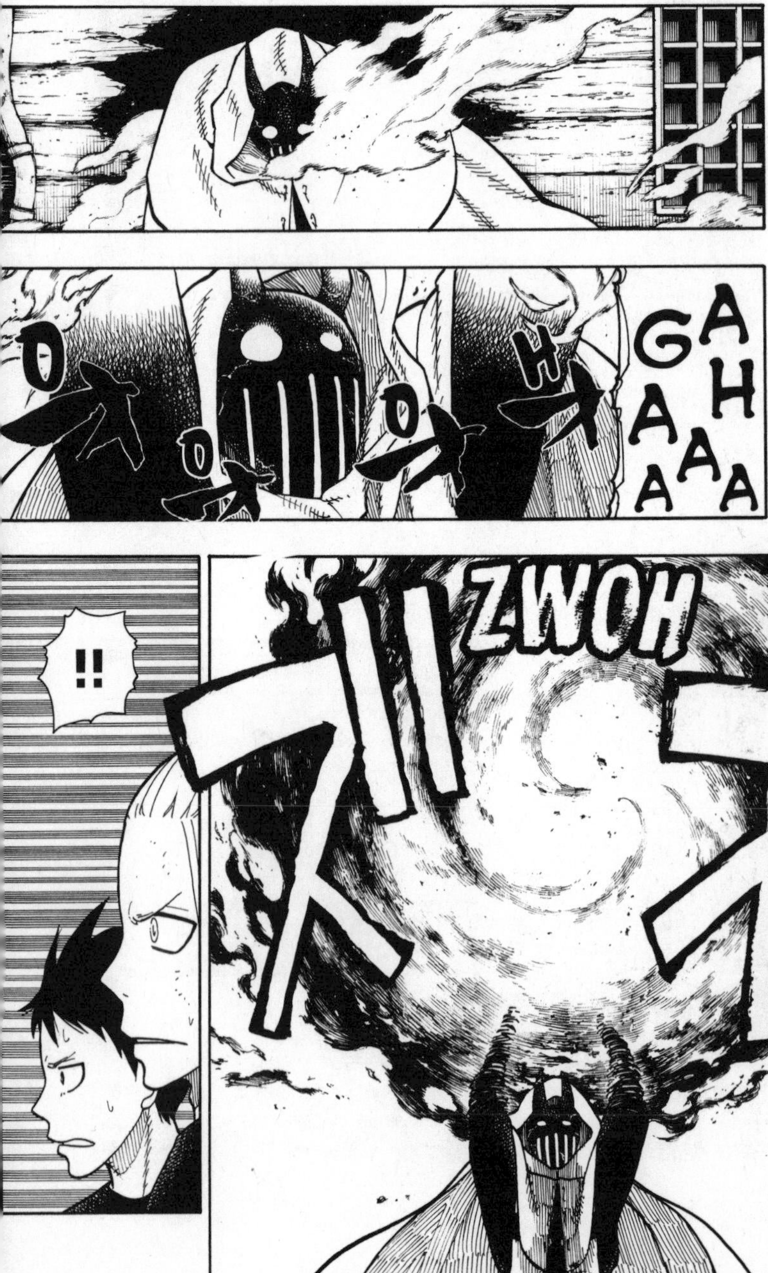
GAHAAAAA
OOOH
ZWOH
!!

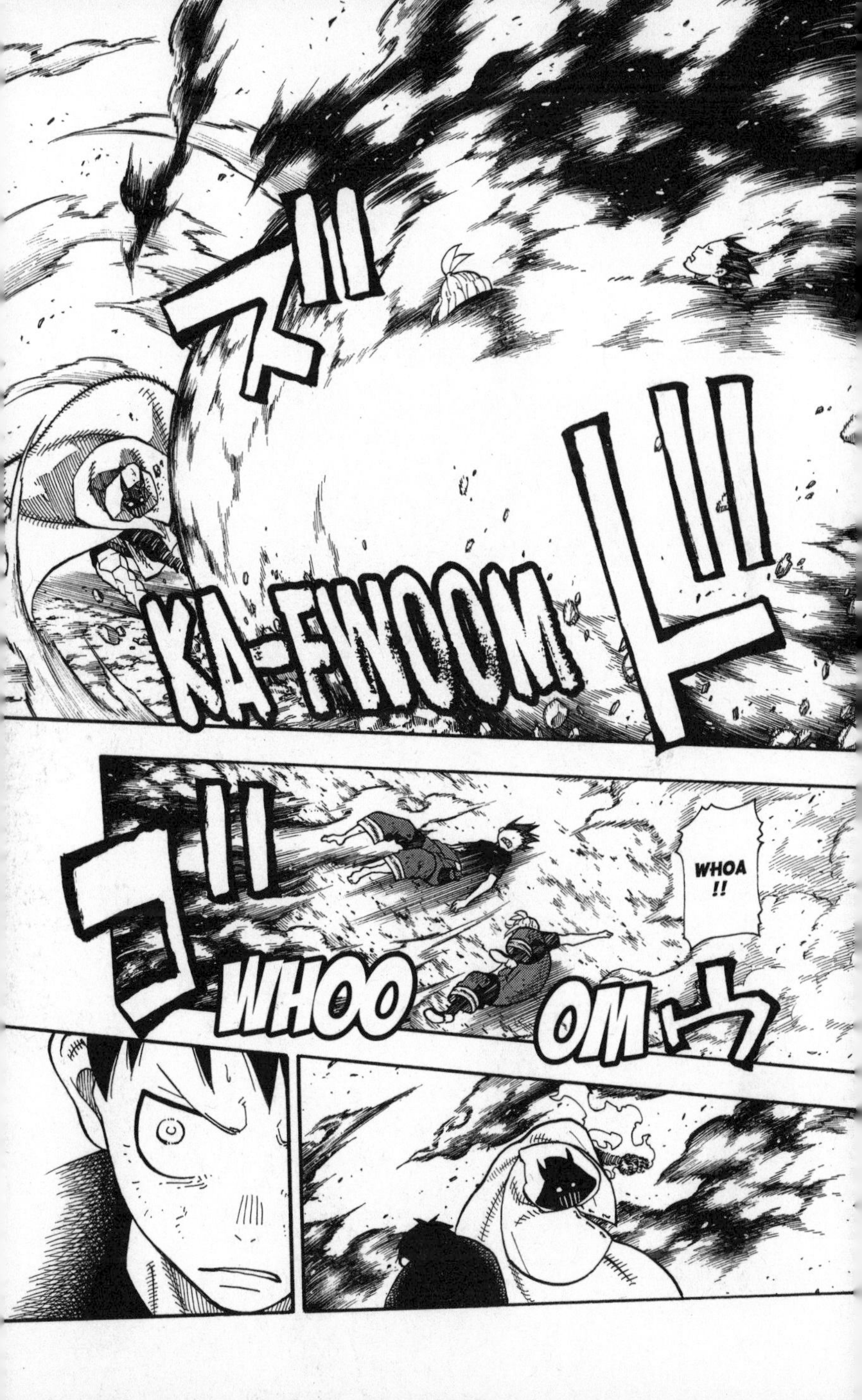
KA-FWOOM
WHOA !!
WHOO OM

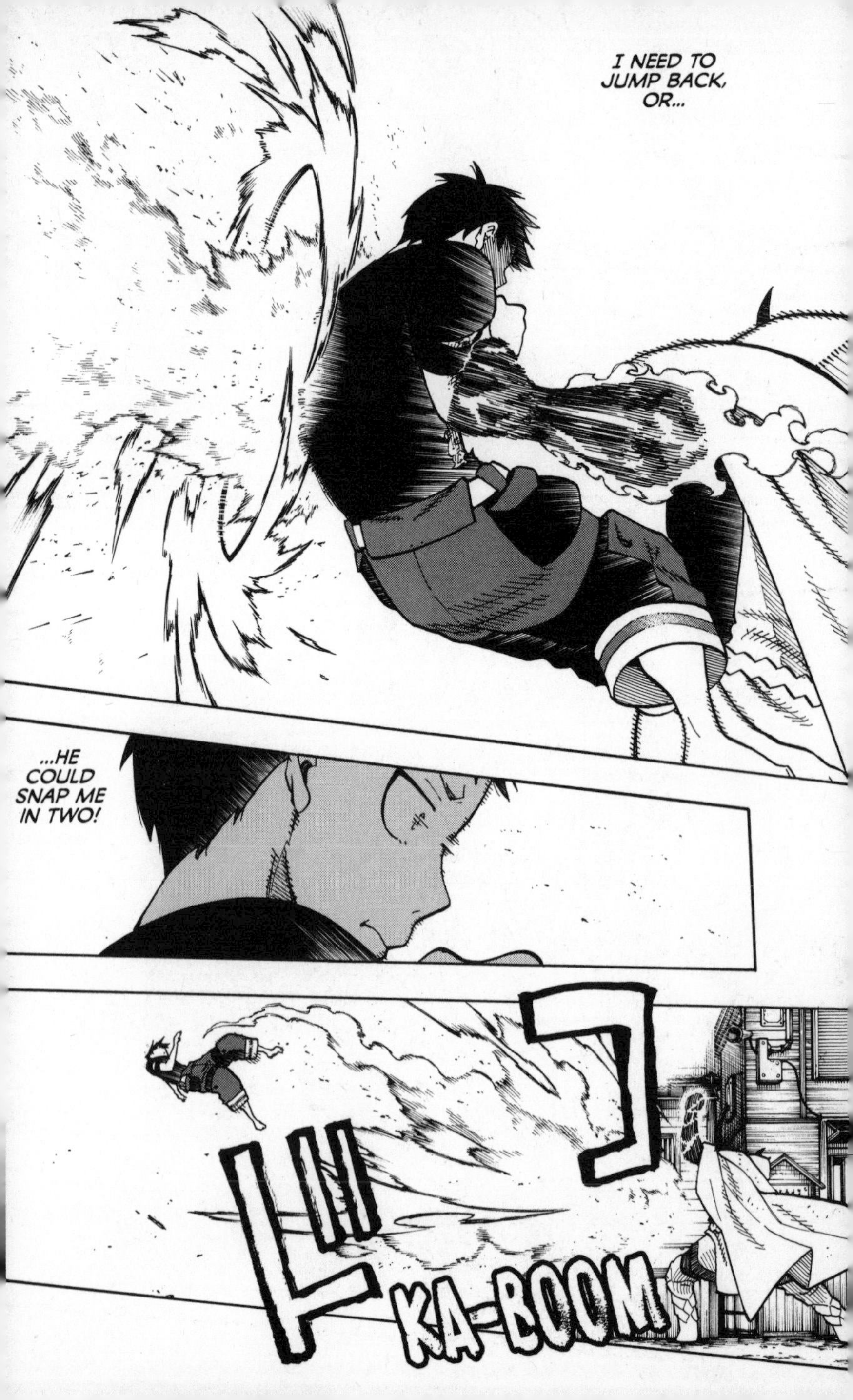
I NEED TO JUMP BACK, OR...
...HE COULD SNAP ME IN TWO!
KA-BOOM

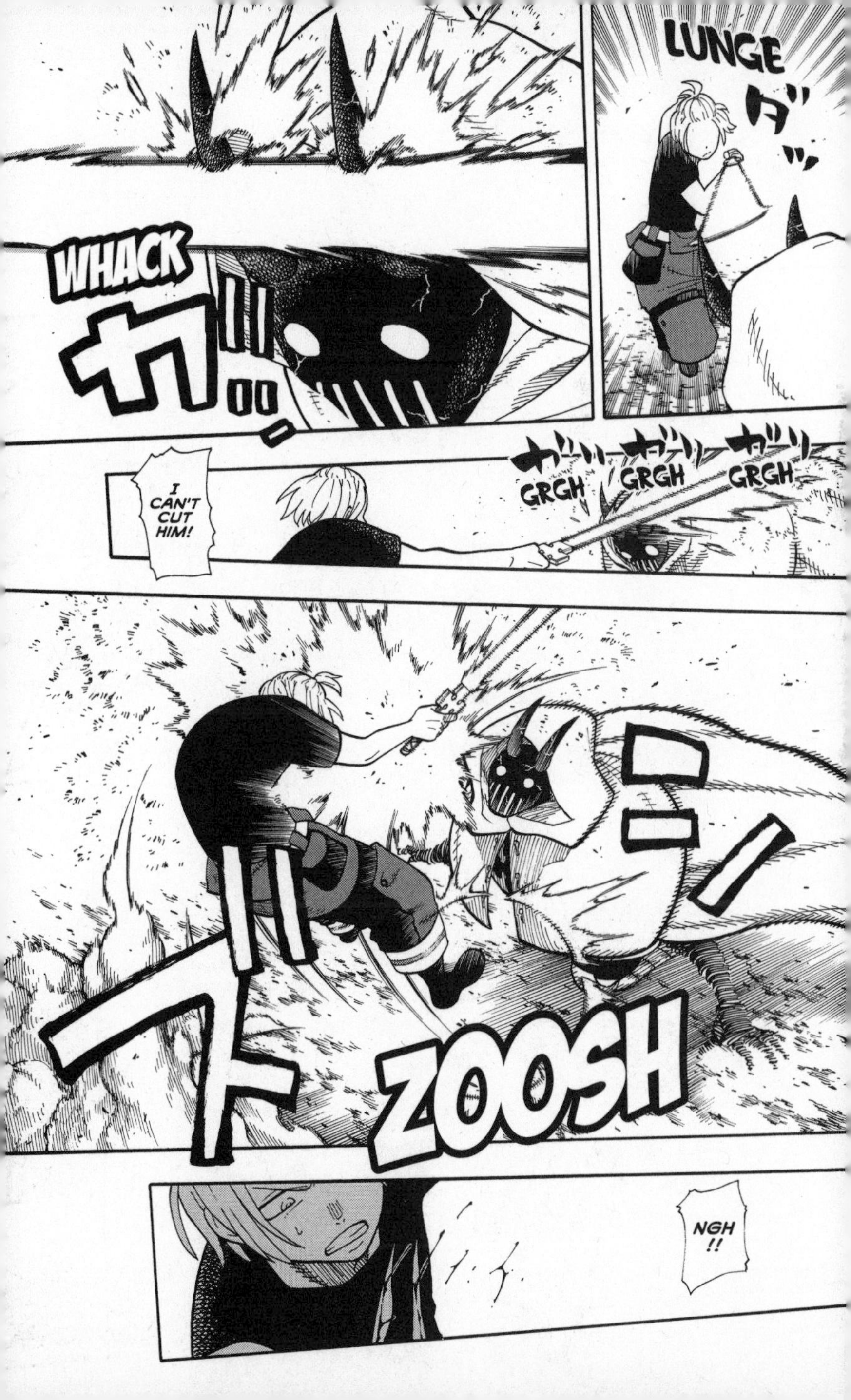
LUNGE
ダッ
WHACK
ガッ
GRGH
GRGH
GRGH
I CAN'T CUT HIM!
ZOOSH
NGH!!

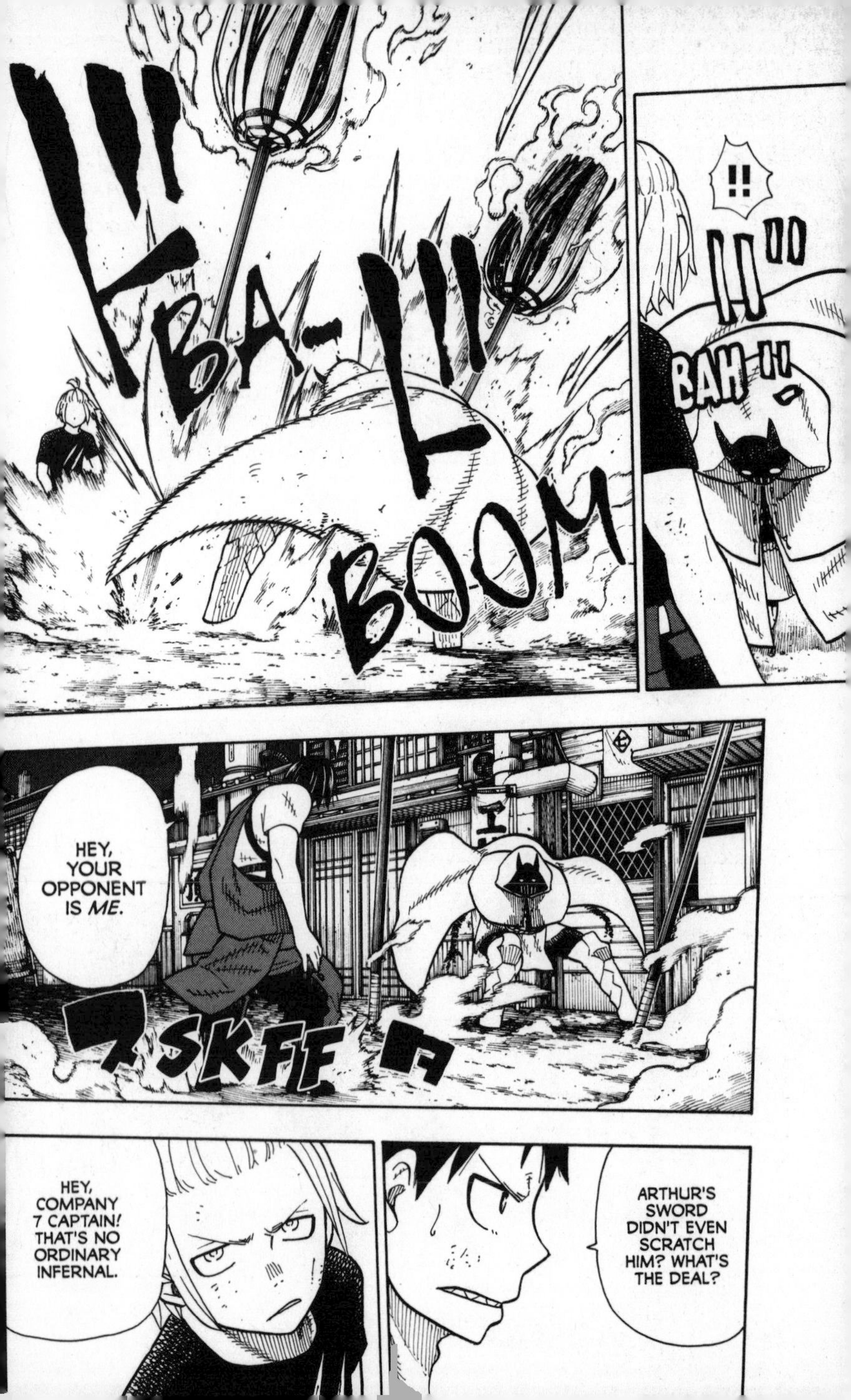
!!
BAH!!
!!
BA-
BOOM
HEY, YOUR OPPONENT IS *ME*.
SKFF
ARTHUR'S SWORD DIDN'T EVEN SCRATCH HIM? WHAT'S THE DEAL?
HEY, COMPANY 7 CAPTAIN! THAT'S NO ORDINARY INFERNAL.

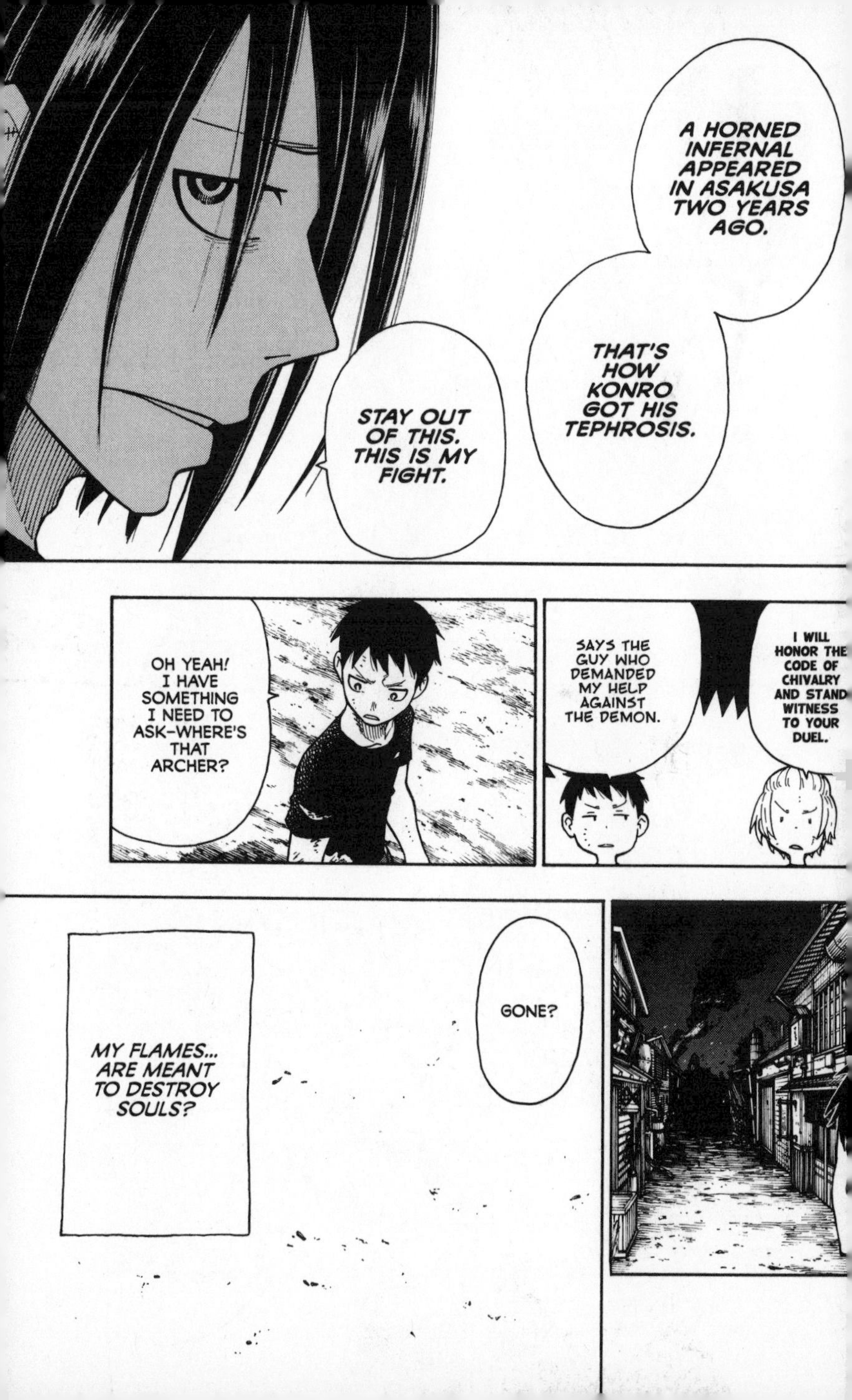
A HORNED INFERNAL APPEARED IN ASAKUSA TWO YEARS AGO.
THAT'S HOW KONRO GOT HIS TEPHROSIS.
STAY OUT OF THIS. THIS IS MY FIGHT.
I WILL HONOR THE CODE OF CHIVALRY AND STAND WITNESS TO YOUR DUEL.
SAYS THE GUY WHO DEMANDED MY HELP AGAINST THE DEMON.
OH YEAH! I HAVE SOMETHING I NEED TO ASK–WHERE'S THAT ARCHER?
GONE?
MY FLAMES... ARE MEANT TO DESTROY SOULS?

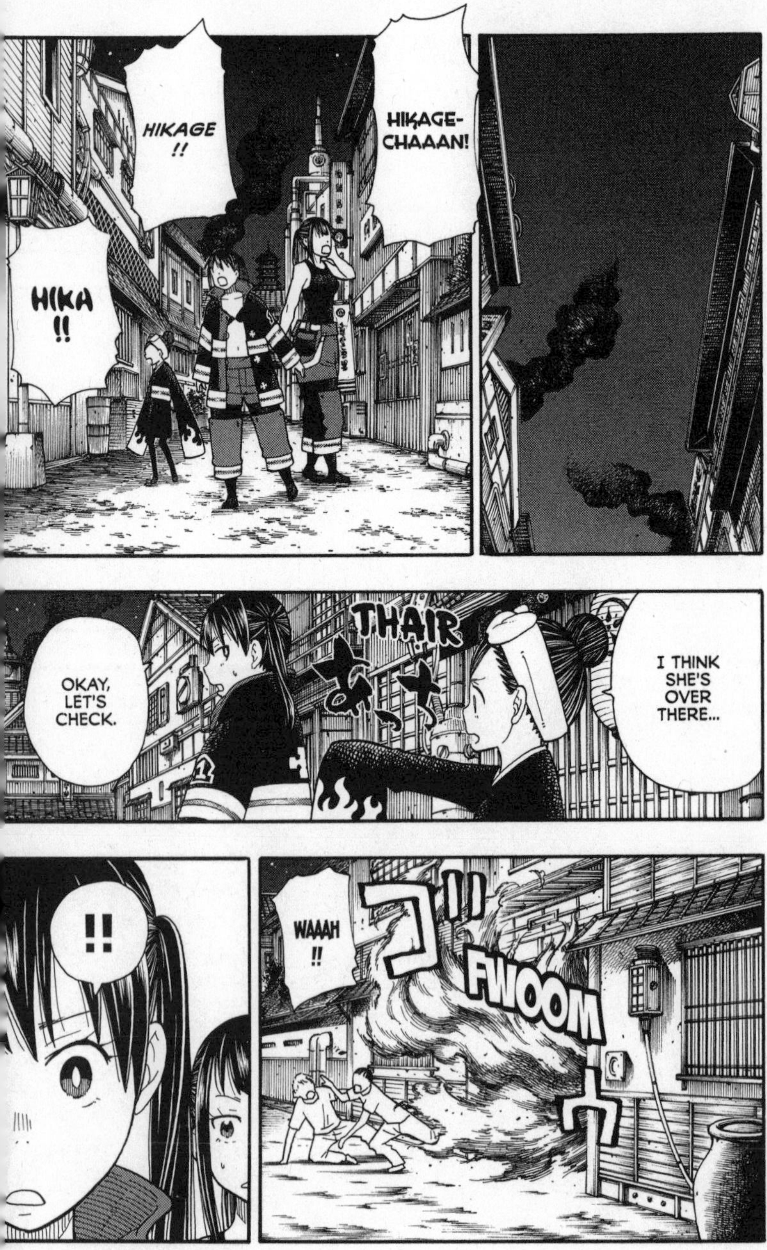
HIKAGE-CHAAAN!
HIKAGE !!
HIKA !!
I THINK SHE'S OVER THERE...
THAIR
OKAY, LET'S CHECK.
FWOOM
WAAAH !!
!!

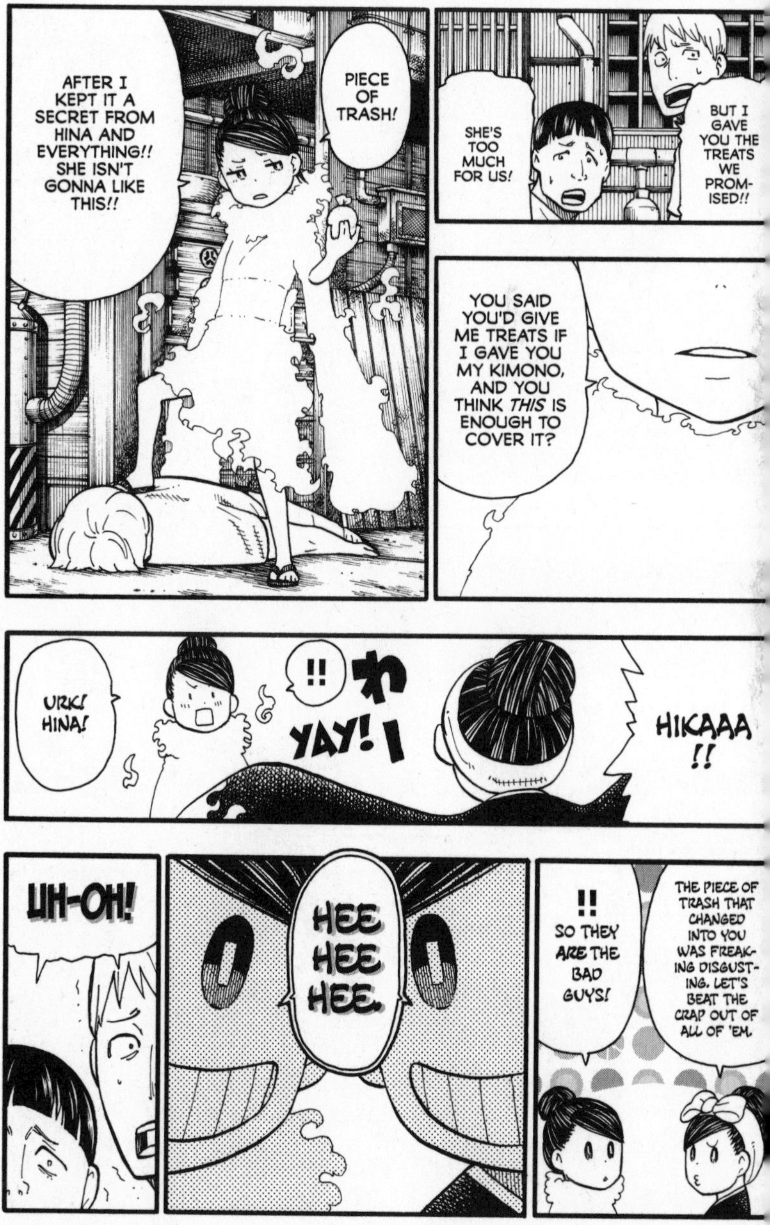
BUT I GAVE YOU THE TREATS WE PROMISED!!
SHE'S TOO MUCH FOR US!
YOU SAID YOU'D GIVE ME TREATS IF I GAVE YOU MY KIMONO, AND YOU THINK *THIS* IS ENOUGH TO COVER IT?
PIECE OF TRASH!
AFTER I KEPT IT A SECRET FROM HINA AND EVERYTHING!! SHE ISN'T GONNA LIKE THIS!!
HIKAAA !!
わ
YAY!
!!
URK! HINA!
THE PIECE OF TRASH THAT CHANGED INTO YOU WAS FREAKING DISGUSTING. LET'S BEAT THE CRAP OUT OF ALL OF 'EM.
!! SO THEY *ARE* THE BAD GUYS!
HEE HEE HEE.
UH-OH!

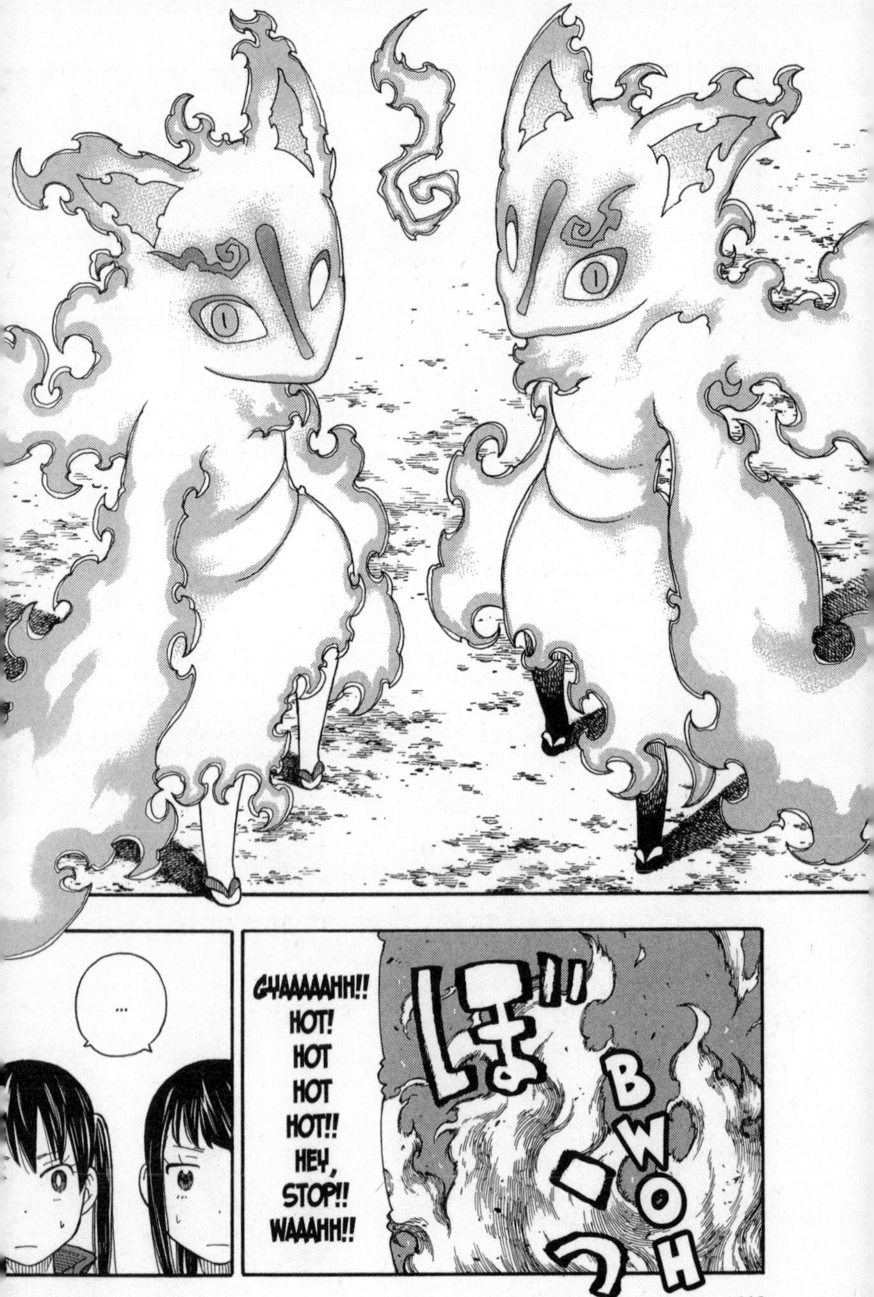
ぼっ
BWOH
GYAAAAAHH!! HOT! HOT HOT HOT!! HEY, STOP!! WAAAHH!!
...

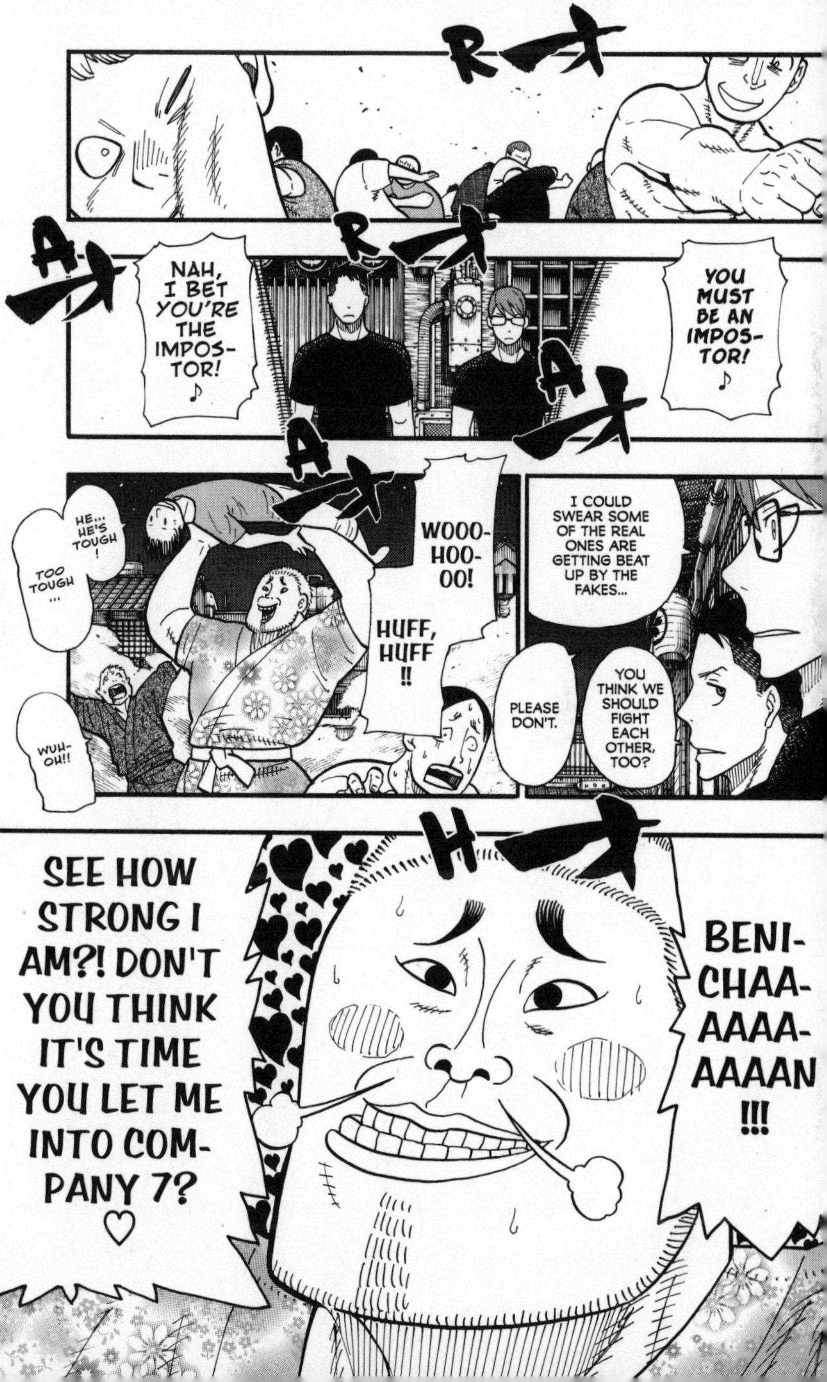
YOU MUST BE AN IMPOSTOR! ♪
NAH, I BET YOU'RE THE IMPOSTOR! ♪
I COULD SWEAR SOME OF THE REAL ONES ARE GETTING BEAT UP BY THE FAKES...
YOU THINK WE SHOULD FIGHT EACH OTHER, TOO?
PLEASE DON'T.
WOOO-HOO-OO!
HUFF, HUFF!!
HE... HE'S TOUGH!
TOO TOUGH...
WUH-OH!!
BENI-CHAAAAAAAAAAN!!!
SEE HOW STRONG I AM?! DON'T YOU THINK IT'S TIME YOU LET ME INTO COMPANY 7? ♡

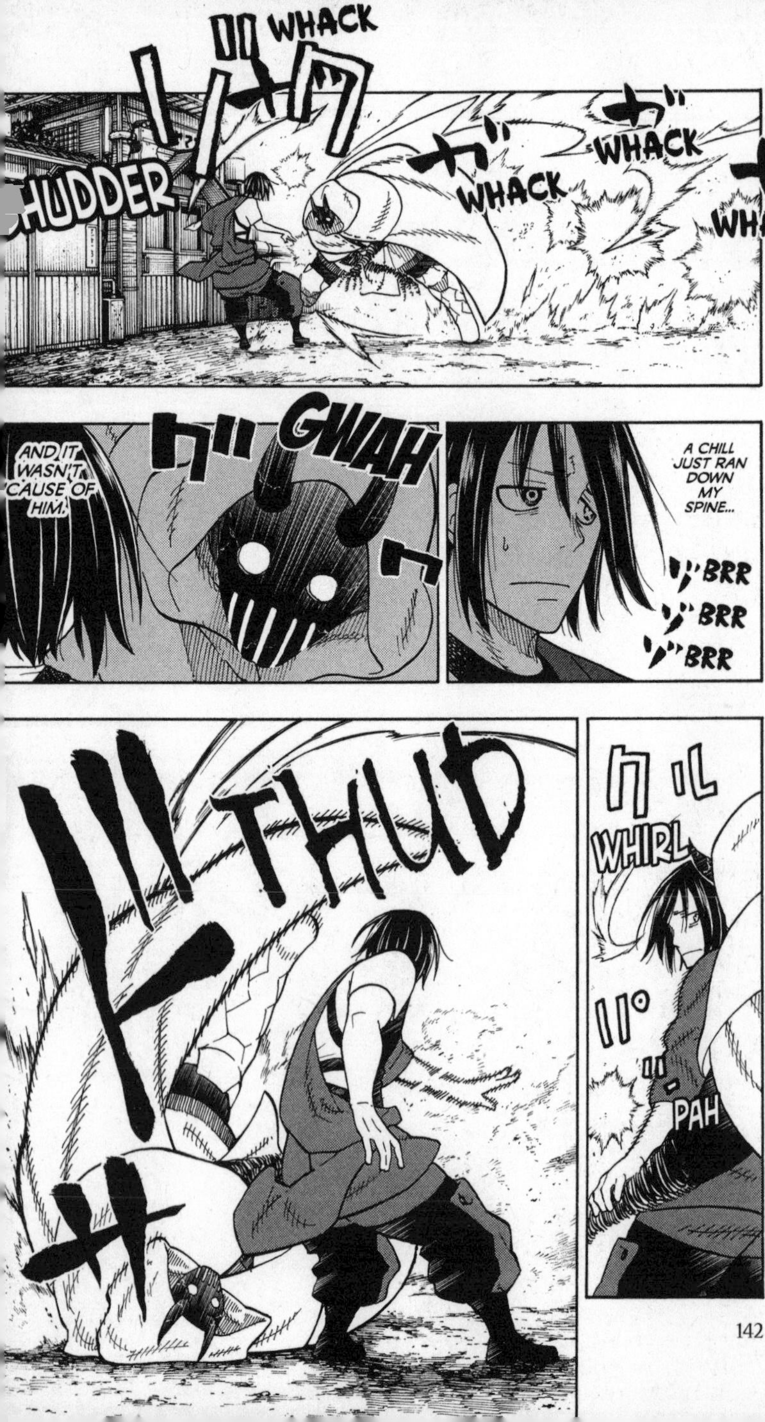
WHACK
WHACK
WHACK
WHACK
SHUDDER
A CHILL JUST RAN DOWN MY SPINE...
BRR
BRR
BRR
GWAH
AND IT WASN'T 'CAUSE OF HIM.
WHIRL
PAH
THUD

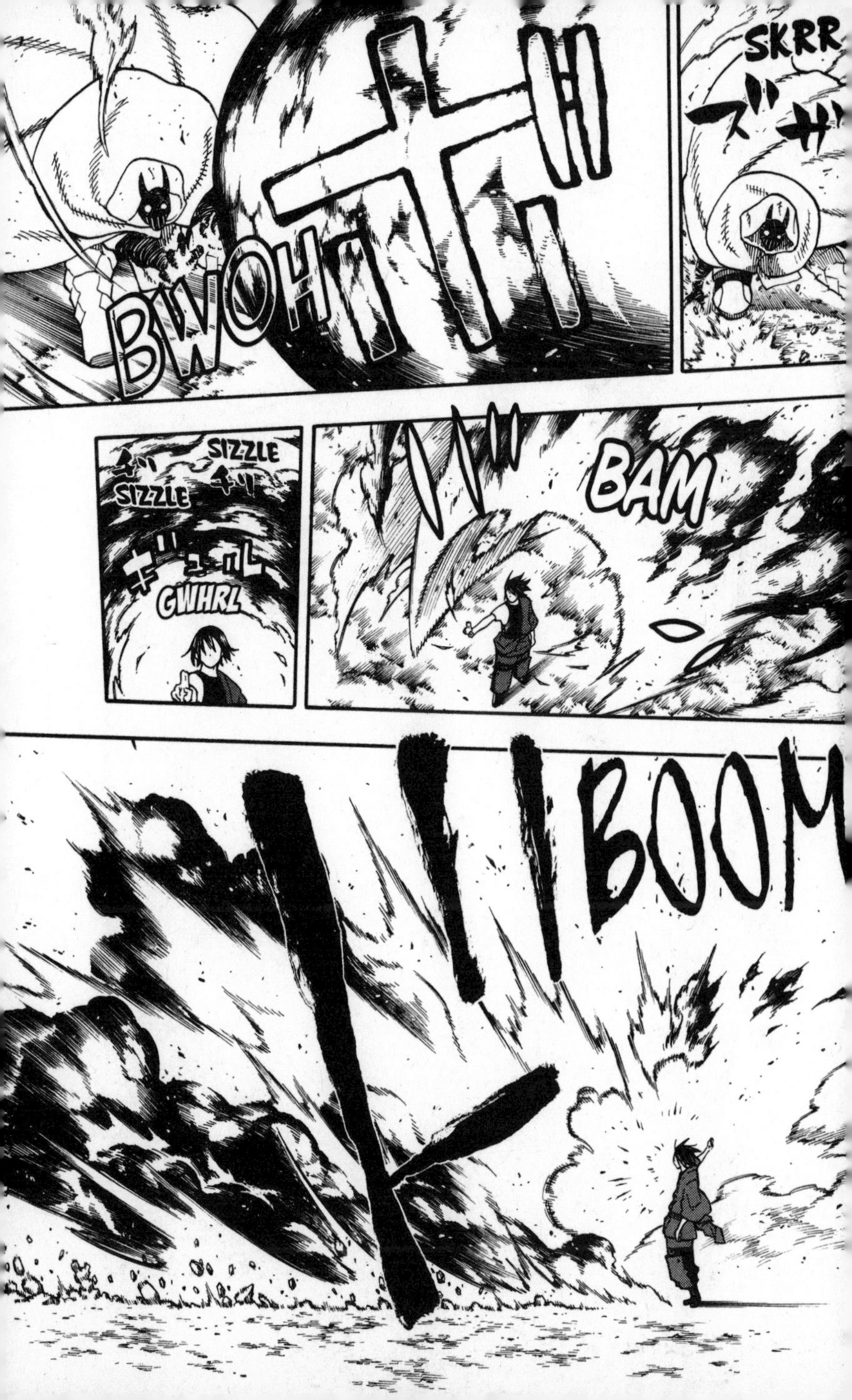
SKRR
BWOH
BAM
SIZZLE
SIZZLE
GWHRL
BOOM

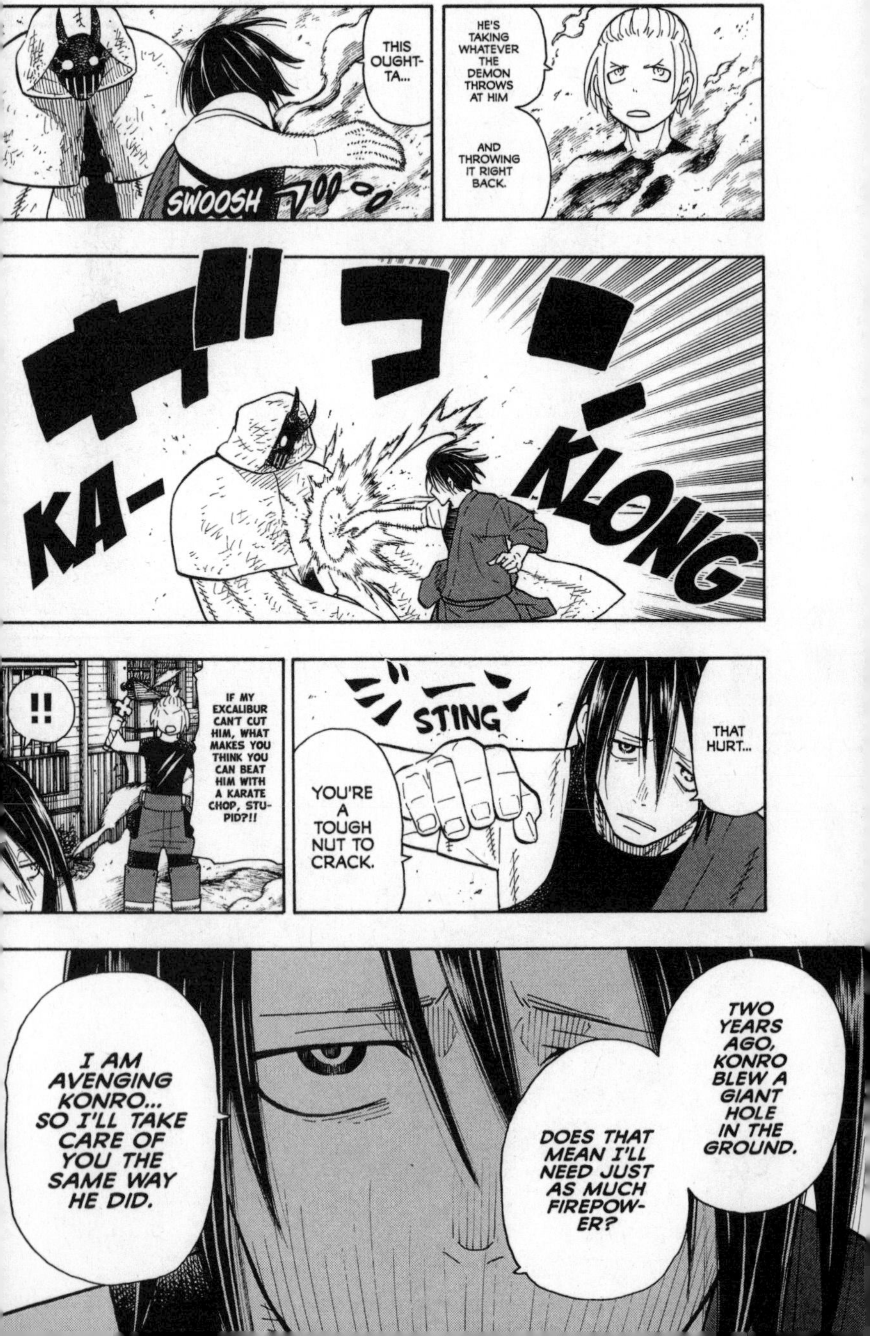
HE'S TAKING WHATEVER THE DEMON THROWS AT HIM
AND THROWING IT RIGHT BACK.
THIS OUGHT-TA...
SWOOSH
KA-
KLONG
STING
THAT HURT...
YOU'RE A TOUGH NUT TO CRACK.
!!
IF MY EXCALIBUR CAN'T CUT HIM, WHAT MAKES YOU THINK YOU CAN BEAT HIM WITH A KARATE CHOP, STU-PID?!!
TWO YEARS AGO, KONRO BLEW A GIANT HOLE IN THE GROUND.
DOES THAT MEAN I'LL NEED JUST AS MUCH FIREPOW-ER?
I AM AVENGING KONRO... SO I'LL TAKE CARE OF YOU THE SAME WAY HE DID.

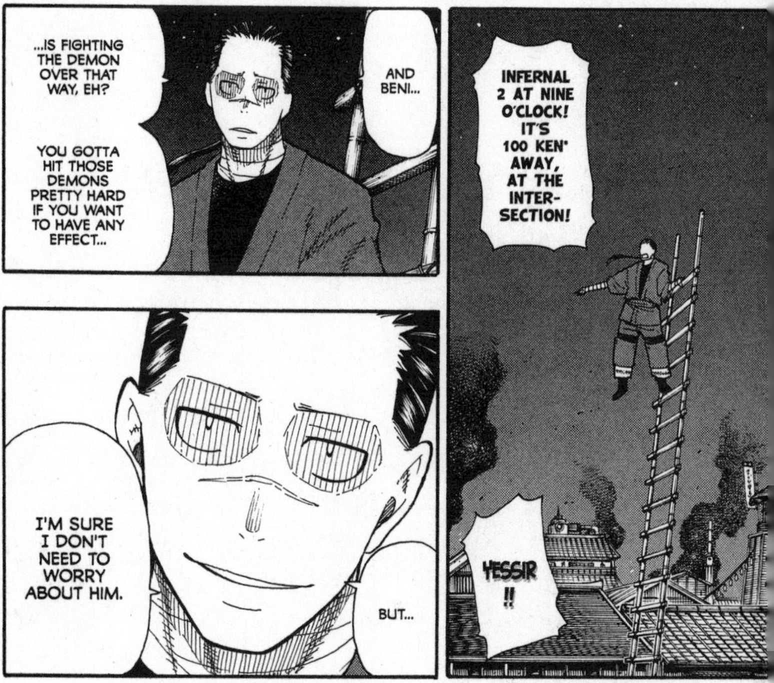
INFERNAL 2 AT NINE O'CLOCK! IT'S 100 KEN* AWAY, AT THE INTERSECTION!
YESSIR !!
AND BENI...
...IS FIGHTING THE DEMON OVER THAT WAY, EH?
YOU GOTTA HIT THOSE DEMONS PRETTY HARD IF YOU WANT TO HAVE ANY EFFECT...
BUT...
I'M SURE I DON'T NEED TO WORRY ABOUT HIM.

*A unit of measure a little shorter than two meter

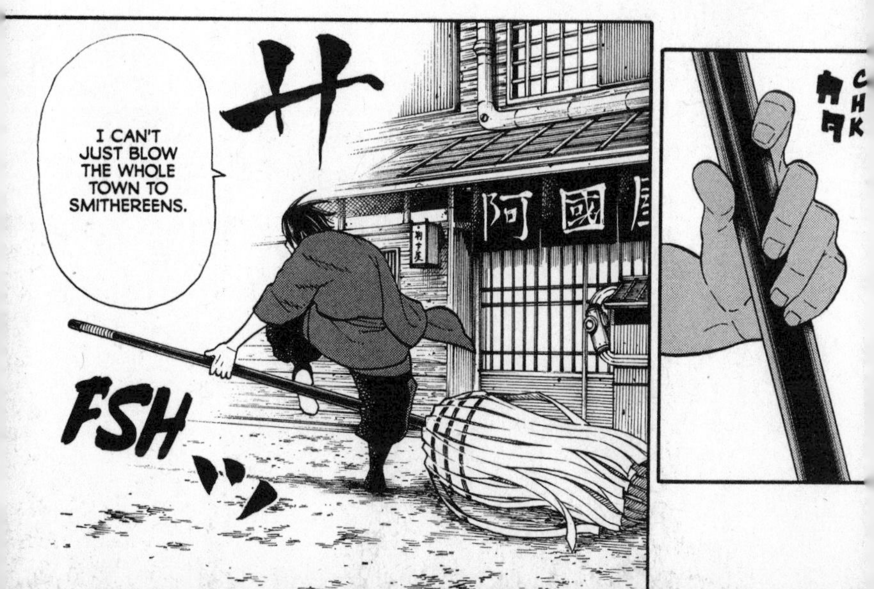
CHK
I CAN'T JUST BLOW THE WHOLE TOWN TO SMITHEREENS.
FSH

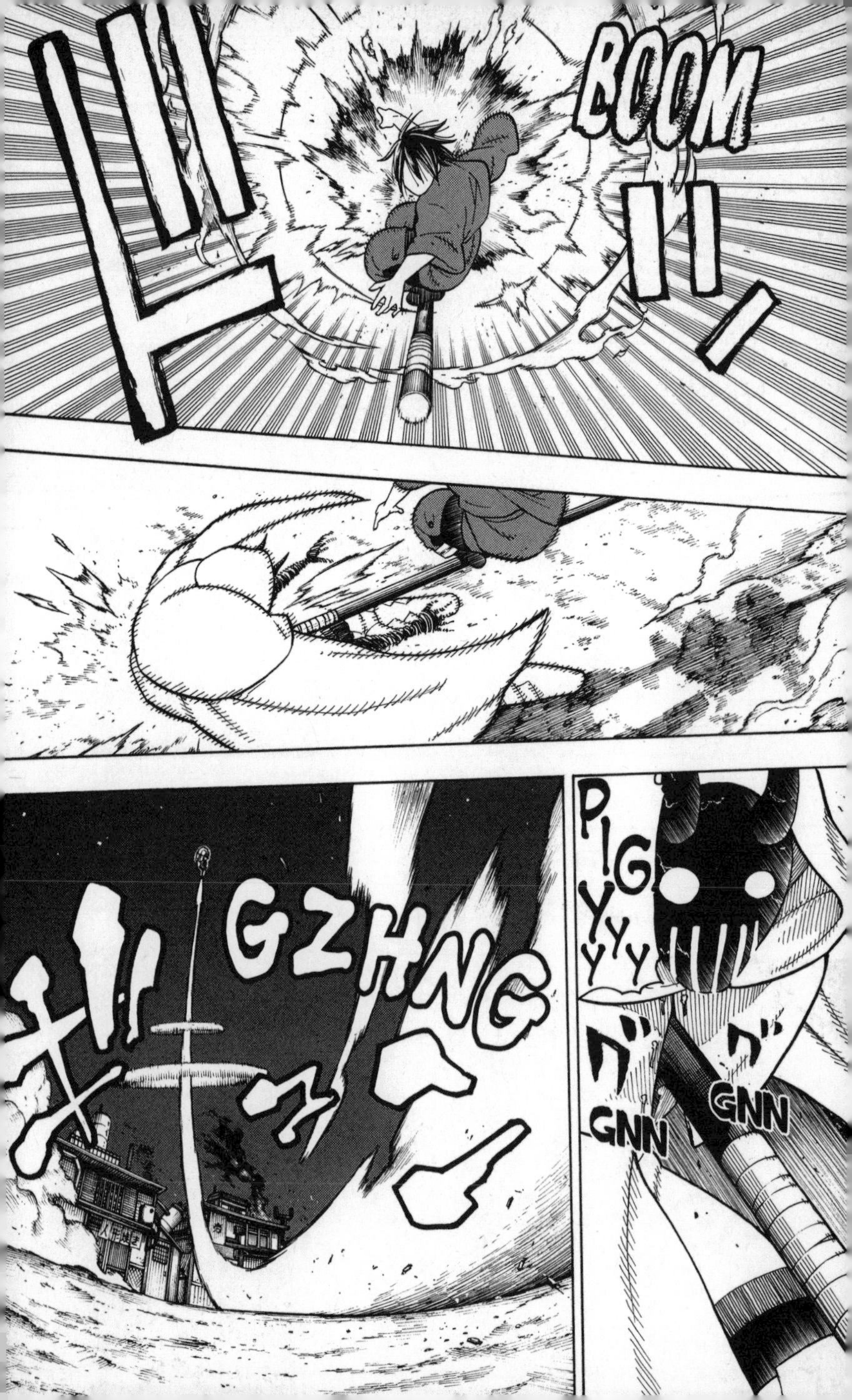
BOOM
PIGYYYYY
GNN
GNN
GZHNG

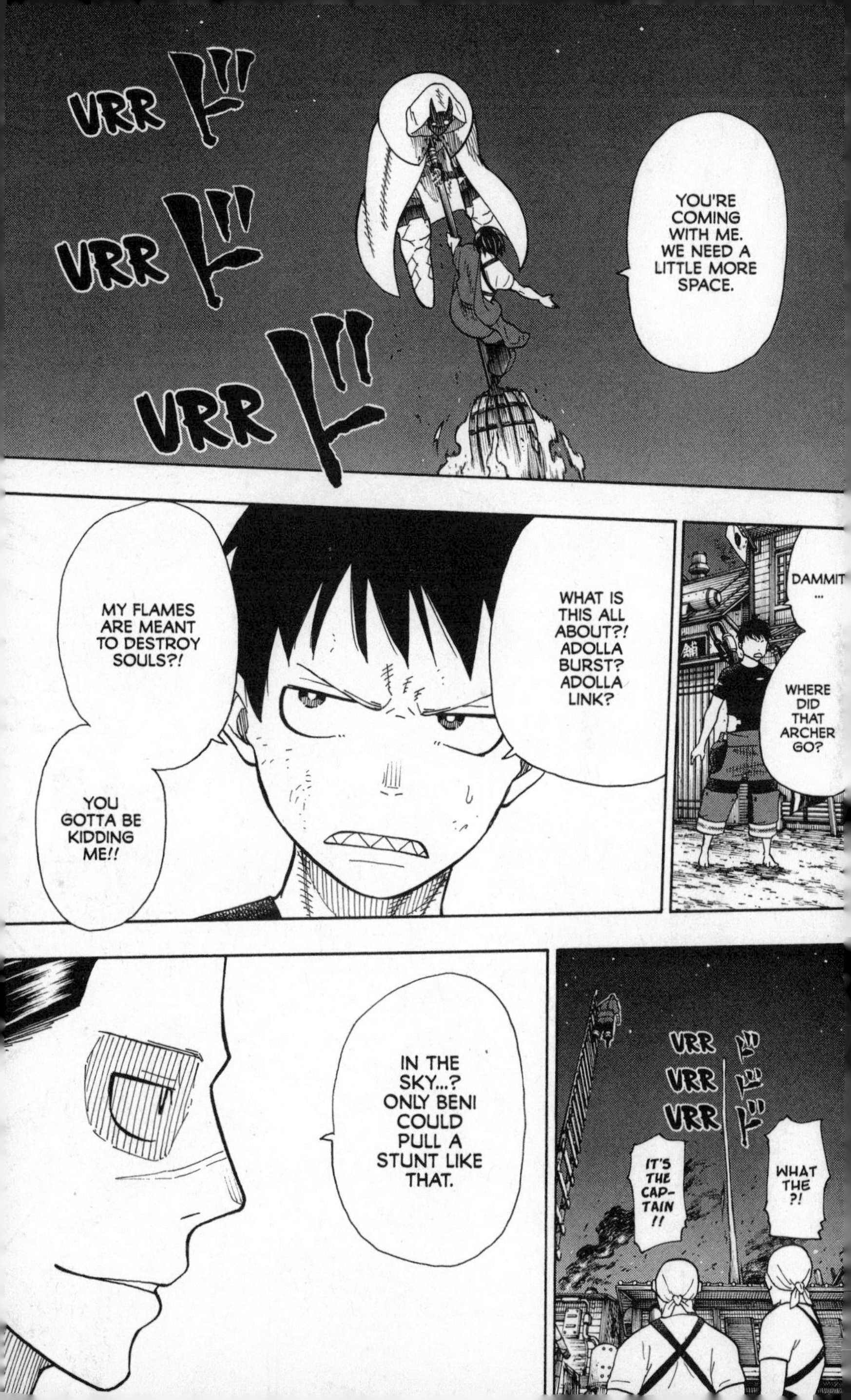
YOU'RE COMING WITH ME. WE NEED A LITTLE MORE SPACE.
VRR
VRR
VRR
DAMMIT...
WHERE DID THAT ARCHER GO?
WHAT IS THIS ALL ABOUT?! ADOLLA BURST? ADOLLA LINK?
MY FLAMES ARE MEANT TO DESTROY SOULS?!
YOU GOTTA BE KIDDING ME!!
VRR
VRR
VRR
WHAT THE ?!
IT'S THE CAPTAIN!!
IN THE SKY...? ONLY BENI COULD PULL A STUNT LIKE THAT.

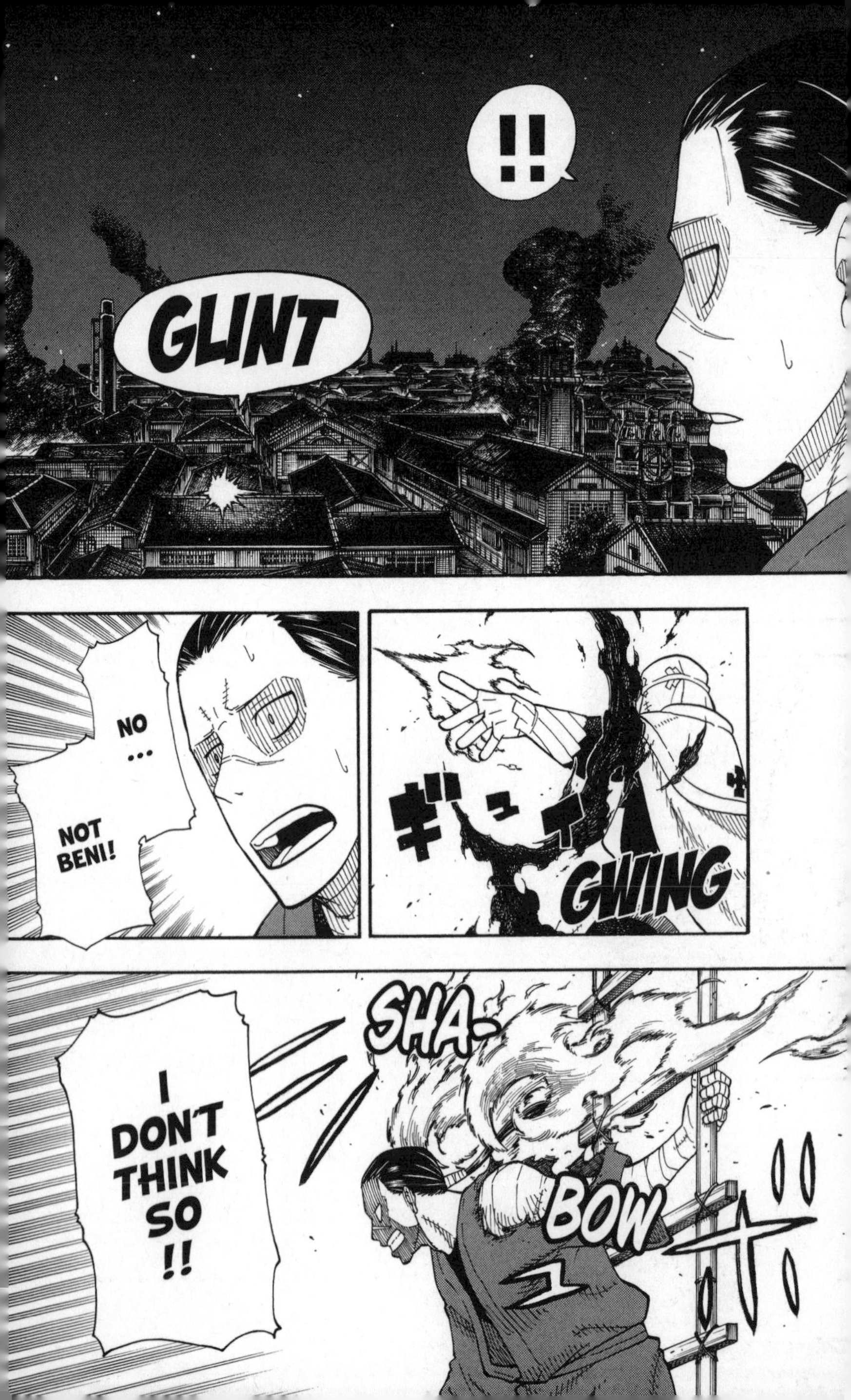

!!
GLINT
ギュイ
GWING
NO... NOT BENI!
SHA-
BOW
I DON'T THINK SO!!

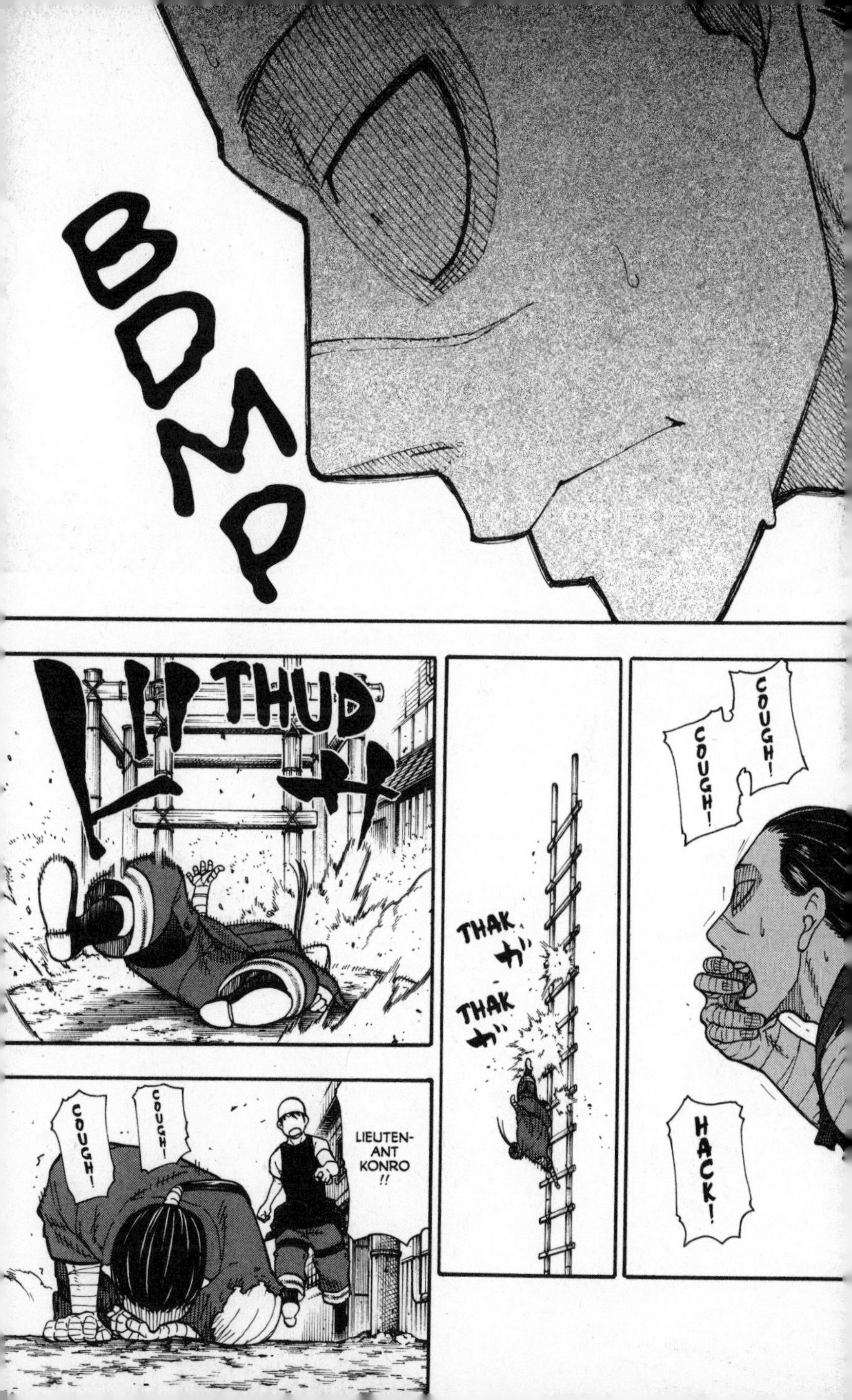
BDMP
COUGH!
COUGH!
HACK!
THAK
THAK
THUD
COUGH!
COUGH!
LIEUTEN-ANT KONRO!!

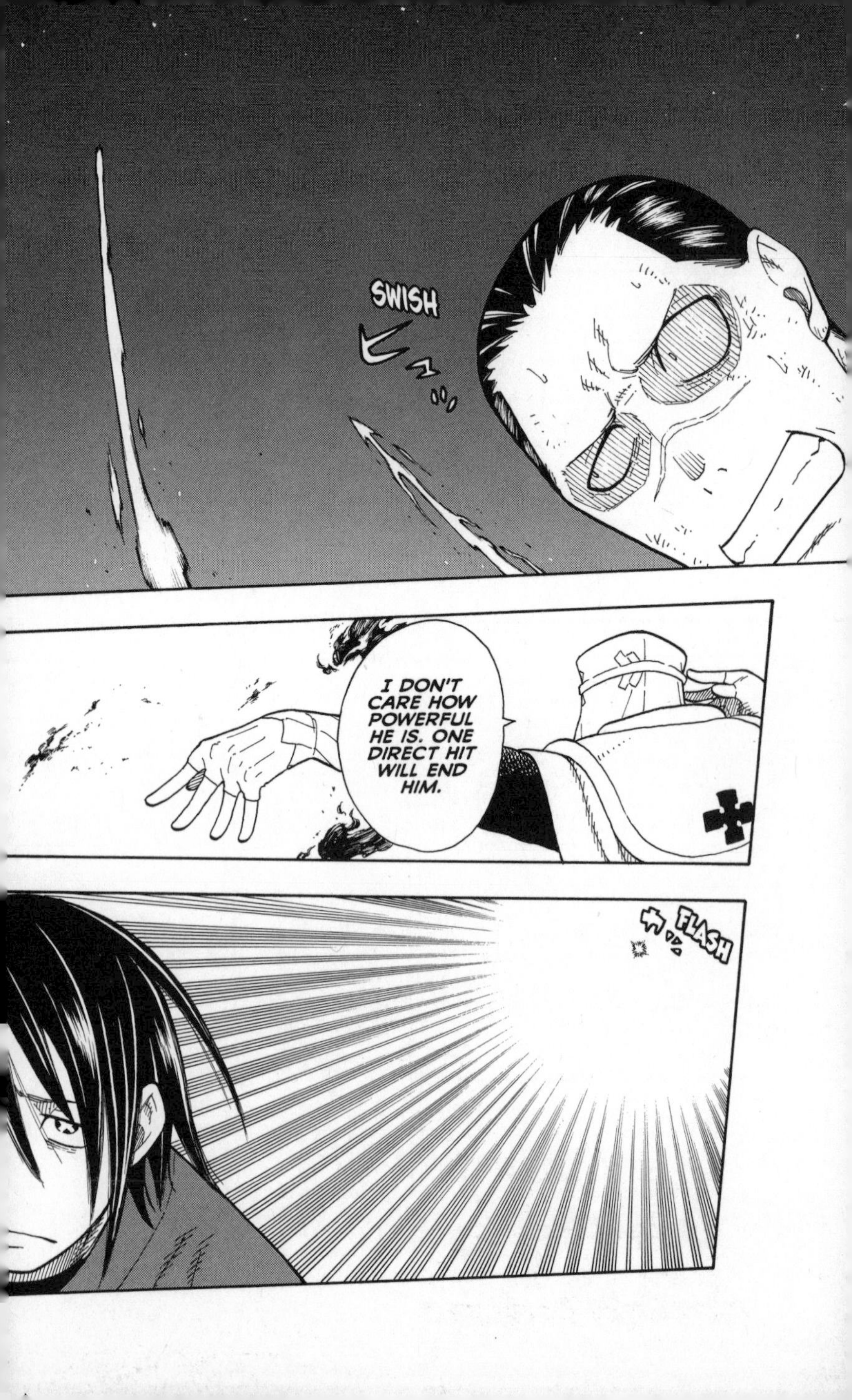
SWISH
I DON'T CARE HOW POWERFUL HE IS. ONE DIRECT HIT WILL END HIM.
FLASH

FIRE FORCE

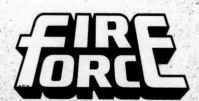

FIRE FORCE

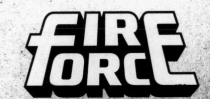

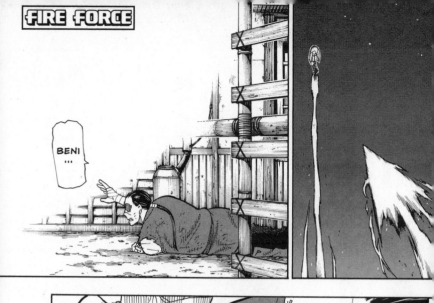

BENI
...

I...CAN'T MOVE...

SOME-BODY... HELP BENI...

BENI...

LIEU-TENANT KONRO !!

USE ME BEFORE YOU PUT YOUR LIFE ON THE LINE AGAIN!! I WANT TO HELP!!

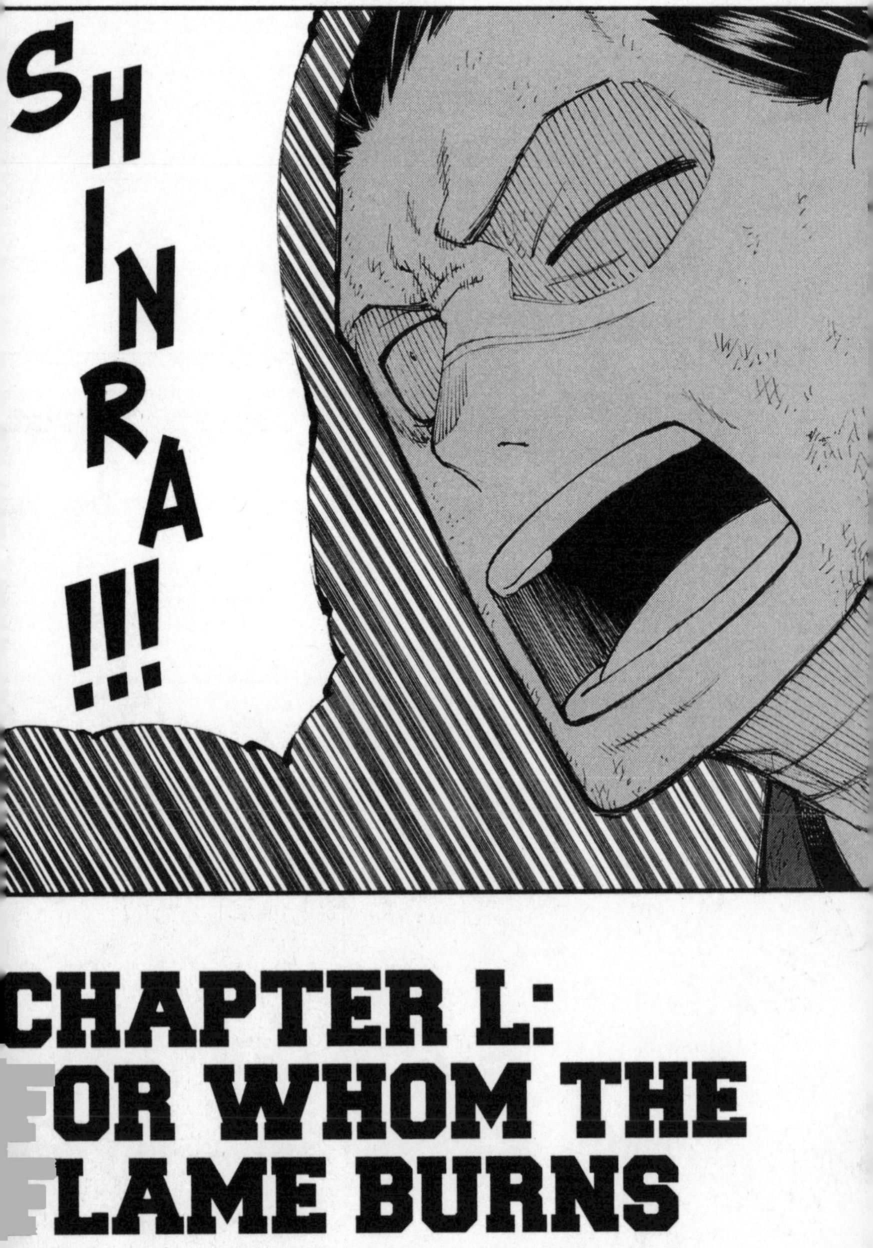
SHINRA!!!

CHAPTER L: FOR WHOM THE FLAME BURNS

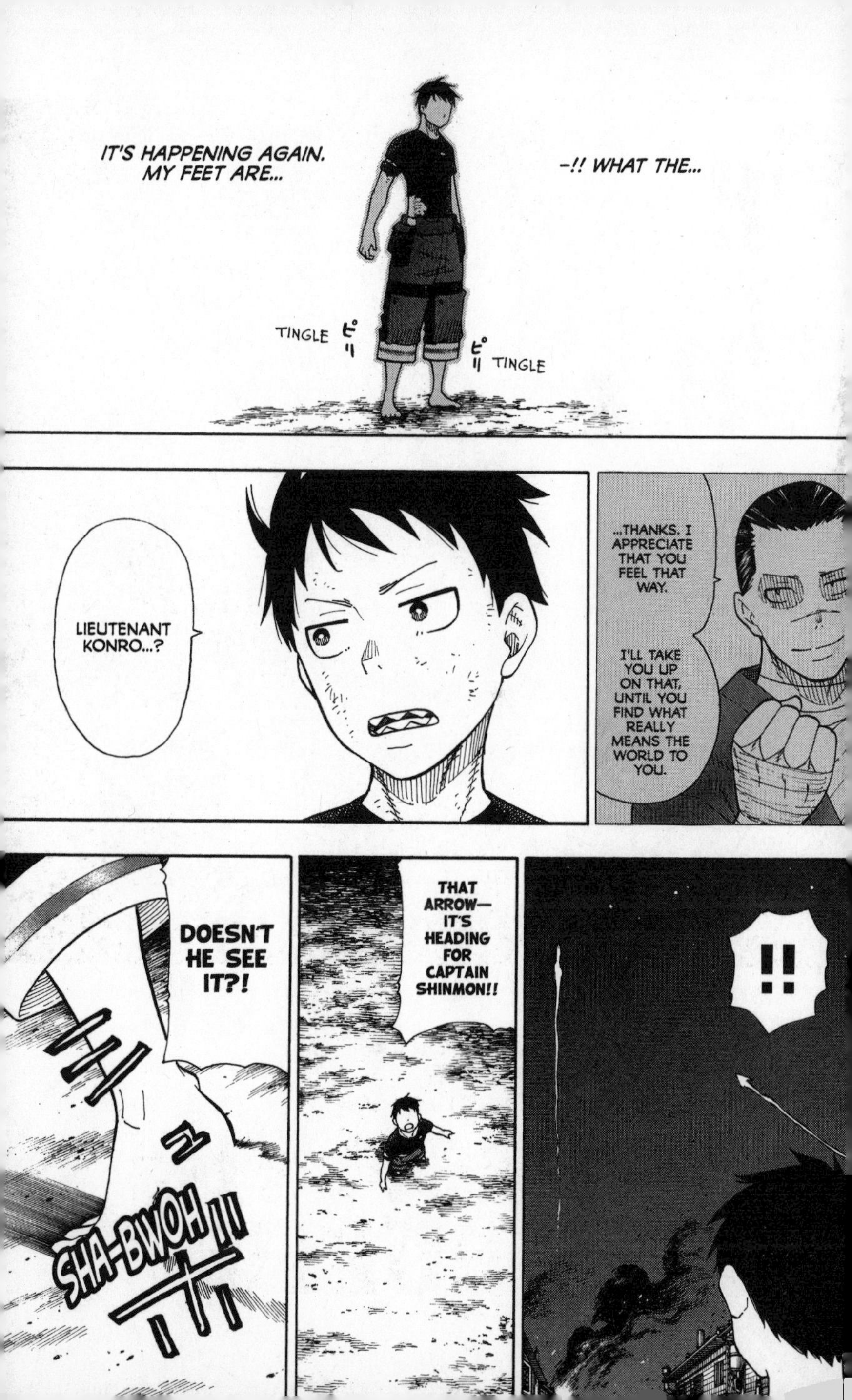

-!! WHAT THE...
IT'S HAPPENING AGAIN. MY FEET ARE...
TINGLE
TINGLE
...THANKS. I APPRECIATE THAT YOU FEEL THAT WAY.
I'LL TAKE YOU UP ON THAT, UNTIL YOU FIND WHAT REALLY MEANS THE WORLD TO YOU.
LIEUTENANT KONRO...?
!!
THAT ARROW— IT'S HEADING FOR CAPTAIN SHINMON!!
DOESN'T HE SEE IT?!
SHA-BWOH!!

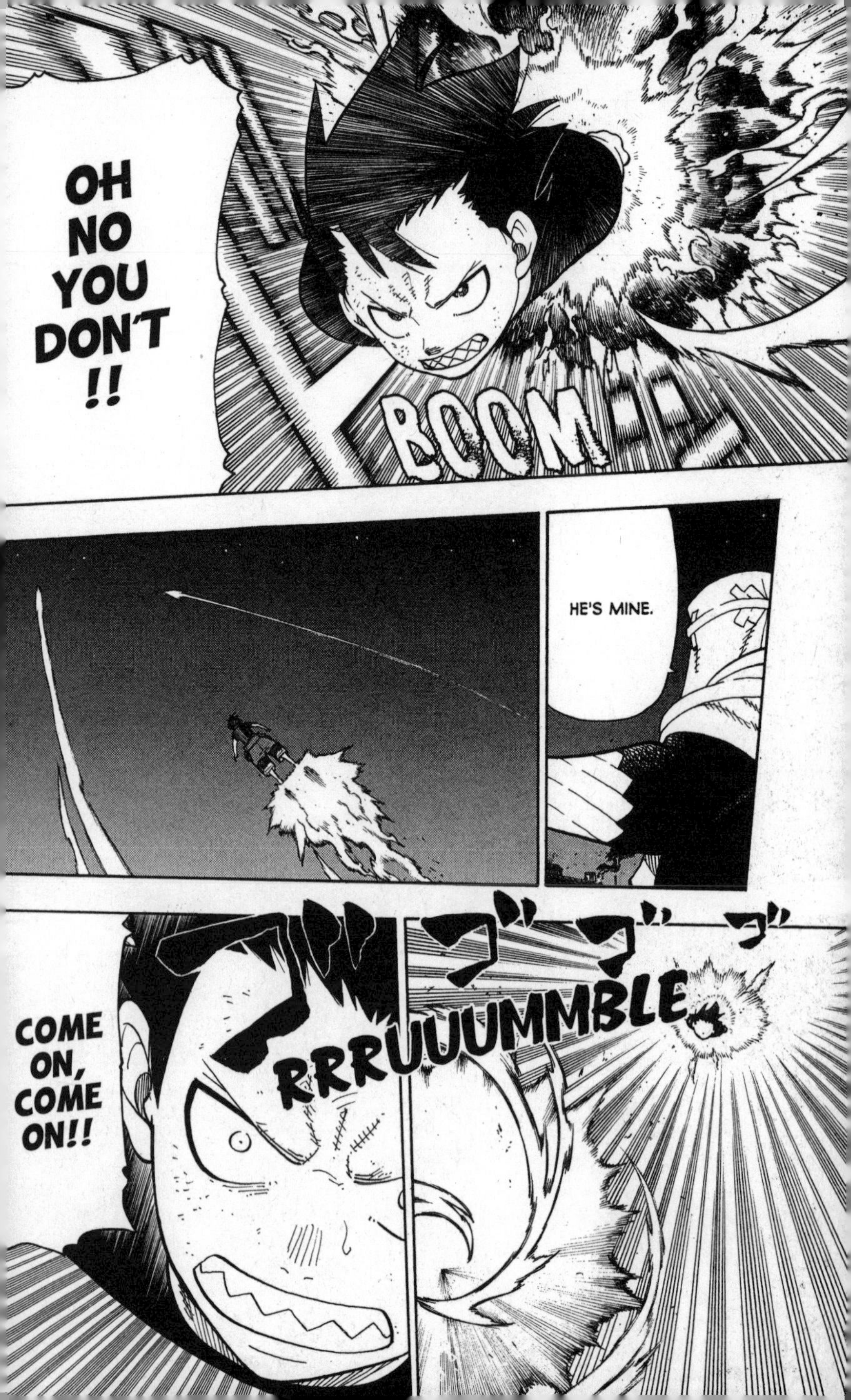
OH NO YOU DON'T!!
BOOM
HE'S MINE.
RRRUUUMMBLE
COME ON, COME ON!!

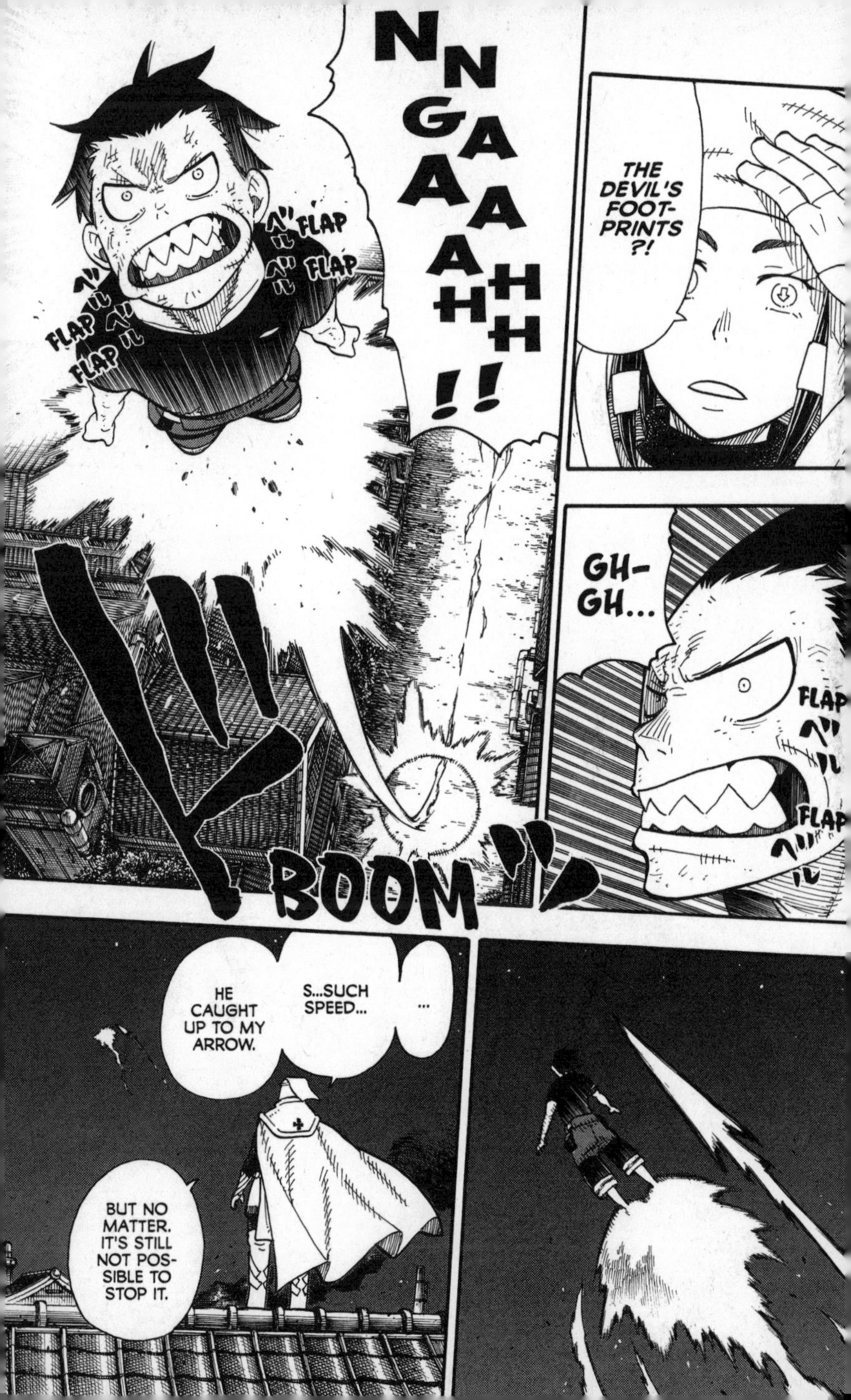
THE DEVIL'S FOOT-PRINTS ?!
GH-GH...
FLAP
FLAP
NNGAAAAHHH!!
FLAP
FLAP
FLAP
FLAP
BOOM
...
S...SUCH SPEED...
HE CAUGHT UP TO MY ARROW.
BUT NO MATTER. IT'S STILL NOT POSSIBLE TO STOP IT.

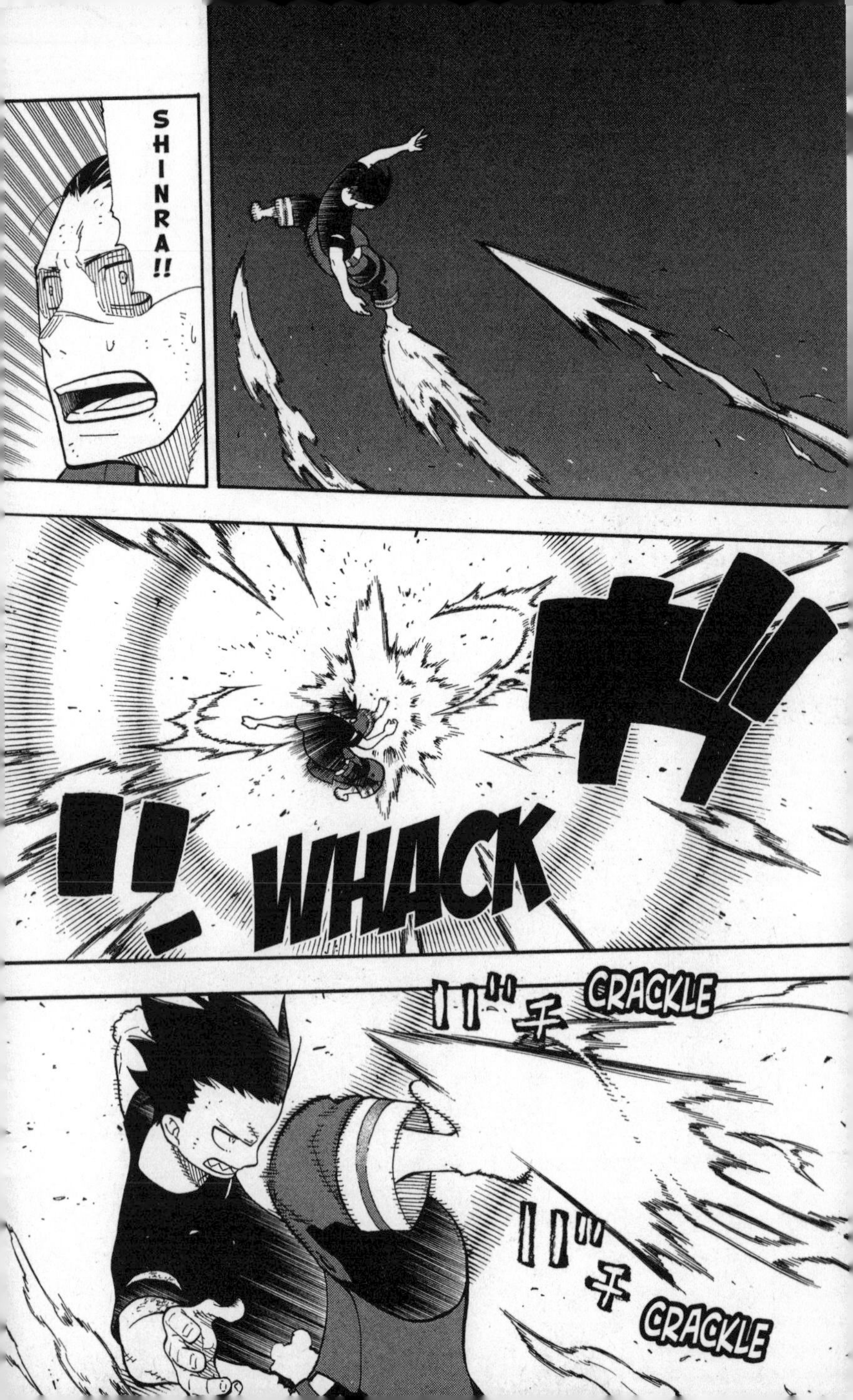
SHINRA!!
WHACK
CRACKLE
CRACKLE

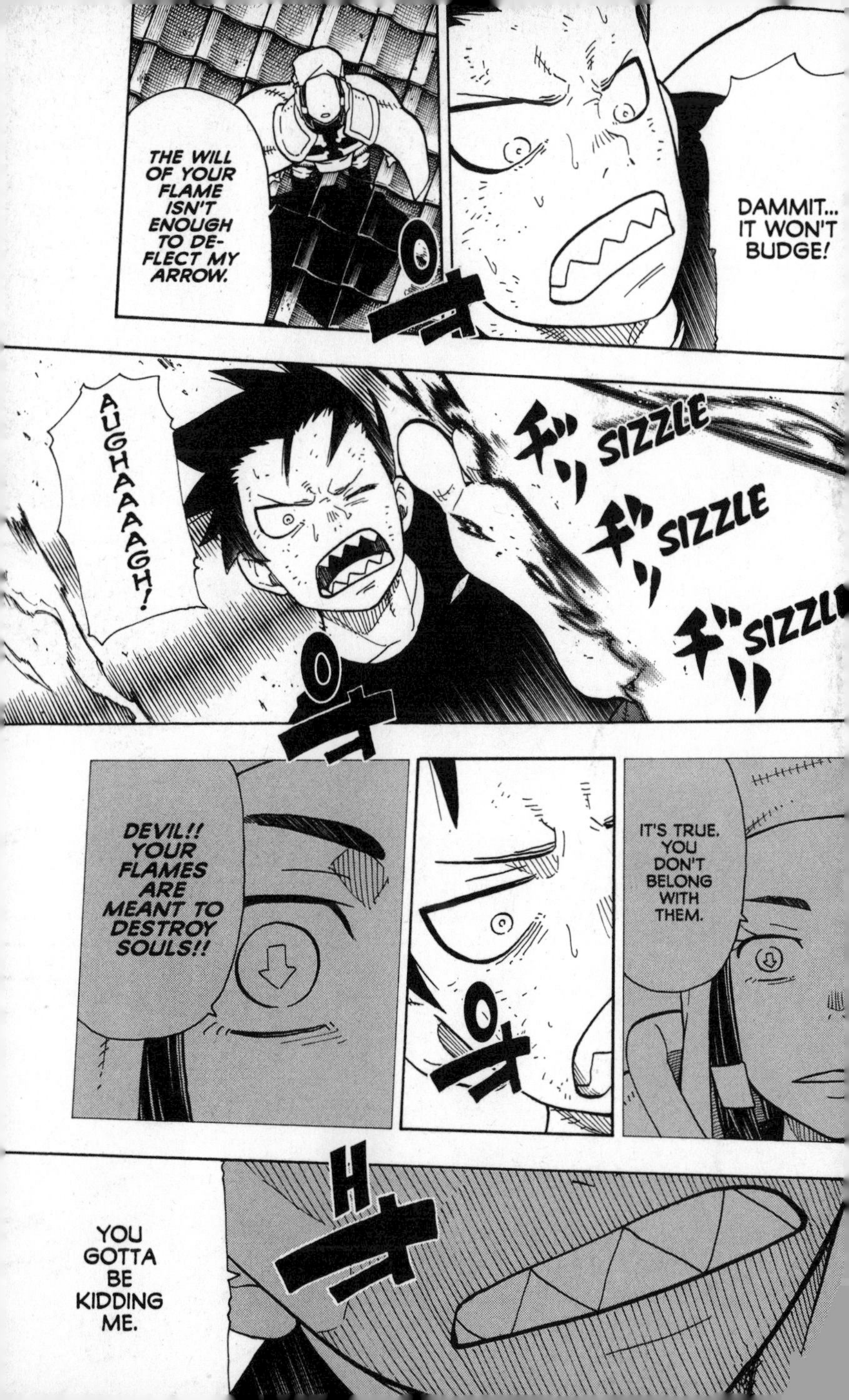
DAMMIT... IT WON'T BUDGE!
THE WILL OF YOUR FLAME ISN'T ENOUGH TO DEFLECT MY ARROW.
SIZZLE
SIZZLE
SIZZL
AUGHAAAAAGH!
IT'S TRUE. YOU DON'T BELONG WITH THEM.
DEVIL!! YOUR FLAMES ARE MEANT TO DESTROY SOULS!!
YOU GOTTA BE KIDDING ME.

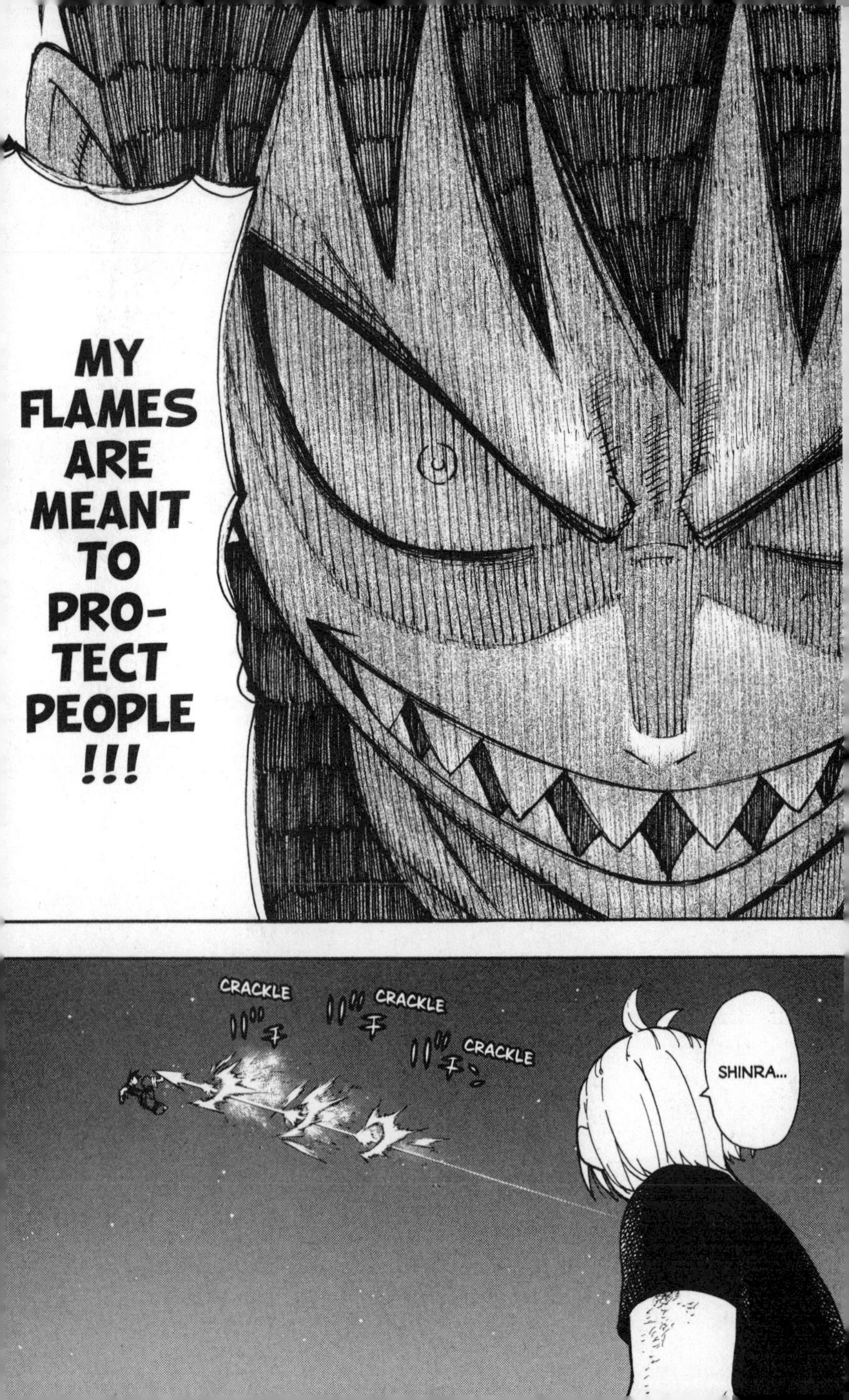
MY FLAMES ARE MEANT TO PRO-TECT PEOPLE!!!
SHINRA...
CRACKLE
CRACKLE
CRACKLE

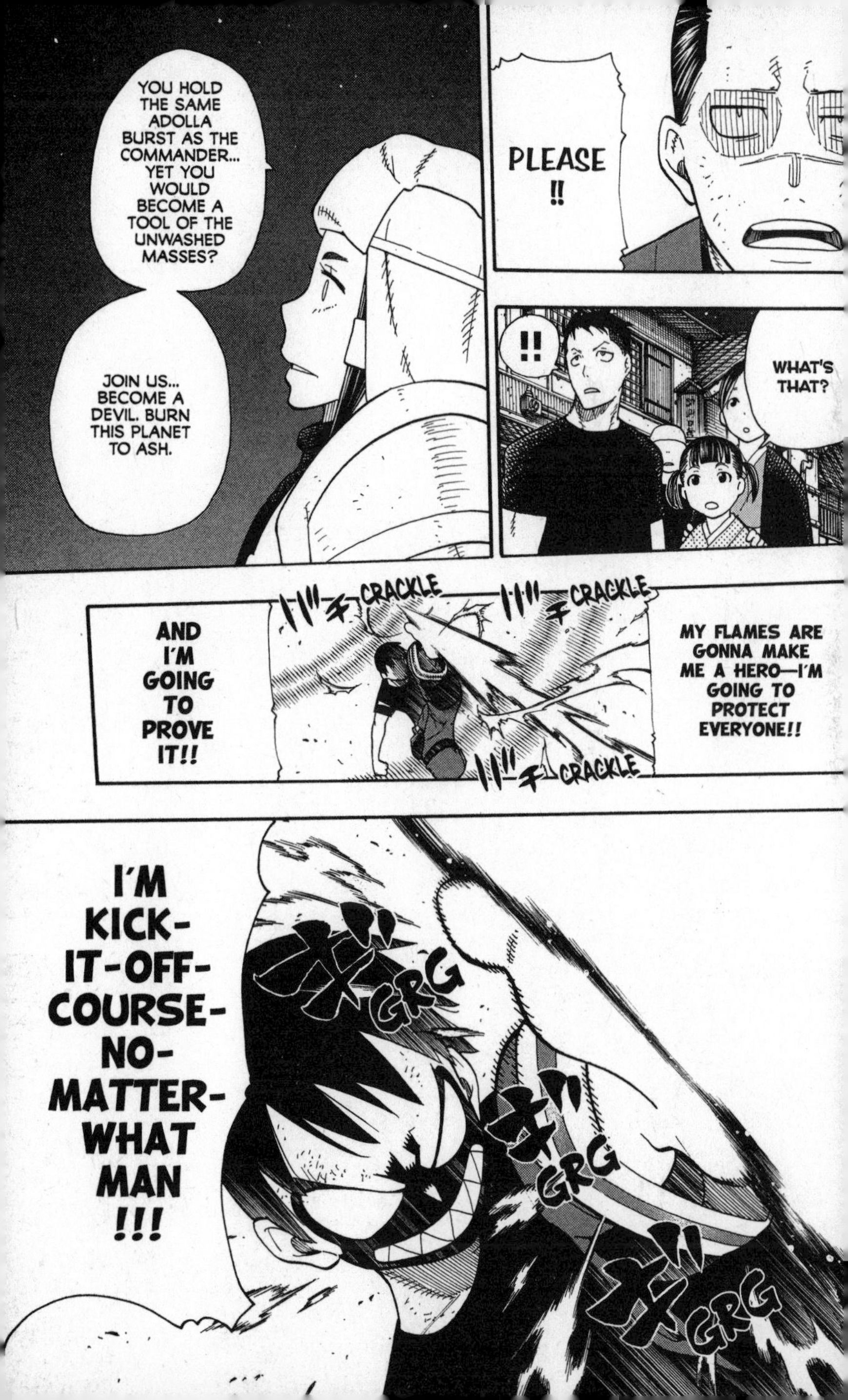
PLEASE !!
WHAT'S THAT?
!!
YOU HOLD THE SAME ADOLLA BURST AS THE COMMANDER... YET YOU WOULD BECOME A TOOL OF THE UNWASHED MASSES?
JOIN US... BECOME A DEVIL. BURN THIS PLANET TO ASH.
MY FLAMES ARE GONNA MAKE ME A HERO—I'M GOING TO PROTECT EVERYONE!!
CRACKLE
CRACKLE
CRACKLE
AND I'M GOING TO PROVE IT!!
I'M KICK-IT-OFF-COURSE-NO-MATTER-WHAT MAN !!!
GRG
GRG
GRG

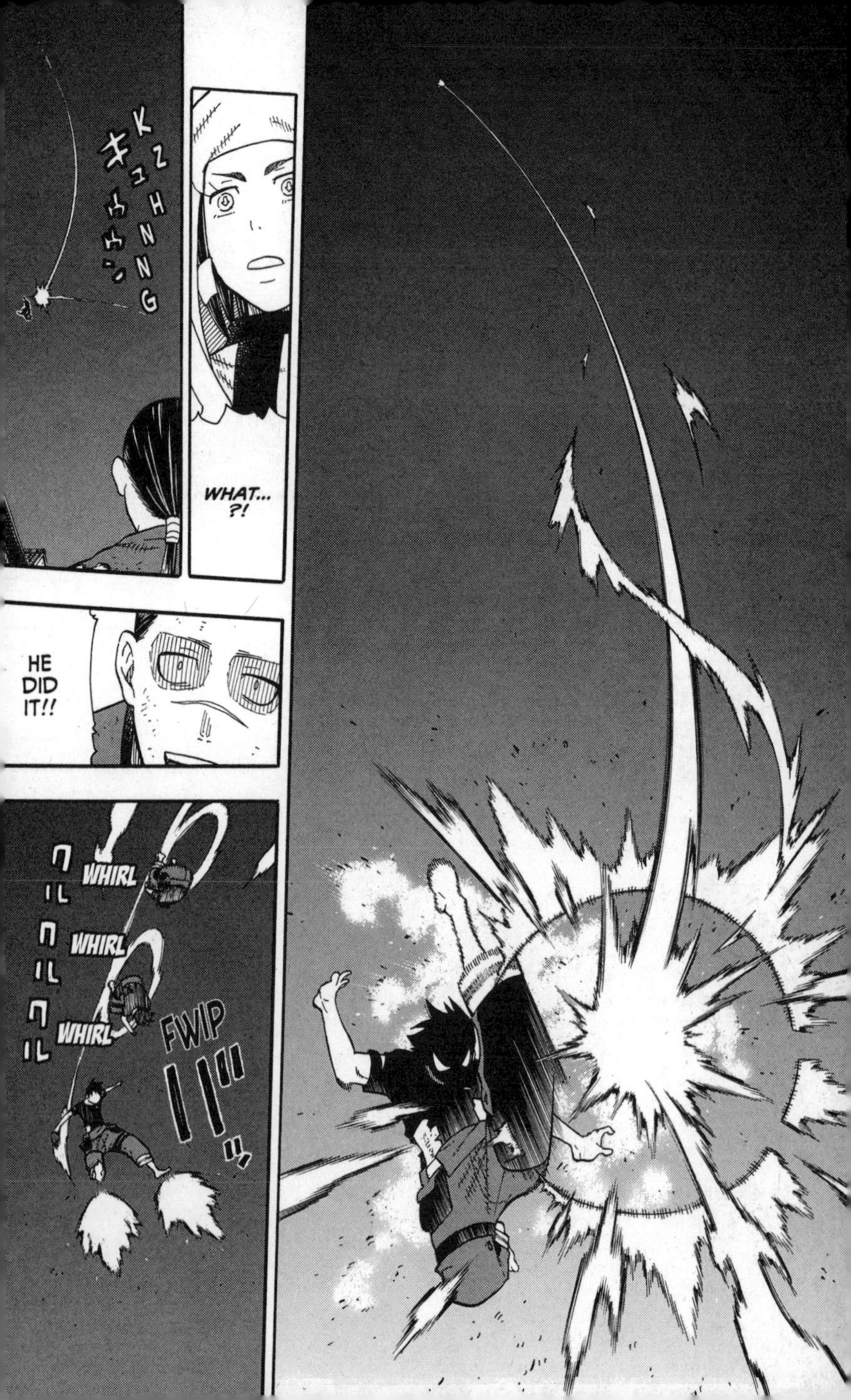
WHAT...?!
KZHNNG
HE DID IT!!
WHIRL
WHIRL
WHIRL
FWIP

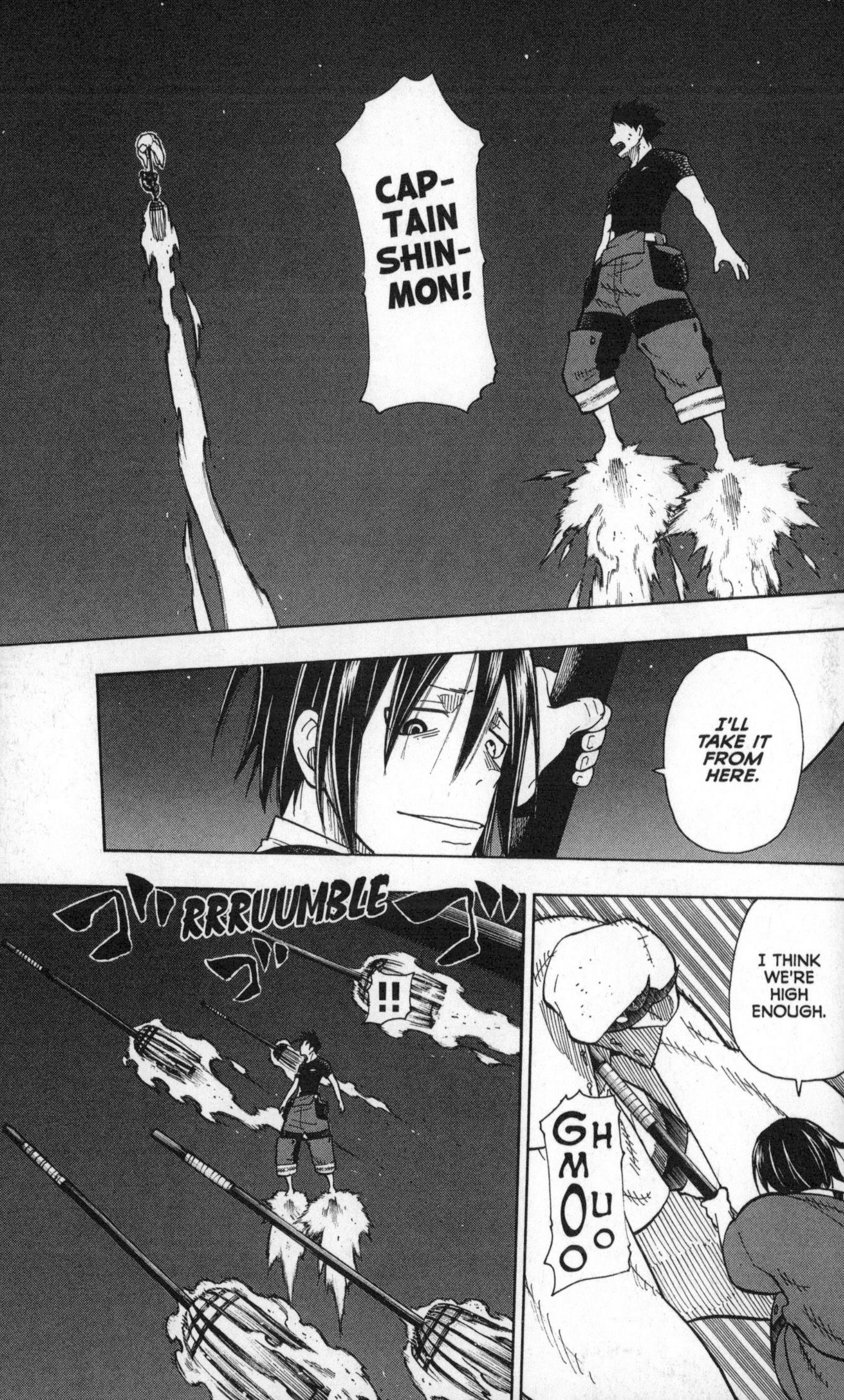
CAP-TAIN SHIN-MON!
I'LL TAKE IT FROM HERE.
I THINK WE'RE HIGH ENOUGH.
GHMOUOO
RRRUUMBLE
!!

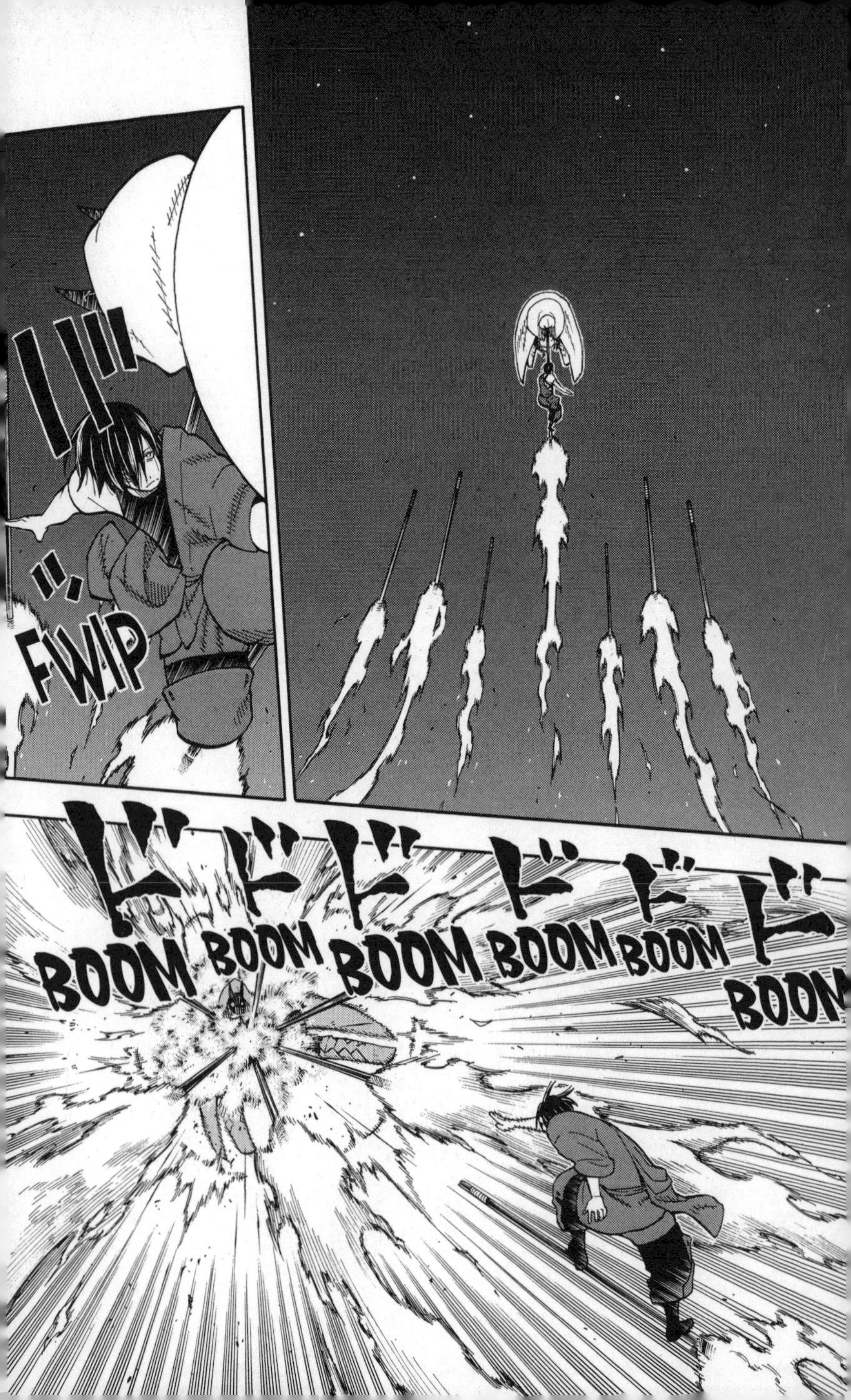
FWIP
ドドドドドド
BOOM BOOM BOOM BOOM BOOM BOOM

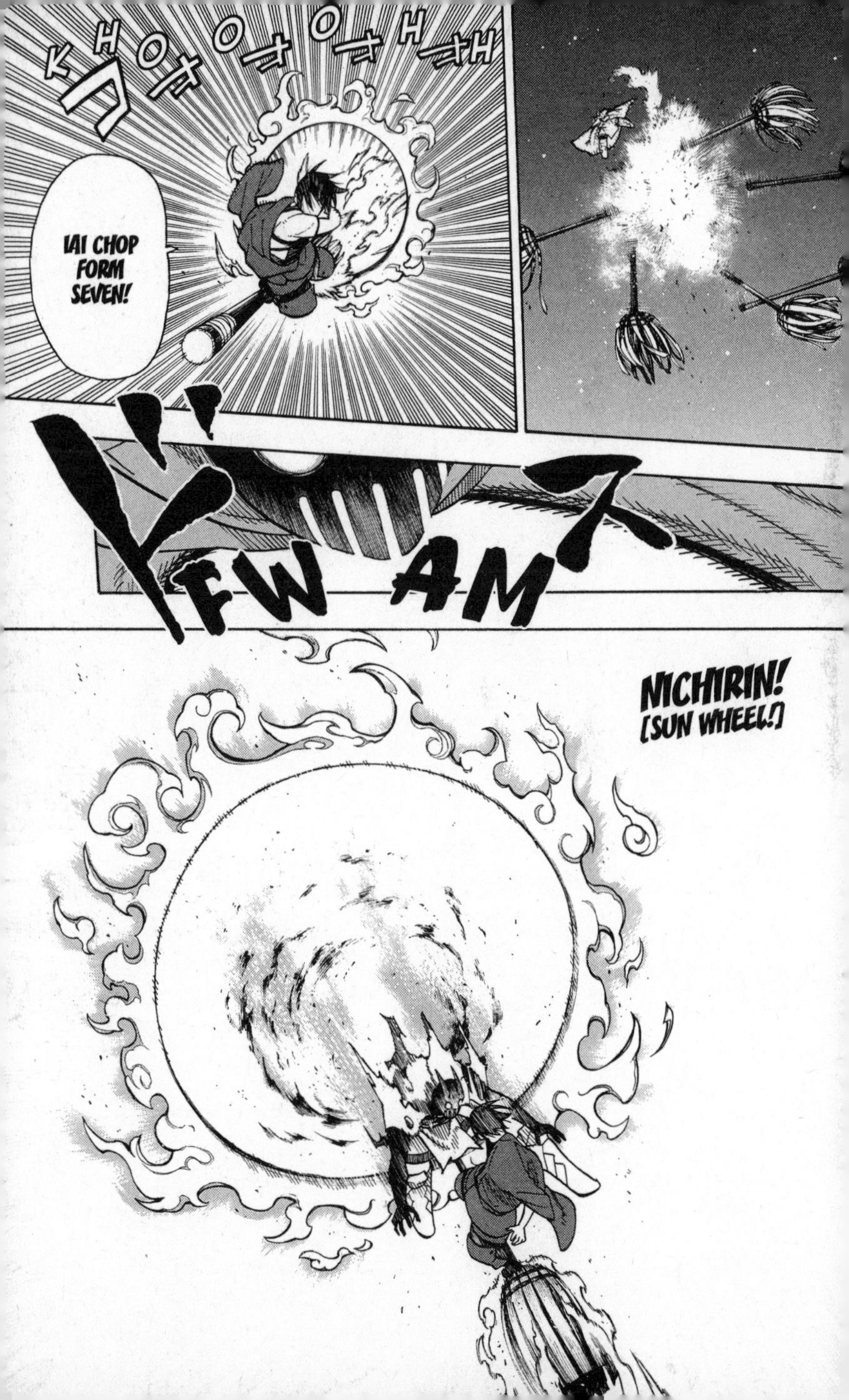
KHOOOHH
IAI CHOP FORM SEVEN!
FWAM
NICHIRIN!
[SUN WHEEL!]

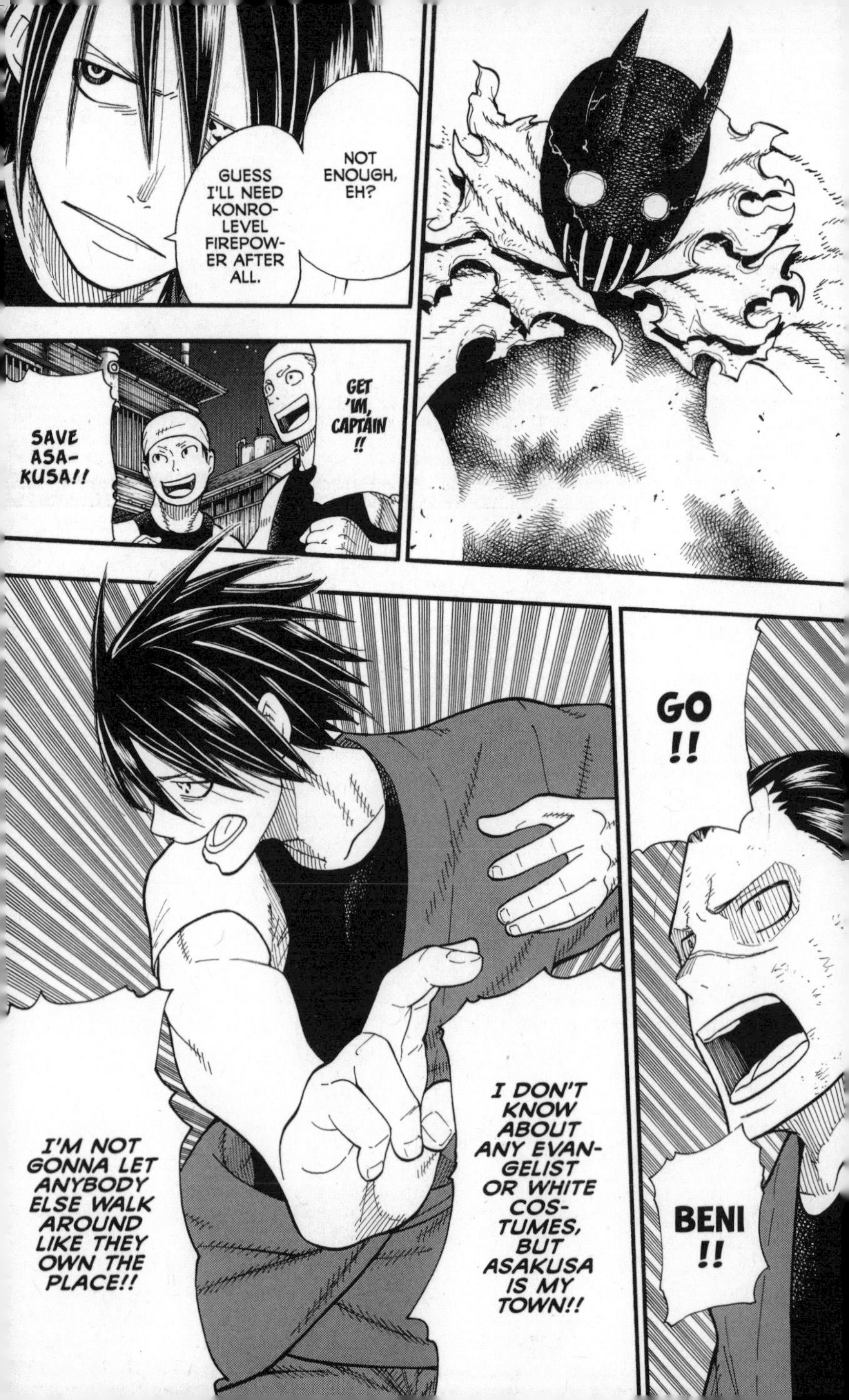
NOT ENOUGH, EH?
GUESS I'LL NEED KONRO-LEVEL FIREPOW-ER AFTER ALL.
GET 'IM, CAPTAIN!!
SAVE ASA-KUSA!!
GO!!
BENI!!
I DON'T KNOW ABOUT ANY EVAN-GELIST OR WHITE COS-TUMES, BUT ASAKUSA IS MY TOWN!!
I'M NOT GONNA LET ANYBODY ELSE WALK AROUND LIKE THEY OWN THE PLACE!!

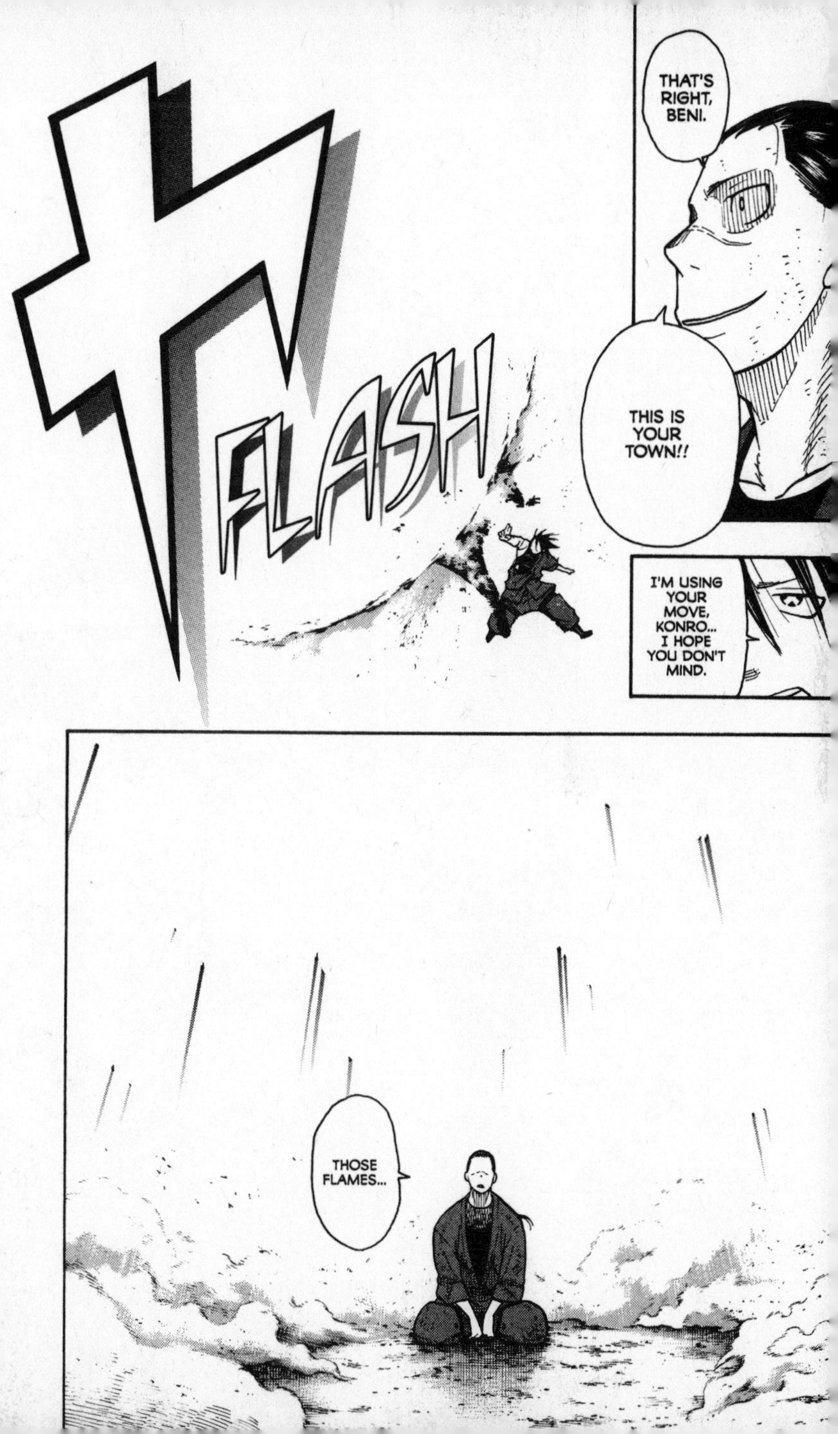
THAT'S RIGHT, BENI.
THIS IS YOUR TOWN!!
I'M USING YOUR MOVE, KONRO... I HOPE YOU DON'T MIND.
FLASH
THOSE FLAMES...

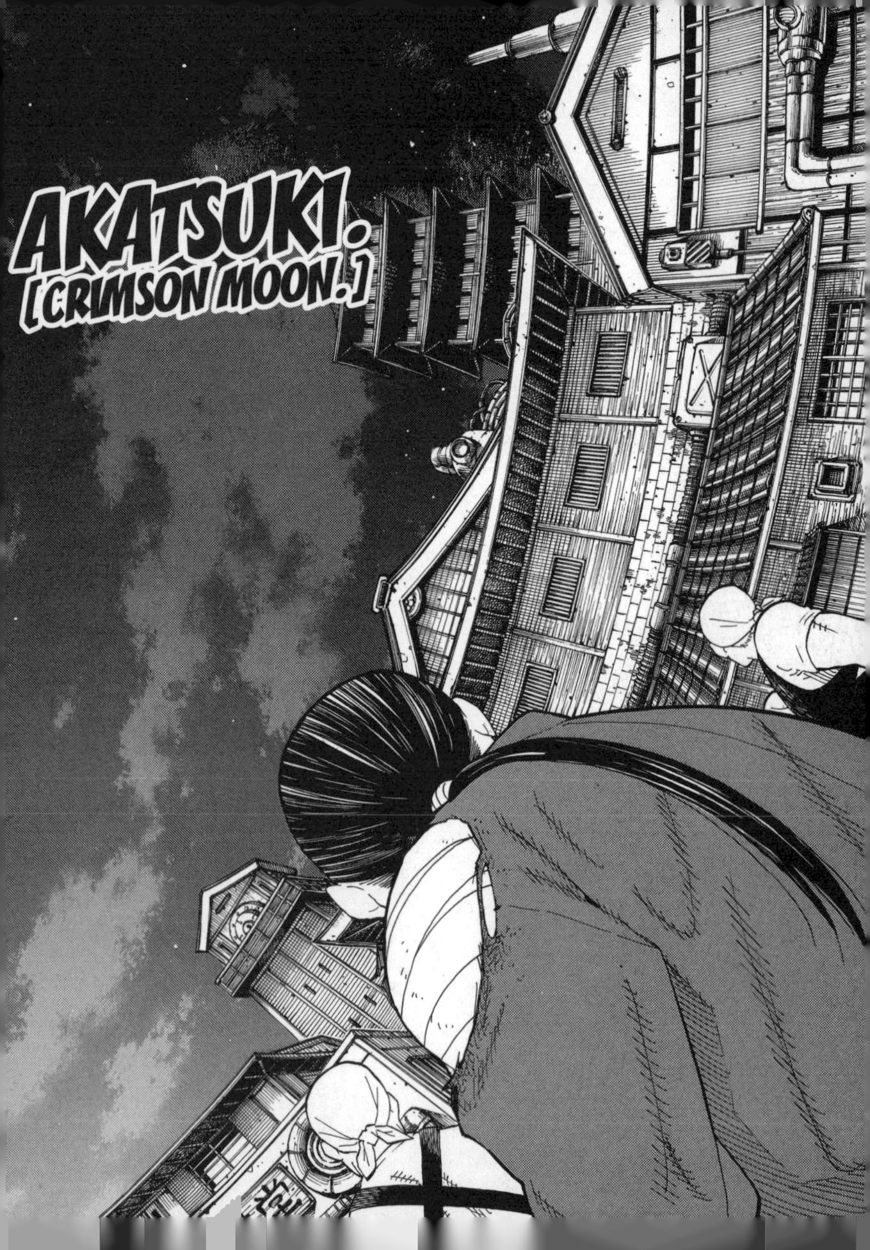
AKATSUKI.
[CRIMSON MOON.]

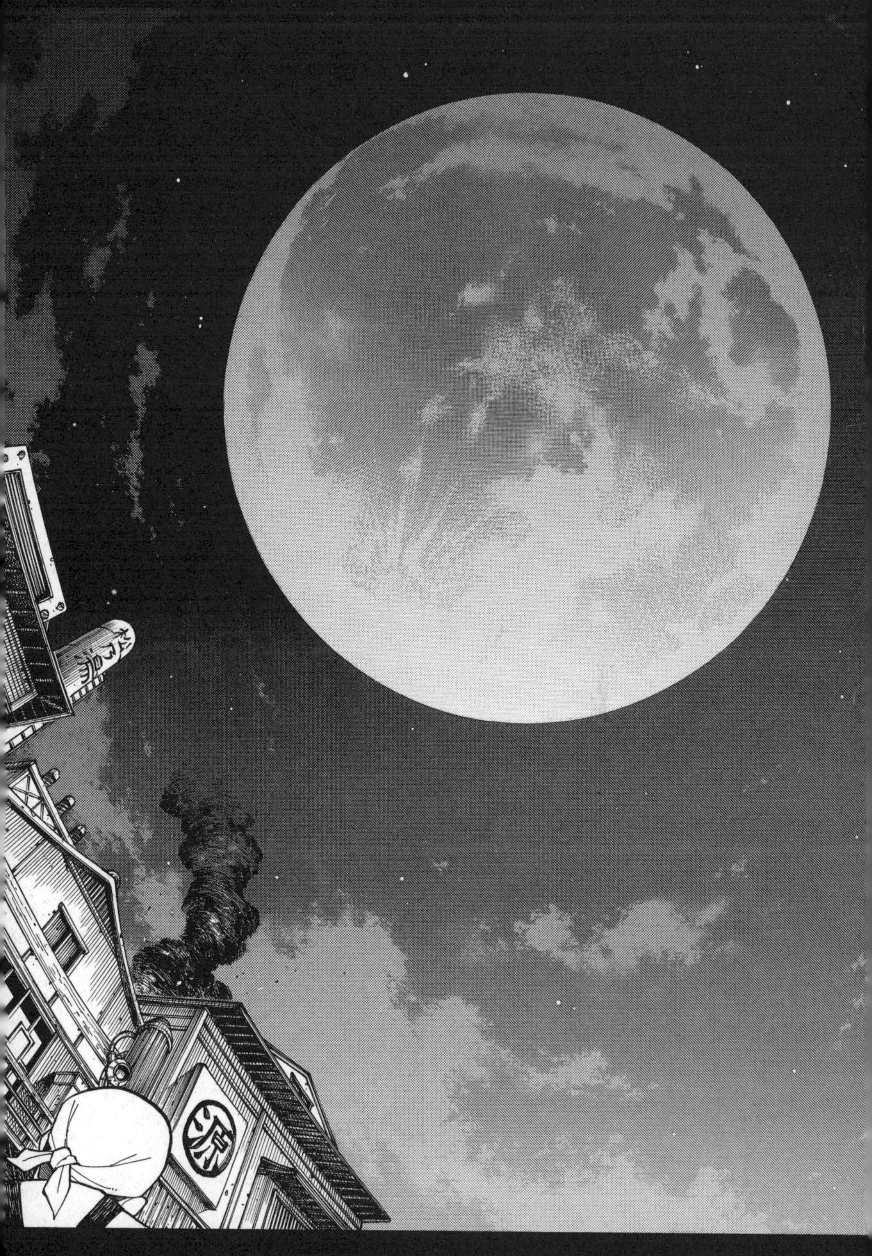
源

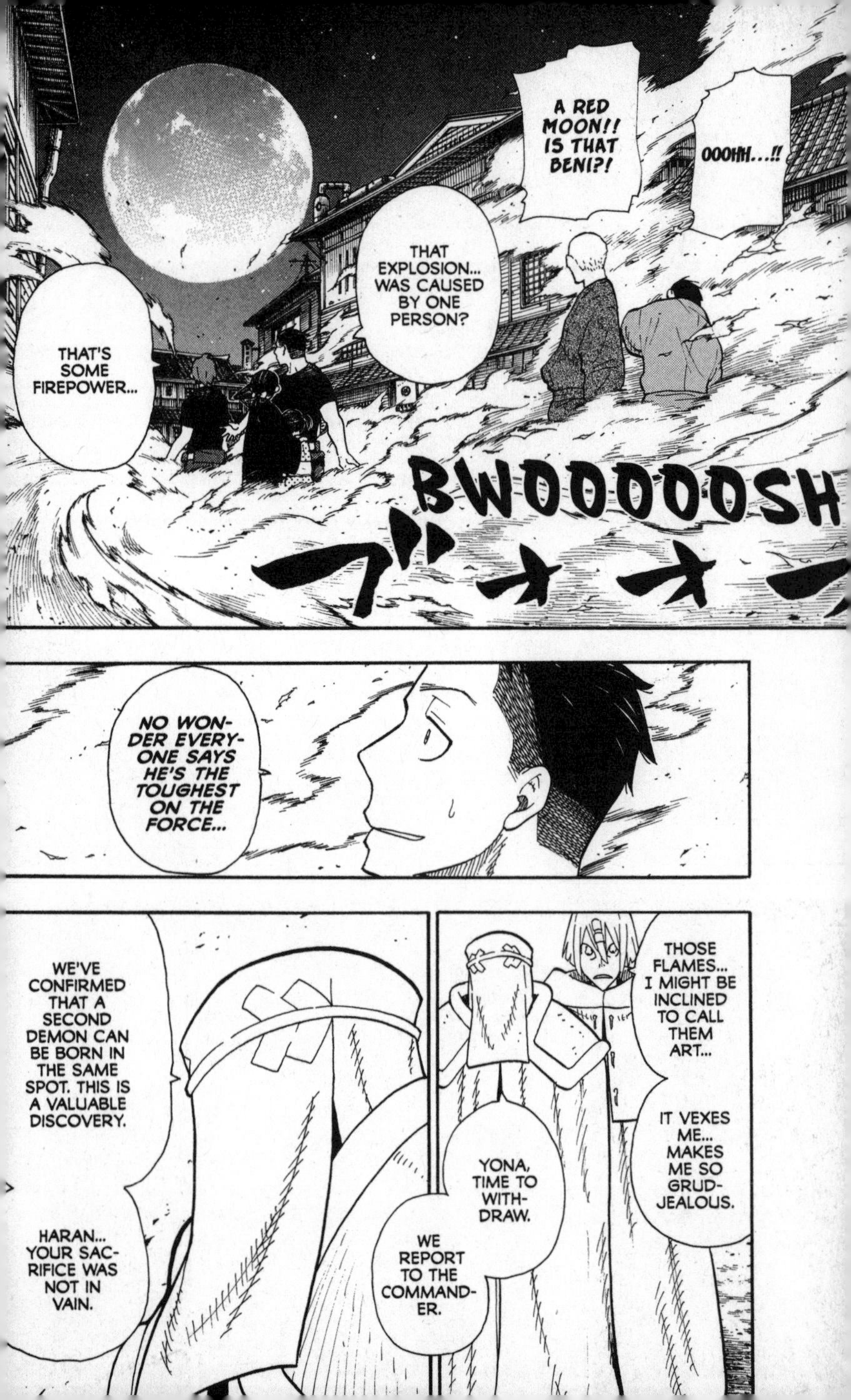
OOOHH...!!
A RED MOON!! IS THAT BENI?!
THAT EXPLOSION... WAS CAUSED BY ONE PERSON?
THAT'S SOME FIREPOWER...
BWOOOOOSH
ブオオー
NO WONDER EVERYONE SAYS HE'S THE TOUGHEST ON THE FORCE...
THOSE FLAMES... I MIGHT BE INCLINED TO CALL THEM ART...
IT VEXES ME... MAKES ME SO GRUD-JEALOUS.
YONA, TIME TO WITHDRAW.
WE REPORT TO THE COMMANDER.
WE'VE CONFIRMED THAT A SECOND DEMON CAN BE BORN IN THE SAME SPOT. THIS IS A VALUABLE DISCOVERY.
HARAN... YOUR SACRIFICE WAS NOT IN VAIN.

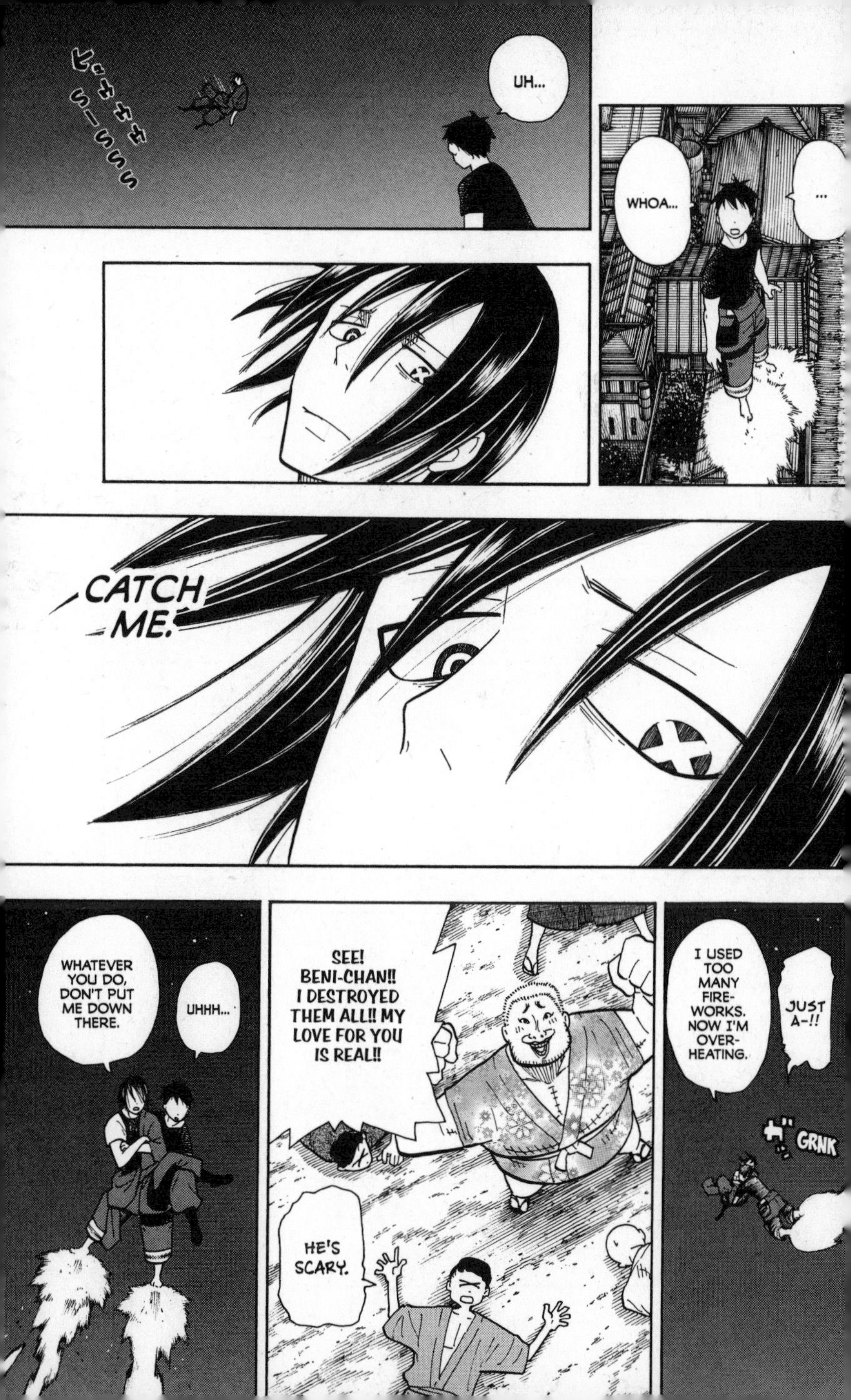
...
WHOA...
UH...
S—SSSS
CATCH ME.
JUST A-!!
I USED TOO MANY FIRE-WORKS. NOW I'M OVER-HEATING.
GRNK
SEE! BENI-CHAN!! I DESTROYED THEM ALL!! MY LOVE FOR YOU IS REAL!!
HE'S SCARY.
UHHH...
WHATEVER YOU DO, DON'T PUT ME DOWN THERE.

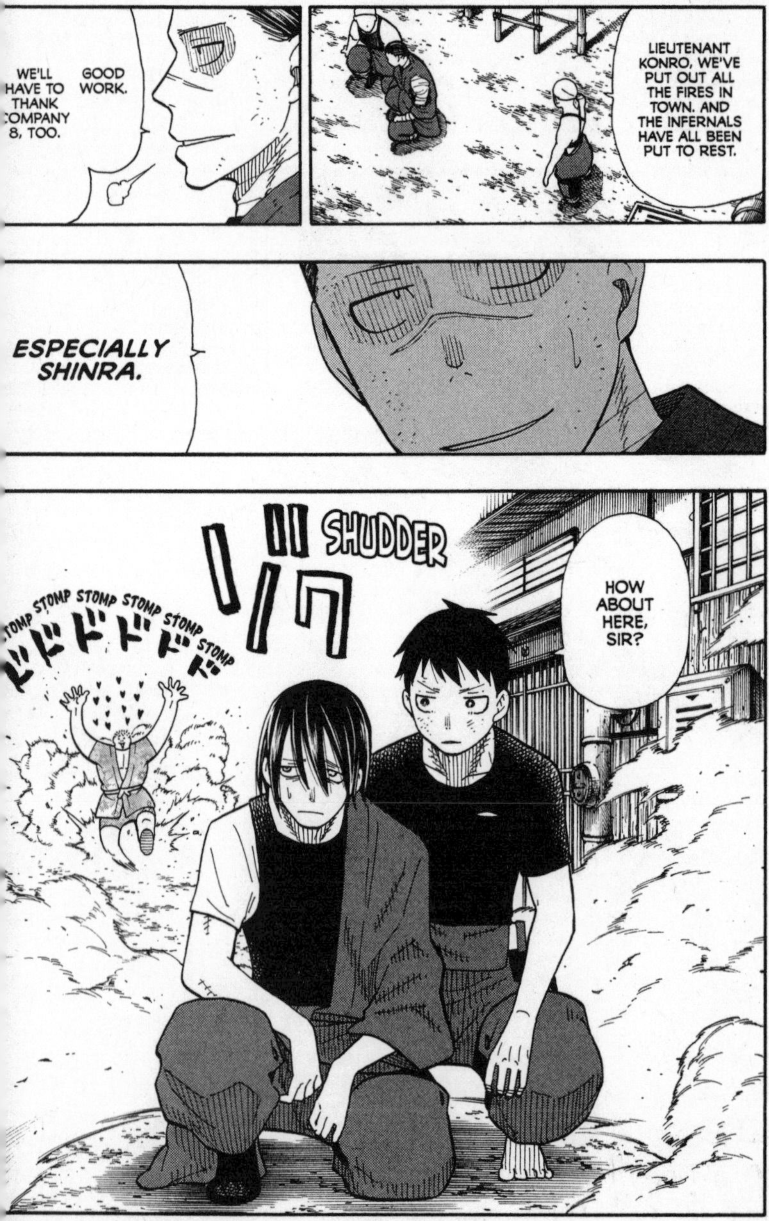

LIEUTENANT KONRO, WE'VE PUT OUT ALL THE FIRES IN TOWN. AND THE INFERNALS HAVE ALL BEEN PUT TO REST.
GOOD WORK.
WE'LL HAVE TO THANK COMPANY 8, TOO.
ESPECIALLY SHINRA.
HOW ABOUT HERE, SIR?
ビク
SHUDDER
ドドドドドド
STOMP STOMP STOMP STOMP STOMP STOMP

FIRE FORCE

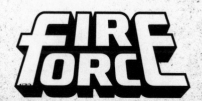

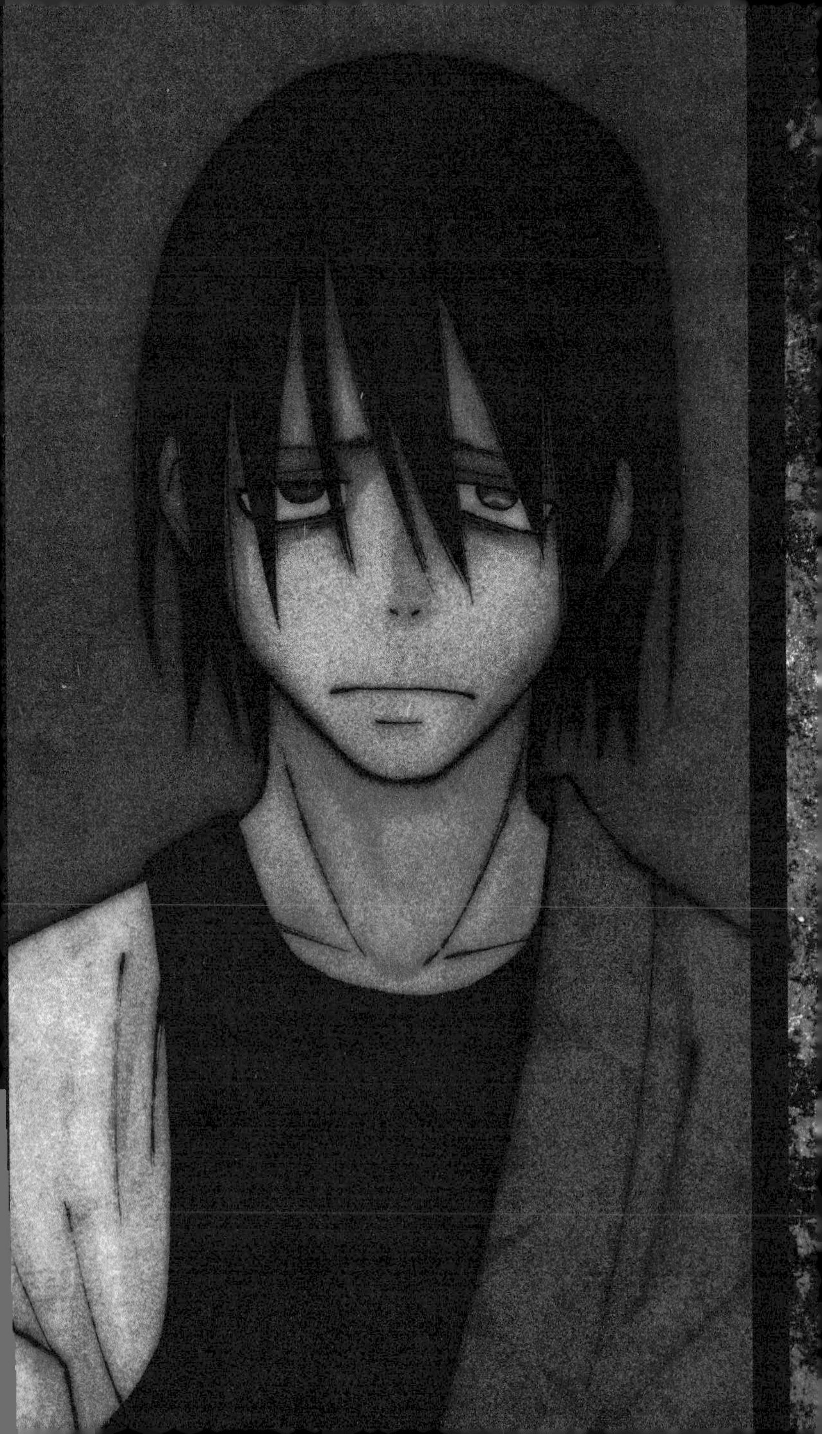

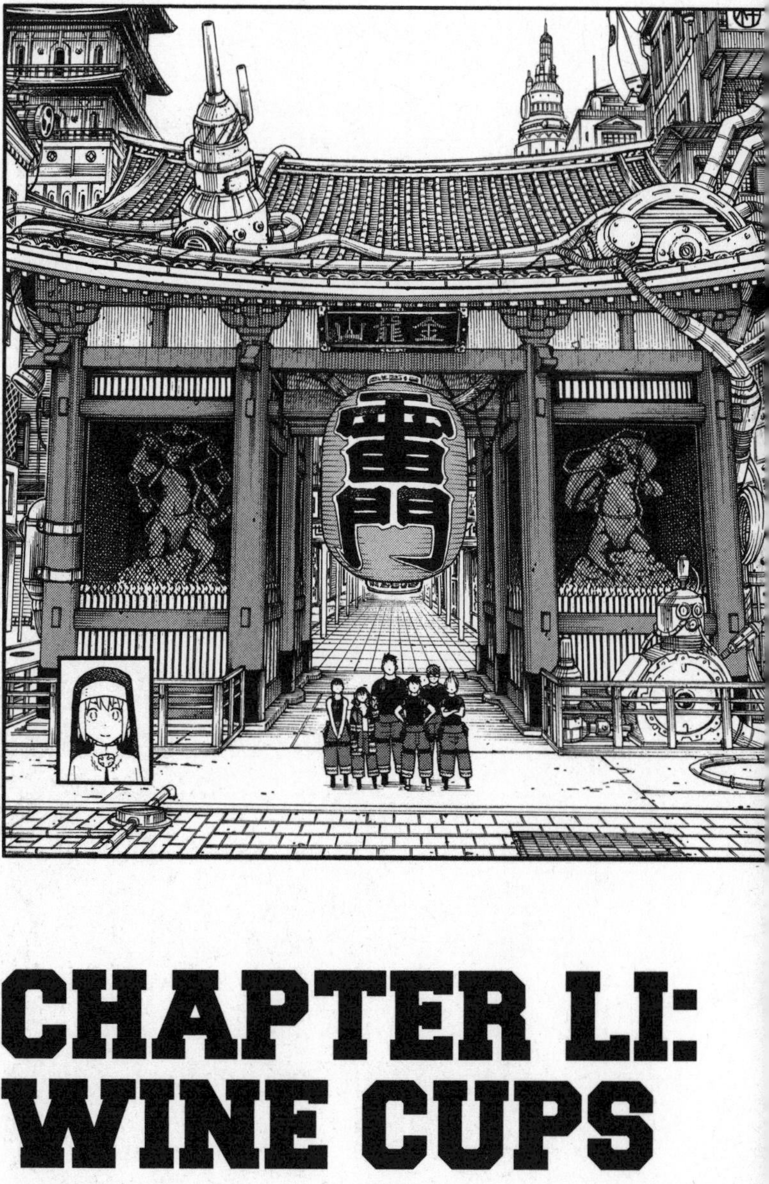
金龍山
雷門

CHAPTER LI: WINE CUPS

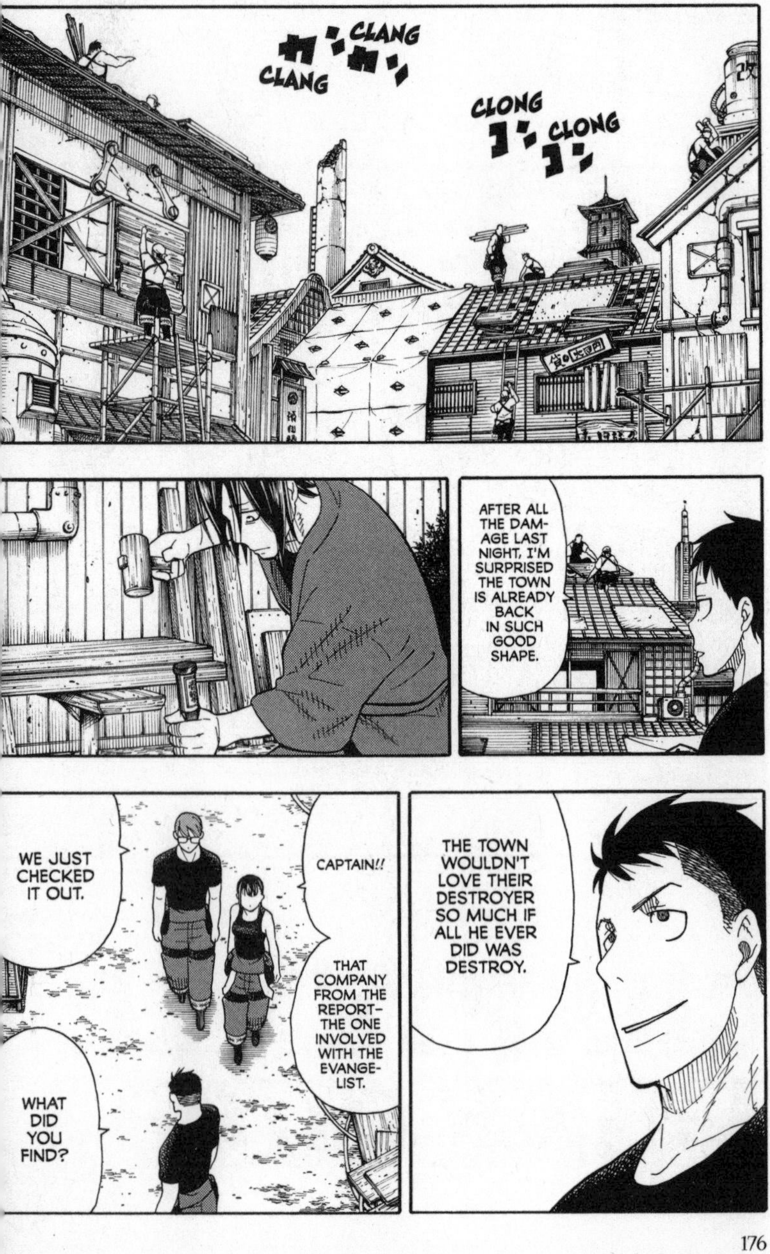
CLANG
CLANG
CLONG
CLONG
AFTER ALL THE DAMAGE LAST NIGHT, I'M SURPRISED THE TOWN IS ALREADY BACK IN SUCH GOOD SHAPE.
THE TOWN WOULDN'T LOVE THEIR DESTROYER SO MUCH IF ALL HE EVER DID WAS DESTROY.
CAPTAIN!!
THAT COMPANY FROM THE REPORT—THE ONE INVOLVED WITH THE EVANGELIST.
WE JUST CHECKED IT OUT.
WHAT DID YOU FIND?

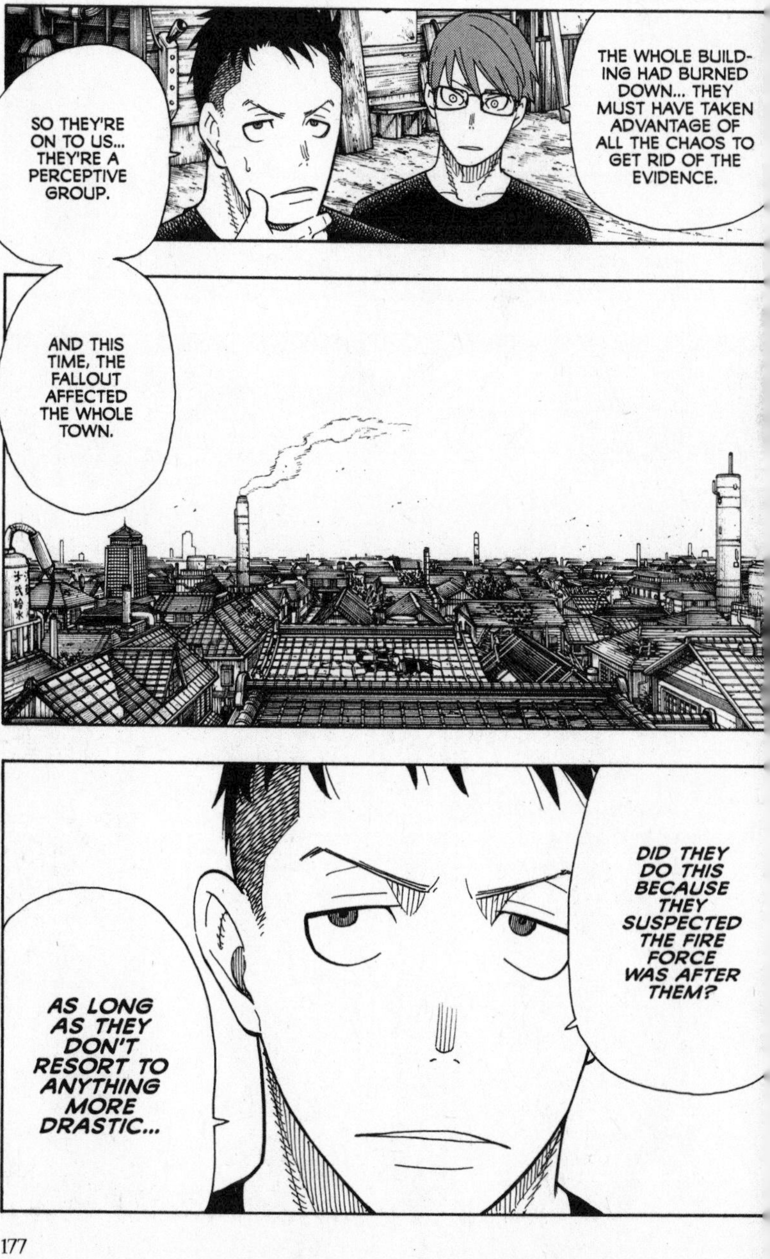
THE WHOLE BUILDING HAD BURNED DOWN... THEY MUST HAVE TAKEN ADVANTAGE OF ALL THE CHAOS TO GET RID OF THE EVIDENCE.
SO THEY'RE ON TO US... THEY'RE A PERCEPTIVE GROUP.
AND THIS TIME, THE FALLOUT AFFECTED THE WHOLE TOWN.
DID THEY DO THIS BECAUSE THEY SUSPECTED THE FIRE FORCE WAS AFTER THEM?
AS LONG AS THEY DON'T RESORT TO ANYTHING MORE DRASTIC...

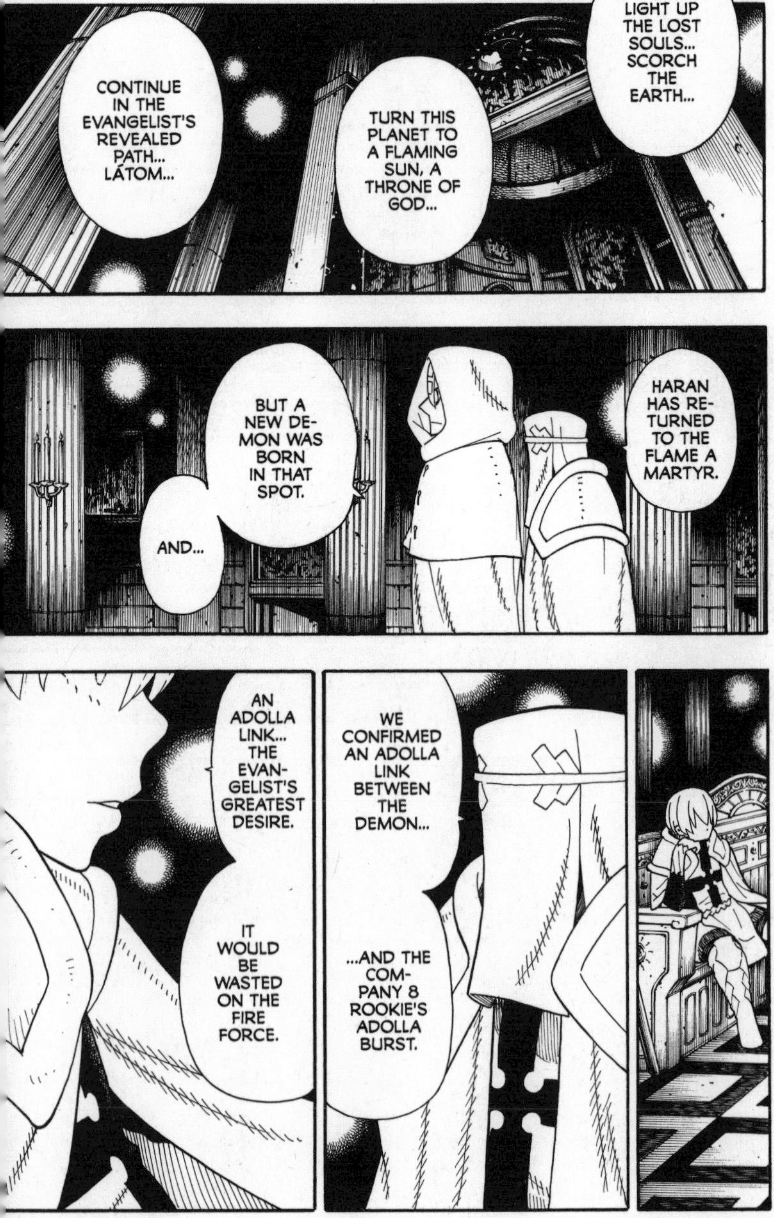
LIGHT UP THE LOST SOULS... SCORCH THE EARTH...
TURN THIS PLANET TO A FLAMING SUN, A THRONE OF GOD...
CONTINUE IN THE EVANGELIST'S REVEALED PATH... LÁTOM...
HARAN HAS RETURNED TO THE FLAME A MARTYR.
BUT A NEW DEMON WAS BORN IN THAT SPOT.
AND...
WE CONFIRMED AN ADOLLA LINK BETWEEN THE DEMON...
...AND THE COMPANY 8 ROOKIE'S ADOLLA BURST.
AN ADOLLA LINK... THE EVANGELIST'S GREATEST DESIRE.
IT WOULD BE WASTED ON THE FIRE FORCE.

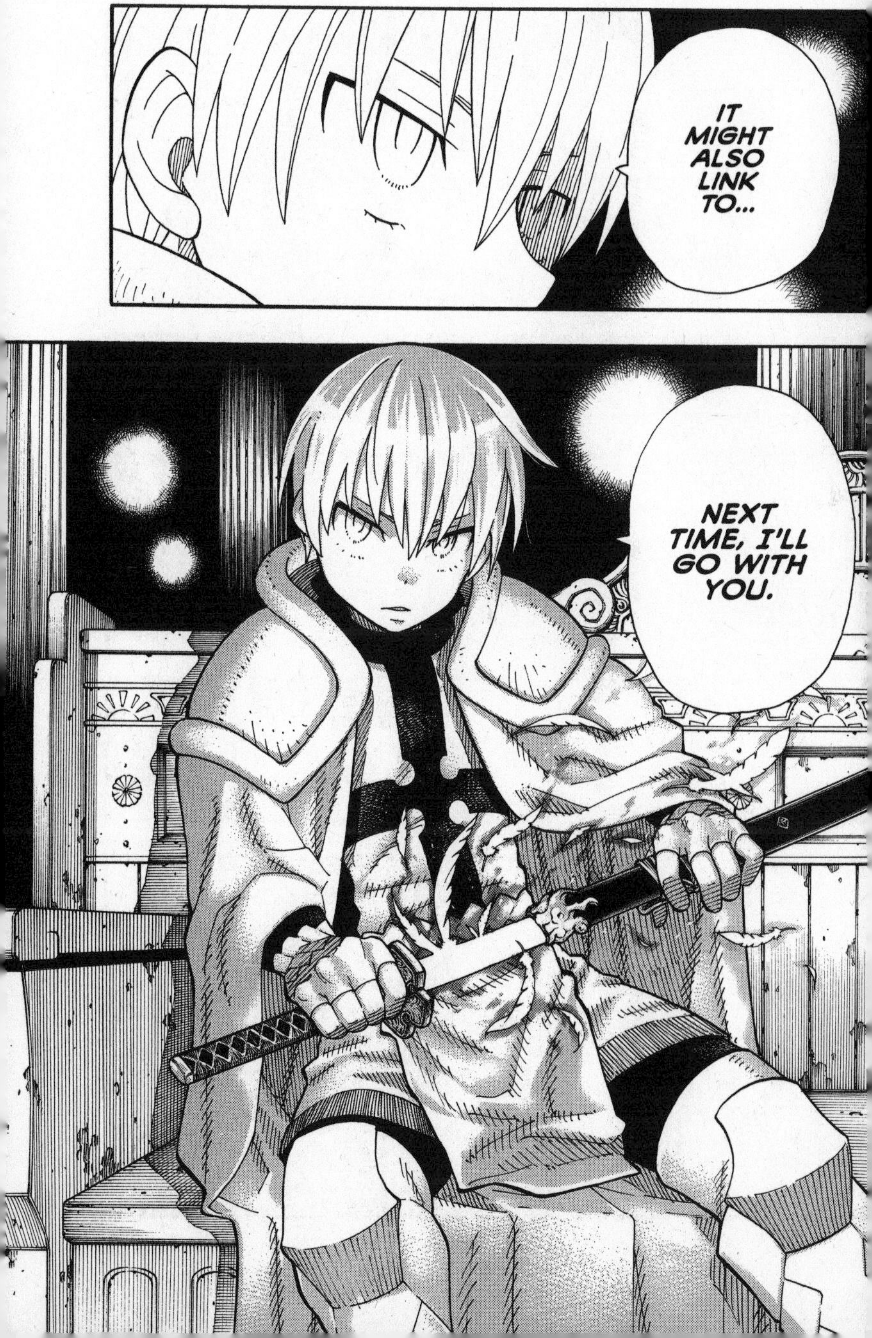
IT MIGHT ALSO LINK TO...
NEXT TIME, I'LL GO WITH YOU.

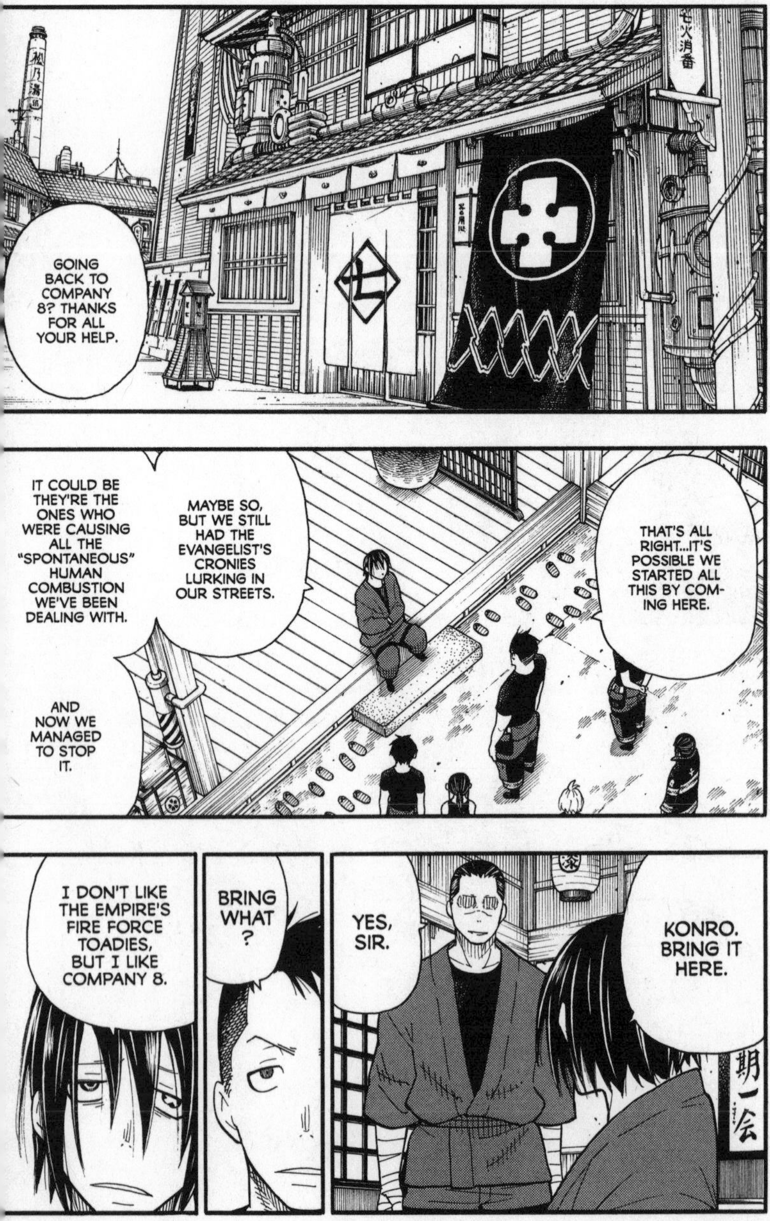
GOING BACK TO COMPANY 8? THANKS FOR ALL YOUR HELP.
THAT'S ALL RIGHT...IT'S POSSIBLE WE STARTED ALL THIS BY COM-ING HERE.
MAYBE SO, BUT WE STILL HAD THE EVANGELIST'S CRONIES LURKING IN OUR STREETS.
IT COULD BE THEY'RE THE ONES WHO WERE CAUSING ALL THE "SPONTANEOUS" HUMAN COMBUSTION WE'VE BEEN DEALING WITH.
AND NOW WE MANAGED TO STOP IT.
KONRO. BRING IT HERE.
YES, SIR.
BRING WHAT?
I DON'T LIKE THE EMPIRE'S FIRE FORCE TOADIES, BUT I LIKE COMPANY 8.

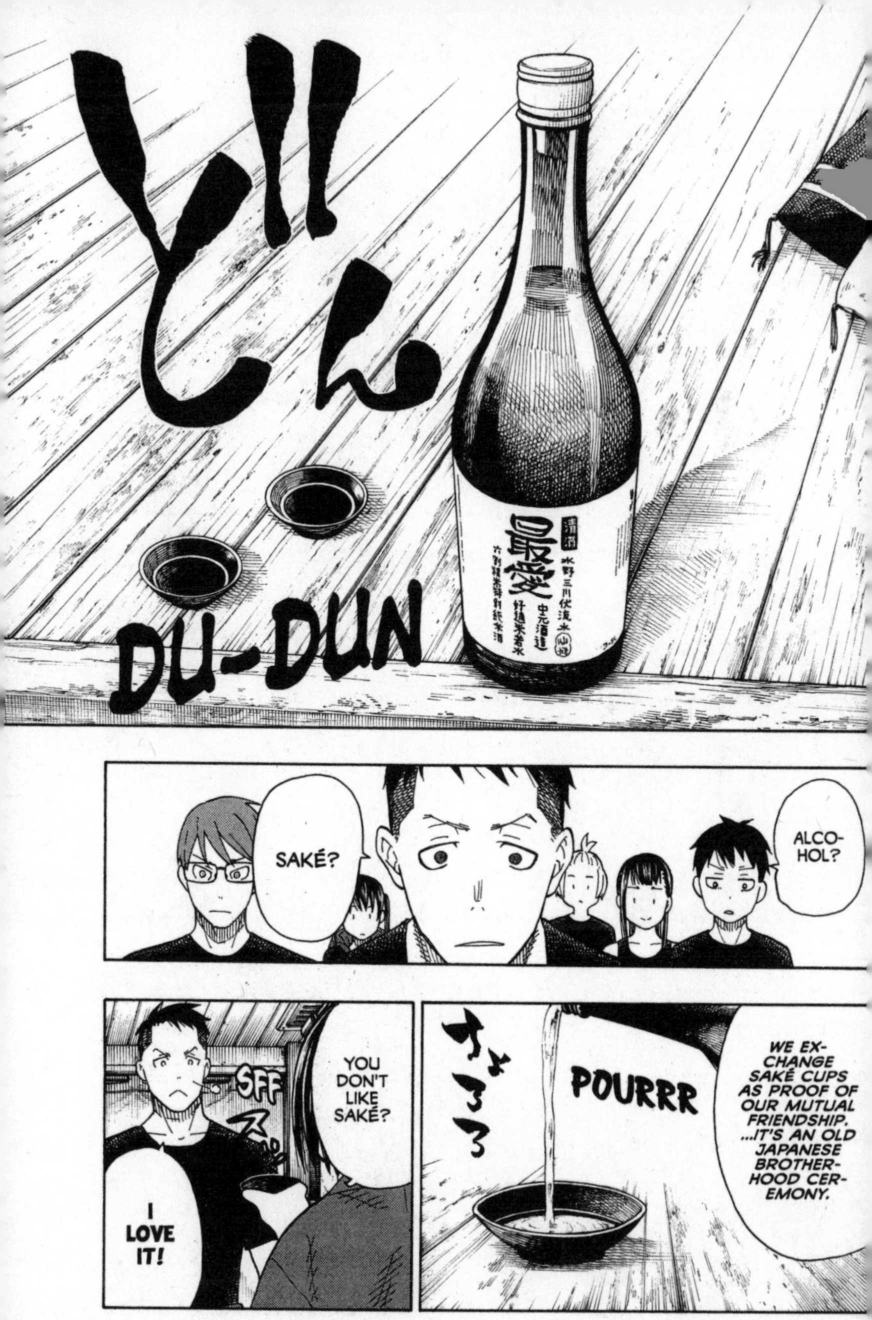
どん
DU-DUN
清酒
最愛
ALCO-HOL?
SAKÉ?
POURRR
WE EX-CHANGE SAKÉ CUPS AS PROOF OF OUR MUTUAL FRIENDSHIP. ...IT'S AN OLD JAPANESE BROTHER-HOOD CER-EMONY.
YOU DON'T LIKE SAKÉ?
SFF
I LOVE IT!

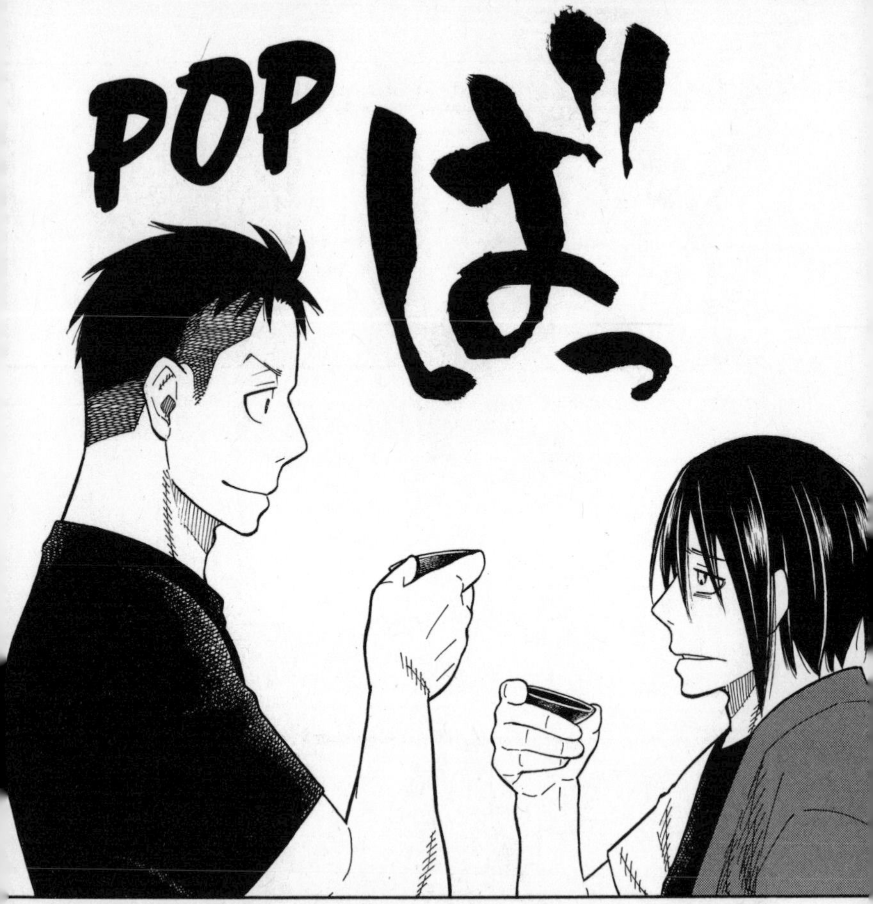
POP
ばっ

Sign: Ruffians

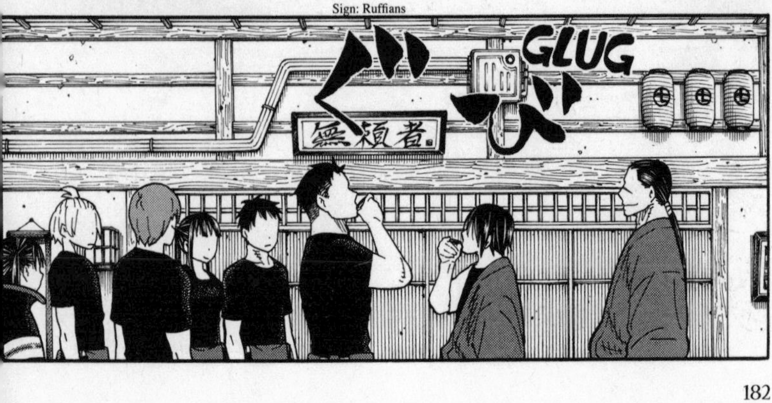
GLUG
くいっ
無頼者

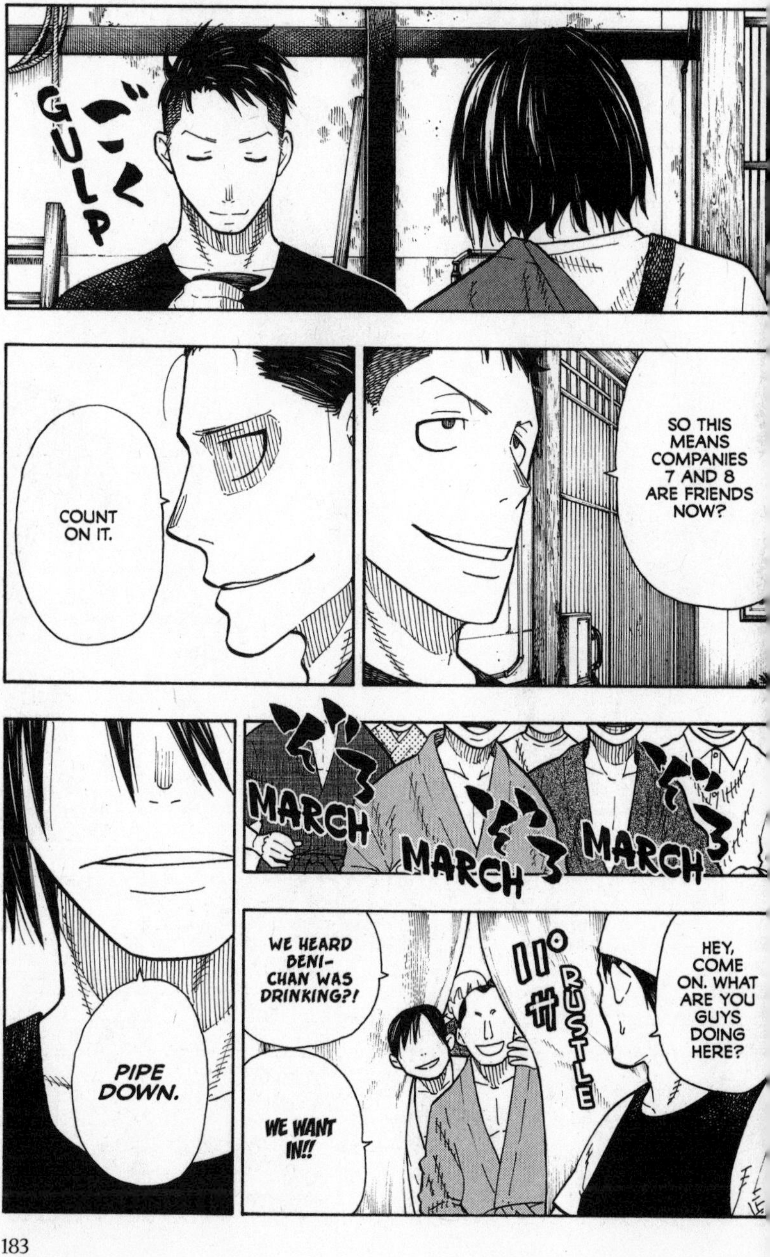
GULP
SO THIS MEANS COMPANIES 7 AND 8 ARE FRIENDS NOW?
COUNT ON IT.
MARCH
MARCH
MARCH
HEY, COME ON. WHAT ARE YOU GUYS DOING HERE?
RUSTLE
WE HEARD BENI-CHAN WAS DRINKING?!
WE WANT IN!!
PIPE DOWN.

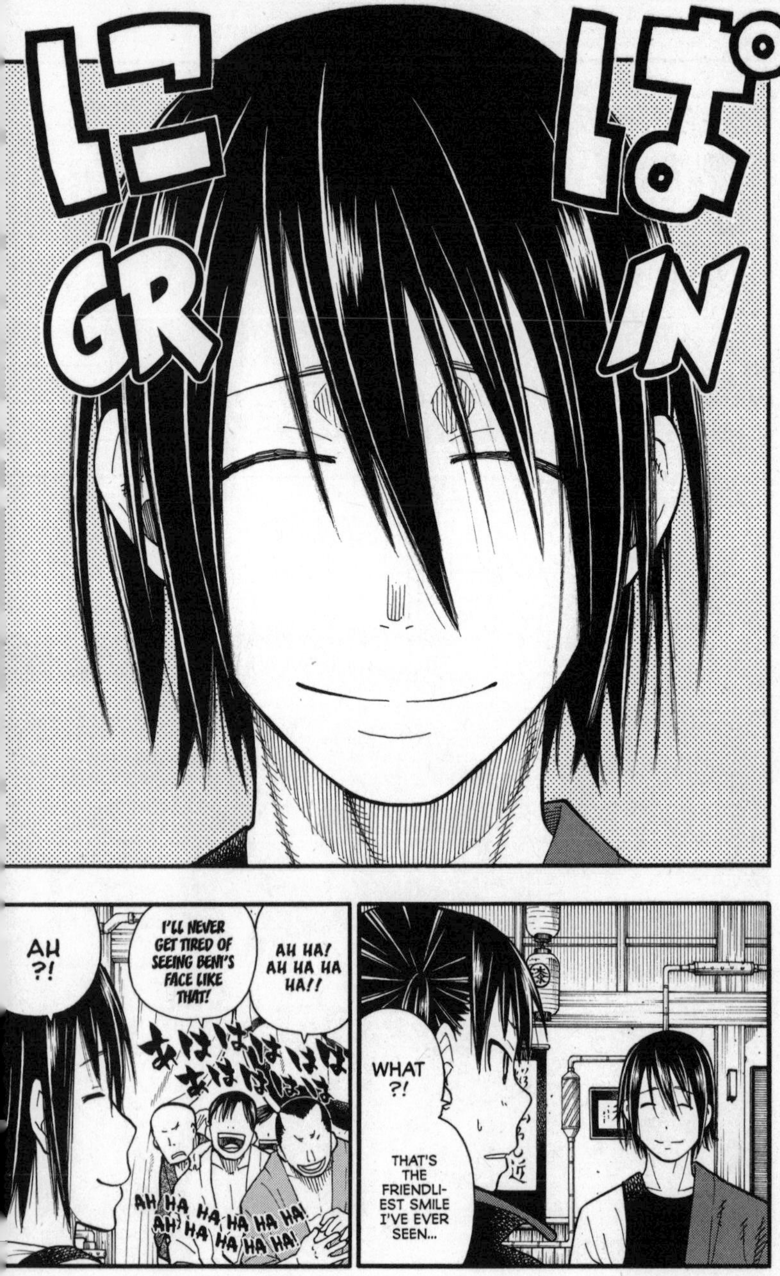

にぱ
GRIN
WHAT?!
THAT'S THE FRIENDLI-EST SMILE I'VE EVER SEEN...
AH HA! AH HA HA HA!!
I'LL NEVER GET TIRED OF SEEING BENI'S FACE LIKE THAT!
AH?!
あははははは
あはははは
AH HA HA HA HA HA!
AH HA HA HA HA!

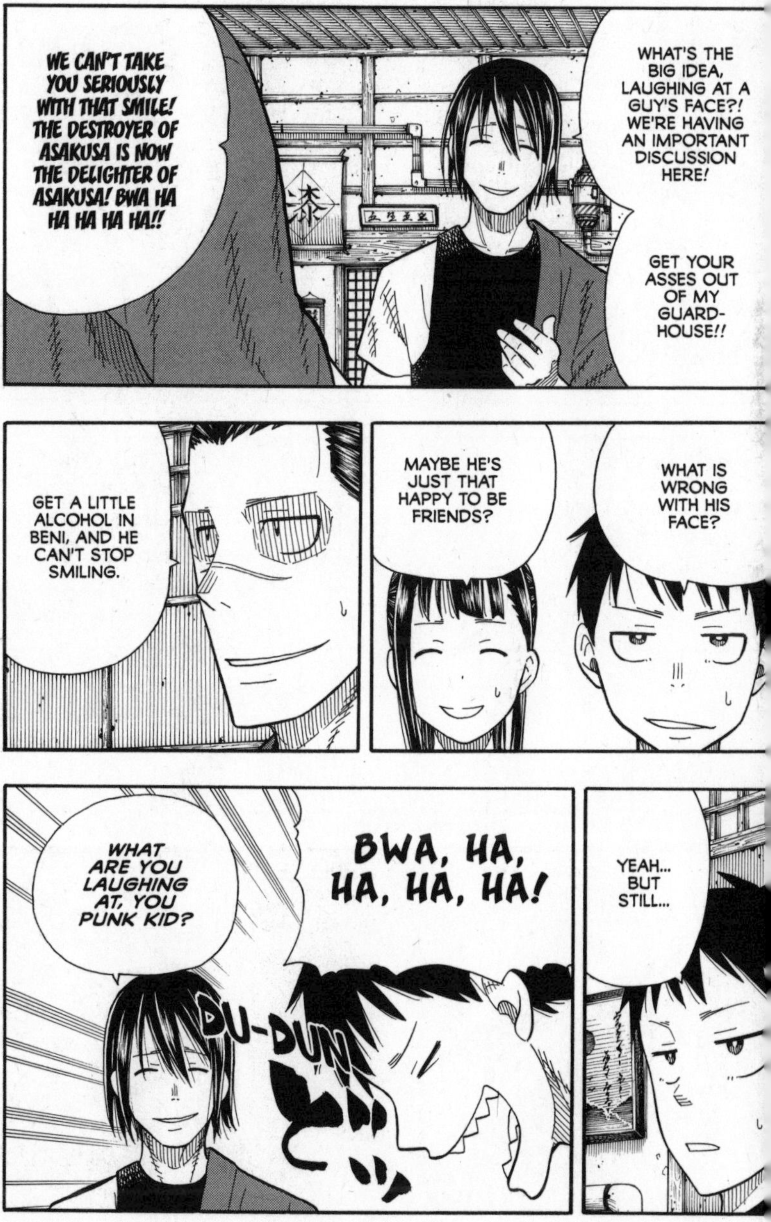
WHAT'S THE BIG IDEA, LAUGHING AT A GUY'S FACE?! WE'RE HAVING AN IMPORTANT DISCUSSION HERE!
GET YOUR ASSES OUT OF MY GUARD-HOUSE!!
WE CAN'T TAKE YOU SERIOUSLY WITH THAT SMILE! THE DESTROYER OF ASAKUSA IS NOW THE DELIGHTER OF ASAKUSA! BWA HA HA HA HA HA!!
WHAT IS WRONG WITH HIS FACE?
MAYBE HE'S JUST THAT HAPPY TO BE FRIENDS?
GET A LITTLE ALCOHOL IN BENI, AND HE CAN'T STOP SMILING.
YEAH... BUT STILL...
BWA, HA, HA, HA, HA!
WHAT ARE YOU LAUGHING AT, YOU PUNK KID?
DU-DUN

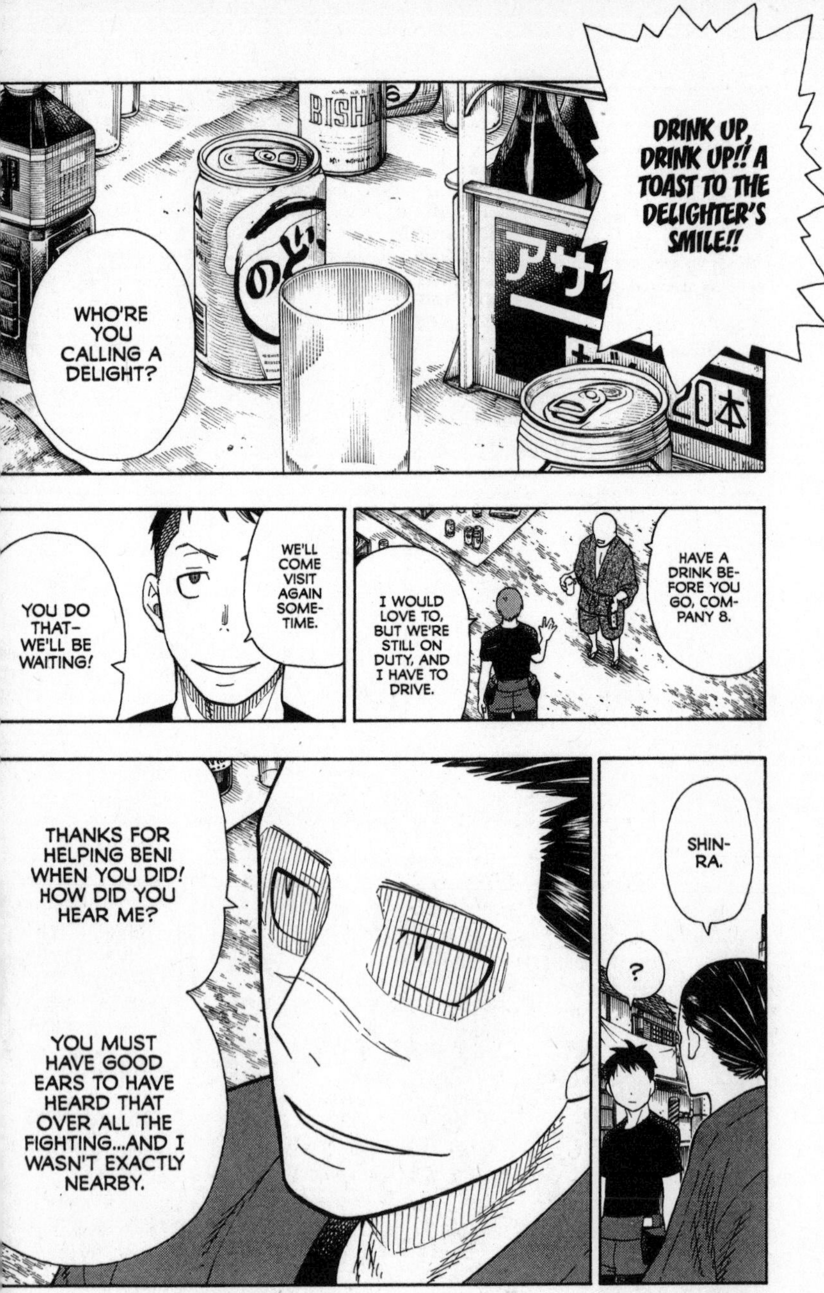
DRINK UP, DRINK UP!! A TOAST TO THE DELIGHTER'S SMILE!!
WHO'RE YOU CALLING A DELIGHT?
HAVE A DRINK BEFORE YOU GO, COMPANY 8.
I WOULD LOVE TO, BUT WE'RE STILL ON DUTY, AND I HAVE TO DRIVE.
WE'LL COME VISIT AGAIN SOMETIME.
YOU DO THAT—WE'LL BE WAITING!
SHINRA.
?
THANKS FOR HELPING BENI WHEN YOU DID! HOW DID YOU HEAR ME?
YOU MUST HAVE GOOD EARS TO HAVE HEARD THAT OVER ALL THE FIGHTING...AND I WASN'T EXACTLY NEARBY.

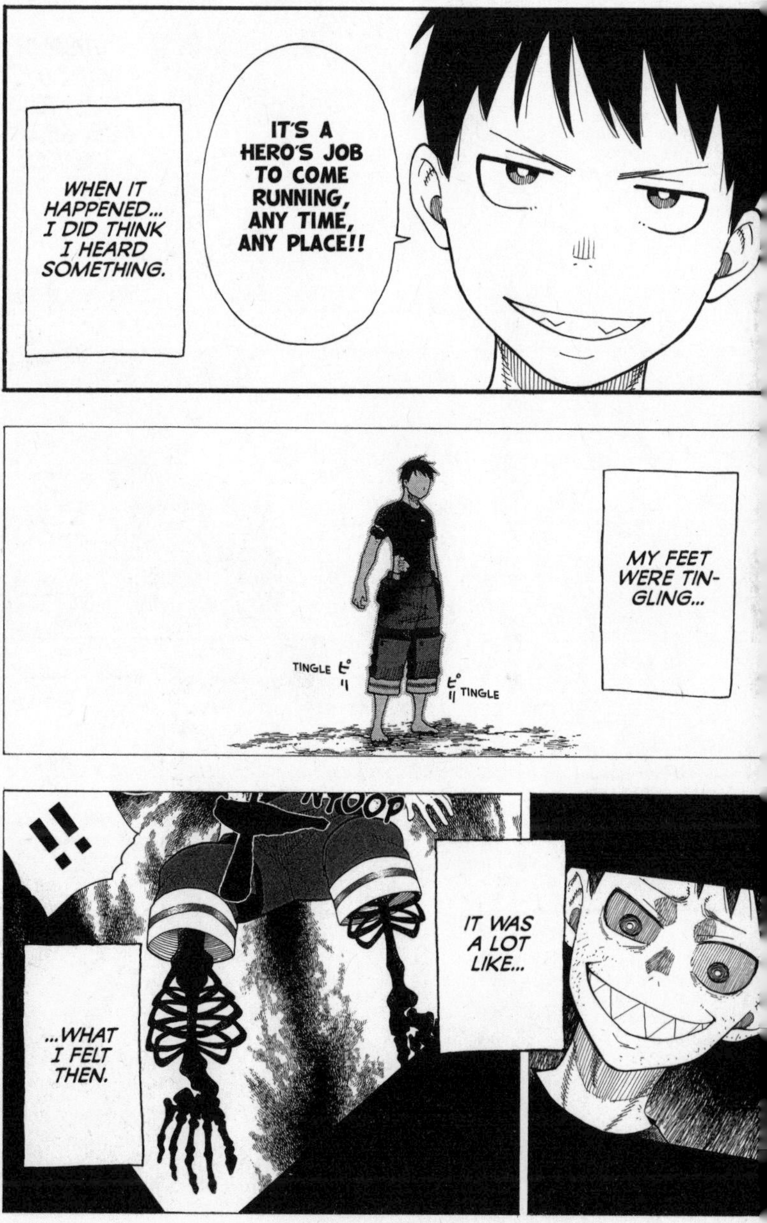
IT'S A HERO'S JOB TO COME RUNNING, ANY TIME, ANY PLACE!!
WHEN IT HAPPENED... I DID THINK I HEARD SOMETHING.
MY FEET WERE TINGLING...
TINGLE
ピリ
TINGLE
ピリ
IT WAS A LOT LIKE...
!!
...WHAT I FELT THEN.

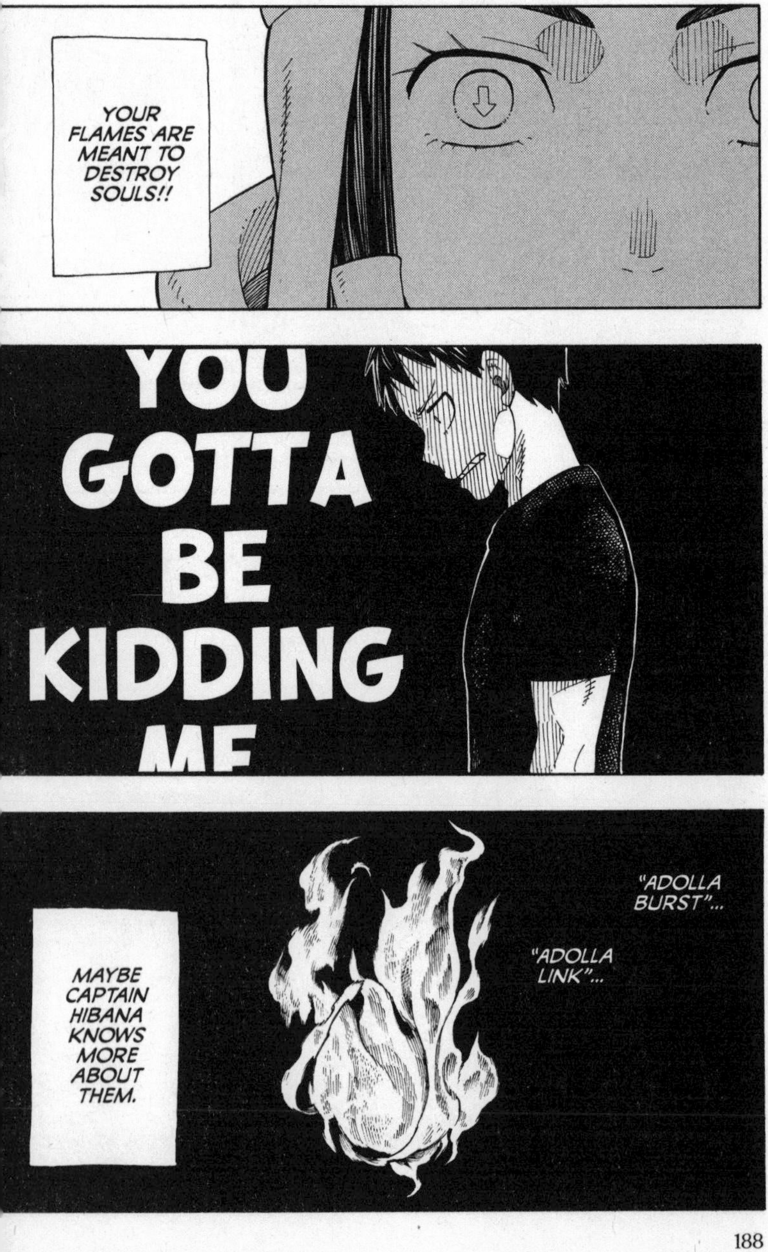
YOUR FLAMES ARE MEANT TO DESTROY SOULS!!
YOU GOTTA BE KIDDING ME
"ADOLLA BURST"...
"ADOLLA LINK"...
MAYBE CAPTAIN HIBANA KNOWS MORE ABOUT THEM.

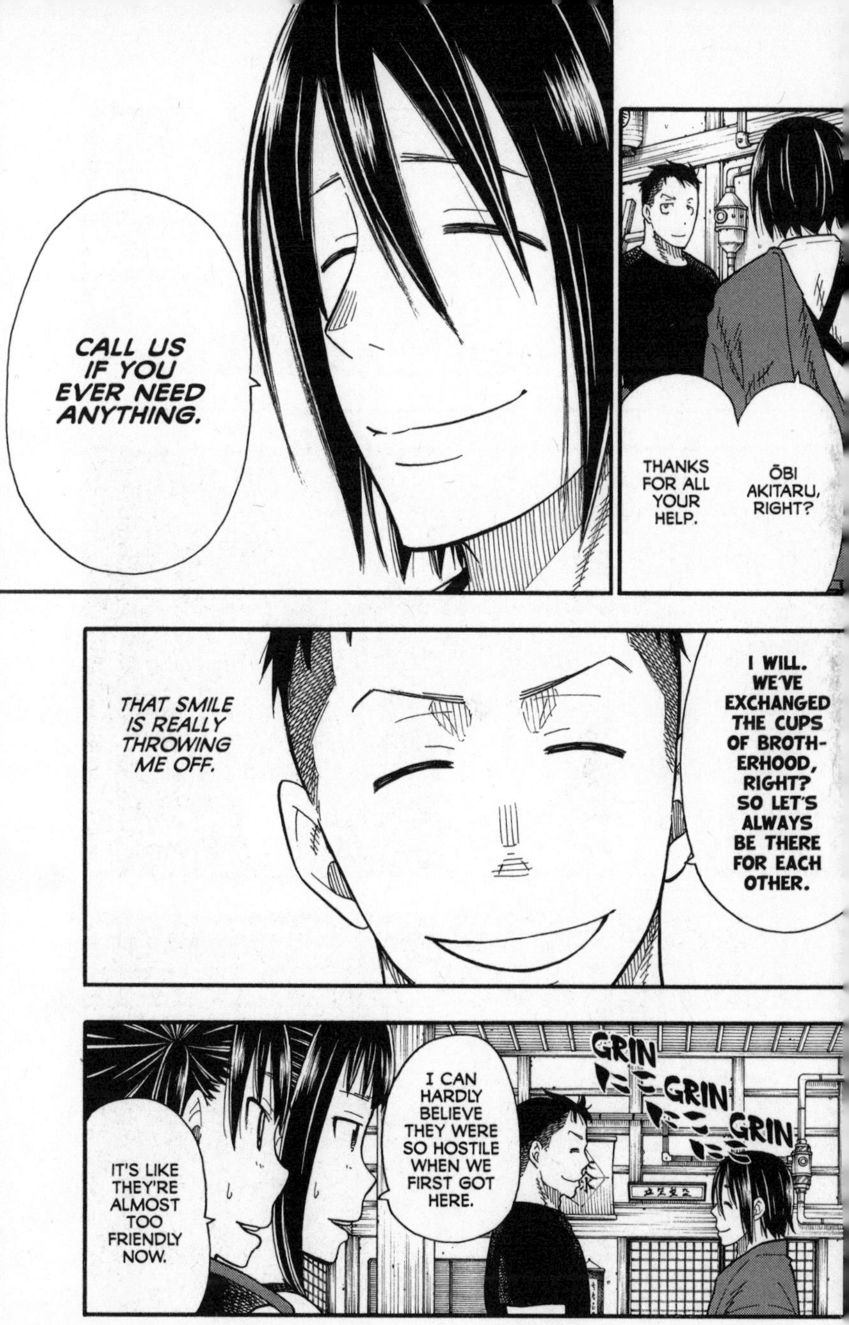
ŌBI AKITARU, RIGHT?
THANKS FOR ALL YOUR HELP.
CALL US IF YOU EVER NEED ANYTHING.
I WILL. WE'VE EXCHANGED THE CUPS OF BROTHERHOOD, RIGHT? SO LET'S ALWAYS BE THERE FOR EACH OTHER.
THAT SMILE IS REALLY THROWING ME OFF.
GRIN
GRIN
GRIN
I CAN HARDLY BELIEVE THEY WERE SO HOSTILE WHEN WE FIRST GOT HERE.
IT'S LIKE THEY'RE ALMOST TOO FRIENDLY NOW.

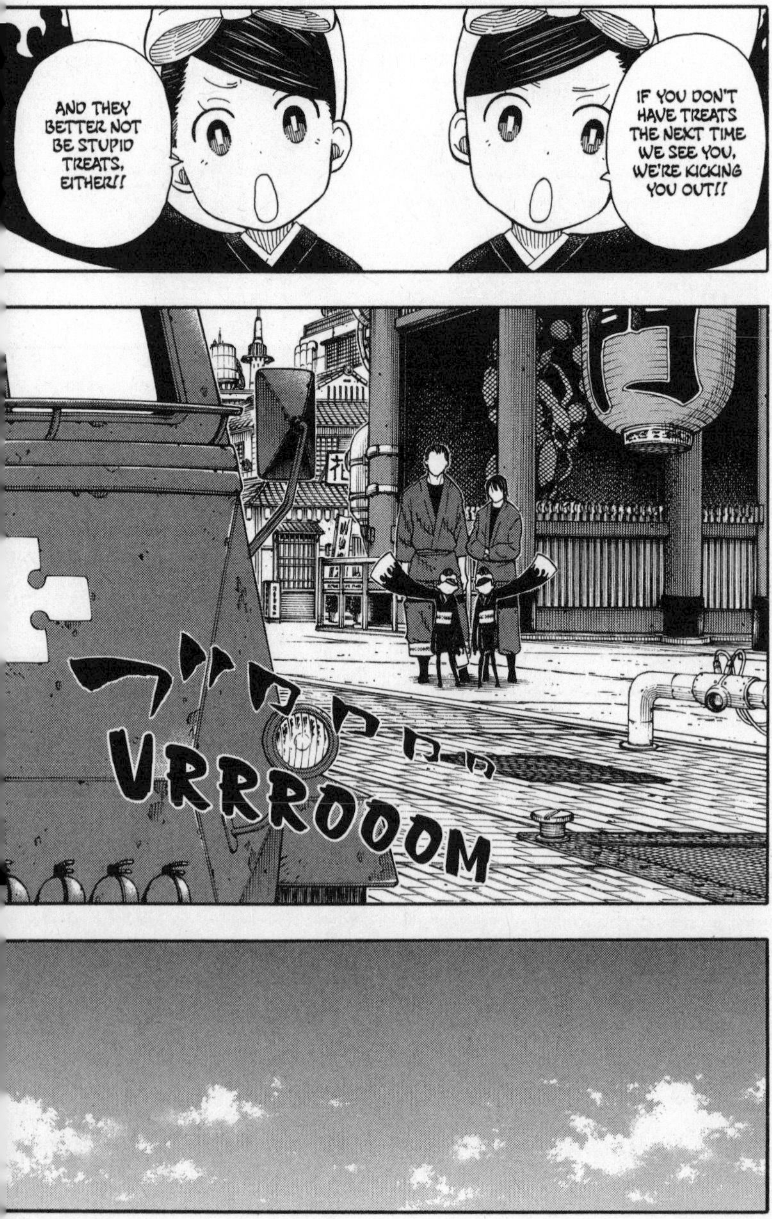
IF YOU DON'T HAVE TREATS THE NEXT TIME WE SEE YOU, WE'RE KICKING YOU OUT!!
AND THEY BETTER NOT BE STUPID TREATS, EITHER!!
VRRROOOM

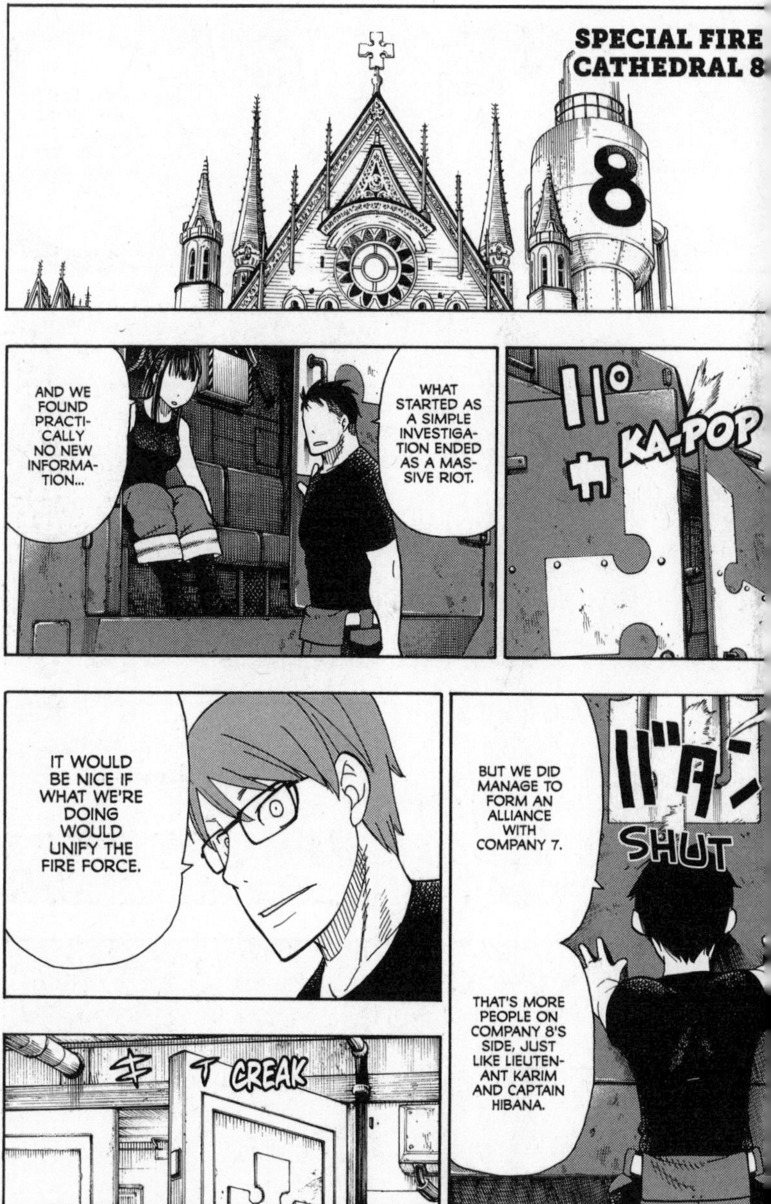
SPECIAL FIRE CATHEDRAL 8
8
パカ
KA-POP
WHAT STARTED AS A SIMPLE INVESTIGATION ENDED AS A MASSIVE RIOT.
AND WE FOUND PRACTICALLY NO NEW INFORMATION...
バタン
SHUT
BUT WE DID MANAGE TO FORM AN ALLIANCE WITH COMPANY 7.
THAT'S MORE PEOPLE ON COMPANY 8'S SIDE, JUST LIKE LIEUTENANT KARIM AND CAPTAIN HIBANA.
IT WOULD BE NICE IF WHAT WE'RE DOING WOULD UNIFY THE FIRE FORCE.
キィ
CREAK

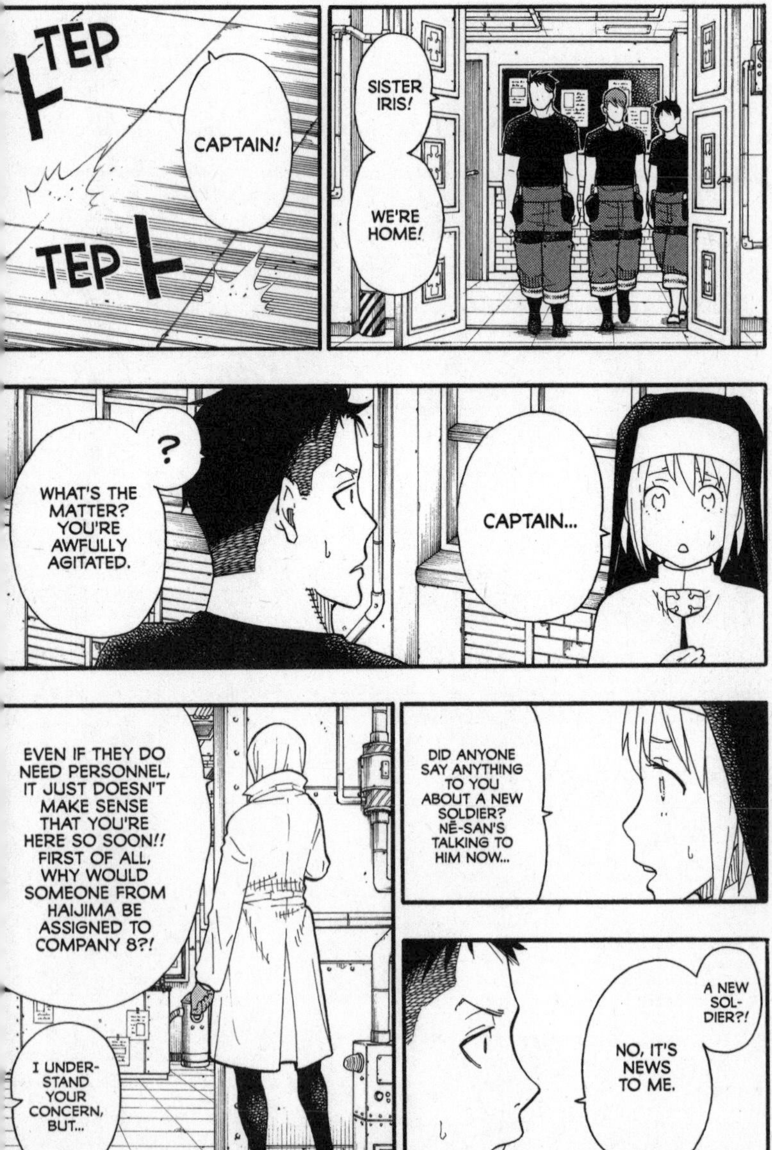
SISTER IRIS!
WE'RE HOME!
TEP
TEP
CAPTAIN!
CAPTAIN...
?
WHAT'S THE MATTER? YOU'RE AWFULLY AGITATED.
DID ANYONE SAY ANYTHING TO YOU ABOUT A NEW SOLDIER? NĒ-SAN'S TALKING TO HIM NOW...
A NEW SOL-DIER?!
NO, IT'S NEWS TO ME.
EVEN IF THEY DO NEED PERSONNEL, IT JUST DOESN'T MAKE SENSE THAT YOU'RE HERE SO SOON!! FIRST OF ALL, WHY WOULD SOMEONE FROM HAIJIMA BE ASSIGNED TO COMPANY 8?!
I UNDER-STAND YOUR CONCERN, BUT...

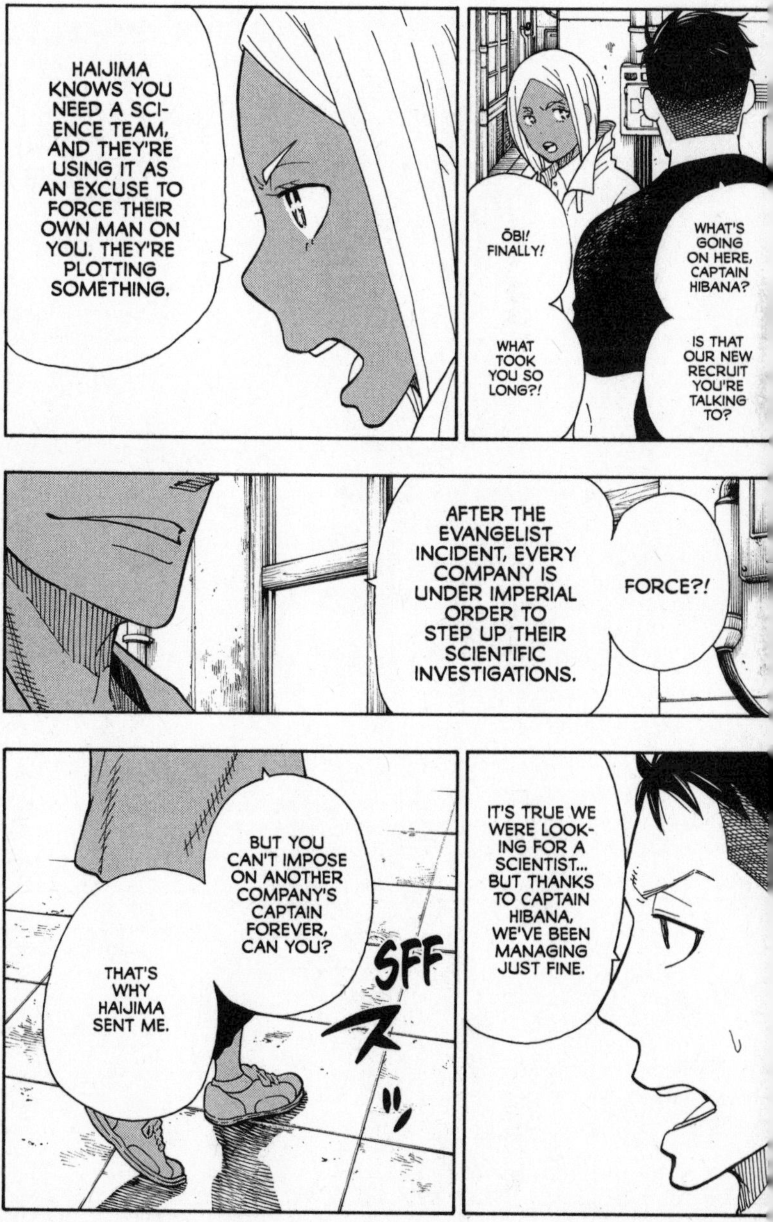
WHAT'S GOING ON HERE, CAPTAIN HIBANA?
IS THAT OUR NEW RECRUIT YOU'RE TALKING TO?
ŌBI! FINALLY!
WHAT TOOK YOU SO LONG?!
HAIJIMA KNOWS YOU NEED A SCIENCE TEAM, AND THEY'RE USING IT AS AN EXCUSE TO FORCE THEIR OWN MAN ON YOU. THEY'RE PLOTTING SOMETHING.
FORCE?!
AFTER THE EVANGELIST INCIDENT, EVERY COMPANY IS UNDER IMPERIAL ORDER TO STEP UP THEIR SCIENTIFIC INVESTIGATIONS.
IT'S TRUE WE WERE LOOKING FOR A SCIENTIST... BUT THANKS TO CAPTAIN HIBANA, WE'VE BEEN MANAGING JUST FINE.
BUT YOU CAN'T IMPOSE ON ANOTHER COMPANY'S CAPTAIN FOREVER, CAN YOU?
THAT'S WHY HAIJIMA SENT ME.
SFF

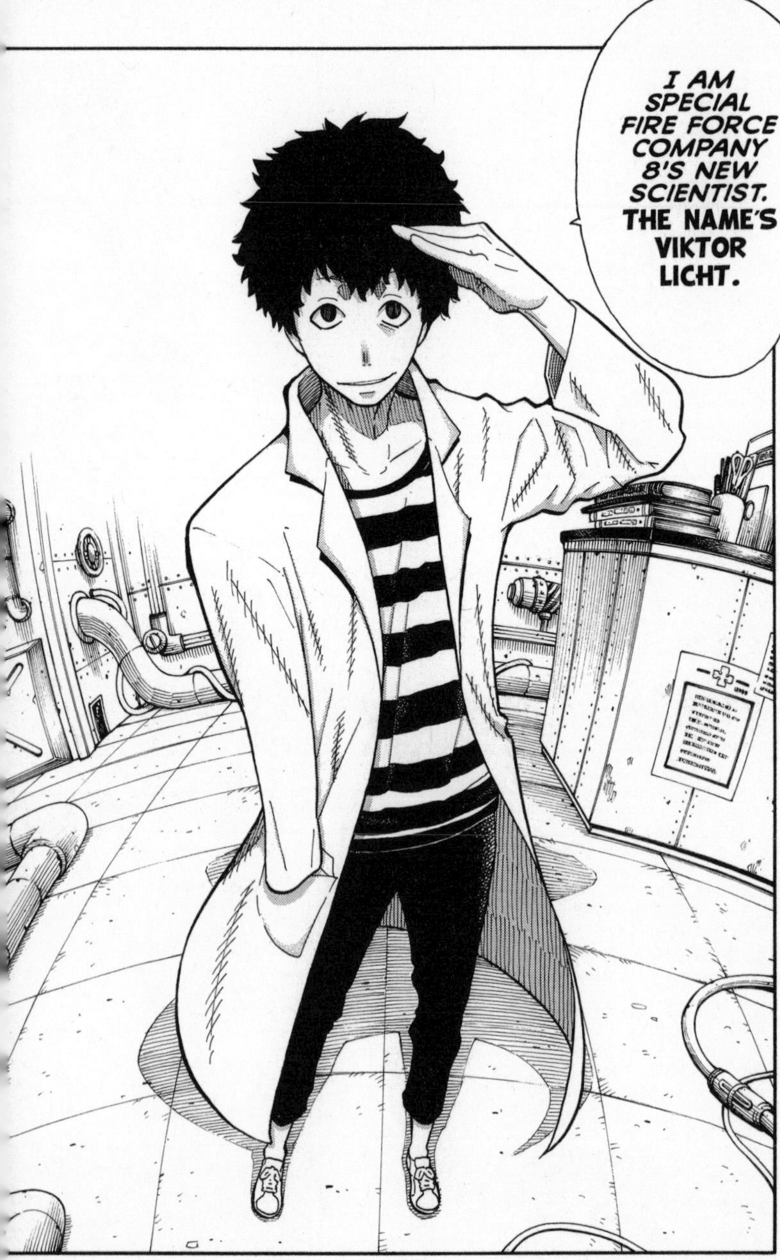
I AM SPECIAL FIRE FORCE COMPANY 8'S NEW SCIENTIST. THE NAME'S VIKTOR LICHT.

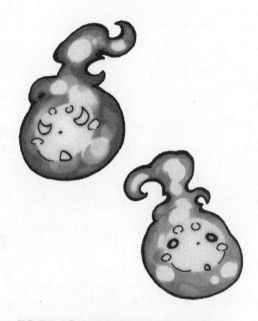

TO BE CONTINUED IN VOLUME 7!!

Translation Notes:

.s there a fox going around, page 48

n Japanese folklore, it is believed hat foxes are not only cunning and ly, but have shape-shifting powers. n the legends, they will transform nto a human, possibly a friend or cquaintance of their victim, to leceive people and cause mischief, eading to the saying, "As if tricked y a fox." While it is unclear whether r not Captain Shinmon believes in ctual transforming foxes, with all he accusations flying around, it's a reasonable idiom for him to think of.

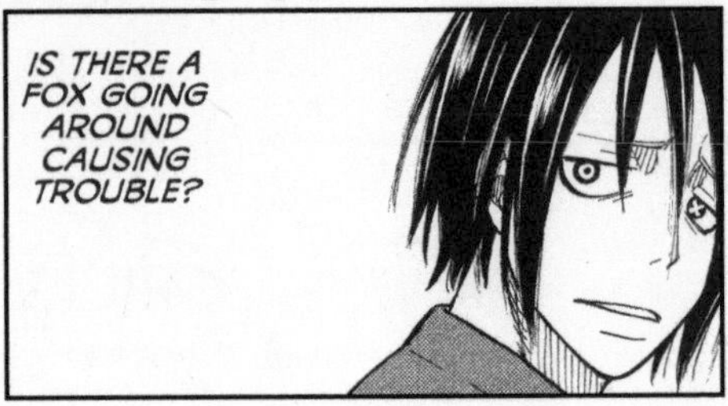
IS THERE A FOX GOING AROUND CAUSING TROUBLE?

ighting festival, page 118

n this case, a fighting festival is exactly what it sounds like—a big party where veryone beats each other up. The reader may also be interested to know that there are, in fact, fighting festivals in Japan, but not of this variety. A common feature of a Japanese festival is the carrying of the *mikoshi*, a portable shrine for transporting a deity. At a *kenka matsuri*, or fighting festival, there are multiple *mikoshi*, and hose carrying them will smash them into each other, as if the gods inside are fighting. This contest is considered to be pleasing to the gods.

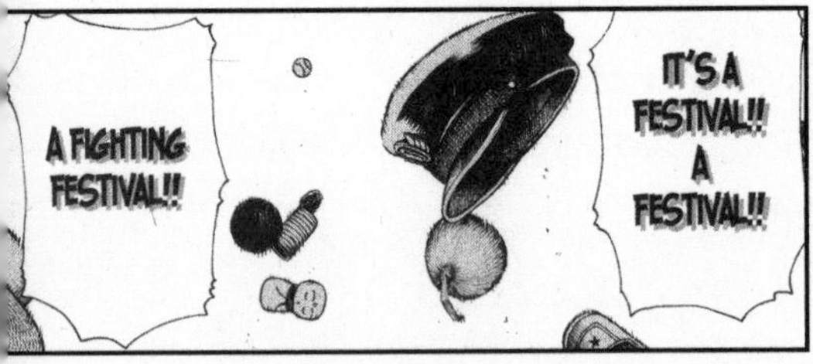
IT'S A FESTIVAL!! A FESTIVAL!!
A FIGHTING FESTIVAL!!

Grudjealous, page 170

The readers may have noticed that Yona ends to use some odd words. This one is a ombination of "grudge" and "jealous," based n the original Japanese *jerashitto*, which ombines the English word "jealousy" with he Japanese word for the term, *shitto*. It nay or may not have been inspired by the character from the *Super Sentai* (Japanese *Power Rangers*) series, *Kaizoku Sentai Gokaiger* (*Pirate Rangers Gokaiger*).

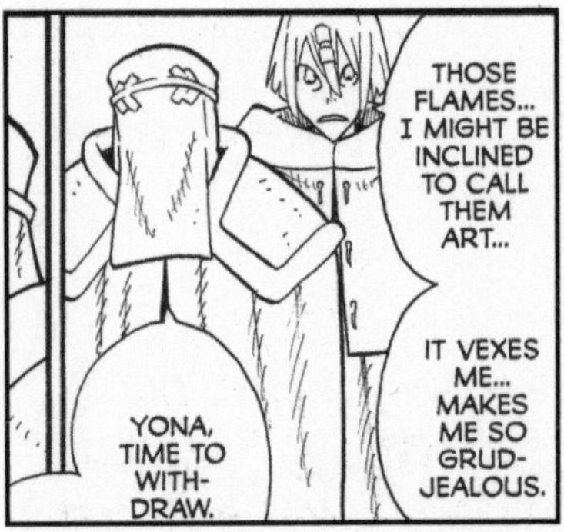
THOSE FLAMES... I MIGHT BE INCLINED TO CALL THEM ART...
IT VEXES ME... MAKES ME SO GRUD-JEALOUS.
YONA, TIME TO WITH-DRAW.

FIRE FORCE

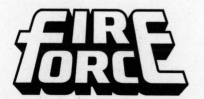

AFTERWORD MANGA: ATSUSHIYA

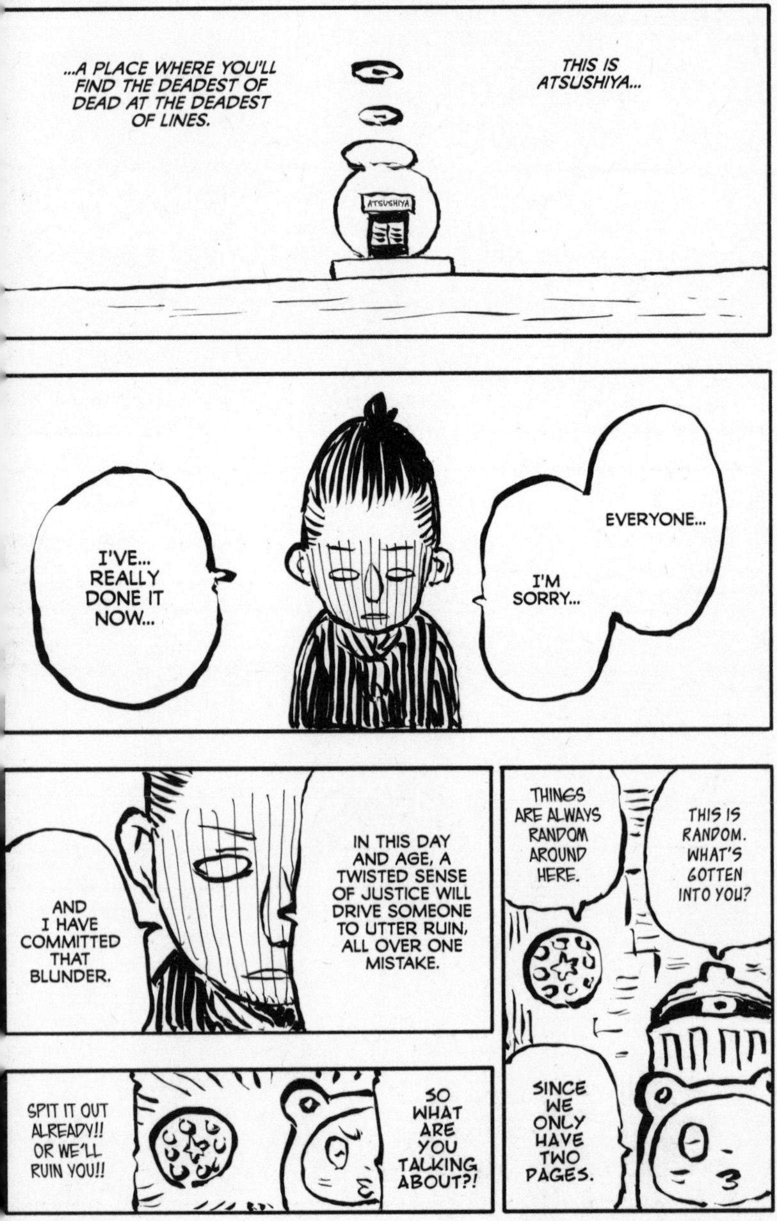
THIS IS ATSUSHIYA...
...A PLACE WHERE YOU'LL FIND THE DEADEST OF DEAD AT THE DEADEST OF LINES.
ATSUSHIYA
EVERYONE...
I'M SORRY...
I'VE... REALLY DONE IT NOW...
THIS IS RANDOM. WHAT'S GOTTEN INTO YOU?
THINGS ARE ALWAYS RANDOM AROUND HERE.
SINCE WE ONLY HAVE TWO PAGES.
IN THIS DAY AND AGE, A TWISTED SENSE OF JUSTICE WILL DRIVE SOMEONE TO UTTER RUIN, ALL OVER ONE MISTAKE.
AND I HAVE COMMITTED THAT BLUNDER.
SO WHAT ARE YOU TALKING ABOUT?!
SPIT IT OUT ALREADY!! OR WE'LL RUIN YOU!!

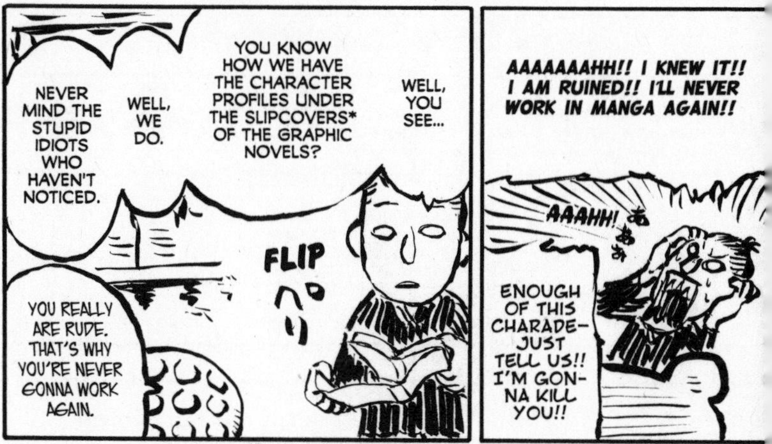
AAAAAAAHH!! I KNEW IT!! I AM RUINED!! I'LL NEVER WORK IN MANGA AGAIN!!
AAAHH!
ENOUGH OF THIS CHARADE— JUST TELL US!! I'M GONNA KILL YOU!!
WELL, YOU SEE...
YOU KNOW HOW WE HAVE THE CHARACTER PROFILES UNDER THE SLIPCOVERS* OF THE GRAPHIC NOVELS?
WELL, WE DO.
NEVER MIND THE STUPID IDIOTS WHO HAVEN'T NOTICED.
FLIP
YOU REALLY ARE RUDE. THAT'S WHY YOU'RE NEVER GONNA WORK AGAIN.

*Found in the back of the English releases.

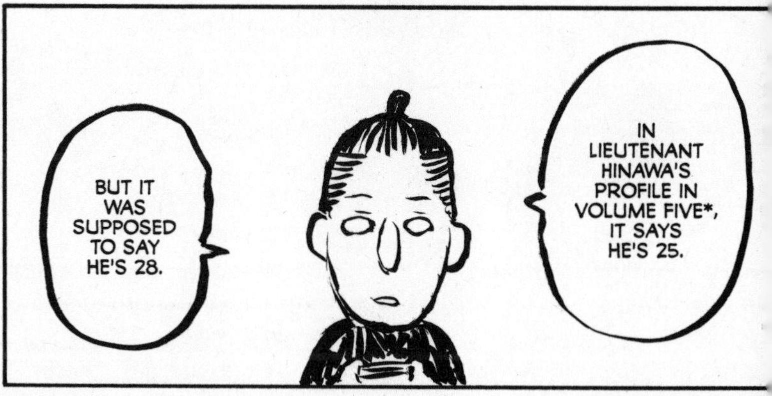
IN LIEUTENANT HINAWA'S PROFILE IN VOLUME FIVE*, IT SAYS HE'S 25.
BUT IT WAS SUPPOSED TO SAY HE'S 28.

*This volume of the English release

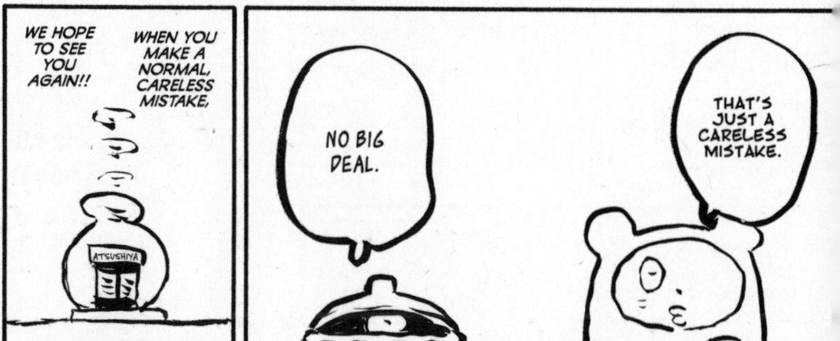
THAT'S JUST A CARELESS MISTAKE.
NO BIG DEAL.
WHEN YOU MAKE A NORMAL, CARELESS MISTAKE,
WE HOPE TO SEE YOU AGAIN!!
ATSUSHIYA

MAKI OZE

AFFILIATION:
SPECIAL FIRE FORCE COMPANY 8

RANK:
FIRST CLASS FIRE SOLDIER

ABILITY:
SECOND GENERATION PYROKINETIC (CONTROLS FIRE; EXCELS AT DEFENSE)

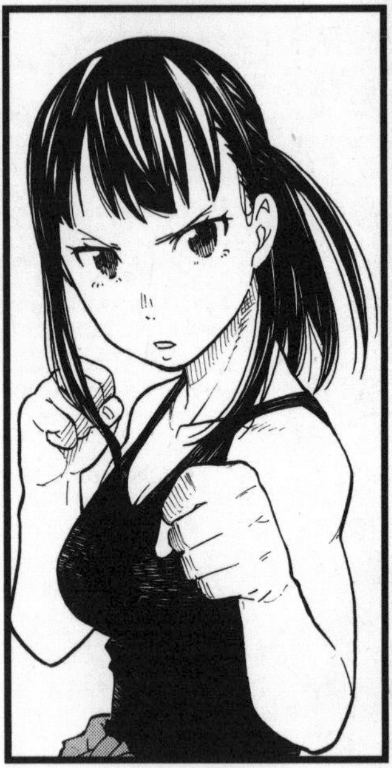

Height	167 cm [5'6"]
Weight	The same as five apples ♥ (60 kg [132.3 lbs.])
Age	19 years
Birthday	September 16
Sign	Virgo
Bloodtype	O
Nickname	Ogress
Self-Proclaimed	Who are you calling a gorilla cyclops?!
Favorite Foods	Strawberries Flan Chicken breast
Least Favorite Food	Food that smells like the ocean, like sea urchin
Favorite Music	Pop music
Favorite Animal	Sloth
Favorite Color	Pastels
Her Type	Someone cheerful and funny
Who She Respects	Lieutenant Hinawa, Captain Ōbi
Who She Has Trouble Around	People who stare at her body
Who She's Afraid Of	Lieutenant Hinawa
Hobbies	Fortune telling Sewing
Daily Routine	Stargazing (while doing sit-ups)
Dream	To be a beautiful bride
Shoe Size	26 cm [10]
Eyesight	1.2 [20/16]
Favorite Subject	Language Arts
Least Favorite Subject	Math

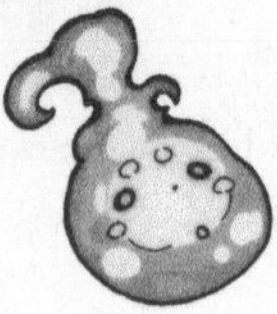

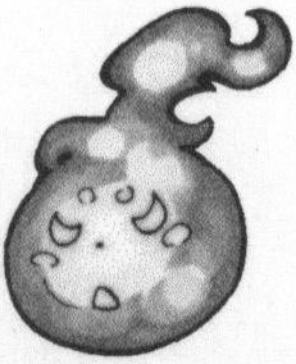

TAKEHISA HINAWA

FIRE FORCE

AFFILIATION:	RANK:	ABILITY:
SPECIAL FIRE FORCE COMPANY 8	**LIEUTENANT**	**SECOND GENERATION PYROKINETIC (CONTROLS BULLETS FROM FIREARMS)**

Height	180 cm [5'11"]
Weight	74 kg [163.17 lbs.]
Age	25 years (actually 28, see page 199)
Birthday	September 23
Sign	Libra
Bloodtype	O
Nickname	The lieutenant with the weird hats and scary eyes.
Self-Proclaimed	A man of little importance.
Favorite Foods	Sushi
Least Favorite Food	Anything eaten with someone who has bad manners.
Favorite Music	Jazz
Favorite Animal	Dog
Favorite Color	Earth tones, like green
His Type	Calm women
Who He Respects	Captain Ōbi, Tōjō
Who He Has Trouble Around	Captain Princess Hibana
Who He's Afraid Of	No one in particular
Hobbies	Hiking Camping
Daily Routine	Firearms maintenance, being talked into buying overstocked clothing items by store employee
Dream	To achieve Company 8's objective
Shoe Size	27.5 cm [9]
Eyesight	1.5 [20/12.5] (but has a strong astigmatism)
Favorite Subject	Loves all academic subjects, especially good at math
Least Favorite Subject	None

AKITARU ŌBI

AFFILIATION: SPECIAL FIRE FORCE COMPANY 8

RANK: CAPTAIN

ABILITY: NON-POWERED

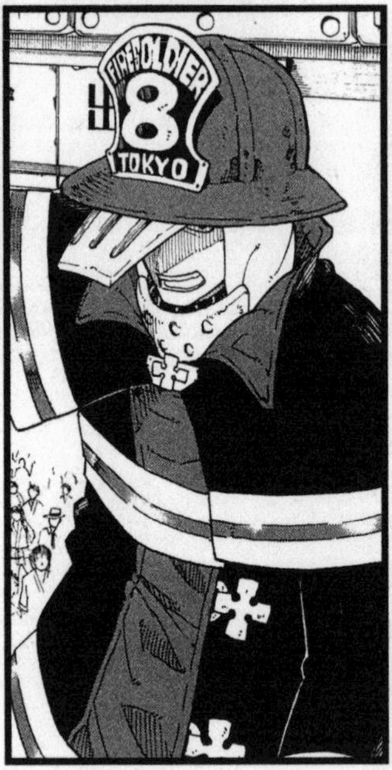
FIRE SOLDIER
8
TOKYO

Height	189 cm [6'2"]
Weight	108 kg [238.14 lbs.]
Age	31 years
Birthday	March 27
Sign	Aries
Bloodtype	B
Nickname	Bodybuilding Gorilla
Self-Proclaimed	Non-powered
Favorite Foods	Chicken ramen
Least Favorite Food	Protein
Favorite Music	Rock
Favorite Animal	Dog
Favorite Color	Beige
His Type	Someone with a strong sense of justice
Who He Respects	The Chief of the Fire Defense Agency, his parents
Who He Has Trouble Around	Captain Princess Hibana
Who He's Afraid Of	Lieutenant Hinawa
Hobbies	Collecting records Basketball DIY Home Improvement (not good at it)
Daily Routine	Bodybuilding
Dream	To eradicate spontaneous human combustion from the world
Shoe Size	29 cm [11.5]
Eyesight	1.5 [20/12.5]
Favorite Subject	Industrial arts (got bad grades), history
Least Favorite Subject	None

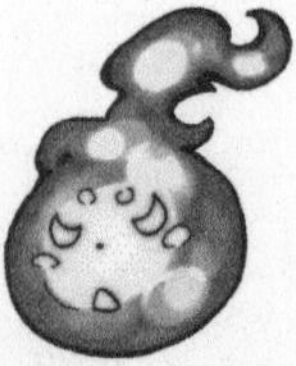

SAVE THE DATE!

HALLOWEEN
ComicFest
halloweencomicfest.com

October 28
2017

CELEBRATE HALLOWEEN AT YOUR LOCAL COMIC SHOP!

HALLOWEENCOMICFEST.COM

"An emotional and artistic tour de force! We see incredible triumph, and crushing defeat... each panel [is] a thrill!"
—Anitay

"A journey that's instantly compelling."
—Anime News Network

WELCOME TO THE BALLROOM

By Tomo Takeuchi

eckless high school student Tatara Fujita wants to be good at mething—anything. Unfortunately, he's about as average as a slouchy en can be. The local bullies know this, and make it a habit to hit him up r cash, but all that changes when the debonair Kaname Sengoku sends em packing. Sengoku's not the neighborhood watch, though. He's a ofessional ballroom dancer. And once Tatara Fujita gets lled into the world of ballroom, his life will never be the me.

KC KODANSHA COMICS

The award-winning manga about what happens inside you!

"Far more entertaining than it ought to be... wh
kid doesn't want to think that every time th
sneeze a torpedo shoots out their nose?"
—Anime News Netwo

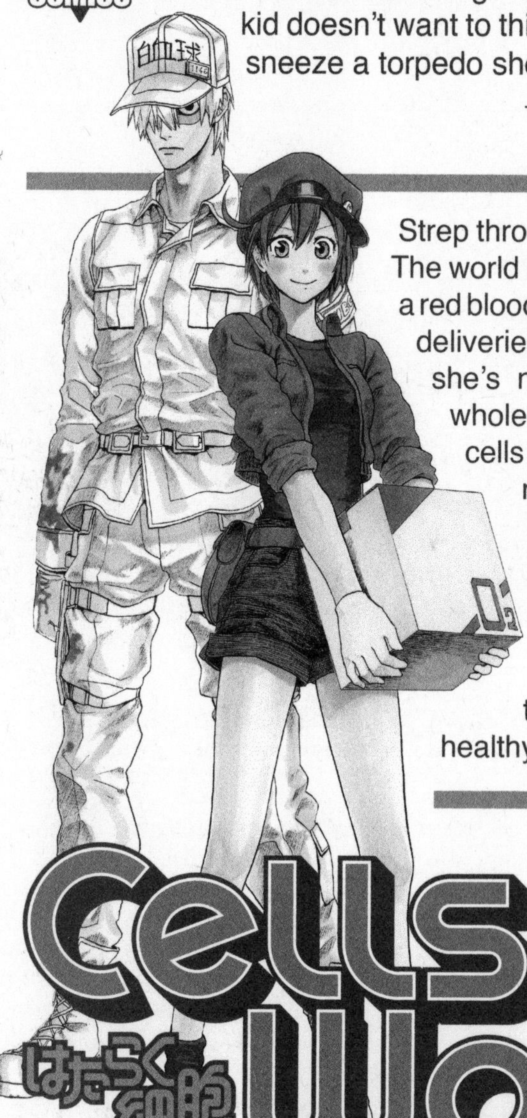

Strep throat! Hay fever! Influenz
The world is a dangerous place f
a red blood cell just trying to get h
deliveries finished. Fortunate
she's not alone…she's got
whole human body's worth
cells ready to help out! Th
mysterious white bloc
cells, the buff and bras
killer T cells, even th
cute little platelets
everyone's got
come together
they want to keep yo
healthy!

Cells at Work!

はたらく細胞

By Akane Shimiz

The Black Museum The Ghost and the Lady

By Kazuhiro Fujita

eep in Scotland Yard in London sits an evidence room dedicated to the greatest
ysteries of British history. In this "Black Museum" sits a misshapen hunk of
ad—two bullets fused together—the key to a wartime encounter between Florence
ightingale, the mother of modern nursing, and a supernatural Man in Grey. This
ory is unknown to most scholars of history, but a special guest of the museum will
l the tale of *The Ghost and the Lady*...

Praise for Kazuhiro Fujita's *Ushio and Tora*

charming revival that combines a classic look with modern depth and pacing... **Essential viewing**
th for curmudgeons and new fans alike." — Anime News Network

REAT! The first episode of *Ushio and Tora* captures the essence of '90s anime." — IGN

KC
KODANSHA
COMICS

*New action series from Hiroyuki Takei, creator of
the classic shonen franchise Shaman King!*

In medieval Japan, a bell hanging on the collar is a sign that a
has a master. Norachiyo's bell hangs from his katana sheath, but he
nonetheless a stray — a ronin. This one-eyed cat samurai travels acros
dishonest world, cutting through pretense and deception with his blac

By
Hiroyuki Takei

Fire Force volume 6 is a work of fiction. Names, characters, places, and incidents are the products of the author's imagination or are used fictitiously. Any resemblance to actual events, locales, or persons, living or dead, is entirely coincidental.

A Kodansha Comics Trade Paperback Original.

Fire Force volume 6 copyright © 2016 Atsushi Ohkubo
English translation copyright © 2017 Atsushi Ohkubo

Published in the United States by Kodansha Comics, an imprint of Kodansha USA Publishing, LLC, New York.

Publication rights for this English edition arranged through Kodansha Ltd., Tokyo.

First published in Japan in 2016 by Kodansha Ltd., Tokyo.

ISBN 978-1-63236-478-4

Printed in the United States of America.

www.kodanshacomics.com

9 8 7 6 5 4 3 2 1

Translation: Alethea Nibley & Athena Nibley
Lettering: AndWorld Design
Editing: Lauren Scanlan
Kodansha Comics edition cover design: Phil Balsman